PUBLISHING

Collection Directors and authors: Dominique AUZIAS et Jean-Paul LABOURDETTE

Publishing manager: Yan EVEN

Authors: Gwénaëlle LABBE, Carine PAGES, Caroline CHOLLET, Jordan EL OUARDI, FAVRAU, Aurélie REYNES, Marine GASC, Fabienne CALVAYRAC, Yan EVEN, Lise ALVAREZ, Laurie ACCO, Amélie ROUJOU, Jean-Paul LABOURDETTE, Dominique AUZIAS et alter

Publishing director: Stéphan SZEREMETA

Publishing team (France): Elisabeth COL, Maurane CHEVALIER, Silvia FOLIGNO and Tony DE SOUSA

Publishing team (World): Patrick MARINGE, Caroline MICHELOT, Morgane VESLIN, Pierre Yves SOUCHET and Talatah FAVREAU

STUDIO

Studio Manager: Sophie LECHERTIER assisted by Romain AUDREN

Layout: Julie BORDES, Sandrine MECKING, Del[illegible] Laurie PILLOIS, Sara DOLLE et Noémie FERRON

Pictures management: Anne DIOT

Mapping management: Jordan EL OUARDI

WEB

Web Director: Louis GENEAU de LAMARLIERE

Technical Director: Lionel CAZAUMAYOU

Web management and Development: Cédric M[illegible] Nicolas GUENIN, Florian FAZER, Caroline LAFFAIT[illegible] Andrei UNGUREANU and Nicolas VAPPEREAU

Community Manager: Cyprien de CANSON

NATIONAL PUBLICITY

Publicity director: Caroline CHOLLET

Local publicity management: Michel GRANSEIGNE

Customer relations management: Vimla MEETTOO and Sandra RUFFIEUX

Heads of National Publicity: Caroline AUBRY, François BRIANCON-MARJOLLET, Perrine DE CARNE MARCEIN, Caroline GENTELET and Caroline PREAU

INTERNATIONAL PUBLICITY

Heads of Publicity: Jean-Marc FARAGUET, Guillaume LABOUREUR assisted by Michelle MAYER

CIRCULATION AND PROMOTION

Sales promotion Director: Bénédicte MOULET assisted by Aissatou DIOP and Vianney LAVERNE

Sales Manager: Jean-Pierre GHEZ

Press and sponsor partnership management: Jean-Mary MARCHAL

ADMINISTRATION

Chairman: Jean-Paul LABOURDETTE

Administrative and financial Director: Valérie DECOTTIGNIES

Human Resources Director: Dina BOURDEAU assisted by Sandra MORAIS and Eva BAELEN

Information and Technology Manager: Pascal LE GOFF

Accounting: Jeannine DEMIRDJIAN, Christelle MANEBARD and Adrien PRIGENT

Collection: Fabien BONNAN assisted by Sandra BRIJLALL and Belinda MILLE

Siwtchboard: Jehanne AOUMEUR

PETIT FUTE BEST OF AUDE 2021-2022

Petit Futé was founded by Dominique AUZIAS.
It is published by Les Nouvelles Editions de l'Université
18, rue des Volontaires - 75015 Paris.
✆ 01 53 69 70 00 - Fax 01 42 73 15 24
Internet: www.petitfute.com
SAS au capital de 1 000 000 € - RC PARIS B 309 769 966
Cover: Remparts de Carcassonne
© Satilda - iStockPhoto.com
Printing: Imprimerie Champagne Nouvelle – 52200 Langres
Legal deposit: 18/07/2020
ISBN: 9782305035277

To email us, type the surname (lowercase) followed by @petitfute.com
Write to the editor: info@petitfute.com

WELCOME TO AUDE!

In this department of the Aude, where the scents of the sea embalm, even more so by caressing the wild plants of the Corbières, the change of scenery is permanent. There is such a diversit[illegible]nd at his conve-[illegible]. From the fine [illegible]esorts, such as [illegible] its kite enthu-[illegible]door activities, [illegible] the beginning [illegible]ner swimming [illegible] that combine [illegible]es, the City of [illegible] are combined [illegible]ste, in the wine [illegible], the nectars produced by the terroirs of the Minervois, Boutenac, Corbières, or the oldest sparkling wine in the world: La Blanquette de Limoux! An ancient Roman province, with Narbonne as its capital, the Aude is rich in history and ancestral traditions, which can still be found today in its daily life and in its gastronomy, with the Cassoulet of Castelnaudary as a highlight. But this land, seemingly blessed by the gods, is not safe from heavenly wraths, and 2020 got off to a bad start with floods, which desecrated places that had been preserved until then. Many towns and villages have been badly damaged, today the wounds are healed, and the smile of welcome is once again on everyone's lips. All the service providers will offer you today, as in the past, the best they have to offer, so that your stay will be embellished by the communicative love that the people of Aude have for their department. This one, alas, has not been spared by the coronavirus, but has been able to cope, so that no pandemic will disrupt your holidays. "Welcome" remains the key word of this future season, which we wish you the most memorable.

Yan Even and his team of "Petits Futés".

PEFC
10-31-2009
Certifié PEFC
Ce produit est issu de forêts gérées durablement et de sources contrôlées.
pefc-france.org

PRINTED IN FRANCE

FREE
THE DIGITAL VERSION OF THIS GUIDE BOOK
See page 101

TABLE OF CONTENTS

DISCOVER AUDE

FROM PLACE TO PLACE

Canal du Midi.

Courtesy of the Departmental Tourist Board - Reprodcution Prohibited- January 2011

Aude

Saint-Pons-de-Thomières
Tarn
Citou
Caunes-Minervois
Trausse
Azille
Minerve
Bize-Minervois
Béziers
Pouzols-Minervois
Mirepeisset
Ouveillan
Port-la-Robine
Ginestas
le Somail
GRANGE DE FONTCALVY
Sallèles-d'Aude
Rieux-Minervois
Homps
Tourouzelle
Argens-Minervois
CANAL DU MIDI
St-Marcel-sur-Aude
Cuxac-d'Aude
Coursan
Montpellier
St-Frichoux
La Redorte
Puichéric
Escales
LÉZIGNAN-CORBIÈRES
Macorignan
Moussan
Fleury-d'Aude
Blomac
Roquecourbe
Vinassan
Les Cabanes de Fleury
Capendu
Montbrun
Montredon
NARBONNE
Douzens
Conilhac-Corbières
Ornaisons
PAYS DE LA NARBONNAISE
Saint-Pierre-sur-Mer
MONTS D'ALARIC
AUTOROUTE DES DEUX MERS
Bizanet
Narbonne-Plage
Boutenac
Gasparets
Gaussan
NOTRE-DAME DES AUZILS
Fabrezan
Fontfroide
la Nautique
Bages
Gruissan
Montséret
Peyriac-de-mer
Étang de Bages et de Sigean
Gruissan-Plage
Lagrasse
Saint-Laurent-de la-Cabrerisse
Étang de l'Ayrolle
RESERVE AFRICAINE DE SIGEAN
Fontjoncouse
Portel-des-Corbières
ILE STE-LUCIE
PAYS CORBIÈRES-MINERVOIS
Sigean
Durfort
Port-la-Nouvelle
Termes
Villerouge-Termenès
Roquefort-des-Corbières
Durban-Corbières
Lapalme
Mediterranean Sea
Cascastel-des-Corbières
Villeneuve-des-Corbières
Étang de Lapalme
Laroque-de-Fa
Palairac
Castelmaure
La Franqui
Parc Naturel Régional
Aguilar
Leucate
Leucate-Plage
Tuchan
Fitou
Padern
Paziols
Duilhac-s-Peyrepertuse
Cucugnan
Quéribus
Port-Leucate
Perpignan SPAIN
Étang de Leucate ou de Salses
Le Bacarès
Tautavel
Paul-de-Fenouillet
Pyrénées Orientales
DUBLIN
KOBENHAVN
LONDON
AMSTERDAM
BERLIN
PARIS
ZÜRICH
AUDE
CACASSONNE
BARCELONNE
ROME
MAP KEYS
Abbey - Church
Castle
National Heritage Site
World Heritage Site
Train
Chef lieu of canton
Commune - Tourist Attraction
Seaside Resort
Highway
Main Road
Secondary Road (1st and 2nd category)
Secondary Road (3rd category)
Cathar Path

Stroll on the Canal du Midi.

DISCOVER AUDE

THE MUST-SEES

AUDE ★★★

The medieval city of Carcassonne

LA CITÉ MÉDIÉVALE DE CARCASSONNE ★★★★
Cité de Carcassonne
CARCASSONNE
✆ 04 68 11 75 87
www.remparts-carcassonne.fr
♿

Open all year round. Free visit of the city and the old cathedral. Château comtal closed on 1 Jan. 1 May, 1 and 11 Nov. and 25 Dec. 1 October to 31 December Open daily 9: 30am – 5pm / 2 January to 31 March Open daily 9: 30am – 5pm. From 1 April to 30 September Open daily 10am – 6: 30pm. Free until 18 years old. Adult: 9.50 €. Group (20 people): 7,50 €. Free every first Sunday from November to March. Route commented by a receptionist included in the entrance fee: departures from 10: 15am every day. Audioguides and visit with a cultural action officer with extra charge. American Express. Some areas are accessible to wheelchair users. Please ask at the reception. Guided tour. Boutique. Entertainment. Open from October to March from 9am to 5pm and from April to September from 10am to 6: 30pm.

Visible from a distance and especially from A61, the Cité Médiévale looks like an anachronism in the landscape, placed in this Mediterranean environment. It is true that it is impressive with its 52 towers, mostly headed with slates, and its 3 km ramparts. A picture coming out of a storybook! Futé strongly urge you to stop in this historical site, because what you see from afar is nothing compared to what you find here... A trip back in time which will open the door of medieval art in its entire splendour to you!

Fontfroide Abbey

ABBAYE DE FONTFROIDE ★★★★
Chemin de Fontfroide, D613
NARBONNE
✆ 04 68 45 11 08
www.fontfroide.com
info@fontfroide.com

Open all year round. Closed on December 25 and January 1. In low season: from 10am to 12: 30pm and from 1: 30pm to 5pm. In high season: from 9: 30am to 7pm. From April 1st to June 30th and from September 1 to October 31: 10am to 6pm. Free up to 6 years old. Adult: 11.50€ (student and PMR rate: 8€). Children (from 7 to 18 years old): 7€. Group (20 people): 8.50€. Family rate 2 adults and 2 children: 30€. Guided tours + 2€ / person. Night rate: 15€. The rooms are accessible to disabled people except the dormitory on the first floor and the terraced gardens. Guided or free visit with digital tablet. The visit includes the abbey and the garden. Restaurant open from mid-February to mid-December: lunch formula from 21€ to 25€. In the evening: menus from 35€ to 39€.

Nestled in its Massif, Fontfroide Abbey, incredibly well preserved, stands out with all its splendour! Dating from 1093, this Cistercian masterpiece is one of the greatest in France. Today, you can visit the refectory, the dormitory, the cloister of the 12th-13th centuries, the Louis XIV court, the abbey church, the chapter house and the gardens... In 1908, the abbey was the subject of a public sale. Gustave Fayet and his wife Madeleine d'Andoque de Sériège bought Fontfroide, not hesitating to outbid to save the abbey from a departure for the Americas. A cultural and artistic renaissance took place. Extensive restoration and beautification work were undertaken and the abbey quickly became a place for artistic and intellectual encounters. In the winter months, Fontfroide opens the private apartments of Le Fayet to visitors, an opportunity to discover the Parlor, the Dining Room or the old kitchens. The Visite des 3 Peintres, organised on Tuesdays and Saturdays (by reservation only), will allow you to admire the Day and the Night, two majestic works by the painter Odilon Redon. At the back of the church, on sunny days, the colours of the 2,000 roses will reveal their sweet fragrance. Throughout the year, Fontfroide offers a rich cultural programme: concerts, flower market, medieval weekend, orchid exhibition, entertainment for adults and children... In July and August, embark on a new journey with Fontfroide la Nuit, a poetic nightlife for the whole family. The abbey can be visited every day by guided tour or with the help of a digital tablet (adult and child route) or with a leaflet.

Tasting and sale at the cellar: The wines of Fontfroide- AOP Corbières and IGP Pays d'Oc. Club "œno" upon reservation.

Food service: Fontfroide's restaurant offers a revisited Mediterranean cuisine, a must in the region.

The Palace of the Archbishops of Narbonne

PALAIS-MUSÉE DES ARCHEVÊQUES ★★★★
Place de l'Hôtel-de-Ville
NARBONNE ✆ 04 68 65 15 60
culture@mairie-narbonne.fr

Open from 10am to 6pm, from June 1 to September 30. From 10am to 12pm and from 2pm to 5pm. Closed on January 1, May 1, November 1, November 11 and December 25. From July 19 to August 22, a dramatized visit on the history of the palace.Guided tours organized during the school holidays in zone C, program available at the Tourist Office or on the websites www.narbonne.fr and www.narbonne-tourisme.com. Shop.

Dream
of Tuscany ?
Experience
Narbonne !
www.narbonne-tourisme.com
Narbonne
TOURISME

Palais-Musée des Archevêques is a familiar place for the Narbonnais as the town hall has been there since 1842. On both sides of Passage de l'Ancre, a charming paved alley, you can find Palais Vieux (12th and 13th centuries) and Palais Neuf (14th century, modified in the 17th and 18th centuries). Originally a modest ecclesiastical residence, the archbishopric, in Roman, Gothic, classical and neo-Gothic styles, is now a sophisticated architectural complex. The facade of the palace has three towers: that of the Madeleine, the oldest, the Saint-Martial tower and the Gilles-Aycelin dungeon, crowned with bartizans. The archbishop proclaimed his military strength at the end of the 13th century from the top of the 40 m of the keep to the powerful bossage walls. The top offers a panorama of the city and you can enjoy the remains of the Via Domitia and the Saint-Just-Saint-Pasteur cathedral. Palais-Musée des Archevêques hosts two collections: the archaeological collections in the Vieux Palais offer the public one of the finest collections of antique frescoes. The collections of Art and History are located in the Palais Neuf, where paintings, sculptures and temporary exhibitions can be found. The palace rests against the first enclosure of Narbonne, beyond which the garden of the archbishopric spreads. Fountain, boxwood carved in French style, sundial, stele of Paul Tournal, founder of the Archaeological and Literary Commission. A break in the shade of the monuments is required. At the bottom of the Passage de l'Ancre, a door leads to the 14th century cloister, freshly restored, where you can admire picturesque carved gargoyles, but also enjoy the shade and peace and quiet.

The Oeil Doux Abyss

■ LE GOUFFRE DE L'ŒIL DOUX ★★
FLEURY

In the heart of the Clape massif, the impressive "Œil Doux" chasm is set in a green setting and offers a surprising spectacle. The view from above is exceptional: Domaine de l'Oustalet, the sea, the clape and the Etang de Pissevaches. This natural curiosity was born from the collapse of a huge vault. It is made up of high limestone cliffs overlooking a stretch of emerald green, brackish and motionless water. Perfectly circular, this water point remains a puzzle for geologists. This water would come from the drainage of underground rivers of the Clape. A siphon would be in the center of it. More than two hundred species of birds, some of which are very rare, make this site one of the best ornithological sites in the department. Feel free to bring your binoculars. The chasm is signposted on the road between Fleury and Saint-Pierre-la-Mer, the access to the car park is marked and winding in order to preserve the local flora and the beauty of nature. Possibility to picnic under the pines and oaks. If hiking boots are not necessary, however, we advise you to wear walking shoes but also something to cover your head in the middle of summer, the path is not shaded because here, the vegetation is mainly low. It is important to remain vigilant and to follow safety instructions, especially with regard to fire. Finally, do not approach the edge, do not jump, do not swim, and open your eyes wide to enjoy this spectacular site! Swimming is forbidden and dangerous.

The giant Cabrespine Abyss

■ GOUFFRE GÉANT DE CABRESPINE ★★★
D 112
CABRESPINE
✆ 04 68 26 14 20
www.gouffre-de-cabrespine.com
gouffrecabrespine11@gmail.com

Qualité Tourisme. Qualité Sud de France. Open from the beginning of February to the beginning of December. November, December: 2pm/5.30pm; February, March, April, mid-June, September: 10am/6.30pm; May, early June, October: 10am-12pm/2pm-6.30pm; July and August: 10am/7pm with regular departures every 45 min in the morning and 30 min in the afternoon. Free up to 4 years old. Adult: 11.60 €. Children (from 5 to 12 years old): 6.90 € (young people – from 13 to 17 years old: 9.90 €). Group (20 people): 7.90 € (on reservation). Aventures Parc (on reservation): Accro Grotte de Cabrespine (from 12 years

© catalyseur7 - stock.adobe.com

The "Oeil doux" abyss.

old): 37 €/person; La Rivière Souterraine (from 10 years old): 48 €/person. Equipment provided: wetsuit, helmet, harness, gloves. Labeled Tourisme & Handicap. Labeled Le Pays Cathare. Children welcome area. Guided tour in French (about 50 minutes). Audio-guides in Spanish, Catalan, English and German (extra charge of 1.50 € outside the audio-guided period). Food service (bar and snack bar). Free parking for light vehicles and buses. Charging station for electric vehicles. Shop with souvenirs and regional products.

This is the largest developed abyss in Europe, renowned worldwide for its mineralogical wealth. There are discs, eccentrics, aragonites, draperies, columns, and waterfalls. Giant, is not an overused term here, since it is 250 metres deep for a volume of more than 1,500,000 m^3, it could almost house the Eiffel Tower. Thanks to cleverly designed facilities, most of the course is accessible on one level and therefore to the greatest number of people (parents with pushchairs as well as wheelchair users). In addition, an 8 m long glass footbridge rises from the rock face 200 m above the void, once the first fears have passed, it allows you to discover areas of the chasm that were previously inaccessible to the public. The disc gazebo created in 2018 allows you to get as close as possible to the vault to observe its unique disc-shaped concretions. Exceptional visits are planned at the end of August such as "L'envol des chauves-souris", an impressive show featuring the charming chiropterans of the chasm at nightfall. Since 2019, the Aventures Parc is proposed, combining 2 activities located 250 m at the bottom of the abyss, combining fun and discovery. Acrobatic course or exploration of the underground river, you will surely find what you are looking for. As far as safety is concerned, no worries, you are well supervised by real qualified professionals who know the abyss in great detail! Be sure, after all these emotions, the Gouffre Géant de Cabrespine will remain forever engraved in your memories!

The Canal du Midi

■ CANAL DE LA ROBINE ★★
NARBONNE

The Canal de la Robine occupies the former bed of the river Aude in ancient times. This 32 km waterway entry in the heart of the town gives Narbonne its whole identity, as the city is divided into two districts by La Robine: Bourg in the south and Cité in the north. This canal, which is classified as a UNESCO world heritage, links the Canal du Midi to the Mediterranean and allows you to understand the town in a different way: by going along its landscaped banks on foot, by bicycle, or on board small electric boats that you rent. A beautiful walk, from the island of Moulin-du-Gua, via the theatre to the island of Sainte-Lucie. You can get from one bank to the other by many footbridges. The Pont des Marchands resembles the "Ponte Vecchio" in Florence: a pedestrian bridge lined with shops, linking the two districts of the city. However, only an arch is still visible, the six others are buried in the basements of houses. The canal is made even more pleasant by green spaces and quays fitted out with all the equipment needed by boaters. Each moment is a pleasure.

CANAL DU MIDI ★★★★

www.sudouest.vnf.fr

Guided tour. Commented cruises in several languages are offered on the Canal du Midi.

Designed by Pierre-Paul Riquet (1609-1680) and motivated by the wheat trade, Canal du Midi was shaped by the hand of man. It began the era of the Industrial Revolution by allowing to rally, by its 240 kilometers, the Atlantic Ocean, via the Garonne, to the Mediterranean Sea. Its journey begins in Toulouse and ends in Marseillan - the other part connecting the Atlantic begins in Toulouse and ends in Castets-en-Dorthe (Canal de Garonne). It was made between 1667 and 1694 and two thousand workers were hired from January 1667. This number rose to twelve thousand, including six hundred women, to alleviate the shortage of men. The work was carried out in three major projects: the first from Toulouse to Trèbes (east of Carcassonne) which includes the basins and water supply systems, the second towards the south of Trèbes to the pond of Thau, and the third that was the construction of the harbour of Sète. To address the problem of leveling throughout the course, more than 60 locks had to be built, Riquet was perfectly conscious of helping to forge a symbol of the power of the 17th-century France, while giving the country a functional communication channel. He thus particularly made sure that the quality of the canal's architecture is worthy of this function. The bridges, the locks and the structures associated with them, as well as the tunnel entrances were designed and drawn with a great sense of aesthetic combined with technical constraints, the whole includes no less than 328 works of art and 63 locks. He was also extremely conscious of the impact of his work on the landscape and took great care to ensure that it was properly bordered by trees and by vegetation in harmony with the landscapes crossed. Since 1996, this performance has rightly been listed as a UNESCO World Heritage site.Having the width of 10 to 20 meters and deep of about 2 meters, the canal passes to its highest point at the threshold of Naurouze, at the border of the department of Aude and Haute Garonne in the Lauragais. Its history with Carcassonne was quite complex since, at the completion of the first route, the canal was 2 kilometers from the city. A link between the city and the canal was suggested in 1686 by Vauban but it was only a century later, in 1787, that the construction of a new route was ordered and was completed in 1810 and that wouldl definitely set the canal in its current configuration.

The castles of Pays Cathare

CHÂTEAU DE QUÉRIBUS ★★★

1, rue Achille-Mir
CUCUGNAN
✆ 04 68 45 03 69
communication@cucugnan.fr

Open all year round except December 25 and January 1. Audiopass: 4€ in addition to the entrance ticket, the 2nd one free. Free up to 5 years. Adult: 7.50€. Child (from 6 to 15 years old): 4.50€. Group (20 people): 6€ (for groups: 85€ for a guided tour in costume; 75€ for a 1h15 guided tour). Reduced rate: 6.50€- January / February: 10am-5pm; March: 10am-5: 30pm; April: 9: 30am-6pm; May-June-September: 9: 30am-7pm; July-August: 9am-8pm; October: 10am-6.30pm; Nov/December 10am-5pm. Guided tour (for groups only).

Overlooking the Corbières, the majestic citadel of Quéribus is one of the major castles on the northern border of the Kingdom of Aragon. Chabert de Barbaira, a supporter of the King of Aragon, occupied the fortified site of Quéribus in 1239, where he sheltered the Cathar heretics who fled after the fall of Montségur. Quéribus will be the last stronghold to fall to the Crusaders in 1255. After 16 years of reign, Chabert of Barbaira surrenders, not without having negotiated his freedom, and abandons Quéribus to the royal engineers and soldiers and returns to the King of Aragon. Now a royal fortress, Quéribus watches over the border between the kingdoms of France and Aragon. Saint Louis then became the master of the Corbières. The castle will lose its strategic interest in 1659, under the reign of Louis XIV, with the Treaty of the Pyrenees which sets a new border between France and Spain. A very nice visit: a path leads to the castle after a good 10 minutes walk, explanatory panels mark out the circuit. The dungeon's terrace, which culminates at 728 metres, offers a breathtaking panorama of the Corbières, the Pyrenees and the Mediterranean. The state of conservation of the elements related to daily life (cistern, main building, location of the fireplace, etc.) is remarkable.

CHÂTEAU DE PEYREPERTUSE ★★★

D14
Le Château
DUILHAC-SOUS PEYREPERTUSE
✆ 04 30 37 00 77
www.chateau-peyrepertuse.com
info@peyrepertuse.com

Open all year round, every day from 24th, 25th and 31st December. High season: open from 9am to 8pm. For the other months, see the calendar on the website. Free up to 5 years old. Adult basic rate: 7 €. Child (from 6 to 15 years old): 4 €. Group (adults/children): 5/4 €.

Peyrepertuse is the name of the rock on which the fortress stands and means "pierced stone". Suspended 800 m above the ground – hence the breathtaking view of the Corbières and Fenouillèdes to the sea – with its 1.2 km rampart, it is the largest of the "sons of Carcassonne". The first mention of this castle dates back to 1070. The fortress suffered a little from the Crusade against the Albigensians and did not experience any great battle. The citadel of this trundle castle consists of three parts which superimpose three buildings from the 11th and 13th centuries: the low, triangular-shaped enclosure is protected to the north by a 120 m wall (the old keep and dwelling), the medieval enclosure houses a series of ruins, including those of a huge polygonal building and at the top, the Saint-Jordi keep that offers to see fascinating medieval rooms whose loopholes are oriented following the sunrise at the summer solstice. It can be reached by the Saint-Louis staircase built by order of Louis IX in 1250). Peyrepertuse is the most successful and best preserved example of medieval architecture in Languedoc. On the heights, in the distance, it is possible to see the castle of Quéribus, another model of royal architecture, but also to enjoy the view, the calm and the beauty of nature.

In summer, entertainment are orgnized in the castle (Medieval festival, falconry show, 811 festival "music and artistic performance". For more information, visit the website www.peyrepertuse.com.

■ CHÂTEAU DE TERMES ★★
2, Camin dal Caste
TERMS
✆ 04 68 70 09 20
www.chateau-termes.com
chateau.termes@payscathare.org

Closed in January-February, except for groups. Open every day the rest of the year, except on certain dates. In March and November from 10am to 5pm; in May, June, September and October from 10am to 6pm; in July and August from 10am to 7:30pm. Free for children up to 5 years old. Adult: 4 €. Child (from 6 to 15 years old): 2 €. Group (10 people): 3 €. Reduced rate: 3 €.

After winding roads in the middle of nature, the castle stands on a rocky promontory in a majestic site with a stunning view of a wild relief. The noble family of Termes appeared in writings in 1061. The headquarters of a vast feudal district, Termenès underwent the siege of Simon de Montfort in 1210 at the time of the Crusade against the Albigensian, which is responsible for the reputation of the place. Raymond de Termes, who was locked up and died in the City of Carcassonne, was a Cathar sympathiser and his brother Benoît de Termes was designated as a Cathar bishop. As the fortress was placed under the reign of France in 1228 and was used to watch the borders with Aragon, it was rebuilt in the 13th century, and then destroyed in the 17th century by order of the king. The low walls are the best preserved: curtain walls have kept their beauty, thereby giving the general outline of the castle, with its poterne opening onto the gorges (be careful of the vertigo! You are advised to help the children). The second surrounding wall contains various elements found by archaeologists, the scattered remains of the destroyed donjon, and most importantly, the castrale chapel. As you go forward, you will discover two Roman windows, one of which is cross-shaped. Besides, this cross-shaped window is the emblematic part of the castle. For more than a year, the reception has a wifi access (free and unlimited) which allows you to download the application of the castle for a guided tour of the places on smartphone! Take the opportunity to give your opinion about the castle on the Petit Futé application!

■ CHÂTEAU DE PUILAURENS ★
PUILAURENS
✆ 04 68 20 65 26
chateau.puilaurens@orange.fr
By D118 until Quillan, then by D117.

Open every day from March 28, 2020. July and August: 9am-7pm; end of March, April, Oct. and Nov.: 10am-5pm; May, June and September: 10am-6pm. Free up to 5 years old. Adult: 7€. Child (from 6 to 15 years old): 4€. Group (10 people): 6€. Le Pays Cathare label. Guided tour (in French only for groups on reservation). Shop. Animations. Program of animations to be consulted on their website. Shop of local producers.

The fortress of Puilaurens, a real master piece of medieval military architecture, towers at the doorsteps of Fenouillèdes. It is perched on a rocky peak, at 697m high; it dominates Lapradelle village and the Boulzane valley. The first traces of the Puilaurens castle were found in the middle of the 10th century, but the main fortification still visible today was built between the 12th and the 13th centuries: walls, barbicans and machicoulis, towers, residential buildings, cisterns, etc. point out the essential defenseive role played by Puilaurens on the frontier between France and the Kingdom of Aragon until the 17th century. With Peyrepertuse, Quéribus, Aguilar and Termes, Puilarens protected the frontier. These five fortresses are also called the Five Sons of Carcassonne because of their strategic position. In 1659, Puilarens lost its military interest with the signing of the Treaty of the Pyrenees and the royal fortress was gradually abandoned. A rocky path converted to a botanic path leads to the first walls of the castle. Signs posted on the path, as well as the cultural markers given at the reception will help you to better understand this military architecture. In terms of architecture, this castle is the best preserved citadel in Aude. There is also a legend about it, the one of its " White Lady "...

Château de Puilaurens.

DISCOVER AUDE

LES QUATRE CHÂTEAUX DE LASTOURS ★★★

LASTOURS ✆ 04 68 77 56 02
www.chateauxdelastours.fr
chateaux.lastours@online.fr
From Carcassonne, follow Mazamet by D118, then take Conques-sur-Orbiel by D101 until Lastours.

Closed in January and December 25th. At the time this guide was published, the 2018 timetables and prices are not known. Changes are possible. February: from 4 to 28 from 10am to 5pm. March: from 1 to 5, 7 days a week and weekends from 11/12, 18/19 and 25/26 from 10am to 5pm. April, May, June, Sept: 7 days a week from 10am to 6pm. July, August: 7 days a week from 9am to 8pm. Oct: 7 days a week from 10am to 5pm. Nov: 7 days a week from 1 to 12 then the WE: 10am to 5pm. Dec: from 2 to 10, weekends from 16/17 and from 23 to 31 from 10am to 5pm. Free until 5 years old. Adult: 7 € (6 € on presentation of the passport of the sites of the Cathar Country). Child (from 6 to 15 years old): 3 €. Group (15 people): 6 € (free visit, and 9 € with guided tour). Single access to the belvedere: 3 €; free up to 15 years old. Access for PRMs only to the belvedere. Children's welcome area. Guided tour (only for groups of 15 people, ask for conditions). Animations. Guided tours (about 2 hours) in French, English, Spanish, Portuguese and Dutch. Cultural shop, children's booklet, picnic area, telephone, toilets. Animals accepted, only kept on a leash. Animations in July and August.

Perched at 300 m on a ridge above the Orbiel Valley, in a steep landscape, each planted on a summit, these four castles dominate the flow of the Orbiel and the torrent of the Grézilhou. From north to south: the monumental Cabaret, Tour Régine - the most recent one (13th century), Surdespine - the oldest one (12th century), and Quertinheux. Cabaret, Surdespine and Quertinheux existed before the Crusade against the Albigensians. Tour Régine was built after, by the King of France. Despite the multiple assaults suffered during the Crusade against the Albigensians, then those of religious wars – the end of the 16th century (platform for Protestants) – they haven't lost any of their majesty. For centuries, they controlled the passage of Montagne Noire's ores. Access to this impressive architectural complex is somewhat arduous, consider bringing walking shoes! But a remote stopover on the shady belvedere also allows you to admire this exceptional view of the castles. The reception of visitors takes place in a former textile factory where the pieces of sheets and felt were made. Restored, it is used as an exhibition room where part of the archeological furniture found during excavations carried out on the site is presented. A shop offers an interesting selection of books on the Aude heritage and the crusade against the Cathars in the region. You will also find books and games for children and books in different languages.

RUINES DU CHÂTEAU D'AGUILAR ★★

TUCHAN ✆ 04 68 45 51 00
www.payscathare.org

High season: open every day. See full calendar on the website. Adult: 4 €. Child (from 6 to 15 years old): 2 €. Group (10 people): 2,50 €. Reduced rate: 3 €.

Aguilar, means "eagle" in Latin. The Aguilar castle stands in this beautiful Cathar Country, but it didn't play any military role during the Crusade against the Albigensian. There are written traces attesting to its existence from 1020 under the name "Puig Agilar", it was then a property of the count Fonollède. This castle, proudly overlooking the plain of Tuchan from the top of its hill of 321 meters, helped monitoring access to Corbières. However, despite its "height", it was designed like a castle of plain. In second half of the 12th century, it passed to the hands of the Termes family. In the 13th century, in 1260, Saint-Louis bought the castle from Olivier de Termes, and had major works undertaken there, Aguilar became one of the "Cinq Fils de Carcassonne" which protected the southern border of the kingdom against Aragon. But due to its rather easy access, it regularly underwent attacks and from 1542, its degradation was reported. It definitively lost its strategic interest after the signing of the Treaty of the Pyrenees in 1659 and was completely abandoned. It has been listed among Historical Monuments classified since 1949 and fully deserves a detour.

CHÂTEAU DE VILLEROUGE ★★

VILLEROUGE-TERMENÈS
✆ 04 68 70 09 11
www.chateaudevillerouge.fr
chateau.villerouge@villerouge.fr

Closed from December 15 to March 1. Visits for groups only possible by reservation from 15 to 30/12 and in February. In high season: open every day and on public holidays from 10 am to 7: 30pm. In March, only on weekends from 10am to 5pm. April, May, June, September until 15/10: 10am-1pm 2pm-6pm and non stop on weekends. From mid-October to mid-December (All Saints' Day holidays, weekends, public holidays). Free up to 5 years old. Adult: 6€. Child (from 6 to 15 years old): 2€. Group (10 people): 5€. Last visit 1 hour before closing – Inter-site ticket 5€. Animations. Multilingual audio-guided visits.

Fully restored, the castle lights up with its medieval military architecture of Corbières. Its location can be surprising because it is located in the heart of the village. The quadrangular wall with high arrow loops is perfectly preserved. A round tower is positioned on every corner; the highest is the southeastern tower with its 23 m, it was used as a keep. Even though it is partially destroyed, you will notice the crenellation wich is still visible in some places. The east wing of the castle is open on three levels to an audiovisual guided tour. You will discover the life of Guilhem Bélibaste, the last "Cathar perfect", as well as the history of catharism and the power of the Narbonne Archbishop Bernard de Farges. Bélibaste, killed a shepherd of the village during a fight, a procedure was thus launched against him, to save his skin, he abandoned his wife and children and joined the Cathar perfect circle. Denounced then captured, he ended up burnt alive in Villerouge in 1321. This visit of the museum that uses audios, guide, videos, slide shows, models, but also frescoes of the time, immerses visitors into seven centuries era back, in Cathar time. Benefit from the covered path to enjoy the view of the Eglise Saint-Etienne of the village.

Châteaux de Lastours.

Quéribus Castle.

Château de Villerouge.

The medieval city of Carcassonne seen from the sky.

Terra Vinea

■ TERRA VINEA ★★
15, Chemin des Plâtrières
PORTEL-DES-CORBIÈRES
✆ 04 68 45 87 68
www.terra-vinea.com
resaterravinea@gmail.com

Open all year round. Closed Christmas and New Year's Day and all January. Low season: every day and public holidays from 10am to 5: 30pm. High season: every day and public holidays from 10 am to 6: 15 pm. Consult the website, regular variations according to the periods. Free up to 5 years. Adult: 11,20 €. Child (from 5 to 12 years old): 6.90 € (13 to 17 years old: 9.50 €). Group (20 people): 7,90 €. Students, jobseekers and people with reduced mobility (upon proof): €9.50. Cheques not accepted. Children's welcome area. Guided tour. Food service. Shop. Animations. Shop opening hours: 10: 30am-5: 30pm.

Terra Vinea offers you an exceptional trip 80 metres below the Corbières massif... The journey begins on board a small train that takes you into the bowels of the earth and discover the 800-metre gallery! A magical, surprising and enriching show created in the old gypsum mines, an ore that you will see sparkling in the rock. Follow the guide or the instructions of your audio guide (in low season) and enter the monumental galleries where different scenes have been reconstructed. From the Gallo-Roman era to the Middle Ages, you will learn more about lifestyles in these distant times, new features are announced in this section and especially in the Gallo-Roman villa, starting in spring 2020. The highlight of the visit takes place in the underground cathedral where a brand new and amazing sound and light show will showcase this part of the mine with its impressive volumes. Finally, the last table concerns the work of the mine, with testimonies from former miners, and the workshop of a cooper. The visit ends with a tasting of wines from the department and a visit to the shop where you will find a fine selection of local products, most of which are recommended by Le Petit Futé, so don't hesitate to do your shopping! And since emotions make you feel hungry, go to Terra Vinéa's restaurant: Le Grenache, you will be served a simple and well prepared homemade and seasonal cuisine with, for example, large salads, a crispy foie gras, sea bass grilled à la plancha, a beef fillet with foie gras sauce, a homemade burger, a cassoulet from Audary de Castelnaudary without forgetting the medieval menu (only on order)... So, you are satisfied and your head is full of memories when you will leave Terra Vinéa!

Stroll through the marsh

We invite you to criss-cross the irrigation canals of Domaine de Sainte-Marthe aboard small electric boats. An unexpected site, within walking distance from Narbonne, where nature preserves fauna and flora typical of the marshes: egrets, herons, moorhens, mallard, but also lots of small passerines: finches, nightingales, chickadees, warbler. And if you're lucky, you can watch some of the birds of prey: hawks, buzzards and sometimes even sparrowhawks.

DOMAINE SAINTE-MARTHE ★★
Route des Plages, Lieu-dit Sainte-Marthe
NARBONNE
✆ 06 82 90 19 76
www.domainesaintemarthe.com
cecileclara.dubmal@gmail.com

Closed from November to March. Low season: open every day from 10am to 6pm. High season: every day and public holidays from 9am to 7pm. Boat 5 places: €22 the 30 minutes, €32 the hour. Boat 7 places: €24 for 30 minutes, €36 per hour. 10% discount in April / May / June. Pets allowed. Cheques not accepted. Sale of drinks on the spot. Animals tolerated on board the boats and kept on a leash – Lifejacket for children – Open even in strong winds!

After the roundabout at the Narbonne-Est motorway exit, where the cradle of the vine is marked by a huge amphora signed Brigitte Privat, go to the beaches, 1 km on your right the Domaine de Sainte-Marthe will be announced. An unsuspected site where nature preserves a typical marsh fauna: egrets, moorhen, mallards... Take a seat aboard small, environmentally friendly electric boats. You can easily fly them, including children. It's a real pleasure to criss-cross these ancient irrigation canals, to discover the wild flora and fauna, to manoeuvre under small stone bridges and to ring the bell under the last bridge to announce your arrival! The small boats of the Domaine de Sainte-Marthe provide well-being, smiles and wonder to all members of the family, children and adults. Before or after the visit, do not hesitate to pass by the small farm with three donkeys, a mini horse, about twenty goats, little pigs, geese, chickens, turkeys and ducks. To prolong this moment, you can bring your picnic and have lunch on the spot, to enjoy a little more of this bucolic place. New feature planned for July/August 2020: catering.

LOCAL SPECIALTIES

The Lucques

Bright green, crisp and fleshy, the lucques is grown in Aude and Hérault. In 2015, it obtained the "Lucques du Languedoc" Appellation d'Origine Contrôlée (Protected Designation of Origin) for table olives. Its culture is growing in these two departments where it replaces the vineyard whose territory has been reduced following grubbing-up campaigns. Nicknamed "Diamant vert" (Green Diamond), this olive that is elongated, slightly curved and pointed in shape, stands out from all, unique in the world. With multiple fragrances, sweet and very slightly salty, its flesh is thin, tasty and pulpy. It is harvested by hand in autumn between mid-September and mid-October, and this great vintage is selected among the most beautiful orchards. We like it in the kitchen, for its oil with fruity creaminess, or at the aperitif, for its fruit that can be shared among friends, by tasting a muscat of Saint-Jean-de-Minervois, for example. The Lucques brings sunshine to our tables. Again this year, the Lucques has received many gold medals at Salon de l'Agriculture!

Eel bourride

Ingredients for 4 persons: 1 kg of cleaned eels, 600 g of potatoes, 100 g of bacon, 6 garlic cloves, 1 botte of parsley, tomato concentrate, pepper, an average pinch of salt, 20 toasted and garlic bread croutons. *(Preparation: 30 minutes, cooking: 20 minutes)*. Prepare a finely chopped parsley, cut the potatoes in four, cut the eel into pieces of 5 cm. In a cast iron casserole, sauté the parsley in boiling oil, without browning it, add the tomato concentrate, stirring constantly. Make a bed of potatoes, a bed of eels, add bacon or a ham bone and cover everything with cold water. Add salt, pepper, add the pepper. Put over high heat until boiling. When boiling is complete, take the lid off and leave to cook over a high heat for 12 minutes, serve very hot on a bed of bread croutons and serve with a fine wine from the terroir.

Cassoulet

In gourmet history, the origin of cassoulet is quite controversial. According to legend, during the siege

L'OULIBO, olive producers

Oulibo is not just about selling olives and processed products. No! It's above all, a passion, a profession. In the Oulibo, there are real olive growers who take care of everything: olive growing, pruning, grafting, harvesting...

Then it is time to prepare the table olives, to de-bitter them (an essential step) or to sort the olives that will end up in your salads as virgin oil, passing through the mill. Also, since 1940, this cooperative has more than 1,700 member-cooperators and produces more than 80 tons of picholines per year, 350 tons of lucques, as well as 100 tons of oil. In 2017, the Oulibo was labelled "Entreprise du Patrimoine vivant" (Living Heritage Company) and to crown and congratulate the work, the green lucques olives from Languedoc were awarded the Gold Medal at the Salon de l'Agriculture, as were the Picholines and the Tradition and Cuvée lucques olive oils. A beautiful prize list! In order to explain the entire production, harvesting and preparation process, the Oulibo offers an interactive guided tour that will interest both young and old gourmets!

The Odyssey of the Olive Tree

L'Oulibo invites you to live the adventure of the olive and olive oil on its guided tour site: L'Odyssée de l'Olivier – 5 stopovers for a journey into the world of the olive tree. You will follow your guide step by step in an olive grove of 400 trees to discover the secrets of the tree blessed by the gods: the harvest, the varieties, the care, and all the steps to follow the olive to the mill. You will go back in time from Ancient Greece to our times and follow the olive adventure on the Giant Screen. The sound and light show allows you to experience the effervescence of the mill as it is during the harvest period. The last stage is undoubtedly the best as it is an introduction to olive oil and olive tasting! You will be able to take up the challenge and leave with your family during the visit in pursuit of the green diamond, the new treasure hunt for 6-12 year olds. Possibility to buy the visits on the website. So? See you at the Oulibo for a visit?

Beers Made in Aude

Les brasseurs de la Cité

Carcassonne has revived the tradition of beer brewing, since July 2015, thanks to Xavier and Désirée Benoist, whose brewery produces artisanal beers made with wheat and barley grown in France. They have given their beers the pretty name of Ciutat, which means City in Occitan, and they adapt them according to the seasons, with a spring beer, an autumn beer and a Christmas beer. But all year round, you can also taste the Classics: the Ciutat Blanche, a refreshing wheat beer, the blonde, the Pils, a traditional Czechoslovakian beer made from 100% barley malt, or the Amber, with its sweet bitterness and strong flavours.
Visit of the brewery by appointment, to discover the process of making their beer.
For the younger ones, Xavier offers, since 2017, two sodas, the Carca-Cola (caffeine-free) and the refreshing and slightly lemony Pitchoune lemonade.

- www.brasseursdelacite.com
- Adress: 11000 Carcassonne – 240, rue Edouard-Branly – ZI La Bouriette, Tél: 04 30 34 14 21 - 06 19 12 51 93,
- Opening hours: Open Monday to Friday from 8am to 12pm and from 1pm to 7pm. By appointment only. Free guided tours by appointment only, in French and English.

La Mer à Boire

Want to immerse yourself in local products? Discover the craft brewery: La Mer à boire and its four beers: white, blond, red and a light one with a pronounced coffee aroma. Respectively, "L'écume de mer", with its little citrus taste, the "Oh soleil" so refreshing! "La Barbe rousse", which is aptly named, and finally "La Macar".
Discover seasonal beers such as "la mer fruitée", a peach or apricot white, an amber beer with spices for winter, "la mer givrée", and a very hoppy Ipa called "la tram". Would you like to offer or treat yourself? You have the possibility to buy boxes to carry them easily when you come back from your holidays, or to consume why not with your feet in the sand?
Visit of the factory followed by a tasting of the different beers. More information on the website.

- www.brasserielameraboire.com
- 11430 Gruissan – Zone artisanale des chalets – 21, rue de l'Hippocampe. Tél: 06 63 09 88 12
- *Open from Wednesday to Friday from 5pm to 7pm; Saturday from 10am to 12pm. Free visit and tasting. (France)*

of Castelnaudary during the Hundred Years War (1337-1453), the city was starving to death, and the fighters were no longer strong enough to defend the city's walls. That was when all the inhabitants decided to gather the food they still had on hand. Male cooks and female cooks composed a single dish, consisting of dry beans and various meats to give forces to the brave defenders of the city, After this very well watered copious meal, the Chauriens rushed to the English army, who, panicked, ended the siege and stopped only in front of the English Channel. The first "estofat" was born! Some historians have become attached to a very different version that it was not until the 17th century that bean cultivation was introduced in France, so the first "estofat" could only be made with broad beans, widely cultivated around the Mediterranean from antiquity and in southwest France, not beans. Other historians – who are fewer – say that beans were known in our country long before Christopher Columbus discovered America, and were grown in the southwest, and others claim that it entered into the composition of cassoulet only from the 16th century – much more likely – . In short, if the origin of cassoulet seems to be difficult to establish, the etymology of the name is more naturally agreed: the potters of Issel, a small village located 8 km from Castelnaudary, made terracotta containers called " cassoles ", and therefore the dish that simmered in it took the name of Cassoulet. In any case, this dish that continues to delight us has a very old and family origin. peasant one? and popular. Its recipe has stabilized over time to become this great dish whose reputation is constantly growing.
The ingredients are simple: ingot beans, pork knuckle and shoulder, duck confit, pork rind, sausages and bacon, garlic, salt and pepper. All should simmer, if possible over a wood fire, more than 3 hours until a crust is formed on top, and you can then taste it.

Gragnotte narbonnaise

This little delicacy represents the frog of Saint-Paul church, in a holy water font, composed of 68% chocolate of selectted cocoa beans. The frog is filled with a praliné gianduja/hazelnut. You can choose the black chocolate version or the milk chocolate one. Delicious!

OUTDOOR ACTIVITIES

Rugby

"A thug sport, played by gentlemen… ". It is difficult to escape the rugby culture in this region. The games, commented before, during and after the partys that gravitate around the stadiums and also, for insiders, the beauty of the game and the pleasure shared by a whole population at the games on weekends. The Racing Club Narbonne Méditérannée (RCNM) is Narbonne's rugby club, which is essential in the life of the city. The first traces of football-rugby were visible in Narbonne as early as 1894 with students from the Narbonnais stadium that confront the Carcassonnais stadium and Toulouse residents: the Sporting Club Narbonnais. After the terrible events of 1907, caused by the wine-growers'revolt, which deeply affected the city and its region, the city hosted the garrison of the 80th infantry regiment whose rugby team is a finalist of the French championship. History has it that a challenge game opposed Sporting Narbonnais to the military of the 80th Infantry Regiment on the Champ-de-Mars field. The rivalry between the two teams would last only 80 minutes and, in the following days, the merger of the two clubs was unanimously decided, the Narbonnais Racing Club was born! Over the generations, many Narbonne residents wore the colors of the team of France, all remember the Spanghero, Codorniou, Benesis, Maso, Sangalli, Website… evidence that RCNM was a good training school and a true nursery.

SENSATIONAL SPORTS

Water sports

Kitesurfing. Kite sports, commonly known as kite, is in fact the most recent gliding sports. It uses multiple supports: in your hands, a surface kite adapted to the wind force, which is compulsorily inflatable if you start in the water; on your feet, a surfboard, a snowboard or a buggy, rollers, skis or ice skates… The three-dimensional evolution of those who practise this sport, *riders*, is only limited by their imagination. Kite is a true wing that allows you, not only to move upwind and therefore to sail over long distances, but also to take off and make impressive figures and jumps. The kite temple is in Leucate – La Franqui – the place of Mondial du Vent in spring.

Sand yachting. Sand yachting is a water sport that is very quickly enjoyable. It is a playful activity accessible to all. Sand yachting provides the thrill of fantastic accelerations over the sand. In a half-sitting sleeping position, you hold the hoist which regulates the sail and you can steer the vehicle with your feet.

The best dominant winds. Tramontana – WNW to NNW: this wind coming from the earth violently blows for the greatest happiness of funboarders. It tumble down, reinforced by a corridor effect in the Corbières and can reach force 8 very quickly.

Marin – ESE and SSE sector: it is the wind of the sea that is the least common, but it can blow at an interesting speed with the formation of a strong low-frequency swell at sea.

The spots

Spots on the pond. Le Goulet – slalom spot. Mandatory *waterstart* in the middle. Only by the north wind. La Mine – foot almost everywhere in this area. Speed spot by sea wind or north wind. Ideal for getting started. The oyster park – very well exposed to wind by the northern wind. Non-mandatory *Waterstart* obligatoire - 1 metre deep. Shallow spot, exploitable by all winds. The Corrège – ideal for all levels. Same as the oyster park.

Spots on the sea. All the spots require extreme caution with north wind, because it leads to the offshore. Do not sail alone. Coussoles – by tramontana, reserved for experts. Area of {1}kitesurf{/1}. Deep-water waves. *Speed-sail* and sand yachting on the sand. La Franqui – site World Cup of Mondial du Vent. A magical spot where local people and holidaymakers make the public dream all year round. Cap Leucate – spot reserved for experts, because difficulties to return to the coast by all winds. Dangerous for *kitesurfing*. Discouraged by sea wind. Beginners abstain. The Funclub Les Pilotis – south of Leucate, beach perfect by sea wind for *kitesurfing* and *funboarding*. The amusement park – deep-water waves by north wind. Ideal by sea wind. Car park and sanitary facilities on site.

Bike stroll on the banks of the Canal du Midi.

Rugby

Safari route, Le gour en étoile, giant abyss of Cabrespine.

Rafting.

FESTIVALS AND EVENTS

Festivals

■ EMBRASEMENT DE LA CITÉ DE CARCASSONNE

July 14th at dusk. Further information at the Carcassonne Tourist Office ✆ 04 68 10 24 30.

Considered one of the most beautiful fireworks displays in France, the embrasement of the City is a fabulous and hallucinating sound and light show. For nearly 30 minutes, at nightfall, magic works on everyone, from 7 to 77 years old the eyes open. Millions of stars, skillfully choreographed, illuminate the skies and ramparts of the City, on the entire western front, it is simply astonishing. The finale ends in apotheosis with the burning of the ramparts, which seem to catch fire in continuous cascades. Created in 1898 in honour of the arrival of the Cadets of Gascony in the city, the city's fire fascinates more than 700,000 spectators from all over the world every year. Feel free to organize a picnic or book your restaurant and location, or even your hotel room, very early. Guaranteed traffic jams at the end of the show, unless you continue on place Carnot with the July 14th ball...

■ FÊTE DU CASSOULET CASTELNAUDARY

www.fete-du-cassoulet.com

6 days of celebration around the last Sunday in August. Free parking and concerts. Concerts, animations.

Free concerts on the 3 main squares of the town from Wednesday to Sunday, entertainment and shows open to all, bringing together children and adults, locals and tourists, in the heart of the festival, for the happiness of all. A celebration of sharing par excellence, it's a Cassoulet menu at all hours concocted by the town's restaurateurs, a gourmet market, brass bands, a children's village, a parade of flower floats, water jousting on the Canal du Midi, balls and concerts in the evenings until 2am. Since 1999, it has been the tested cocktail of this popular event that lasts several days and pays homage to this divine recipe! Every year, more than 60,000 people get together in the world capital of cassoulet for this event. And last but not least, don't forget to come dressed in white and blue, those are the colors of the party!

■ CARNAVAL DE LIMOUX

Place de la République
LIMOUX
www.limoux.fr

♿

From January to March. Restaurant.

The city of Limoux is known for its blanquette, but also for its carnival, the longest in the world by its duration. It begins in January and ends more than ten weeks later, culminating in the night of the blanquette. Certified as early as the 17th century, its origins date back to the 14th century, when millers celebrated the handing over of their royalties to the Prouilhe monastery on Mardi Gras day, crossing the city by throwing flour at the faces of passers-by. Since then, it has evolved and remains extremely codified, this carnival honours every Saturday and Sunday, a different band of carnival performers, called Fécos, accompanied by musicians, with an established musical repertoire, the scores played are chosen in advance by the members of the band. Each band of Fecos makes an exit under the arcades of the Place de la République, in 4 passages from one corner of the square to the other, marking a break in each café

Carnival of Limoux.

to quench their thirst. Three carnival "parades" are on the agenda on the day of the release of each band, in the morning around 11am when the carnivalists are masked according to a registered theme, often pasticulating the news, around 5pm more conformist with the pierrot covered inherent to each band, each one having its own different characteristics, and finally in the evening around 9pm in the light of the torches which undeniably create a particular atmosphere. During the folk week, there are also outings at different times and on different days. Behind the procession, after the musicians march the Goudils, characters masked according to their mood, who can't get together with the bands. His Majesty Carnival is burned on the last day of the carnival, during the famous Nuit de la Blanquette, which gives rise to a judgment in Occitan, during which the irrevocable and annual sentence is pronounced, a huge fire takes place in the centre of the square, the unfortunate condemned will be burned, the carnivals will alternate meditation and dances of joy around the fire. The king is dead, long live the king... See you next year! Calendar and detailed programme of the carnival on the city's website.

© Andrew Felix Shears – Shutterstock.com

Carnival of Limoux.

Cultural events – Festivals

■ FESTIVAL DE CARCASSONNE
Théâtre de La Cité
CARCASSONNE
✆ 04 68 11 59 15
www.festivaldecarcassonne.com
communication@mairie-carcassonne.fr
From July 17 to 31, 2020 (info/reservations on www.festivaldecarcassonne.fr). Online ticketing.
Festival ranked in the top 10 festivals in France. La Cité, already very lively in the summer, has its festival in the Jean Deschamps amphitheatre. 120 shows, 80 of which are free (Off festival) and a programme as varied as it is prestigious, mixing music (classical, variety, rock...), theatre and dance from various horizons... Every year, a quality program with a selection of the best artists of the moment, this year: -M-, Francis Cabrel, Patrick Bruel, Supertramp's Roger Hodgson, Mika, James Blunt, Matt Pokora, PNL, Christophe Maé... Find out about the entire program and anticipate your reservations on www.festivaldecarcassonne.fr.

Festival Off: in July (free)
It is the "off" festival which animates the lower town and takes place in parallel with the festival of the City. A big advantage is that the shows (animations, concerts, theater...) are free, which doesn't prevent headliners on the program. Several stages host shows in different places in the city, and there is something for everyone. And always nice surprises! info on www.festivaldecarcassonne.fr.

Festival du film insolite de Rennes le Château

■ FESTIVAL DU FILM INSOLITE DE RENNES LE CHÂTEAU
RENNES-LE-CHÂTEAU
www.festivalfilminsoliterenneslechateau.fr
TARIF: 6 € la séance - Pass journée : 20 €. Gratuit jusqu'à 18 ans.
This 6th edition of the festival will take place from 04/09 au 08/09/2020 in the famous esoteric village of Rennes le Château, but also in partnership with the municipalities of Couiza, Quillan, and Montazels around a theme as unusual as it is fundamental: water, humans and their environment. Fanny Bastien, and her companion Geoffroy Thiebaut, both famous French actors who fell in love with the upper Aude valley, draw the quintessence of the natural landscapes of this territory, to offer the most beautiful scenes to original and prestigious film representations. Great names of the 7th art follow one another during these few days, in a festive summer atmosphere, a spirit of sharing reigns supreme around their love and their cinematic experiences, rare encounters and moments of exchange, which give this event its letters of nobility. This event, which in just a few years has become one of the summer's must-attend events, always raises the colours of cinema, and awakens awareness of societal problems, essential and original questions through short films, round tables, atypical and creative scenarios, exhibitions... a timeless moment, where reflection and conviviality are stimulated in all simplicity!

SOL Y FIESTA
LEUCATE
✆ 04 68 40 91 31
www.solyfiesta.com
alexandra.cancer@mairie-leucate.fr
Ascension weekend, every year.
This street festival, well anchored for many years in the program of the unmissable festivities in Leucate, has always been successful! The town of Leucate offers you two festive days between brass bands, gastronomy, orchestras, dances, bodegas, theatres, folklores, entertainments for children... Above all, do not miss the three big night parades in the streets of Leucate-Village with, at each new edition, the presence of great renowned groups of music. Incredible shows in a general frenzy. An unmissable event.

BARQUES EN SCÈNE
Office de Tourisme
NARBONNE ✆ 04 68 65 15 60
Free concerts. End of August. Places: Les Barques and the city centre.
Created in 2008, "Barques en Scène" is becoming the major event in summer. The festival is held over three days with street animations, bands, bodega atmosphere, celebrities, shows, DJ nights, free concerts, exhibitions, street arts. It is continuously evolving and offering novelties. Every year, emblematic and talented icons meet at the edge of Canal de la Robine for a moment of show and conviviality. In 2019, Gims Amir and Hoshi are there to set the stage on fire. More and more people go to Cours Mirabeau and Promenade des Barques, 33,000 people for Gims! There is "d'la joie et du soleil" (joy and sun) in the narrow streets of Narbonne! Do not miss the street shows that give this festival its whole character!

FESTIVAL NATIONAL DE THÉÂTRE AMATEUR
Cour de la Madeleine du Palais des Archevêques
NARBONNE
✆ 04 68 65 32 53
www.narbonne.fr
communication@mairie-narbonne.fr
Free of charge. From June 25 to July 4, 2020 (doors open at 9:30pm). Followed by meetings-conferences with actors, directors and authors. Tickets for the first show can be picked up at the MJC reception desk. The programme can be consulted on the city's website.
Created by theater fans and organized by the amateur troupe of Théâtre des Quatre Saisons in 1982, the Festival Amateur de Narbonne has become a reference. Hence, its nickname "Avignon of amateur theater". This major event takes place at nightfall, in the open-air and in the sumptuous courtyard of Madeleine du Palais des Archevêques. It lights up to offer you the best of the classic and contemporary amateur theater. Follow the Facebook page to find out the schedule.

FESTIVAL LA ROMERIA
QUILLAN
✆ 06 38 58 30 58
From 25 to 26 July 2020 (food service stands and various bodegas on site). Free throughout the city.
As has been the tradition for several years, the city of the three skittles will be transformed, on the last weekend of July, into an enclave of Occitan-Spanish culture, a crossroads of folk dances and Iberian traditions. The Romeria, the Spanish festival of Quillan, on the initiative of Véronique Fernandez, organised by the Cosaq association in partnership with the municipality, will start with a fanfare on Saturday for its seventh edition, with a rich and varied programme. For an entire weekend, the city will live to the rhythm of Spain, in a festive whirlwind of popular culture. The romeria has won the favour of the public with its exuberance and rich colours. It consists of a procession or pilgrimage (in decorated carriages, on horseback or on foot) that leads to a sanctuary to celebrate Notre-Dame Marie, patron saint of the church of Quillan. Around this fervour, there are concerts of Spanish, flamenco, Sevillian, Latin and oriental music, shows, bodegas and games. Occitania is not to be outdone, an essential link across the Pyrenees, and has been present since 2018, with a conference on Catharism and an exhibition of paintings and sculptures on Spain.

© Philippe – stock.adobe.com
Fireworks during the city's conflagration.

FROM PLACE TO PLACE

The bust of Dame Carcas at the entrance to Cité Médiévale of Carcassonne.

THE REGION OF CARCASSONNE

CARCASSONNE ★★★★

Located on the East bank of the Aude, the city of Carcassonne is first known as a fortified medieval town. This rocky spur has been occupied since the 6th century BC, first by the Gauls, then by the Romans who endowed the city with ramparts from the 3rd-4th centuries AD. On the west side of this fortification the castle, built in the 12th century by the Trencavel viscounts, takes support. At the beginning of the 13th century, Carcassonne was taken by Simon de Montfort during the Albigensian crusade and was then annexed to the royal estate. The fortification works continued throughout the 13th century, with the construction of the outer enclosure and the modernisation of the interior rampart. Carcassonne became less important after the signing of the Pyrenees Treaty in 1659. In the second half of the 19th century, it was the object of a huge restoration site under the leadership of Eugène Viollet-le-Duc. It is today inscribed on the list of UNESCO World Heritage. To be seen urgently: the Comtal Castle and the Saint Nazaire Basilica.

■ **OFFICE DU TOURISME GRAND CARCASSONNE**
2, square Gambetta
✆ 04 68 78 58 90
www.grand-carcassonne-tourisme.fr
contact@grand-carcassonne-tourisme.fr
Bikes welcome. Vineyards and Discoveries. From June to September: from 9: 30am to 1pm and from 2pm to 6: 30pm every day. April, May, October: from 9: 30am to 1pm and from 2pm to 6pm every day Closed on May 1st. From November to March: from 9: 30am to 1pm and from 2pm to 5pm Monday to Friday. Reception at the airport on Wednesdays. Closed from December 23rd to January 2nd. Shop, interactive terminals, children's area. Guided tours for individuals and groups, dramatised visits and treasure hunts, cultural events, exhibitions... Tourism & Handicap Label.

The Office de tourisme Grand Carcassonne welcomes you at the gates of the Bastide, on the edge of the Square Gambetta. Grouping Carcassonne and 82 communes of its agglomeration, the tourist office informs you about a wide range of activities and organized cultural events that allow the visitor to discover the diversity and richness of the surrounding heritage. Here, you will find many ideas for your holidays in the Aude: addresses of the best accommodation, from campsites to hotels, including gîtes and more unusual accommodation such as tree houses or trailers, but also contact details for gourmet tables, restaurants or tables d'hôtes. The Office de tourisme Grand Carcassonne also organises guided tours for individuals, groups and families. Possibility of tailor-made tours on reservation. Very active on social networks, we invite you to follow them on Facebook (@Office de Tourisme Grand Carcassonne) and Instagram to keep you up to date with news in Grand Carcassonne.

▸ **Le *Petit Futé* liked**... The interactive terminals available to visitors, the free wifi, the shop with a variety of products, the range of brochures and maps on offer, as well as the friendly welcome from the office staff, who were very available.

▸ **Info in addition to Grand Carcassonne Tourisme:** At the corner of Square Gambetta, between the bastide and the access to the medieval city of Carcassonne (by the Pont Vieux or the Pont Neuf) the tourist office offers you a personalized welcome and informs you about the activities to do in Carcassonne and its region. Nearest car park (Gambetta underground car park), public toilets 200 metres away. The Office de Tourisme de Carcassonne agglo has 4 permanent and 2 seasonal offices throughout the territory (82 communes)

■ **ROADTRIP NATURE** NEW
✆ 04 68 78 58 90
www.grand-carcassonne-tourisme.fr
contact@grand-carcassonne-tourisme.fr
After the visit of the castle and the ramparts, go on an escapade around Carcassonne. Superb villages to wander around, such as Caunes-Minervois: its cobbled streets, its Romanesque abbey and its world-famous red marble. Montolieu, village of books and arts: 16 old bookshops and as many art galleries and workshops including the Cerès Franco museum of art brut. Discovery of mystical abbeys and castles, caves and chasms surrounded by valleys and vineyards criss-crossed by numerous hiking trails. Not to be missed: the "Balades Vigneronnes", where you will be accompanied to discover the PDOs of our Great Wines in Grand Carcassonne: Cabardès, Minervois, Malepère; Corbières.

FIND THE BEST VISITS

★ INTERESTING ★★ EXCELLENT ★★★ UNMISSABLE ★★★★ UNFORGETTABLE

© Yan EVEN

Place Carnot every Saturday morning.

■ CALÈCHES DE LA CITÉ – CIRCUIT TOURISTIQUE

Porte narbonnaise
✆ 04 68 71 54 57
www.carcassonne-caleches.com
spidatel@cegetel.net

Annual closing from the beginning of November to the beginning of April. Activity very much linked to the weather, possible additional closing days if the weather does not allow the horses to move around. High season: open every day and on public holidays from 10 am to 6 pm. Except July and August, closed on Saturdays. May and June: 11am to 4pm, September: 10: 30am to 5pm, October and until November 11th: 10: 30am to 4pm. Adults: 8 €. Children (from 2 to 10 years old): 5 €. No reservation possible. Cheques not accepted. Commented route.

In front of Porte Narbonnaise, three 12-seat carriages offer departures every 10 minutes, for two people to discover Cité de Carcassonne in an original way and without getting tired. The professional coachmen comment on the visit while the draft horses snap their hooves on the paved street. It lasts 20 minutes and it is a good overview of what the wonderful medieval city can offer. An ideal tourist attraction for children, or older ones.

■ CARCASSONNE CROISIÈRES (LOU GABARET & HÉLIOS BOATS) ★★

Promenade du Canal
Marina
✆ 04 68 71 61 26
lougabaret.canaldumidi@wanadoo.fr

Qualité Sud de France. Open from April 1 to October 31. In high season: open every day. Child from 6.50 to 24€ for lunch cruise. From 8.50€ to 37.50€ for a lunch cruise. Free parking, animals accepted on board. Qualité Tourisme. Tourisme & Handicap Label. Guided tour (comments in French, English and Spanish).

Want to discover the surroundings of Carcassonne on water? Carcassonne Croisières offers you different formulas on its two panoramic boats: Lou Gabaret and L'Hélios. They run on five different routes to live the unique experience of crossing locks on Canal du Midi, including (trips of 1 hour 30 to 2 hours 45 according to the chosen route. Guided tours are in French, English and Spanish. Depending on the season, there are two to eight departures per day, boarding is next to the SNCF train station. For you who are more romantic, we suggest that you embark for a rural stopover at Epanchoir de Foucaud, a very pleasant picnic cruise. As for LE Défi, the boat-restaurant (see restaurants section), it takes you for a "lunch" or "dinner" cruise, as desired, combining pleasure of the eyes and pleasure of the palates.

■ CHÂTEAU AUZIAS – CAVEAU

Chemin de Paretlongue
Pennautier (11610)
✆ 04 68 47 28 28
www.auzias.fr
visite@auzias.fr

Open Monday to Saturday from 9am to 5: 30pm. For groups, by appointment only: visit and tasting all week long. Blending and tasting workshop on reservation. For individuals: Free tasting from Monday to Friday from 9am to 5pm. Visit from Monday to Friday at 10am/11am/15pm/16pm, Saturday and Sunday at 11am and 3pm. Outside of the times and days indicated above, we advise you to inform us of your arrival by telephone. There are different organized visits: the tasting visit at the price of 5 €, lasting about 1 hour – The workshop discovery of the terroir at 10 € to discover the estate and its wines in harmony with local products, this workshop lasts 1h30 to 2 h – Workshop creation of your own wine at 55 € (min 4 pers) lasting between 2h30 and 4h.The domain also receives motorhomes free of charge all year round. Maximum capacity of 5 at a time. Delivery possible. Online shop with the possibility to buy wines directly. Follow the link: www.shop.auzias.fr

Château Auzias, the trade mark of the Auzias heirs, an old family of Carcassonnais traders with several areas and vineyards, particularly in the Far East, is located in Paretlongue. This estate, which has been there since the Roman conquest, became famous in the 12th century with the foundation in 1111, in the middle of the Cathare period, of the Pareti-Loungi Abbey (the name of the great walls protecting the buildings). Since that date there has been; in a thousand years, only 4 families owners of this vineyard. This means that the tens of hectares of plains and hillside land that form the property are the best in the area and, as they say in the country to explain that the vineyard has virtually never changed ownership: In Paretlongue, grain is good to grind. Over the last few years, the estate administrator has set up a Wine Tour which has been very successful. This very complete visit consists of a presentation on the history of the castle, a route within the vineyard (in golf cart – depending on the time and the number of people). On return, you will visit the cellar by following the various steps in preparing their wines until bottling. A free wine tasting of Château Auzias wines will complete this beautiful discovery on a sweet note. New, original and smart, have you always wondered how winemakers crafted their wines? Part of the secret is unveiled at Château Auzias as you can participate in a creative workshop. After the visit, an initiation into tasting wines of the estate, you will create your own wine. With two mono-grape wines and measuring cylinders, you will blend your own wine in several trials. Once your wine is finished, you will put the cork on your bottle and paste your personalized label with your name and the bottling date of your creation. You can thus leave with your creation, which will be a beautiful souvenir of your visit to the castle. Finally, note that the estate is very trendy: Facebook, Google +, You Tube… find the latest information on the web like the new Multispace of Château Auzias, created by Poli Perrenoud, which is art gallery, tasting space and meeting room at the same time. Fun activity: the photocall with Dominique Auzias' side-car where you can take pictures of yourself, a funny and original souvenir.

Getting There

By Plane

■ AÉROPORT SUD DE FRANCE CARCASSONNE
Route de Montréal
✆ 08 20 67 34 11
www.aeroport-carcassonne.com
Access: A 61 exit n° 23 Carcassonne-ouest.

Wifi, car rental, parking area, taxis, shuttles, shops, restaurants.

Sud de France Carcassonne airport ensures an average of seven commercial flights per day operated by Ryanair airline. It serves the following destinations from Carcassonne: Belgium, Ireland, United Kingdom and Portugal. The airport is open to national as well as to non-scheduled international commercial traffic, to private planes, IFR and VFR. Shuttles are available at the main exit of the airport so as to link it to Carcassonne town centre. For the Carcassonne-town service, please see the "Airport Shuttle" section. Paid parking. On-site catering avaible, bar-snack area.

By Train

■ GARE SNCF DE CARCASSONNE
1, avenue du Maréchal-Joffre
✆ 36 35
www.voyages-sncf.com

Open every day and on public holidays from 5: 15am to 12: 15am. Young Traveller reception, Junior & Cie service and group reception point. Taxi station nearby. ATM in the station car park. Ticket office: Monday to Friday from 8: 30 am to 5: 40 pm, Saturday and Sunday from 9: 25 am to 5: 40 pm. Public holidays: from 9: 25 am to 5: 40 pm. Self-service kiosks. Prices vary according to the period of reservation. Free Wifi. Shop (tobacco, newspapers, food...). Disabled reception in the hall, from 6: 15 am to 9: 41 pm, Monday to Sunday.

If all roads lead to Rome, all trains lead (or almost) to Carcassonne! Of course, our dear British neighbors will swear only by plane for practical reasons in terms of speed and economy. But the inhabitants of France will be happy to settle quietly in a comfortable train and arrive rested and fit in the prefecture of the Aude. If the journey of Paris is not direct, however, you will be delighted to pass through Narbonne, Montpellier or Toulouse, other charming regional capitals. As for fares, it is understood that the first to arrive will be the first to be served, starting from the principle that the sooner you book, the cheaper you will pay for your train ticket. The very busy Relais H opens at 5.45 am on weekdays (a little later on weekends) to allow you to stock up on magazines and sweets…

By Bus

■ NAVETTE AÉROPORT
✆ 04 68 47 82 22
www.aeroport-carcassonne.com
contact@airportcom.com

Every day of the year, 6 €.

To make your arrival, departure or stay from Carcassonne airport easier, shuttle services have been organized. Adapted to aircraft schedules, each departure is made between 30 and 45 minutes after the arrival of each flight. The shuttle bus serves the city of Carcassonne, Gambetta Square, SNCF station (and the Canal port) and Davilla square. In the Carcassonne-airport direction, the schedules allow you to arrive for check-in. Connections are possible all day long on all Carcassonne Agglo (Agglo'Bus) networks. At the exit of the SNCF railway station, the stop is located immediately after the car park on your left. You can connect to the Internet free of charge thanks to the Wifi network available on board and recharge your smartphone thanks to the USB sockets. Tickets on sale on the RTCA mobile application or directly on board.

Aéroport
Sud de France
Carcassonne
La Région Occitanie Pyrénées - Méditerranée
DIRECT ACCESS
TO SOUTH OF FRANCE
with Carcassonne Airport
EDINBURGH
MANCHESTER
DUBLIN
EAST MIDLANDS
CORK
LONDON STANSTED
BRUSSELS CHARLEROI
Toulouse
Carcassonne
PORTO
www.aeroport-carcassonne.com/en
AeroportCarcassonne
aeroportcarcassonne
Airport news :

© Yan EVEN

Rue Trivalle.

■ **PETIT TRAIN DE L'AGGLO (CENTRE VILLE-CITÉ SHUTTLE)**
Halte centrale du Dôme
30, rue Georges-Brassens
✆ 04 68 47 82 22
www.carcassonne-agglo.fr
agglobus@agglo-carcassonnais.fr

Runs from the 01.06 to mid-October. In low season the train also runs, but on Sundays it stops at 6pm. July and August, every day except 14/07: 10 rotations/day from 10am to 7pm. For the other periods: 7 rotations/day from 11am to 6pm. 4€ for one trip, 6€ for the 2 proposed.

To visit this beautiful city without missing anything, escaping the hectic pace of summer, in complete tranquillity, come aboard the Little Train of Carcassonne which connects the lower town to the medieval city. Two circuits to discover the city center (La Bastide) and the historic city of Carcassonne will be offered to you, with a departure approximately every hour. Your ticket will be valid all day long (round trip). The first circuit connects the square André Chénier to the medieval city, and the second is in the opposite direction. You will have a unique and original opportunity to admire many atypical places full of history; some heritage subjects will no longer hold any secrets for you.

▶ Le Petit Train de l'Agglo offers a new circuit to Lac de La Cavayère, for the price of a bus ticket, it is an extension of line 4 in July and August.

By Boat

■ **CAPITAINERIE DU PORT DE PLAISANCE (MARINA AUTHORITY)**
Esplanade du Port – Promenade du Canal
✆ 04 68 25 10 48
www.port-carcassonne.com
port.carcassonne@wanadoo.fr

Open every day and on public holidays from 8: 30am to 12: 30pm and from 1: 30pm to 7: 30pm. Open from March to October. Paying check-in gives access to the pontoons equipped with water and electricity as well as to the sanitary facilities, showers, hairdryer, washing machine and dryer. Possibility of wintering from November.

As river tourism is growing exponentially, it is plesant to stop in small ports on a human scale and with undeniable charm. Built since 2000 on the Canal du Midi, near the railway station, the marina of Carcassonne offers 47 berths, supervised by the captain's office during the day and by a security company at night. Nearby, Bastide Saint-Louis (heart of the city) offers you a wide range of activities, entertainment and attractive shops. In addition, you can have access to guided tours on board tourist boats, rent a boat for a weekend or a week, board in season, electric vehicles made available free of charge allowing you to discover the lower city. Don't forget to visit the Medieval City, an extraordinary site listed as a UNESCO World Heritage Site, via the city bus or the summer train. As for the airport, it is easily accessible thanks to its daily shuttle connections.

Getting Around

Green Transport

■ **NAVETTE ELECTRIQUE "LE TOUC"**
✆ 04 68 47 82 22
www.carcassonne-agglo.fr

Open Tuesday, Thursday and Friday from 9am to 12: 30pm and from 3pm to 7pm; Wednesday and Saturday from 10am to 12pm and from 3pm to 7pm. Open from the beginning of May to mid-October and in December. Not on Mondays, Sundays and public holidays. Free transport service by electric vehicles accessible to people with reduced mobility (PRM) in and around the Bastide Saint-Louis.

These 100% electric and free shuttles set up by Carcassonne Agglo called "touc" will once again travel through the city center this summer. Allowing to cross the Bastide without having to walk, it is very easy to use them. Indeed, when one of them passes by you, a simple hand gesture is enough to stop it. Fast, available and free, Le Touc offers a great service. The drivers are available and accommodating. Just give them your destination and the shuttle starts immediately, even if you are alone on board. Drivers pay particular attention to users and revive the notion of public service. This service is without reservation, Touc makes regular visits to predefined stopping points. Without noise and without polluting, it will drop you off where you want in the Bastide.

Note that this service operates from early June to late September. Le Touc does not operate on Sundays, Mondays and public holidays.

Car Rental

ADA
Zone artisanale Saint-Jean de l'Arnouze
Rue Claude-Chappe
✆ 04 68 11 71 92
www.ada.fr
carcassonne@reseauada.fr

Open Monday to Friday from 8am to 12pm and from 2pm to 6pm; Saturday from 8am to 10am and from 4pm to 6pm. Delivery possible.

This agency has been able to build customer loyalty through a pleasant hospitality, professionalism and honesty with regard to its staff. Here, there is no risk when returning the rented vehicle, whether you are wrongly accused or damaged, with the sole purpose of cashing in your deposit. The vehicles offered (commercial or passenger) are in perfect condition and the rates are very competitive. Promotions are regularly offered, and young drivers benefit from numerous advantages. Free for the second driver on any type of vehicle. In addition, these can be delivered to your home, the airport or the train station. You also have the possibility to book directly online.

Sightseeing

CENTRE D'HISTOIRE VIVANTE MÉDIÉVALE ★
3, rue du Comte-Roger
✆ 09 50 88 50 23
www.ilc-lacite.fr
contact@ilc-lacite.com

♿

Open all year round. Visit in French or English. Every day and holidays from 10 am to 6: 30 pm. Ask for group rate, maximum 25 people. Visit "Along the ramparts", Duration: 45 min – 7.5 euros / pers, 6 euros / miner, free under 6 years old, – Discovery of the world of chivalry, between values and art of war, Wheelchair access, Duration: 30 min, 5 euros / pers (under 5 years old free). Children's welcome area. Guided tour. Animations. Possibility of Private Visits: Duration: 1 hour on reservation only 150 euros (up to 10 people).

The Centre d'Histoire Vivante Médiévale aka ILC welcomes you to experience the Middle Ages with their knight, an emblematic character of the city. Travel back in time and discover the Middle Ages in a different way. This knight, a resident of the City, a tour guide, historian and passionate about historical reconstruction, promises you a unique experience in the heart of the City of Carcassonne! All year round, in the heart of the City, ILC offers 2 guided tours for everyone; the first is a "Along the ramparts" guided tour with the Lord of the City, which will make you understand the history of the City, between myths and realities, as well as siege techniques: defense and attack. The second is a discovery of the world of knighthood, between values and the art of war, with the presentation of a knight's reconstructed equipment, the codes inherent to this order and a demonstration with the sword/shield. With ILC you will be totally immersed in medieval history, to experience the universe of the City in a different way.

Monuments

BASILIQUE SAINT-NAZAIRE-ET-SAINT-CELSE ★★★
Cité médiévale
Place Auguste-Pierre-Pont
✆ 04 68 25 27 65
www.tourisme-carcassonne.fr

Open all year round. Free of charge. No visits on Sunday morning during mass. Organ concerts.

For nearly ten centuries, the Saint-Nazaire and Saint-Celse basilica has been a masterpiece, a symbol of the meeting of two styles: Romanesque and Gothic, in the heart of La Cité. Its construction began at the end of the 11th century. The pope Urbain II, who preached in 1095, in Clermont, the first crusade in Holy Land, passed by Carcassonne and blessed the first stone of the building in June 1096. The construction site was really completed only in the middle of the 14th century, after the reconstruction of the Romanesque choir in Gothic style between 1269 and 1330. The nave is today the oldest part of the building. Its Romanesque vault, in semicircular arch, contrasts with the Gothic bedside and the transept that are illuminated by stained-glass windows dating from the 13th, 14th and 16th centuries. Changes were made under the episcopate of Pierre de Rochefort, at the beginning of the 14th century (1300-1321). We also owe the southern rose window of the transept, representing Christ in majesty, to this bishop. As for the northern rose window, dedicated to the Virgin, queen of the Skies, it dates back to the 13th century, and it is one of the most beautiful stained-glass windows of this monument. In 1803, whereas La Cité experienced a period of abandonment, the church lost its rank of cathedral for the benefit of the Saint-Michel church located in the Saint-Louis country house. However, classified as a Historic Monument since 1840, thanks to the Carcassonne Jean-Pierre cros-Mayrevielle, the former cathedral found its magnificence, and was given the status of basilica in 1898 by the pope Leo XIII.

© Yan EVEN

Basilique Saint-Nazaire et Saint-Celse.

Among the curiosities of the basilica: The tomb of the bishop Razouls - or Radulphe – (13th century) that is in a niche in relief, the crosier in the hand surrounded by twelve canons, and the tomb with recumbent statue of Pierre de Rochefort. A pretty Pietá of the 16th century, located in the north arm of the transept, is also worth visiting. Do not fail to raise your eyes towards the stained-glass windows of the chapels of the transept representing the Tree of Jesse, between the end of the 13th century and the beginning of the 14th century (Notre-Dame chapel) and the Tree of Life of the 14th century, restored in the 19th century (chapel of Sainte-Croix). They are renowned as the most beautiful of Midi for their compositions and their colours. The large organ of the basilica, set in the 17th century, is the work of two local cabinetmakers. It was extended in the following century, then restored in the 19th and the 20th centuries. Every summer, every Sunday, organ concerts are offered to lovers and allow them to discover the extraordinary acoustics of the building (find out more at the Tourist Office). Free admission.

CENTRE JOE BOUSQUET ★

Maison des Mémoires
53, rue de Verdun
✆ 04 68 72 45 55
maisonmemoires@aude.fr

Open all year round. From Tuesday to Saturday from 10am to 1pm and from 2pm to 6pm. Closed on Sundays, Mondays and public holidays. Open on Heritage Days, including Sundays, from 10am to 12pm and from 2pm to 6pm. Free of charge. A special welcome is reserved for young people and schoolchildren: reading classes, questionnaires, etc. Groups (30-40 people maximum): by appointment from Tuesday to Saturday. Tourism & Handicap Label. Guided tour. Animations. Exhibitions.

This house of memories is where the surrealist poet Joë Bousquet lived until his death in 1950, after an injury during the First World War left him paralysed. Bedridden, he welcomed in his room the greatest creators, painters, writers, poets and philosophers of his century, all succeeded one another at his bedside, from Magritte to Louis Aragon, from Paul Valéry to Max Ernst, including Tanguy, Dali, André Gide, and Simone Weil... A friend of Aragon, Eluard and Paulhan, he had a great influence, devoting his life to the knowledge of being and language, and founded the literary magazines Chantiers and Les Cahiers du Sud. In this beautiful residence, time has suspended its flight, and you will be able to find the room and the universe of the artist as it was during his lifetime. You will immerse yourself in his work through the permanent exhibition dedicated to him, the influence he exerted on the literary, philosophical and artistic circles of his time.

In addition to the permanent exhibition, you can enjoy two temporary exhibitions per year (spring and autumn).

CHÂTEAU COMTAL ET REMPARTS DE LA CITÉ DE CARCASSONNE ★★★★

Cité médiévale
1, rue Viollet-le-Duc
✆ 04 68 11 70 70
www.remparts-carcassonne.fr

Open all year round. Closed on 1 January, 1 May, 1 and 25 December. On 14 July, the county castle closes early for fireworks and the ramparts are not accessible. Low season: every day from 9: 30 am to 5 pm. High season: every day from 10 am to 6: 30 pm. Audioguides and visit document in several languages. Adult: 13 € (discovery visit of the fortifications). Audioguide: 3 €. American Express, Cheque Vacances. Tourism & Handicap Label. Only the Cour d'Honneur of the castle is wheelchair accessible. Guided tour. Shop. Animations.

You cannot come to Carcassonne without visiting the Comtal castle and its ramparts, and without imagining yourself dressed in the these soldiers' armour who protected the fortress by peering the surroundings at 360 °. Visit one of the largest fortified cities in Europe, surely the best preserved thanks to the restoration of Viollet-le-Duc in the 19th century. As an ultimate defence, the Comtal castle was enlarged in the 12th century by Trencavels, Viscounts of Carcassonne, and was constantly changed in the following centuries. Consisting of one seigniorial palace that separates two courtyards (the large one, known as Cour d'Honneur and the Cour de Midi), it overlooks Ville Basse (Saint-Louis country house). It is protected by 11 towers including 2 dungeons. The main entrance is guarded by twin towers forming a miniature castle whose defensive systems are very elaborate: Tour du Guet, located in the Cour du Midi, is the highest point of the castle, it is one of the rare square towers of the city. Since June 2015, there have been some innovations for the comfort of visitors, with the creation of the ticketing space that should facilitate the access, a refurbished shop, and especially the reopening to the public, in free access, of the western front's rampart that has been recently restored. Wonderful Romanesque wall paintings are visible in the main dungeon that is in free access, just like the lapidary museum. On the second floor, you can attend the screening of an educational film, explaining its evolution and its mission over centuries. Moreover, many activities are offered all year long including an electronic festival in September. Gardens, inspired by medieval gardens, are accessible to all in the moats of the castle. In addition, since June 2015, visitors have been benefiting in season from a reception point of Centre des Monuments Nationaux and another, from the Tourist Office of the City, both located near Porte Narbonnaise, in front of the cemetery.

■ LA CITÉ MÉDIÉVALE DE CARCASSONNE ★★★★

Cité de Carcassonne
✆ 04 68 11 75 87
See page 8.

■ HALLES

Place Eggenfelden
Between the streets of Verdun and Aimé Ramond
Closed Sunday and Monday. Open from Tuesday to Saturday. Food service (bar in the halls for coffee, aperitifs and snacks from early morning until lunch). Shop.

Former meeting place for grain trade, this corn exchange was built in the mid-18th century in a "U" shape, around the square that is now called Place Eggenfelden very close to Rue de Verdun. Today, there are regional products, butchers, fishmongers, poulterers, greengrocers and a few caterers. In winter, traditional fat fairs and other culinary events are still held there. Look up to admire the outstanding beams that make up the impressive wooden structure. These rest on impressive stone columns. Another curiosity, on the central square, you can notice on the ground a circle that indicates the location of a pillory, this wooden portico where thieves were once tied and exhibited... Beautiful entertainment on Saturday mornings in and around the covered markets. Regular customers meet for a drink on the neighbouring terraces and are happily tempted by a few oysters or various delicatessenm meats. A cheerful atmosphere of village square!

■ PONT-VIEUX, BERGES DE L'AUDE, JARDIN PIERRE ET MARIA SIRE ★★

Free of charge.

Pont Vieux, a beautiful 14th century structure reserved for pedestrians, crosses the river Aude to bring visitors and walkers to the foot of the medieval city. It is a great observation post on this one and on the surrounding mountains whether it is on one side the Pic de Nore, or on the other, on a clear day, the Pyrenean foothills. You can picnic on the lawns of the garden dedicated to Pierre and Maria Sire, two authors from Aude, and take your children to the fenced playground... Take the Bellevue quay which offers a very beautiful view and continue to the Païchérou quay, continue to the Mayrevieille plain, an inlet runs along the campsite from the back and then the Barbacane, one of the oldest popular districts of Carcassonne, at the foot of the ramparts. Return to the Pont-Vieux to continue the walk towards the Trivalle, another picturesque district or towards the bastide Saint-Louis.

La Bastide Saint Louis, viewed from the terraces of the Hotel de La Cité.

Museums

MUSÉE DE L'ÉCOLE

Cité médiévale
3, rue du Piô
✆ 04 68 25 95 14
musee.ecole@mairie-carcassonne.fr

Open all year round. November, January and February: 10 am – 5 pm. February to October: 10am – 6pm. Free up to 12 years old (accompanied children). Adults: 3,50 €. Group: 3,00€ per person. Free for accompanying adults School, self-guided tour: 25, 00€ per class with accompanying adults. For schools and groups, visits by appointment. Students, disabled persons: 3 €. With the City Pass 2 €. Tourism & Handicap Label. Visit accessible to the disabled. Children's welcome area. Shop. Animations.

Musée de l'Ecole is located in the former boys' school, in the heart of the medieval city. You will be able to discover through its five rooms, all the pedagogical tools used in communal schools, from 1880 to 1960. As soon as you enter, you can immerse yourself in the textbooks of yesteryear and from the first room, read a reminder of Jules Ferry's laws, temporary exhibitions and a very beautiful collection of old school elements: wooden desks, stage, blackboard, chalk, inks, blotters, Sergent-Major pens, etc. The second room, called "La Communale", houses a faithful reconstruction of a single class from the late 19th century (1882). In the third, the animation room, you will discover the evolution of the classroom, with its furniture and its purple ink writing kit. You can try the Gallic nib pens and Sergeant Major, in this writing room, indulge in a dictation chosen from the annals of the "certificate", or arithmetic exercises just as proposed, while you sit at one of the desks with your beautiful nib pen! Finally, the visit will end with a room where the "school battalions" will be discussed. A large library of period school books (5,000 titles) may help some people to upgrade their skills. An authentic place to discover for a visit that will take you back in time in a pleasant and fun way, for the whole family!

Note: Explanatory sheet available in English, Spanish and German – Average duration of the visit: 30 to 40 minutes.

MUSÉE DE L'INQUISITION

Cité médiévale
7, rue Saint-Jean
✆ 06 03 84 13 86
www.musee-inquisition-carcassonne.com

Open all year round. September to March 10am to 5pm, April to June 10am to 6pm, July & August 10am to 8pm, school holidays and Saturdays 10am to 7pm. Adults: 10,50 € (+12 years old and students: 9,50 €). Children (from 5 to 14 years old): 7,50 €. Groups: adults: 9,50 €. Audioguide (2h) 10 languages available. Adult €12.50. Guided tour.

History buffs and the curious will cross the threshold of this museum (in two separate buildings) in the heart of the City. Also named "Museum of Torture" to be more explicit, we advise sensitive souls to refrain! Not only will you get a glimpse of the instruments of torture dating from the 12th century up to the French Revolution, but you will also see scenes of torture recreated with mannequins in period costumes. Torture room, prisoner cell, animations, engravings and instruments of torture of the Inquisition show all the genius deployed by the torturers to subdue heretics. The torture equipment is put into realistic situations and a tour full of true stories is offered to visitors... We therefore advise you not to bring your cherubs, unless you blindfold them to let them admire on the second floor illuminated models of the main castles of the Cathar country. The visit is not guided but many small posters explain the instruments and the context of their use. If you take the time to read the explanations, count between 40 min and 1 hour maximum for the visit.

© Yan EVEN

Medieval city of Carcassonne, Narbonne Gate.

Please **note:** every month the museum welcomes new instruments of torture used by the Inquisition against the Cathars, one of them is particularly presented and explained.

MUSÉE DES BEAUX-ARTS
15, Camille-Pelletan Boulevard
✆ 04 68 77 73 70
musee@mairie-carcassonne.fr

Open all year round. From mid-June to the end of September, open every day from 10 am to 6 pm, closed on public holidays. Outside this period, open from Tuesday to Saturday inclusive from 10am to 12pm and 2pm to 6pm and on the 1st Sunday of the month from 2.30pm to 5.30pm, closed on Sundays, Mondays and public holidays. Free of charge. 10 audioguides presenting 9 stations are available for blind people. Guided tour (on request). Shop. Animations. Sale of postcards, posters and catalogues related to the exhibitions organized by the museum.

The Musée des Beaux-Arts is housed in the former Presidium of the town. Originally, it was the generosity of the Société des Arts et Sciences which, by offering Carcassonne more than a hundred paintings for its museum, made it possible to raise this building to the rank of a fine arts museum. Donations and legacies from private individuals and the State have added to the collection of works of art and paintings. The current collection is therefore very eclectic and presents works from the 17th to the 20th century. In addition to the rich collection of Western paintings, there is a collection of earthenware, tapestries and various art objects, including archaeological remains from the region. Open all year round, this Musée des Beaux-Arts offers three annual exhibitions, a series of lectures and educational workshops with a multidisciplinary vocation.

Walks & Strolls

ATELIER DU LIVRE
103, rue Trivalle
Notre-Dame de l\'Abbaye
✆ 04 68 26 88 90
www.atelierdulivre.net
atelier@atelierdulivre.net

Open from 1 July to 31 August and from 19 October to 2 November. High season: open from Monday to Friday from 10:30am to 12:30pm and from 2pm to 6pm. Initiation workshop from 3€ to 7€. Children's workshop 12€ 1/2 day, 21€ the day, adult workshop from 40 to 60€ (3 to 5 hours of workshop). Exhibition: free entrance. Initiation day for schoolchildren from 7 to June from 18 to 21€. Credit card not accepted. Children's welcome area. Guided tour. Shop. Animations. Exhibition.

At the foot of the medieval city of Carcassonne, through a fabulous association, which retraces and preserves the memory of an ancestral know-how, come and indulge in the joys of educational and recreational workshops, to discover paper and book trades. Different formulas are proposed to you, from the initiation workshop to the whole day, discover and experiment all the stages of the artisanal manufacture of this paper work: manufacture, realization of marbled paper with a wide choice of colors, engraving, typography (composition letter to letter and then printing on proof press)... everyone can then let his imagination run free and realize a personal creation! As for school groups, educational activities are offered over a period of 2 to 5 days, discovery classes with the possibility of accommodation at the Notre-Dame de l'Abbaye approved center, where the Atelier du Livre is located.

LE PARC AUSTRALIEN
Chemin des Bartavelles
✆ 04 68 25 86 83
www.leparcaustralien.fr
leparcaustralien@gmail.com
Follow the direction of the Lac de la Cavayère until the exit of the hamlet of Montlegun.

Open from the beginning of April to the beginning of November. Low season: open from Monday to Saturday from 2pm to 6pm; Sundays and public holidays from 10: 30am to 6pm. High season: every day and public holidays from 9: 30am to 7pm. Free up to 3 years old. Adult: 10.90 €. Child (from 4 to 11 years old): 7,90 €. Discovery day animal care profession for children or teenagers: 50 € / Children's birthday parties every Wednesday/Saturday and holidays 14,90€/child (8 min). L'escape game (team of 2/3 pers) 5,90€/pers (team 4 pers and +) 3,90€/pers. Children's welcome area (days at their destination to experience the profession of animal caretaker as closely as possible). Guided tour (free). Restaurant. Shop. Animations.

Come and discover at the gates of Carcassonne a thousand facets of this fabulous continent that is Australia. In a playful and interactive way. The ambassadors of this faraway land are waiting for you: kangaroos of course (each one cuter than the next), but also ostriches, dromedaries and a whole host of wildlife. For a total immersion, we recommend the guided tour (free of charge) which is very instructive; thanks to it you will be able to enter the enclosures and even a large aviary and feed the budgerigar which are its tenants. If your child or teenager wishes to take the experience further, some days are devoted to discovering the profession of caretaker, to apprehend all these adorable boarders, feed them, groom them, protect them... Already a bit Australian at heart? In a reconstructed aboriginal village, children and adult will discover their ancestral way of life and practice boomerang throwing or the mysterious didgeridoo. In the pioneer village, you will plunge into the very "cowboy" history of the first settlers, children will follow in the footsteps of the gold diggers. The park, which covers 5 hectares, has picnic areas, a snack bar and a refreshment bar. In short, a great day of fun and learning for all ages, and you don't see time passing!

Note a nice novelty for the 2020 season: The Australian escape game, a life-size strategy game accessible to families as well as single adults (The level of difficulty is different if children are present or not). Every day of Easter holidays Zone C and summer holidays at 2pm and 4pm (Duration: 1h30) upon reservation (min 2 pers).

PLACE CARNOT

The city of Carcassonne has few large squares, but place Carnot is certainly one of the prettiest and most typical, an essential place in the heart of the city, it is the nerve centre of the lower town called Bastide Saint-Louis, founded in the 13th century at the request of King Louis IX. Once framed by cutlery, it is lined with beautiful bourgeois buildings recently renovated and featuring beautiful and flattering colours. Formerly known as Place aux Herbes, Place Carnot has evolved over the centuries. Restored, modified, paved and then planted with trees, the central square, it has never ceased to be highlighted and has adapted to the habits and customs of the time, as well as to the various modes of consumption over time. In the middle of it is a monumental 18th century fountain dedicated to Neptune, the King of the Waters, which consists of basins in pink Caunes-Minervois marble with sculpted ornaments made of white marble imported from Italy. It was created by the Italian artist Barata, the same man to whom we owe Rolland's hotel. A meeting place for the Carcassonne inhabitants, the square is animated by restaurants and café terraces where it is pleasant to relax at the first rays of sunshine. A place to live that never stops, since there is an early morning market three times a week, on Tuesday, Thursday and Saturday mornings, as well as many festivities: Wine festival, Christmas market... Every summer, during the festival, a stage is set up on the square to receive the artists of the Off Festival, all of whose shows are free. During the fairy tale of the end of the year celebrations, Place Carnot is transformed into a gigantic open-air skating rink, to the delight of all children, surrounded by small chalets, places of exhibition and sale of many craftsmen where the adults will be served a mulled wine.

Knife & Fork

LE 37

37, bis rue Trivalle
✆ 04 68 47 35 05
le37restaurant@orange.fr

Closed 15 days in February and the last 2 weeks of June. Closed on Tuesday and Wednesday all day, open for both lunch and dinner the other days. Booking recommended. Lunch formula: €17.90 (starter, main course and dessert. weekdays, weekends and public holidays excluded). Wine by the glass. American Express. Group welcome (40 place settings in the dining room and 40 on the terrace). Baby chairs. Terrace.

Located at the foot of the Cité, Le 37 is an address just the way we like it! Benoît and his team offer a revisited bistro cuisine made with fresh products, mostly from local producers, and authentic recipes where flavour and quantity reign. Here, you will find traditional dishes such as the excellent homemade cassoulet, the gardiane de taureau (in summer). We also like Benoit's creations such as his gravlax salmon smoked with chinese tea, the risotto with saffron and chorizo, the beef tartare cut with an Italian knife, pesto and parmesan or the new veggie style tartare... several vegetarian dishes are proposed. The wine list offers a selection of Languedoc wines, most of which are organic. Le 37 is one of the best addresses in the Trivalle offering a very good value for money where you don't cheat on the merchandise and where it comes from. You will enjoy a great time here, especially since the decoration has been completely redesigned to offer a more trendy but still warm and intimate setting.

AUBERGE DES DUCS D'OC

6, place du Château
✆ 04 68 47 91 90
contact@auberge-des-ducs-doc.fr

Open all year round. Every day for lunch and dinner. Booking advised. Menus from € 16.50 to € 36 (lunch and dinner. 10% discount on any order between 11.45 a.m. and 12.30 p.m. and between 6.45 p.m. and 7.30 p.m.). A la carte: around € 30. Children's menu: € 9.50. Wine by the glass. Fresh pasta from € 13.90 to € 15.60, salads from € 8.60 to € 16.70. Meats from € 15.90 to € 19.80. Magrets from € 16.50 to € 19.50. Fish from € 14.50 to € 17.50. Desserts from € 7.90 to € 8.50. An aperitif is offered in the menus. American Express. Groups welcome. Baby chairs. Terrace. Animals accepted.

Auberge des Ducs d'Oc welcomes you in the heart of Cité Médiévale, Place du Château. The restaurant offers terroir cuisine by Bruno Tresca with essential dishes on the menu like the duck confit cassoulet nicely presented in traditional cassoles or duck magrets with variations like the one with Cartagena sauce or roasted with wild spices. You will also drool in front of specialities like the homemade foie gras terrine, panfried duck foie gras cutlet or the Indian style mahi-mahi fillet. The menu is generous and offers unique and genuine flavours: on the other hand, it goes with an interesting range of different wines from various Audes terroirs. The exposed stones and the large old beams of the dining room adds unusual charm and character to the place. Elisabeth Tresca always welcomes you with a smile and an aperitif offered. The auberge des Ducs d'Oc also has a pretty inner courtyard which can accommodate up to 40 persons. It is a pleasant and cool place on sunny days, far from the summer crowds storming the old town.

■ BRASSERIE CHEZ JU

Route de Limoux
✆ 04 30 34 41 90

♿

Open Monday from 12pm to 3pm; Tuesday and Wednesday from 12pm to 3pm and from 7pm to 10pm; Thursday and Friday from 12pm to 3pm and from 7pm to 11pm; Saturday from 7pm to 11pm. Closed on Sunday, Monday evening and Saturday at lunchtime. Menus from 14 € to 35 € (gourmet menu [starter+main course+dessert+coffee to be chosen from the menu]). Children's menu: 10 €. Lunch formula: 17.50 € (every lunch from Monday to Friday starter + main course and drink or main course + dessert and drink / express formula at 14 € served in 30 min with dish of the day). Wine by the glass. Starters 8,50 (in plate meal: 13 €). Ju dishes from 13 € to 22 €. Cote à l'os from 1.2kg to 50 € (for 2). Pizzas 12€. Tapas (in the evening): 6 €. Boards from 12 €. Groups welcome (welcomes groups, ideal for birthdays, weddings on request, baptisms, CE, can accommodate up to 200 seated people). Terrace. Take away sale.

The restaurant of Julien Ouddane (known as "Ju") is located at the exit of the city, route de Limoux just in front of the nightclub le Black. When you go to Chez Ju, you are sure to have a good time around a brasserie-style cuisine in a modern setting with a terrace. What we like here is that from one year to another the menu evolves to meet the customers' expectations. The menu therefore offers dishes for all tastes and budgets. Clever: if a starter makes you particularly envious, you can take it as a meal. What we like at Chez Ju are the delicious meats grilled over a wood fire, meat that comes from the Salette butcher's shop in Bram. Ju also offers pizzas, his "Folie des pâtes" (pasta madness) such as the pasta gratinées au four aveyronnaises, as well as homemade burgers such as the "tout canard", you can also opt for a venison stew, a leg of lamb, a veal chop or just as much for this fabulous 1.2 kg simmental bone-in beef chop – a gustative slaughter! The tapas formula, perfect for an aperitif with friends, will seduce you with its convivial side. The plates are copious and nicely laid out, and the wine list gives pride of place to the region's vintages. Note that the terrace has been moved further back and more quiet, in the shade of the pergola. An address to remember for a lunch break or a tapas evening with friends, which can continue in the "Garden" and end on the Black's dance floor, it's up to you.

▶ **New:** A beer bar with references of beers from around the world or 100% Carcassonnaises in the complex of the Black open from 7pm, entertainment and tapas.

■ **LA BARBACANE**
Place Auguste-Pierre-Pont
Cité Médiévale
✆ 04 68 71 98 71
reservations@hoteldelacite.com

Closed from mid-February to mid-March. Open every day and on public holidays from 12: 30pm to 2pm and from 7: 30pm to 9: 30pm. Reservation recommended. Menus from 95 € to 130 € (for the whole table. Food and wine pairings by Chef Sommelier Fabrice Longo 45€). A la carte menu: around 110 € (Starters from 40 to 48 €, Dishes from 47 to 68 €, Desserts from 15 to 18 €). Lunch formula: 41 € (menu with regional aperitif, 2 glasses of wine/pers, water and coffee included). Wine by the glass. Terrace.

Jérôme Ryon's table is familiar with the summits and again with the stars (1*). A success without false notes, obtained thanks to original flavour combinations. A cuisine inspired by his taste for exoticism combined with the French culinary values to which he is very attached... For example, you can enjoy a Caviar Oscietre (15 gr) from Petrossian, creamy egg white and candied yolk, pink grapefruit marmalade, Isigny cream, a few blinis, followed by a wild Turbot with semi-salted Bordier butter, black mountain trumpets and gnocchi persillades, poultry juice. The meats are sublimated in the image of the unavoidable Filet of beef with foie gras and cheeks of braised beef, new candied carrots and coloured petals, dolphins with truffles and onions, a Périgordine sauce. A chief who honours the place: a large neo-Gothic style room with fireplaces, high ceilings and cathedral chairs. And, beyond the windows, the landscaped gardens and the city walls that extend as far as the eye can see. The Futé advises you to go through the bar in order to taste one of Gaétan's famous cocktails, the "bartender" of the place, which will be served in the library, the garden or the panoramic terrace of the hotel... a must!

■ **BRASSERIE LE DÔME**
35, rue des Trois-Couronnes
✆ 04 68 25 03 48
wpiaux@gmail.com
♿

Open all year round. Monday and Tuesday for lunch; Wednesday to Saturday for lunch and dinner. Reservation recommended. Menus from 14,50 € to 20 € (starter, main course and dessert). Children's menu: 8.50 € (main course + dessert). Dish of the day: 8.50 € (starter of the day: 6 €). Wine by the glass. Breakfast. The restaurant and the terrace are wheelchair accessible. Reception of groups (private events – receptions). Terrace. Free Wifi.

It has now been 4 years since Wilfried also known as "Fifi" took over the management of this typically Carcassonne brasserie. Brasserie du Dôme is a restaurant frequently visited by regulars and these loyal guests give it an atmosphere of authenticity and welcoming friendliness for newcomers. According to the tradition of the address, Fifi offers a family and traditional cuisine with the musts like the homemade cassoulet, "the best cassoulet of the city" according to word of mouth, and that's true! Cooked within the art of the tradition with quality ingredients, served in a clay cassole and cooked in oven just before arriving on your table, it's a wonder! You can also find on the menu starters such as the seasonal vegetable escalivada, the puff pastry with Saint Nectaire and bacons or the freshly-prepared beef tartare and delicious dishes like an excellent duck breast and its sauce with muscat, veal cutlet with shallots or calf's kidneys with Porto. Feel free to enjoy the homemade foie gras, which is unanimously enjoyed like this divine chocolate mousse. A brasserie which is worth visiting for its cuisine and its atmosphere. Good quality-price ratio.

■ CAFÉ GREEN GARDEN NEW

3, route Minervoise
✆ 09 50 18 65 15
sas.happiness.factory@gmail.com

Closed from 1 to 15 September. Open Monday to Friday from 7.30am to 3pm; weekends from 9.30am to 3pm. Reservation recommended. Menus from 10 € to 15 € (homemade bagel with soup or fries or smoothie... depending on the menu chosen). Wine by the glass. Bagel house 9€ – Burgel (bagel burger) from 9 to 15€ – Breakfast from 3 to 8€ – Brunch plate 15€. Holiday vouchers, Restaurant vouchers. Reception of groups. Baby chairs. Terrace. Takeaway sale. Dogs allowed.

Opened at the dawn of summer 2019, Café Green Garden is an attractive place, an oxygen break in the heart of the city. With its retro look, its old-fashioned crockery, its embroidered napkins, this coffee-shop and bagel store is an original concept that breathes a breath of fresh air and novelty, which gives you the opportunity to eat on the go in a different way. Here everything is homemade with application, very good bagels, delicious desserts but also a wide choice of smoothies, milkshakes, local sodas and organic coffees. Sébastien and Yahel welcome you, with friendliness and explain their fair trade approach through their selections of teas, organic coffees, soft drinks, green smoothies and their culinary creations such as cinnamon roll, delicious cinnamon roll cake, pancakes, or their egg bread. Everything is done on the spot, the homemade meal is an institution to be enjoyed directly or taken away, the Fox did not make a mistake and ate everything!

▸ **Brunch offered every morning** with cinnamon roll, pancake, homemade granola, cottage cheese, bacon bagel and eggs, egg bread.

■ LE CAFÉ SAILLAN

31, rue Albert-Tomey
✆ 04 68 72 34 40

Open from Tuesday to Saturday from 7am to 4pm (last service at 1:30pm). Dish of the day: 10 € (at 14 €). Cold meats or cheese boards: 6 €. Desserts: 4 €.

It is very close to the halles and the media library of the city center that you will find this small bistro which is one of the references in Carcassonne in terms of great conviviality and good cooking. Much more than a simple bistro, the Saillan is a true place where the Carcassonnais like to meet. 7am: small coffee and croissant, we read the news of the day on "l'Indep", we quickly discuss the news and the weather and we go about our business. Then it's time for an aperitif: a small glass of red (or white) wine from a local winegrower taken at the bar accompanied by a

dish of charcuterie, perfect to follow up with the dish of the day cooked by Denis: veal blanquette, sauerkraut, stuffed squid, chicken yassa, aligot sausage... 100% home-made canaille cuisine. We like the atmosphere of the place, listening to the gossip, the good jokes of Manu Péna and the good mood of Morgan, the boss. The high point is the Saturday lunchtime rendezvous: the street barred on the occasion of the market allows the barrels to be brought out, around which people flock for wine tastings, tapas and other grilled dishes à la plancha sometimes cooked by great star Chefs. At Café Saillan, we come as we are and enjoy the moment and the people, Le Petit Futé is a fan!

■ COMTE ROGER

14, rue Saint-Louis
Cité médiévale ✆ 04 68 11 93 40
www.comteroger.com
restaurant@comteroger.com
♿

Qualité Sud de France. Open from Tuesday to Saturday from 12pm to 1:45pm and from 7pm to 9:45pm. Closed Sunday & Monday. Reservation recommended. Menus from 25€ to 43€. Menu: 59€ approximately. Children's menu: 16€. Lunch formula: 25€ (Starter + Main Course or Main Course + Dessert). Wine by the glass. Starters from 12 to 20€, Fish from 23 to 28€, Meat from 27 to 32€, Desserts from 11 to 13€. American Express. Groups welcome (reservation required). Baby chairs. Terrace. Take away sale. Comte Roger cassoulet is also on sale to take away! The jar (2 persons): 20€.

Chef Pierre Mesa dusts off and revisits typical dishes which have made the reputation of Aude and Languedoc terroirs. A modern wind blows over these dishes with studied beauty and sublimated flavours. The menu which evolves according the seasonal products guarantee freshness and culinary creativity. May the purists rest assured: the chef also offers a purely traditional and local cassoulet which will please you and leave an unforgettable gourmet souvenir. Furthermore, Pierre Messa is an illustrious ambassador of this regional dish, as he belongs to the Académie universelle du Cassoulet. However, seated on the shady terrace, not far from the Comtal castle and Saint Nazaire basilica, the fox has tried a panfried foie gras cutlets upside-down tart, caramelised potatoes with Saint-Jean de Minervois muscat sesame gold biscuits followed by panfried scallops, risotto with celery ball, mushrooms, parmesan and smoked magret, balsamic cream and finally to lick your lips, a Valrhona dark chocolate sphere with hot cold berries. A real treat! The modern interior lounge is prettily decorated with beige and taupe and the staff is extremely professional. An essential gourmet place.

LA CANTINE DU SAINT ROCH

15, place Carnot
© 06 26 90 23 60

Open all year round. Wednesday to Friday from 9: 30 am to 10 pm; Saturday from 7 am to 10 pm. Low season: Monday evening; Tuesday midday. Low season from January to March included. In high season closed on Sundays and Monday midday only. Booking recommended. Menus from 13 € to 18 €. Children's menu : 9 € (under 12 years old). Dish of the day: €11.90 (€13.50 (starter+main course or main course+dessert) to €16 (starter+main course+dessert)). Wine by the glass. Tickets from 12 € to 16 €. Dishes from 12 € to 22 €. Desserts from 6 € to 8 €. Menu Cassoulet: €18 (+ 1 glass of wine). Butchered entrecote (approx. 400 g) €22; beef tartare: €15; vegetarian lasagna: €12. Access to wheel-chaired people in the room but not in the toilets. Groups welcome (on reservation). Baby chairs. Terrace.

Cantine, did you say *cantine*? It must be said quickly, even very quickly, since here, everything is far from an impersonal and noisy room or tasteless dishes! Here, the modern and cosy decoration, enhanced by new refined and contemporary chandeliers, and the warm welcome immediately open the view of a pleasant break. On the plate, the pleasure is omnipresent from the starter to the dessert: presentation, quality and quantity meet expectations to stir your taste buds up. An easily readable cuisine, tasty, focusing on traditional values of the local and family gastronomy enhanced with some creativity. We liked the menu meant to be short to offer seasonal dishes made with fresh products and, of course, the presence of the must-eat cassoulet. The shirred egg, the daring duck confit spring roll with Saint Moret cheese, the duck burger and its homemade French fries and other tartares are among the beautiful specialties of the house. As for the dessert, we fell for the banofee (Breton shortbread, milk jam, banana, whipped cream) and the success (macaroon paste, praline cream and roasted almonds) made by Laurence, exceptional pastry chef of the Cantine. On sunny days, the terrace on Place Carnot is the fantastic playground of this "canteen" that is emulated.

LA COTTE DE MAILLES

2, rue Saint-Jean – La Cité © 04 68 72 36 24
reus.christopher@gmail.com

Open all year round. Closed in January and February. High season: every day for lunch and dinner. Exceptional opening for groups. Open 7 days a week also during school holidays. Reservation recommended. Menus from 14 € to 25 €. Children's menu: 8.50 € (mini cassoulet, or your choice of minced steak or chicken leg). Dish of the day: 10,50 €. Wine by the glass. Home-made cassoulet from 12 € to 20 €, duck breast 16 €, piglet with honey 18,90 €, salmon escalope 14,90 €, mixed salads from 4,90 € to 15,90 €, plate of cold meats 10,90 €, vegetable soup 8 €. Groups welcome (up to 50 people on reservation). Baby chairs. Terrace. Covered patio.

La Cotte de Mailles is an address the medieval city located within walking distance from Grand Puits. Christopher Reus and his team welcome you in this nice restaurant of the old city where they offer local specialties such as duck breast, piglet with honey (recipe of medieval inspiration) or a true cassoulet of Carcassonne, with pork, duck confit, sausage, and AOC ingots of Castelnaudary. The chef also concocts a royal cassoulet, to which twice as many manchons and duck confit and foie gras are added.... More classic dishes like these beautiful plates of duck breast and seasonal vegetables are offered, a treat! You can choose to be in one of the air-conditioned dining rooms or on terrace. During the winter of 2018 and 2019, the restaurant was given a facelift, thus, offering more modernity and brightness.

■ LE CRÉNEAU

6, place Saint-Jean
✆ 04 68 71 81 53
www.restaurant-lecreneau.com
gobin.creneau@gmail.com
♿

High season: open every day for lunch and dinner. Non-stop service. In Low season closed Sunday evening and Monday. Service from 12pm to 3pm and from 7pm to 11pm. Single menu at €16. Children's menu: €11. Wine by the glass. Tapas from €5 to €17. Restaurant voucher. Terrace. Entertainment. Musical evening with DJ.

Le Créneau is ideally located on Place Saint-Jean and offers one of the most beautiful views of Château Comtal. Paul Gobin, known as "Polo", the owner of this establishment, quickly established his restaurant as one of the city's references, especially after the 2016 works where a rooftop was created, offering a breathtaking spectacle at sunset with a breathtaking view over the Château Comtal and the Pyrenees in the background, unique in the city! As for the menu, fresh products are showcased with tapas to share (carcassonnaise snail, tataki of the moment, pili-pili shrimps, foie gras...) and homemade specialities such as Polo burger, local oysters, parillade of the sea, fresh salad with marinated beef, homemade cassoulet and mature beef meat, lovers will enjoy... Another highlight of the menu: the desserts, they are delicious. Tapas and DJ evenings are already scheduled, as well as ephemeral evenings with winegrowers. A very popular address of the Carcassonne people where you can delight the view, the taste buds and the ears in the evenings when the turntables are out.

■ LA DIVINE COMÉDIE

29, boulevard Jean-Jaurès ✆ 04 68 72 30 36
www.ladivinecomedie.fr

Closed from Christmas to mid-January. Open Monday to Friday from 12pm to 2pm and from 7pm to 11pm; Saturday from 12pm to 2pm and from 7pm to 12am. Closed on Sundays. Reservation recommended. À la carte menu: about 20€. Wine by the glass. À la carte dishes only. Starters from 6.50€ to 13.50€, pizza from 9.50€ to 13€, meats: 18€ to 18.50 €; homemade cassoulet with duck confit 19.50€; pasta: 9.50€ to 13€ Desserts 6.50€. Cheques not accepted. Groups welcome (up to 30 people). Baby chairs. Terrace. Take away sale. Free Wifi. Parking in front of the restaurant.

This restaurant-brasserie-pizzeria opened since 1985 on one of the main boulevards of Carcassonne, facing the court, is a must in the lower town. The establishment has just been renovated at the beginning of 2020, with a cosy, refined, very contemporary decoration that favours a certain sobriety in the tones, a real treat for the eyes. The classic menu, featuring quality products, excellent cuisine and generous dishes: an effective formula for over thirty years. Very well known by all, this restaurant is a real melting pot of regulars, we meet lawyers, doctors, who rub shoulders with workers and sales representatives, in short, a warm and relaxed atmosphere for a traditional cuisine, with local products, or a gourmet pizza. Don't stop at the restaurant's inn look, as it is perfect for a breakfast, lunch, dinner or coffee break with friends, as a couple or colleagues. The shaded terrace is very pleasant on sunny days. So, don't miss it...

▶ Note: pizzas and cassoulet to take away.

L'ÉCURIE

43, boulevard Barbès
✆ 04 68 72 04 04
www.lecurie.fr
infos@lecurie.fr

Maître Restaurateur. Qualité Sud de France. Open all year round. Open every day for both lunch and dinner (except Saturday lunch, Sunday evening and Monday all day long). Reservation recommended. Menus from 30€ to 45€. Lunch formula: 16€ (starter + main course or main course + dessert) to 19.90€ (starter + main course + dessert + coffee). Wine by the glass. Traditional Languedoc Cassoulet + salad 22€ (allow 25 min. waiting time). Groups welcome (up to 56 people). Baby chairs. Garden. Terrace. Take away sale. Animations. Wifi. Seminar room. Musical animations on Thursday evening, Friday and Saturday evening. Easy parking and bus parking.

It is not only in the City that you will find incredible and even unusual places, at L'Ecurie, you will be amazed by the tables set up in the old boxes of authentic 18th century stables and a superb garden with trees in the heart of the lower town. Kam, the owner of the place, has been able to give back in a few years its letters of nobility to this emblematic restaurant of Carcassonne. The team in the kitchen will propose seasonal dishes with a strong regional inspiration with the must-eat cassoulet. The meats are excellent and the cooking is perfect, the amateurs will appreciate the veal kidneys with forest sauce or the blanquette of veal in the old-fashioned way. Please note that vegetarian dishes are also proposed such as potato and goat's cheese cake, vegetables board, chives cream or salmon filet confit. Finally, when the weather is fine, planchas and barbecues are offered in the wooded park sheltered from the sun, wind and noise of the city... a haven of peace. An address to closely follow as events are regularly organized there (see the Facebook page).

LE FLAGRANT DES LICES

3, Marcou Square, (cité médiévale)
✆ 04 68 71 45 33 – lefdl@orange.fr

Closed in January. Low season: open every day from noon to 2.30pm and from 7pm to 10pm. In low season, please call for information. Extended opening hours in high season. Menus from €16.90 to €32. A la carte menu: around €40 (starters from €10 to €20, main courses from €16 to €25, desserts from €5 to €9). Children's menu: €10 (up to 10 years old). Lunch formula: €13.90 (starter + main course or main course + dessert. Menu at €16.90: starter, main course and dessert). Wine by the glass. Free aperitif (homemade hypocras) on presentation of the City Pass. Continuous service in high season. Baby chairs. Terrace. Animations.

Located in the heart of the medieval city, Le Flagrant des Lices is a safe bet. The establishment has a terrace on Place Marcou and a more intimate patio at the back of the restaurant, as well as 2 rooms with stone walls and contemporary furniture. Since 2008, Guillaume Luyat has been constantly developing his restaurant, both in terms of decoration and cuisine, with a regularly updated menu. From the starter to the dessert, his cuisine is authentic, made with fresh and seasonal products (guaranteed). While amateurs will enjoy a cassoulet with duck confit and sausage from the Boucherie Izard in Carcassonne, others will appreciate a nice piece of beef with chorizo cream and foie gras or a nice parillade of fish. Renard has tested the Château's menu for you, with a hearty coppa salad topped with a slice of foie gras as a starter, followed by grilled sirloin steak, maître d'hôtel butter and homemade French fries, to finish with a warm and melting tarte tatin. Add to this a smiling and professional service and a very reasonable prices, Renard was delighted with this moment.

FLORIDA BLANCA (BAR À POULPE)

22, rue Trivalle ✆ 04 30 34 58 55
floridablanca22@gmail.com

Closed from mid-February to early March. Open from Tuesday to Saturday for lunch and dinner. Closed Sunday & Monday. Reservation recommended. Children's menu: 9 €. Lunch formula: 17 € (dish of the day: 12 €). Wine by the glass. Tapas from 5 € to 25 €. Dishes from 12 € to 24 €. Desserts 5 €. – Regularly organization of Aperitif'oysters. Reception of groups (the patio can be privatized from 15 people and Nathalie's Pavlova is offered to you to end the meal). Terrace.

When Spain invites itself to Carcassonne, it happens at Florida Blanca, the octopus bar. The room of this tapas bar is very long and overlooks a small heated terrace at the back. We immediately notice the clientele of regulars who know the boss, it must be said that Jean-Lou knows many people in Carcassonne... we then notice the Spanish at tables, which is a good omen for an establishment that offers Iberian specialities... On the menu we find tapas and typical cooked dishes, octopus of course (this is the concept) like the whole grilled tentacle or Thai style, black rice in ink, cuttlefish and light garlic, beef pika-pika, bull rib, burgers... We recommend tapas to share, friendly and that allows you to taste more things. One Sunday a month, the restaurant turns into an oyster bar with a few tapas (facebook program). An address that is good for morale, where we will be happy to come back.

FREAKS – CAFÉ ET CANTINE

30, rue de Verdun
✆ 04 30 18 95 36

Open all year round. Monday to Saturday from 8am to 6pm. Booking recommended. Lunch formula: €16 (to €20 - Single dish: €12). Wine by the glass. Breakfast from €3 to €9. Reception of groups. Pets allowed. Free Wifi. Small lounge with magazines and music at the disposal of customers. Vegetarians welcome. Gluten-free dishes.

Le Freaks opened at the beginning of 2016, with its vintage-retro decor, the address is already one of the highlights of the city center. It must be said that Betty and Hocine, under their "cool" and relaxed looks, are true professionals who leave nothing to chance. Betty always welcomes you with a smile and provides a professional and efficient service, Hocine, in her open kitchen, keeps an eye on the room while preparing her delicious meals. Her cuisine changes according to the seasons and the products are always fresh. Culinary creations that combine tradition and modernity: planked fish, in tataki or ceviche, homemade velvety dishes, cooked meat dishes, all served with seasonal vegetables that bring a true taste boost. Without forgetting the exotic notes declined here and there in his recipes, according to Hocine's inspiration, a true challenge and a unique aestheticism in his recipes: we fell for a courgette salad with courgettes and cake topped with bagna as a starter, followed by octopus à la plancha with an anchovy sauce, served with potatoes, excellent! In the morning, breakfasts are served with Betty's famous homemade granola. In the afternoon you can have a tea with cakes of course and enjoy the small lounge with its vintage furniture, magazines and a turntable to listen to some good vinyls is available.

LE JARDIN DE L'ESTAGNOL

1, rue Benjamin-Franklin
ZA de l'Estagnol © 04 68 47 33 17
www.jardindelestagnol.com
estagnol@orange.fr

Open Monday to Friday from 12pm to 2pm; Tuesday to Saturday from 7: 30pm to 10pm. Reservation recommended. Menus from 20 € to 35 €. Children's menu: 10 €. Lunch formula: 17 € (starter, main course and dessert). Wine by the glass. Groups welcome. Baby chairs. Terrace. Private car park.

It is difficult to imagine that when crossing an industrial zone, we will arrive in such a pleasant place. Indeed, the establishment forms a small enclave of greenery and calmness, between Canal du Midi and the industrial companies of the city. And what a pleasant surprise once you're seated to eat! Jardin de l'Estagnol offers a quality traditional home cooking which is elaborated from fresh seasonal products by the chef Christian Amigues and his assistant Jean Christophe Bounhoure. The ingredients pruduce tasty recipes such as the pan of gambas with chorizo, crème brûlée with foie gras, roasted camembert pan and potatoes, candied pork cheek nut with citrus caramel, sardine tartar with sesame, fish trio... There is also the home-made cassoulet which is copious and cooked according to tradition. On sunny days, you can have lunch on one of the shady terraces which is very pleasant in summer and enjoy grilled meat over a wood fire. Note that there is a very beautiful wine list of Aude at very reasonable prices, you will be pleased to enjoy a nice wine. The reputation of the establishment is no longer to be made in Carcassonne, and if you want to be on the safe side to have a table, it is better to book because the restaurant is regularly crowded... and it is rather a good indication!

MR H

NEW

8, rue de la République
© 04 68 25 41 17
contact@mr-h.fr

Open Monday, Tuesday and Thursday to Saturday from 11: 30am to 3pm and 6: 30pm to 10: 30pm; Sunday from 11: 30am to 3: 30pm. Closed on Wednesdays. Reservation recommended. Children's menu: 12 €. Lunch formula: 20 € (starter, main course and dessert – 18€ starter + main course or main course + dessert). Wine by the glass. Main course only 12€ – Evening à la carte: Shared dishes from 6 to 15€, starters from 12 to 15€, main courses from 15 to 24€, bottled wine from 18 to 35€. Groups welcome. Terrace. Indoor patio, which can accommodate a few covers in fine weather.

Mr H is undeniably the new culinary nugget in the centre of Carcassonne. An incredible building which hides within it the new den of the fine gourmets. La casa Sanchez showcases the market cuisine, generous, tasty, skillfully orchestrated by Hugo, hat screwed on his head and the desire to share as a thread of his creative cuisine. An apprenticeship alongside the great starred chefs Putelat and Ryon, gave him the mastery of flavours, unusual combinations and gustatory discoveries. As soon as you enter, two rooms served by a long corridor welcome you as if you were at home, one cosy with a bohemian decor in the dining room version, with about thirty seats, and the second with a live view of the gastronomic creations, with a counter for about fifteen guests. The decoration is refined and studied, the trendy colours, the careful and subdued lighting make this place the perfect place to sit and eat. The interior patio welcomes you, with a few places, in the first rays of the sun, sheltered from the hustle and bustle of the city. The reception is excellent and a very friendly chef, of a humility to any test completes to convert you at this address. On the menu of the day, velvety lentil soup with foie gras, poultry fricassee, gratin of penne and cream with death trumpets, a Greek bowl for dessert, a delight! In the evening, a reduced menu and small gourmet dishes will delight you, while the lunch formula is different every day, for our greatest pleasure.

Please note: A room can be privatized for all your events, vaulted ceiling and the charm of the old stables revisited.

LE JARDIN EN VILLE
5, rue des Framboisiers
✆ 04 68 47 80 91
www.lejardinenville.fr
contact@lejardinenville.fr

Low season: open Tuesday to Saturday for lunch; Thursday to Saturday in the evening. High season: Tuesday to Saturday for lunch and dinner. Reservation recommended. Menu: about 42 €. Lunch formula: 19 € (starter + dish of the day + dessert + glass of wine / Bistro light formula 16,50€ Starter + dish of the day / or dish of the day + dessert). Wine by the glass. Dish of the day: 12,50 € Starter from 12 to 16€, Main course from 18 to 25€, Dessert 8 €. La grande complète (meal plate): 18 € / Buddha bowl 18€ / Bento from 13,50€. Groups welcome (60 people seated, 120 for lunch, video projector, air conditioning). Garden. Terrace. Take away sale. Shop. Animations. Concept store. Air-conditioned room. Meal tray to be ordered before 11am or 7pm and picked up on site.

In the former market gardening area of the city, Alban and Michèle transformed this farmhouse into a magical place. If they kept the vegetable garden so as to organise their menus, all the rest is different from the rural world; everything is well designed and beautifully decorated! Because here, you are not only welcomed for lunch. There are also a shop with various objects and tableware, a sales-exhibition area where Alban, who is a talented artist, unveils his paintings and sculptures and regularly organises exhibitions of the works of his artist friends. The menu which values local producers (preferably organic) is equally perfect. Choose your table in the meanders of the exhibited objects (and those on sale) and you will enjoy a modern and tasty cuisine. Our favourite is tuna with wasabi peas, or even tuna T8 way and Alban will tell you the story of this dish if you ask him. You can also choose fish, meat or pies as everything is good! . The artistic sensibility of the owners, is even reflected in the presentation of the plates. The welcome is friendly and the service perfect. During fine weather, the garden is a very nice little paradise in full agreement with the dining room as for decoration. Upstairs, there is a small lounge at your disposal for a drink among the works of the host. This year, *Petit Futé* is awarding a well-deserved crush to this concept store located just a stone's throw from downtown.

▸ **New:** order your bento lunch 1 hour before picking it up

L'ARTICHAUT
14, place Carnot
✆ 06 28 94 44 24
lartichaut.carcassonne@gmail.com

Reservation recommended. Low season: open Monday to Wednesday for lunch; Thursday to Saturday for lunch and dinner. High season: Tuesday to Saturday for lunch and dinner. Menu: about 28 € (for a complete meal excluding drinks). Children's menu: 8 € (main course and dessert). Lunch formula: 14,90 € (starter + main course + dessert). Wine by the glass. Tapas from 5 € to 20 €. Groups welcome (on reservation max 20 people). Baby chairs. Terrace. Animations. Capacity 45 covers. Animals accepted.

L'Artichaut is one of the must-see addresses on Place Carnot. This restaurant combines all the ingredients to have a good time, a modern decoration, 2 rooms in a row, a beautiful terrace overlooking the square, a good atmosphere every day and good homemade dishes. Anthony Segui, 28 years old, leads his restaurant with a lot of professionalism and here all the generations meet there. In the kitchen, the chef treats us to his delicious and copious dishes of the day. On the day of our visit, we chose the excellent bull keeper proposed as a suggestion of the day, a delight. Among the house specialities are the unavoidable cassoulet of the paternal, the vegetarian lasagne (aubergine and gorgonzola), the roasted camembert and Serrano, the sliced entrecote steak of 400 gr and homemade sauces or the candied veal chuck, cream with morels and risotto parmiggiano (according to the season). Lovers will delight in mature meats such as the excellent Rubia Gallega (Galician blonde) and to accompany it all, a nice selection of local and foreign wines. In summer, the dishes become lighter with the arrival of carpaccios, salads and tartars. Don't miss the musical evenings announced on their facebook page and find yourself among epicurean partygoers.

L'ESCARGOT
7, rue Viollet-le-Duc
La Cité
✆ 04 68 47 12 55
www.restaurant-lescargot.com
thomasvilleroux11@hotmail.fr

Open all year round. Closed annually in January. From Thursday to Tuesday from 11am to 3pm and from 7pm to 1am. Closed on Wednesdays. Late service in high season. Reservation recommended. Menus from 16 € to 25 €. Children's menu: 10 €. 3 Salad meals of your choice 14 € including one vegetarian. Wine by the glass. Tapas of the world from 4 € to 10 €. Terrace. Air conditioning.
L'Escargot is undeniably one of the Cité's famous safe bets, a pleasant setting made of wood and wrought iron, tailor-made by craftsmen and has a young, dynamic and always smiling team and Thomas who works hard to ensure that the service is as efficient as it is cordial. L'escargot is a restaurant where you can enjoy homemade tapas cooked in front of you. You can choose one of the menus, or choose a la carte specialties that are served on small slates. If we had to mention all our favourite dishes, the list would be long, so here are a few essentials: caramel-pepper sauce magret skewers, shellfish aïoli gratin, grilled chorizo with barbecue sauce, half-cooked foie gras and black olive jam, snails with parsley and Espelette pepper... everything is delicious, even the desserts! Please, note that it is possible to order vegetarian meal. We like the beautiful selection of local wines at very correct prices that you will taste by the glass. Finally, L'Escargot has a second restaurant a stone's throw away, at 4 rue Saint-Jean: Jardin de L'Escargot is an intimate and friendly place where you can also enjoy exhibitions by local artists.

■ LA MAISON DU CASSOULET

Cité médiévale
6, rue du Grand-Puits
✆ 04 68 47 61 03
www.maisonducassoulet.com
mattheo1974@hotmail.fr

Closed in January. Low season: open Tuesday and Wednesday for lunch; Thursday to Saturday for lunch and dinner; Sunday for lunch. High season: every day for lunch and dinner. Menus from €14.90 to €29.90. Children's menu: 9 €. Homemade cassoulet with 2 confits: 16,50 €. "Discovery" formula: 11.90 € (cassoulet with 2 confits + green salad + 1 glass of wine). "Gourmet" package: 19.90 € (same as "Discovery" + dessert of your choice). Groups welcome (on reservation). Terrace.
If you enter the medieval city through Porte Narbonnaise, which is the main entrance, you can't go wrong, the restaurant is located in the second street on the right. Here, the chef shares his secret of the famous recipe of the region: Le cassoulet de Castelnaudary, displaying it at the restaurant entrance and on the wall of the back room. We like to come here and enjoy the shady patio which is set up and sheltered from the wind around a superb Japanese privet. Mathieu, the owner of the premises will serve you are home-made and will welcome you and in the kitchen the chef prepares home-made dishes. The cassoulet is of course the main dish of the house, but also the duck confit with vegetables, whole duck breast, home-made foie gras, copious salads... A simple place in the heart of the medieval city.

■ LA MAISON DE LA BLANQUETTE

2, place Marcou
✆ 04 68 71 66 09
www.restaurant-maisondelablanquette.fr

Closed from November 15 to March 15. Dates subject to slight variations. Low season: open from Thursday to Monday for lunch and dinner; Tuesday lunchtime. High season: daily for lunch and dinner. Low season closed on Tuesday evening and Wednesday. High season: Non-stop service. Children's menu: €10.90 (kids formula). Menu Bistro: €14.90 ; menu Gourmet: €25.

For several years now, we have been referencing this small restaurant in Place Marcou, in the heart of the medieval city. Here we serve you a gourmet and generous local cuisine. The restaurant is very pleasant, here, there is nothing to hide, the kitchens are open to the small room at the entrance of the restaurant completely renewed. After having taken place on the very lively Place Marcou or in the cosy little room on the first floor, you will enjoy a gourmet and homemade cuisine. On the menu, giant skewers of meat or fish: parents and children love it. Specialities are also available such as the delicious homemade gravlax salmon as a starter, the salad of warm candied pork cheeks, cherry tomatoes, chives, hard-boiled egg, burgers, the clerk's plate with its beef fillet, French fries, salad and a small jar of rillette from Maison Bareil (meal plate) not to mention the essential cassoulet (all duck with foie gras) and a raspberry clafoutis for dessert, about which you will tell us more. Here there is something for every taste, every desire and every appetite! Special mention for the Kids formula which offers a nice choice of dishes: cheeseburger, homemade cassoulet, fish & ships or toulouse sausage and homemade puree and dessert. An address we have frequented for years and which never disappoints us.

■ LE PARC FRANCK PUTELAT

80, chemin des Anglais
✆ 04 68 71 80 80
www.franck-putelat.com
contact@franck-putelat.com
♿

Closed the first week of September. Open Tuesday to Saturday from 12pm to 1: 30pm and from 7: 30pm to 9pm. Closed Sunday & Monday. Reservation recommended. Menus from 90€ to 160€. Children's menu: 38€ (under 15 years old). Lunch formula: 60€. Wine by the glass. American Express. Groups welcome. Baby chairs. Garden. Terrace.

Franck Putelat is one of those chefs who have the sacred fire, those for whom cooking is an art in perpetual evolution and who know how to follow the trends to always delight and surprise a demanding clientele. After a first star in 2002, a Bocuse d'argent in 2003, Franck gets his second star in 2012 and becomes meilleur ouvrier de France 2019. The restaurant room, rebuilt in 2015, with a virginal white design, bathes the dining room with great luminosity, and plays with natural elements, nature takes its full meaning both in the room and on the plates. At the entrance you can take a look at the kitchen through the loopholes imagined by the architect, separating the different spaces. The restaurant has a terrace overlooking the park and since winter 2017, Franck has imagined within it, a mountain chalet, which you can privatize, a nod to his native department and the kitchen of his childhood. He offers a menu mixing Aude and Jura, from early December to early March. In the kitchen, the brigade works to sublimate the seasonal products selected, without ever distorting them, but by bringing a touch of exoticism, even madness, perfectly mastered. If you're just passing through, extend this moment by booking one of the 7 luxurious rooms or suites in the Park, to enjoy a sweet night and breakfast before you set off to explore the nearby medieval city...

■ LE PLÔ

23, rue du Plô
✆ 04 68 25 51 85
restaurant.leplo@gmail.com

Closed in January. Open every day for lunch and dinner. Menus from 16,90 € to 29,50 €. Children's menu: 9 €. Lunch formula: 14 €. Wine by the glass. Grill formula: 22,90 €. Mussels & chips formula: 14,80 €. Terrace.

There are some place in the City where you won't be disappointed, and Plô is one of them. Cyril's restaurant is located in the heart of the medieval city between Place Marcou and Grand Théâtre. Each year improvements are made and delight the customers. After major beautification work, there is now a cosy room with old stones, subdued lighting and a contemporary touch and the

menu too has been improved. The house guarantees that everything you eat there is 100% home-made (except the cheese of course) and this is due to big material and human investment.

The menu is refined and offers for example, soup or creamy seasonal soup, excellent cassoulet, crunchy duck breast with honey, beef cheek stew or pork (cooked at low temperature), there is a "steak" formula or a tataki tuna with sesame. The desserts are as perfect, for example the home-made pies are delicious, and also the ice cream which is made on the spot... To accompany yourmeal there is a nice menu of wines of the region. You will have a good time indoors on the well-sheltered terrace.

LE SAINT-JEAN

La Cité
1, place Saint-Jean
✆ 04 68 47 42 43
www.le-saint-jean.eu
restaurant-le-st-jean@wanadoo.fr
♿

Open all year round. In low season: from Wednesday to Monday and on public holidays from 12pm to 2: 30pm and from 7pm to 10pm. In high season: every day and public holidays from 12pm to 2: 30pm and from 7pm to 77pm. Reservation recommended. Menus from 16€ to 29€. À la carte menu: about 35€ (homemade cassoulet with duck confit 14.50€). Children's menu: 9.50€ (up to 12 years old). Lunch formula: 13€ (and in the evening until 8pm). Wine by the glass. Gourmet salads from 16 to 19€. Board of suggestions changing according to the season: from 7€ to 12€ for a starter, 13 to 29€ for the rossini fillet of beef. Tapas from 3.50€ to 8€. Possibility of group menus. Cheques not accepted. American Express. Groups welcome (reservation imperative, 40 people in the dining room and 50 people on the terrace). Baby chairs. Terrace. Take away sale. Animals accepted.

A restaurant that is unanimously acclaimed by tourists and by the Aude inhabitants where you can eat everything against the walls, with a top-notch view of Château Comtal. According to your needs, you can eat in the open air on the large terrace, without being cramped, or inside in a dining room, which, depending on the days, sometimes takes a festive atmosphere! With a very good atmosphere and an attractive menu, it is sure that you will be satisfied. At your choice, traditional dishes like the homemade cassoulet with duck confit, the duck breast with foie gras, the veal kidneys with mustard in an old way and homemade fries or the delicious cod-fish loin and risotto with chorizo, not to forget the hearty gourmet salads. As for the homemade desserts, they are simply a pure delight. Smart: the new (small) bar set in front of Château Comtal, perfect for taking photos while having the aperitif with a few tapas...

LA TABLE DU VATICAN NEW

13, quai Riquet
✆ 06 32 92 30 11
latableduvatican@gmail.com

Open from Wednesday to Monday and on public holidays in the evening. Closed at noon and on Tuesdays all day long. Booking recommended. No menu only à la carte. A la carte menu: about 33 € (antipasti from 2 to 9€, Dishes from 15 to 21€, Pasta from 14 to 18€, Desserts from 5 to 9€). Wine by the glass. Pizzas from 11 to 18€. American Express. Reception of groups. Garden. Terrace.

Need to confess a sin of gluttony? No worries, La Table du Vatican is here! In a unique setting, this true Italian restaurant keeps all its promises, a peaceful place on the banks of the Canal du Midi, a nice terrace welcomes you before entering an atmosphere as cosy as it is offbeat. The baroque decoration is well thought out, the dishes are elegantly staged and the welcome is as friendly as it is professional. You enter the lair of Nina and Franck, who offer their know-how in this establishment, having thought and chosen the smallest detail in the organization of the room and the menu. Let yourself be tempted by the caravan of spritz, a cocktail available in various flavours, and its excellent antipasti board. You will surely opt for the fresh tagliatelle flambéed directly with cognac in a wheel of parmesan, by Franck. Desserts are not to be outdone with an exceptional gourmet coffee or a grand mamma's tiramisu... so just one word AMEN (E)!

New: the Big black, an XXL homemade *chou* filled with vanilla ice-cream from Madagascar with its hot chocolate served in front of you, to be enjoyed!

LA TABLE DE MARIE

NEW

51, rue du Pont-Vieux
✆ 04 68 79 89 59
restaurantlatabledemarie@gmail.com

Closed from December 24th to 31st. Open from Tuesday to Saturday from 12pm to 1: 30pm and from 7pm to 9: 30pm. Closed on Sundays and Mondays. Reservation recommended. Menus from €18 to €30 (evening formula at €30). A la carte menu: about 30 €. Children's menu: 12 €. Lunch formula: 18 € (starter + main course + dessert – 16€ starter + main course – 15€ main course + dessert). Dish of the day 13€ / Cassoulet formula 22€ / Second room for conferences or working breakfast. Groups welcome.

La Table de Marie opened its doors at the end of January 2019 around a bistronomic concept of fresh seasonal products. Here, farewell to frozen food or the reheating of industrial dishes, we are attached to the product, its origin, its freshness, its authenticity, that is what these two Tarbais, Jean-Luc and Marie, advocate. A successful bet! In the kitchen, like Shiva with seven arms, chef Jean-Luc, alone in charge, masters the cooking, prepares starters and desserts, while he prepares, seasoning, cutting... The aromas, taste and flavours are more than just there. In the Marie Room, moves from table to table, giving you advice and kindness, bringing the dishes to beautifully chosen dishes. You will have lunch or dinner in this beautiful room with 30 seats, steeped in Carcassonne history, surrounded by exposed stones, vaults and beams. In short, a remarkable work both on the plates and in the room, a real discovery. A unique formula at lunchtime at a low price and a "à la carte" menu in the evening with four choices of starters, main courses and desserts, based on local products and suggestions from the chef.

LES TABLIERS BLEUS

NEW

865, boulevard Denis-Papin
Les halles de Jojo ✆ 04 68 76 57 94
www.lestabliersbleus.fr
contact@lestabliersbleus.fr

♿

Open all year round. Monday to Wednesday from 7am to 7pm; Thursday to Saturday from 7am to 12am. Open in the evening on Thursday and Friday. Reservation recommended. Lunch formula: 16.90 € (starter + main course + dessert. and free coffee!). Wine by the glass. Starter + main course or main course + dessert with coffee offered 14,90€ – Dish of the day 12,90€ -. Reception of groups. Terrace. Shop.

Les Tabliers Bleus is the story of two childhood friends, ready to take up a challenge, to roll up their sleeves to satisfy small and big appetites. The two partners, Arthur Méré and Julien Mestre, have been welcoming people since March 2019, in Les Halles de Jojo, to their conceptual brewery, where everything is done to satisfy the most discerning customer. They have ideas and will, they have plenty to sell to make good, true, authentic, the truth both on the plate and in the glass with these two. Here you will only eat seasonal products, which are available in the halls, a complete lunch formula is offered, and changes daily according to the freshly arrived products, as well as all the suggestions on the slate. You will taste wines by the glass, from the weekly selection from the wine wall, or choose your bottle on it, at the grocery price, with a cork right. In the same way, you can choose on the stalls of other producers the products you want to taste, pay them directly and taste them at the brewery, a "right of mouth" will apply. On Thursdays and Fridays evenings, enjoy the afterworks in a cosy, relaxed atmosphere, with tapas and meat to share. A place for meetings and exchanges, this brewery allows you to have lunch while shopping, since it is located in a wonderful place where the food industry is concentrated. Le Petit Futé loves it!

LES TERRASSES DE LA CITÉ

5, place Marcou
✆ 04 68 72 07 99
www.lesterrassesdelacite.com
tdc@sfr.fr

Open all year round. From 1 July to 31 August, non-stop service from 11.30 a.m. to 1 a.m. (7 days a week) From 1 April to 30 September, from 11.30 a.m. to 4.30 p.m. and from 6 p.m. to 11 p.m. (7 days a week) From 1 October to 28 February, from 11.30 a.m. to 4.30 p.m. and from 6 p.m. to 11 p.m. Closed on Tuesdays and Wednesdays. Reservation recommended. Single menu at 20,90 €. Pizza, pasta and gourmet salad menus. Children's menu: 8,90 € (up to 10 years old). Wine by the glass. Groups welcome (special group menus on request for groups of 15 people or more). Garden. Terrace. Wifi. English and Spanish spoken.

This beautifully decorated stone house offers two dining rooms, but not only one with a fireplace.... Welcomed by a superb wisteria at the entrance, you will discover a 500 m^2 landscaped garden planted with trees where you will enjoy a quiet moment in an exceptional heritage environment. The infatuation for this place is the result of a real alchemy: a magnificent setting, a terrace on the Place Marcou to enjoy the entertainment or the shady garden more quiet and a quality cuisine combining Italian specialties and unconditional fans of the local soil. This year the menu has been completely rethought to offer a more trendy and modern cuisine always made from fresh products. We still find the inevitable cassoulet of the house, the cassole of cooked mussels and the grilled meats but the novelty is on the very new menu of pasta and pizzas which already makes our mouth water like the "patas" with homemade pesto or the pizza proscuitto, country ham, mozzarella "fior di latte" and fresh rocket. We would like to point out the late service in summer, which is ideal after the shows of the city festival. This restaurant is a safe bet and a renewed favourite!

LE VERRE D'UN (RESTAURANT-CAVISTE)

2, rue de Verdun ✆ 04 68 71 43 99
www.leverredun.com

♿

Open all year round. Tuesday to Saturday from 12pm to 2pm and from 7pm to 10pm. Restaurant closed on Sunday and Monday. Cellar open from Tuesday to Saturday from 10am to 1pm and from 3.30pm to 8pm. Booking recommended. Dish of the day: €12 (formula at €18: Starter + main course + dessert or at €15 starter + main course or main

course + dessert or starter + dessert). Dishes from 14 to €30 (rib of beef and marrow bone). Tapas card from €6 to €12. Room rental. Seminars. Terrace. Entertainment.
Impossible to miss, Le Verre d'Un is located just at the corner of rue de Verdun and square Gambetta. We come here to find a beautiful bottle, among their 400 references (see cellar section), but also for its table where you will be served a bistro cuisine of seasonal products, homemade, where the terroir is highlighted. The decoration of the place is charming, the atmosphere is warm and we like to settle on the inside terrace, as soon as the weather allows it. Frédéric Becq, the Chef, will offer you a different menu every week when you return from the market, with a choice of 2 starters, 2 main courses and 2 desserts. These menus juggle fish and meat, the various dishes on offer are worth a visit, as they are always well balanced and delicious. A few additional suggestions complete the offer, like wasabi tuna tataki with sesame dressing, rib of beef & marrow bone, or homemade cassoulet with a heart of sugar... As for the evening meal, appetizing tapas will seduce you: duck hearts in persillade, duck confit samossas, shrimps with curry and coconut milk, etc. At the table you can indulge yourself by opting for wine by the glass and at the same time discover new estates, which you can buy on site, on the cellar side. Finally, it should be noted that every Friday and Saturday (both lunch and dinner) is Fish & Chips and/or oysters. An ideal address for a lunch break or an evening with friends over good wines.

Good plan: if you like the wine you have tasted at the table and buy a box of the same wine (6 bottles), the bottle consumed at the table will be offered to you.

Sleeping

LE COUVENT NEW
31, rue du 4 septembre
✆ 06 49 76 66 65
contact@au-couvent.fr

Reservation by phone or messenger via their FB page for the restaurant. Double room 90 €; dormitory 30 €. Breakfast included.
It's the story of a success story for two young entrepreneurs, Maxime Camus and Jérémy Marti, who made the crazy bet to save and restore a superb building in the center of Carcassonne, and to transform the 750m² place into a new concept youth hostel. The bet won, for this duo of shock, which makes of its establishment the place "in" of the Bastide carcassonnaise. No less than 72 beds are available on 3 levels, with a tapas bar on the ground floor open to all, a true living space and a festive concept that will delight more than one, all built around a central patio, a 50m² oasis of freshness. So you will have understood that this is not just a traditional youth hostel, it is above all an extremely contemporary establishment, both in its decoration and in its operation, which has more than one string to its bow to seduce a large clientele.

To be noted: every Thursday, Friday and Saturday from 7:30pm under the cloister discover the tapas menu created by Chef Adrien Coste and their 40 wine references.

HÔTEL DU PONT VIEUX

32, rue Trivalle
✆ 04 68 25 24 99
www.hotelpontvieux.com
info@hoteldupontvieux.com

Open all year round. Welcome until 9pm (and with digicode). 19 rooms (room for 4 people from €105 to €135). Double room from €69 to €99; triple room from €95 to €125. Buffet breakfast: €11. Extra bed: €15 (baby bed: €6). Garage (from €7 to €10). American Express. Biker relays. Internet access. Free Wifi. Shop area with local products, regional wines, postcards, designer jewellery... Canal +.

It is in the very nice medieval district of La Trivalle, between the Aude and the Cité (5 minutes walk) that Jean-Michel and Catherine will welcome you with the greatest kindness. The strong points of this establishment are its location, the charm that emerges from it and its very attractive prices. All the rooms have been recently redesigned and this major renovation enabled the hotel to obtain its third star in 2017. The rooms, known as "Privilege", are located on the garden side and several have a superb view of the city. The "standard" rooms overlook the picturesque rue Trivalle and its restaurants with their mouthwatering menus. The decoration of the rooms is modern and elegant, and the restorations carried out have highlighted the existing details, such as the large exposed beams or attic spaces that add to the charm of these rooms. The icing on the cake is the small terrace from which you can take superb photos of the fortress. A pretty *cosy* garden sheltered from the wind is at your disposal to enjoy a moment of relaxation, under an olive tree... in a calm environment. Finally, when you wake up, you will enjoy a hearty breakfast made with good local products such as cheeses from the Briola farm, ham from the Black Mountain, homemade pastries, organic eggs... in short, something to get in shape to face the city

HOTEL ASTORIA

18, rue tourtel
✆ 04 68 25 31 38
www.astoriacarcassonne.com
info@astoriacarcassonne.com

Open all year round. From 7:30am to 8pm. Reception until 8pm (after 7pm contact reception). 19 rooms (including 3 family rooms for 4 people [€75 to €103]). Double room from €46 to €71. Buffet breakfast: €8 (until 9:30am). Baby cot on request. Private outdoor parking: €5 per car per day / Private covered and closed garage €8 per car per day (free for bicycles and motorcycles). Checks not accepted. Pets allowed (small dogs only). Free Wifi. Satellite TV.

Taken over by Sylvia and Ludovic in October 2017, this small hotel close to the train station, within a walking distance from the Canal du Midi, is perfect as a starting point for discovering the Bastide of Carcassonne. Like a phoenix in full rebirth, waking up from a long sleep, the renovations of the rooms and the warm decoration give back a certain charm to the Astoria hotel. This family hotel, divided into two buildings, very quiet, is now starting to conquer a second star, as the new management is constantly making improvements to it. The 19 rooms, all different, are equipped with bedding that will be completely changed in 2018, and a duvet for greater comfort. It should be noted that the hotel has three family rooms for 4 people, so it can accommodate groups as well as families. This charming hotel is one of the few in Carcassonne to have a closed garage and parking (free for bikes and motorbikes), the owners are specialists in welcoming the bicycle tourist.

■ HÔTEL DE LA CITÉ
Place Auguste-Pierre-Pont
Medieval City
✆ 04 68 71 98 71
www.hoteldelacite.com
reservations@hoteldelacite.com

Open all year round. Reception 24 hours a day. 59 rooms (prices according to season and availability). Double room from 240 € to 475 €; suite from 395 € to 925 €. Half-board (several categories, ask the establishment for more information). Breakfast buffet or in room: 28 € (5 € extra for room service). Extra bed: 80 € (free for children under 16 years old). Closed parking: 20 € (free open unsupervised parking). American Express. Babysitting service. Animals accepted (small ones only 15€). Seminars. Receptions and weddings. Internet post. Free Wifi. Restaurant. Satellite TV, Canal +. Excursions (Cinq Mondes spa).

Built at the beginning of the 12th century on the location of the former episcopal palace, this palace proudly stands its exposed stone walls, its woodworks and stained glass windows. It is the most chic hotel of Cité. Unequivocally, here, everything is nothing but luxury, beauty and sensual pleasure. You can be proud of having slept there like famous personalities (Colette was a regular of the place, for example, as well as some artists now scheduled at the festival of the Cité). The room rates – which are as classic as luxurious and refined and with a minimum size of 25 m² - vary depending on whether they open onto an inner courtyard, the ramparts or the square. Idem for the suites, depending on whether their beautiful terrace has a view of the garden and the ramparts, or enjoys a panoramic view of Carcassonne and Cité, as is the case of the splendid suite "Château". Note the "Villa" suites, three suites in an independent building, ideal for families and groups. The hotel's starred restaurant, La Barbacane, is also exceptional, the cuisine of Jérôme Ryon is traditional and offers combinations of flavors new but always successful (see restaurants section).

HÔTEL DU CHÂTEAU
2, rue Camille-Saint-Saëns
✆ 04 68 11 38 38
www.hotelduchateau.net
contact@hotelduchateau.net

Open all year round. Welcome 24 hours a day. 16 rooms (5 classic, 4 superior, 4 deluxe and 3 junior suites). Double room from 122€ to 230€; triple room from 178€ to 209€; suite from 194€ to 275€. Buffet breakfast: 15€ (breakfast with local influences served at the table from 7am to 12pm – in room: 17€ – Breakfast 8€ for children under 8 years old). Closed parking: 10€. Children under 2 years are charged 10€ per night for cots. Concierge service available. Cheques not accepted. American Express, Diners Club. Babysitting service available. Animals accepted (10€). Free Wifi. Restaurant (snacking service 24h/24h). Satellite TV, Canal +. Hammam, hot tub. Heated outdoor swimming pool open from Easter to All Saints' Day (28°c), outdoor jacuzzi open and heated all year round (34°c), Carita SPA with pool and hammam. Open 7/7.

Choosing Hôtel du Château means satisfying your desires for aesthetics, luxury, comfort and serenity, with a breathtaking panoramic view of the medieval city. All the contemporary rooms have been designed to meet all your wishes and expectations. The fabrics chosen and the furniture give the "prestige" rooms a soft atmosphere, all equipped with the latest high-tech equipment. The bathrooms are sublime, glazed and equipped with electric blinds to isolate you or not from the rest of the room. Here, the silence is golden, the soundproof and air-conditioned rooms offer an incomparable view of the City, or the garden, some with a private terrace. The facilities and services offered contribute to the excellence of this hotel, a *Carita* spa (upon reservation), with its three massage cabins, hammam, counter-current swimming pool with integrated whirlpool bath. The hotel also has a heated outdoor swimming pool and an outdoor hot tub heated all year round. Spaces arranged with large sofas, will allow you to rest, comfortably seated, you can contemplate at leisure, the impressive ramparts of the city, you could not be closer. Smart info: take advantage of the many promotional offers by going directly to the hotel's website.

Guesthouses

■ LE MAGNOLIA
59, rue d'Alsace
✆ 07 68 67 89 94
www.le-magnolia.com
contact@le-magnolia.com

Open all year round. 4 bedrooms. From €75 to €140. Breakfast included. Bike storage.

Le Magnolia is a very pretty house entirely decorated by Amandine and Arnaud, the new owners of this house located in the beautiful neighbourhoods of Carcassonne, a stone's throw from the train station, the Canal du Midi, the town centre and about 20 minutes walk from the medieval city. Arnaud at Amandine have made their house a soothing place, with a refined, chic and trendy decoration. The furniture, the lighting, the paintings, everything has been thought of to enjoy a calm and relaxing stay. We fell in love with the "Nature" and "Terrace" rooms, offering a view of the garden where the magnolia tree reigns supreme. The bathrooms will also undergo a total makeover (spring 2020) with materials such as marble, granite or natural stones. Same effort for the organic breakfast with homemade cakes from the Italian coffee, fruit juice, etc.. Arnaud will organize wine tastings in the company of a Carcassonnais winemaker friend. A beautiful place where calm and serenity are the order of the day.

■ **LA DEMEURE SAINT-LOUIS**
2, rue Michel-Sabatier
✆ 04 68 72 39 04
www.demeure-saint-louis.fr
contact@demeure-saint-louis.fr

Open all year round. Welcome 24 hours a day. 5 bedrooms (including 1 suite for 2 or 4 people of 100 m2, 1 apartment of 100 m² for 4 people). In low season: double room from 90€ to 140€; studio / apartment 200€. In high season: double room from 110€ to 150€; studio / apartment 250€. Breakfast included. Extra bed: 30€ (from 2 years old). Closed parking included. Suite: from 120€ to 300€ depending on the season and number of people, apartment: from 700€ to 900€ the week following the season. Credit card not accepted. Animals not accepted. Free Wifi. Satellite Tv.

Bernard and Françoise welcome you to this beautiful 800 m² private mansion, ideally located at the foot of the medieval city, on one of the main roads in the lower town. In 1850, this elegant residence was owned by the Lauer family, who produced the then famous Fritz-Lauer beer in the adjoining brasserie, which has now disappeared. Accompanied by a renowned architect, your hosts have managed to preserve the charm of yesteryear, subtly combining modernity and nobility of period materials. Each room is unique, combining calm, pleasure and softness of hues. The ground floor apartment has a kitchen opening onto the living room and direct access to the garden. The park, hidden from view behind high walls, preserves privacy and is a true showcase of a very Zen spirit, an enchantment in the heart of the city, with its trees and the freshness of its ornamental pond where peaceful Koi carps swim, symbol of love. Particular care has been taken in the preparation of the breakfast, which will delight many gourmets!

Campsites

■ **CAMPING DE LA CITÉ**
Route de Saint-Hilaire
✆ 04 68 10 01 00
www.campingcitecarcassonne.com
campingdelacite@carcassonne.fr

Open on April 1, 2019. Welcome until 9pm (in July and August and until 8pm in mid season). Land of 7 hectares. 200 pitches (including 151 bare pitches and 49 rental pitches. 35 mobile homes). Exposure: shaded / half-shaded. Soil: grassy. Relief: flat. 2 rentals for people with reduced mobility. Motorhome area, (forbidden to motorhomes over 8 meters, caravans and tents): 39 pitches without electricity, payment by credit card only. Pitch + vehicle + 2 persons from 18€ to 26€. Mobil-homes up to 8 persons from 709€ to 904€ per week; mobil-homes up to 4 persons from 254€ to 514€; mobil-homes up to 6 persons from 449€ to 709€. Pitch Basic package from 18 to 26€. Hiking package from 9 to 15€. Visitor's tax: 0.66€ per day. Tourisme & Handicap Label. Children's club. Games for children. Bathroom for babies. Animals accepted (1 animal maxi per pitch: 2.90€). Motorhome area. Internet connection at an extra charge. Wifi free of charge. Restaurant (brasserie, snack bar). Sale (note: Bar/Snack/Grocery from April 1 to September 30). Animations.

A choice location for this campsite located at the foot of the medieval city, which can be accessed by a pleasant hiking trail and only three kilometers from the Canal du Midi. Camping de la Cité is the only one in the city, so it's useless to look for another, this one is perfect. On a surface of seven hectares, the land is planted and the sites are delimited by quite high hedges to have a little privacy, and as for sanitary facilities, all three blocks were completely renovated in the early 2012. The campsite offers a multitude of entertainments for the whole family (in high season): petanque, swimming pool, multi-sport terrain, table tennis, sports tournaments, dance evenings, gym, excursion... Also practical, the restaurant, snack bar and food shop at your disposal from late March to late September. An ideal location to explore Carcassonne while keeping your head in the stars, especially the evening of July 14 where you will be at the first place to witness the spectacular lighting of the medieval city. And you can also book your week stay from Wednesday to Wednesday. In 2016, a camping area was set up right next to the campsite and has 39 pitches.

Leisure

■ **WIN'KART**
Route de Bram
✆ 04 68 25 67 07
www.winkart.fr
contact@winkart.fr

Open all year round. From November to March: 2pm to 6pm. From April to June, September and October: Tuesday to Sunday 2 to 7pm. In July-August: 7/7d 10am to 8pm. Outside these hours on reservation. Ticketing on line. Junior driving lessons on Wednesdays from 2pm to 3:30pm. Go-kart rental (from 7 years old and 1.30 m min): 13€ (9 mns session) Adult: 16€ for 9 minutes; 28€ for 18 minutes and 78€ for 6 sessions; child: 23€ (2 sessions) and 63€ for 6 sessions. Two-seater go-kart. Leisure challenge (on reservation): 40€. Guarded changing room.

If you follow Formula 1 a little bit, you couldn't miss out on young drivers from karting who are winning more and more prizes. Learning to race and speed begins on the karting tracks and Win Kart is the ideal place to start or improve your first laps on the track. With its 976 meters long, this FFSA approved circuit will give you pleasure, challenge, and adrenaline rushes, but above all laughter and good memories with family or friends. The vehicles are new and have 4-stroke engines ranging from 200 cc to 270 cc. Do you want to experience emotions as a couple? A two-seater kart is available. You can then try to beat the current record, by setting the best time. If you come in a group, do not hesitate to book the "Challenge Loisirs" formula, you will have 5 minutes of free practice to familiarize yourself, 5 minutes of time trials and 2 races of 10 laps. There is no doubt, you will come out satisfied and probably a little tired... Many events are scheduled throughout the year, contact them to get all the programming or visit their Facebook page.

Relaxation & Fitness

■ LE BOUDOIR
6, place Davilla
✆ 04 68 77 09 81
www.hammam-leboudoir.com
contact@hammam-leboudoir.com
Open Monday to Thursday and Saturday from 10am to 7pm; Friday from 10am to 8pm. Facial treatments from €40 to €87, Access to the hammam €18, body scrubs €40, massage from €25 to €75. Beauty of the hands or feet €40. Wellness care packages from €60 to €175. Packages 5 sessions from €120 to €190. Women's hair removal from €8 to €30. American Express. The hammam is accessible to people with reduced mobility. Shop.
Once you have passed Le Boudoir's door, your journey to the land of a thousand and one nights begins! A parenthesis of oriental plenitude is immediately offered to you, under this typical Berber tent, intoxicating scents, shimmering colors, the rhythms of a pleasant ethnic music take you far away. You will be in the expert hands of Emilie who will offer you a treatment card adapted to your needs and your body. The ritual can then begin, if you wish, with a hammam, a superb steam bath in shades of night grey, with a 22°C fresh water basin in the centre. The magic works, all your senses are awakened and you enjoy this break of pure well-being. The fragrances are combined whether it is argan oil, shea butter, prickly pear, orange blossom, oriental notes... for your greatest pleasure. You will have a wide choice, as for the proposed treatments whether they are for the face, a targeted area of your body, a body modelling or to perfect the beauty of your hands or feet. You can also opt for a Balinese, shea or rassoul body wrap according to the benefits you expect, and let yourself be pampered with quality products such as La Sultane de Saba or Simone Mahler. Emilie will serve you, to end this moment of sweetness, a mint tea and small oriental sweets, while you can enjoy perfecting your beauty case in the shop.
▶ **Please note:** gift cards that you can buy directly on the website and the possibility to book your treatment online.

Boat

■ LES CANALOUS
15, quai Riquet
✆ 04 68 71 88 95
www.canalous-plaisance.fr
resa@lescanalous.com
Cruises from the end of March to the end of October. Rentals from 1 weekend to 3 weeks. Due to the large offer of boats and seasonal flows, prices are very variable, please call them. Routes adapted to your desires and your time.
Les canalous is the ideal solution to discover the rich heritage of the Aude in a different way! That's why the curious ones (and frankly smart too!) will go and rent a cruise boat without a licence to let themselves slide down the water. Accessible to all, whether there are two or twelve of you, each boat is adapted to your needs and desires. On board, a complete set of equipment will be waiting for you (furniture, crockery, household appliances, bed linen, kitchen utensils, life jackets and other nautical equipment...), all you have to do is discover the "apology for slowness" and a holiday of relaxation on the Canal du Midi, as the locks pass through... The smart ones will book early, and the other freshwater sailors, without imperative, will be able to take advantage of last minute bookings to benefit from mega rates.
▶ For example from Carcassonne: **Weekend** Carcassonne – Bram – Carcassonne: 48 km, 10 locks, 9 hours / **Mini week** Carcassonne, Homps, Carcassonne: 80 km, 26 locks, 18 hours...

Going Out

Tea Rooms

■ CAFÉ GREEN GARDEN NEW
3, route Minervoise
✆ 09 50 18 65 15
sas.happiness.factory@gmail.com
Open Monday to Friday from 7: 30am to 3pm; weekends from 9: 30am to 3pm. Terrace.
Within a walking distance from the Canal du Midi, Green Garden welcomes you in a relaxed vintage spirit, and offers you a break around fresh produce. This coffee shop uses only the best, carefully selected organic and fair trade coffees, roasted by hand, as well as homemade gourmet "en cas". To ensure that the taste is there, a stop in this unusual and atypical tea room is a must, and your energy will be at its peak again!
▶ Green Garden is also a restaurant where you can enjoy "on the go" bagels, burgers and brunches...

■ LE COSY DU PLO
1, rue du Plô
✆ 04 68 25 15 63
cosyduplo@gmail.com
Open all year round. Low season: open every day and on public holidays from 10am to 7pm. High season: every day from 9am. Checks not accepted. American Express. Shop.
Gourmet food has a new place, in the heart of the medieval city, where it can be totally satisfied all year round. Indeed Cosy du Plo, is the new address for a gourmet break, based on natural, local products, selected with great care, you can at leisure enjoy a smoothie, tea or coffee, enjoy a homemade ice cream customizable, or enjoy waffles and pancakes 100% homemade. Take a bath in this cocoon, take the time for a gourmet creation, enjoy! In this beautiful tea shop, with its colourful faux-vintage accents, customer care is the order of the day, and you will find expert advice on a wide variety of regional products, to treat yourself or to offer as a gift. Carine and Charles delight, in this cosy atmosphere, both the Carcassonnais and the many tourists passing through.
▶ **New:** a brunch menu has been added to the establishment's already attractive offer!

KATIA N PATISSERIE NEW

33, rue de la République
✆ 04 34 42 15 98
contact@katia-n-patisserie.com

Open Tuesday, Thursday and Friday from 10: 30am to 2pm and 3pm to 6: 30pm; Saturday from 10am to 6: 30pm. Sweet treats from €2,50, Cheesecake €3,50 / Maxichou vanilla praline €4... Terrace. Shop.

A beautiful and innovative address, which unashamedly puts gourmet food on the agenda. A tea room with a resolutely contemporary design, conceived as a boutique, a beautiful showcase for pastry jewellery. An artist's canopy allows you to follow the design of the sweet creations live, while the cosy sofa awaits you for a snack break, with its succulent hot chocolate. Katia, the hostess of the place, gives "homemade" its true meaning, because here you can, depending on your desires, taste banofee tart, pure hazelnut praline tart, Japanese raspberry rolled biscuit among the multitude of recipes she offers, and especially among the suggestions of the day! You can also enjoy the savoury menu that Seini, originally from New Zealand, who has joined the team of the place, offers you. On the program various savoury tarts, soups, wraps, club sandwiches, flans, sweet or savoury scones, brownies, financials, cookies, desserts... a festival of flavours awaits you. The savoury formula for lunch, including a main course and a dessert, already has its followers, and will be served until 2pm indoors, or in the patio set up as soon as the first rays of sunshine appear.

Bars & Pubs

LE BAR À VINS

Cité médiévale
6, rue du Plô
✆ 04 68 47 38 38
www.lebaravins.fr

Closed from November 15 to February 15. Open during Christmas week from 10am. In high season: open every day and on public holidays from 9am to 2am. Tapas dish from 6 to 12€, dishes from 5 to 21€. Regional wine by the glass 3€, the bottle 21€. Terrace. Restaurant. Animations. Concerts (dj). Terrace with seating for up to 250 people. Groups are accepted on reservation.

It's been almost 35 years since the adventure began and the Bar à Vins is the address to go to for musical and trendy (DJ) evenings in the heart of the medieval city. This year, the owners have changed, and it is Louis, Eric, Isen and Seb who will be at the helm to welcome you and make you feel at home from spring to the end of the year. You come first of all to drink a glass of wine, in the shade of the chestnut tree, a giant bicentenary tree, an important witness of the wild nights of the establishment, but you also let yourself be tempted by a nice plate of tapas, tapenade or any other board according to your desire… then the bar fills up, the resident DJ gets on the decks, sometimes, of the big names of the electro scene, and here we go, the atmosphere rises crescendo. Mojitos, caïpiroska and homemade cocktails are flowing, and during the festival of the city, spectators and artists meet there at the end of the evening, if it's difficult to find a place, we guarantee you a trendy and convivial moment. For late sleepers or early risers, the wine bar also serves breakfast on summer mornings. In winter? It's always so nice, (call beforehand to make sure of the opening hours) we meet inside, we light the fireplace and the atmosphere is always warm!

LE CRÉNEAU

6, place Saint-Jean
✆ 04 68 71 81 53
www.restaurant-lecreneau.com
gobin.creneau@gmail.com

Closed from early January to late March. High season: open every day from 9am to 2am. From April to the end of June: open from 9am-3pm and 6pm-2am closed on Tuesday / October & December: open from 9am-3pm and 6pm-2pm, closed on Sunday evening and Monday / November: open from 9am-3pm and 6pm-2am closed from Sunday evening to Wednesday. Terrace. Food service. Animations. Musical evening with DJ. Ephemeral evenings with winegrowers.

If you wish to discover the city by night, your steps will inevitably lead you to an unusual place, Le Créneau located on the beautiful Place Saint-Jean. Its rooftop offers you an unbeatable view of the counts' castle and magnificent *sunsets*. You can enjoy a leisurely lunch, or dinner under its shade, on the terrace or in the room with its contemporary decoration, sip a cocktail and picnic with friends a little well cooked tapas until late at night, or take a few steps to dance to the wild rhythms of the different DJs who enliven this colourful place one evening (programs on their Facebook page). Nice customers frequent the places, including many people from Carcassone attracted by a unique place and a young, dynamic team that will always do its utmost to make the moment unforgettable. The perfect address for a late dinner or a last drink, where you may come for the first time by chance, but where you will undoubtedly come back for pleasure and desire!

LA MÉTAIRIE

3, chemin de Montlegun
✆ 04 68 26 80 38
lametairie.carcassonne@gmail.com

Open all year round. Wednesday to Saturday from 5: 30pm and from 1: 30pm; Sunday from 6pm and from 1am. Closed on Monday and Tuesday. From Sunday to Friday Early Hours from 6: 30pm to 9pm. Terrace. Restaurant. Animations. Concerts.

La Métairie is the must-see place to admire the sunset over the medieval city. Indeed, this panoramic bar, located on the heights of the city of Carcassonne, will delight all your senses, both your taste buds and your view, sheltered by the veranda or on the terrace, all with music. The concept is simple, a cosy lounge bar, where Carcassonne residents and visitors like to get together for a glass of local wine, or a cocktail while nibbling something. You can come all year round in *afterwork* mode or just for a moment of relaxation, the dishes offered are provided by external interveners who change according to the time of the year. In autumn and spring, it's "tartines XXL" and sushi on Friday evenings, delicious pizzas for the rest of the week. In summer, pizzas are there and you can treat yourself to fish and chips on Thursdays and seafood on Fridays.

ORIGIN'ELLES NEW
1 bis, rue Maréchal-Foch
✆ 07 69 75 05 29
www.originelles-11.fr
origin.elles84@gmail.com

Label for bicycle area. In low season: open on Tuesday and Wednesday from 12pm to 2: 30pm; Thursday and Friday from 12pm to 2: 30pm and from 6pm to 1am; Saturday from 6pm to 1am. In high season: Tuesday and Wednesday from 6pm to 11pm; Thursday to Saturday from 6pm to 1am. Closed Sunday and Monday. Wine by the glass from 3.50€ to 8€. Tapas from 4€ to 20€ per large board. American Express. Animals accepted – Spanish and English spoken. Terrace. Restaurant. Concerts.

This is the story of two passionate women who one day decided to share their beautiful discoveries with us... thus was born the Origin'elles wine bar, a place of conviviality, exchange and sharing around wine. Since September 2018, on the banks of the Canal du Midi, this wine bar with a different approach, accompanies you in a process of discovery, among its 130 wine references, of the region but not only. Here one feels privileged, advised, guided by following our tastes and desires. Nibble on the edge of a barrel for some homemade tapas, whose menu changes with the seasons, or sit in the room or on the patio to enjoy your carefully chosen glass to the rhythm of the musical evenings. The recipe for success is simple, human warmth sprinkled on, enlightened advice given, and the shop to prolong this moment of pleasure: a place full of charm, cosy and hushed, with a convivial atmosphere, Le Petit Futé loved it!

Nightclubs

LE BLACK
Route de Limoux
✆ 07 71 80 62 52
https://complexe-leblack.fr/
leblackcarcassonne@gmail.com

Open all year round. Thursday from 10pm to 4am; Friday and Saturday from 11: 30pm to 6: 30am. Cloakroom 2€ per item (obligatory) – SAM device: Entry 10€ with 2 non-alcoholic drinks. Entrance: 10€ (with one drink except special evening). VIP area: €35 per person and on reservation. 4 entries + 1 premium bottle: €130 Conso with alcohol 10€ Conso without alcohol 5€ / Club entry: 4 entries + 1 club bottle 100€ Conso with alcohol 9€ Conso without alcohol 5€ Club bottle: 100€. Privatization possible (FREE shuttle from 12am: 06 01 31 00 88). Customer shuttle. Restaurant. Animations. Concerts. 2 rooms. Terrace "Le Black Garden": tapas bar and outdoor grill club. Brasserie "Chez Ju" and Parking.

With a capacity of 800 people, Black is the reference for nights in Carcassonne and beyond. With its two rooms, VIP access, summer "Black Garden" and its brasserie, this establishment is now a real complex dedicated to celebration and conviviality. This nocturnal place has evolved over time thanks to its management, the care that Julien Ouddane brings to the sober and refined decoration, as well as the programming. The place is very popular with Carcassonne residents and tourists who are mixed cheerfully on the dancefloor. 100% hits musical programming, a different atmosphere per room, as well as thematic evenings organized regularly. Black people are diversifying and attracting more and more numerous and demanding customers. There is something for every taste and every madness. A "VIP area" is at your disposal, on reservation, especially for your private events. Without forgetting one of the major assets of Black, its Garden, open only in summer season, is a cozy outdoor space (covered by a dome) where you can have a drink while sharing a few tapas, and afterwork party every Thursday from 7pm.

Shopping

LA FILLE DU MIDI
76, rue Trivalle
✆ 04 68 72 47 09
www.lafilledumidi.com
lafilledumidi11@gmail.com

Low season: open Monday from 2pm to 7pm; Tuesday, Wednesday, Friday and Saturday from 10am to 12pm and 2pm to 7pm; Thursday from 10am to 12pm and 2pm to 6pm. High season: every day from 10am to 1pm and from 4pm to 8pm. Closed on Sunday and Monday mornings except July & August. Delivery possible (online order, tasting possible during the high season on reservation).

This pretty delicatessen and tableware store opened its doors in March 2017 in the medieval district of La Trivalle. You will be pleasantly surprised by the originality of the front, surmounted by a bicycle, whose basket filled with flowers invites you to take a gourmet stroll in the Aude region. Indeed, Cristelle Lucchèse devotes herself, in her shop, to the enhancement and sale of Occitan products essentially, to the delight of our taste buds. At La Fille du Midi, you will find the best of local crafts and productions, in the food industry of course but not only. The foie gras, cassoulets and beef stews of the Maison Escourrou, mix with the chocolates of the pastry chef Thimoreau who created, especially for this brand, chocolates in original shapes, Gruissan Salt, Marseilles rice grown by Laurent Malis, pasta from the Domaine de Périès, savoury and sweet biscuits, oils and vinegars, olive paste... and so many other flavours that it is impossible to name them all! Cristelle has not forgotten the creative craftsmen, with the art of the table and its atypical elements with clear and refined lines like no other. To finish in apotheosis, a selection of wines scrupulously chosen directly by the owner, will let you apprehend the different grape varieties and blends through the richness of the Aude terroir, the crémants and blanquettes of the Maison Antech de Limoux, the local aperitifs Micheline and Or-Kina, the Carcassonne beers La Ciutat or the fruit juices of the Maison Bergé. A decidedly very smart address!

Please note: gift boxes can be created according to your budget, for companies and individuals.

MÉMOIRE DES SIÈCLES
5, place du Château
La Cité
✆ 06 85 73 46 31
www.shopmds.fr
Info@shopmds.fr

Open every day from 9am to 7pm. Open all year round. Sale and rental of medieval costumes and accessories. Gift ideas for all budgets.

How can we not be charmed by this shop? Once you have passed the door, everything brings us back to the Middle Ages! The owners of the place, are passionate about this period and offer in their clothing corner shop (for sale or for rent), accessories (belts, shoes, headdresses, purses....), reproductions of weapons, jewels, games, and decoration objects of medieval inspiration. You can also find there a true curiosity cabinet, as well as everything necessary for vintage writing, or painted canvases and tapestries, etc. You will be charmed by a wide choice of books for children, always fascinated by these 10 centuries of History. They can thus discover all the aspects of the daily life in the Middle Ages, from knights to fortified castles, via the builders of cathedrals. Many gift ideas for a few ecus of hard cash and moreover, a commercial gesture will be made upon presentation of your Petit Futé!

Gourmet Basket

ARTHUR ET ADRIEN NEW
27, rue Albert Tomey
✆ 06 12 83 68 86
www.arthuretadrien.fr
contact@arthuretadrien.fr

Open from Tuesday to Saturday from 10am to 7pm. Delivery possible (order and delivery possible via their website Free shipping for orders over 18 bottles or €250 purchase). From €8,5 to €33 per bottle.

Worthy sons of Bacchus, these two have fallen into a very small world, and the effects are permanent in them. The Limouxins Arthur Lallemand and Adrien Mingaud transport us through their selection of wines in a universe of aromas, agreements, grape varieties, passion. The love of terroir runs in their veins, and beyond being "wine selectors" they are also blenders and producers, thanks to the family vineyards on the Malras side of the Limouxine land, which become a fantastic play laboratory for them. These two have not finished marvelling at the wine nuggets discovered during their research throughout the Languedoc-Roussillon region. With a growing notoriety, amply deserved, they have opened a place for tasting, sales and exchanges in June 2019 in the heart of the Bastide Carcassonnaise, highlighting the work of the most promising winemakers, exalting the richness of the vintages found. Local products from delicatessens will be added to their offer, alway high quality but atypical, like this organic gin from the Basque country made by a Carcassonnais. So for a purchase or an epicurean pleasure, trust their selection of exceptional wines, blindly approved by a jury of fine masters, professionals with the most experience s of in sommelier and gastronomy, before being put on sale, for unique food and wine pairings. An address to engrave in its shelves!

Should be noted: themed tastings to come

DOMAINE CHARLEMAGNE NEW
lycée charlemagne
route de saint hilaire
✆ 06 74 63 39 10
www.epl-carcassonne.fr
expl.carcassonne@educagri.fr

♿

Open Thursday and Friday from 2 to 6 pm; Saturday from 10 to 12 am and 2 to 6 pm. Open the rest of the week by telephone reservation. Wine estate in IGP Cité de Carcassonne, vineyard in organic conversion, private cellar, sales cellar open all year round, also distributes local products. Delivery possible. Cheques not accepted. A lift leads to the cellar, to receive people with motor disabilities, and the cellar has been specially designed for people with reduced mobility.

Charlemagne's agricultural college, a veritable nursery for the winegrowers of tomorrow, opened in spring 2019 a magnificent atypical cellar at the gates of Carcassonne with a panoramic view of the medieval city. The place is a work of art in itself, with the monumental fresco covering the vaulted ceiling, a creation by the world-renowned Montolivain artist Harillo, entitled "Al Vino, l'ode de l'Aude au vin" (Al Vino, the Aude's ode to wine). Didn't Aristotle say that "Art and Wine are the superior joys of free men"? It wasn't long before Jean-Marc Olivier, the Director of the estate, offered his wines in organic conversion this beautiful setting so that the nectars produced on the 20 hectares of the vineyard, in PGI Cité de Carcassonne, would find their quintessence here. The Cabernet Franc, Syrah, Merlot, Viognier, Chardonnay and Muscaris varieties are produced and vinified on site in a modern private cellar using the latest techniques, as is the case for the Carolus Magnus cuvée, which is aged in ovoid vats made of natural cement, thus providing micro-oxygenation to the wine. The different vintages are the result of professional work allowing an educational collaboration between the students of the agricultural high school and their teachers, a beautiful synergy for products rewarded by many medals: the cuvée l'Epée, gold medal at the Mondial du rosé 2019, the Blason (red) 2018, bronze medal at the Vinalies competition, the Source (white) has also just won a magnificent gold medal at the 2020 Agriculture Show in Paris, the Cartagena de Carlesmanhe is not to be outdone, with a silver medal 2019 at the Concours des Grands Vins du Languedoc, without forgetting the "Carolus Magnus" flagship that collects them. This cellar is also a beautiful showcase of local products, with the traditional Carcassonnaise beer la Ciutat, the olive oil of Domaine des Pères or the vinegars of the Cyril Codina de Lagrasse... but it is also a place of life, culture and traditions with superb temporary exhibitions and Occitan evenings of sharing. You will have understood it, hurry to stop there, to taste beautiful vintages, and to delight your palate as well as your eyes!

■ ÉPICERIE DES PRODUCTEURS-BERGÉ FRÈRES

Boulevard Denis-Papin, ZI la Bouriette
✆ 04 68 47 68 77 – sarlbergefreres@orange.fr

Open Monday to Saturday from 8am to 7pm. Label Le pays cathare. Delivery possible. In addition to the shop, it is possible to order fruit and vegetable cakes to decorate all your events (aperitifs, weddings, receptions).

Jean-Luc and Éric Bergé produce fruit and vegetables at the pond of Marseillette: asparagus, melons, tomatoes, squash, artichokes, pears, a dozen varieties of apple trees... Their productions are varied and they sell them in their store in Carcassonne, which also hosts the gourmet products of more than 90 other local producers. All the specialities of the agriculture and breeding of Aude are represented here and the consumer benefits from a wide choice to fill his basket of fruits and vegetables of course, but also of meat and delicatessen, a beautiful selection of wines, jams, honey, biscuits, chocolates and nougats, oils, a there is also a creamery section which proposes yoghurts, raw milk and other dairy products. The meat and sausages are produced in the open air and the fruit and vegetables are grown in an environmentally friendly way. The opening of the first Drive Fermier Audois by these passionate producers now allows you to order online and pick up your products at Bergé shop or at one of the other collecting points in Carcassonne and the surrounding area. This drive is a collective project carried out by producers who want to share with consumers the diversity and quality of local products from organic farming.

Drive Fermier Audois
www.drivefermieraudois.fr
06 18 97 74 08

■ LA FERME

55, rue de Verdun ✆ 04 68 25 02 15
www.laferme-carcassonne.fr

Open from Tuesday to Saturday from 8am to 12: 30pm and from 3pm to 7: 30pm. Nearly 7000 references in cheeses, charcuteries, fresh products, groceries, teas, coffees, alcohols, wines, gifts and accessories.

Welcome at the Aladdin's cave of Gilles and Jacqueline Fiorotto, within the fortified town near Place Carnot. This is a reference place for any self-respecting Epicurean. You will always find here the product which will satisfy you with an extreme quality exigency. You will discover in this amazing shop some 7000 references after being tested, tasted and broken down before ending in your plate and palate. This team of taste experts will advise you, guide you in the best way with a permanent care for absolute satisfaction. You will lose your mind among the shelves of delicious cheese, attractive cured meats, exceptional wines and spirits, interesting delicatessen. You will be tempted! Note the presence of some original items like the Himalayan salt diamond from Himalaya to be grated, the original macarolat creations or variations of colourful calissons. Besides these various delicious products, you will appreciate the warm reception of the available staff which will advise you in the best way.

If you can, you can taste while standing next to an authentic barre, a good glass of wine with a homemade plate. All this in a good and friendly atmosphere.

LA FILLE DU MIDI
76, rue Trivalle
✆ 04 68 72 47 09
See page 55.

FROMAGERIE BOUSQUET
865, boulevard Denis Papin
Les Halles de Jojo
✆ 04 68 71 82 55
nicolas.bertrand14@wanadoo.fr
Open Monday to Saturday from 8: 30am to 7: 30pm, Sunday from 8: 30am to 1: 30pm at the Halles de Jojo. Open from Monday to Saturday from 8am to 12: 30pm and from 3pm to 7pm at the Boutique rue Chartran.
Those who love cheese now have two addresses, the downtown cheese factory a stone's throw from Place Carnot and in the industrial zone. La Bouriette in the new Halles de Jojo. Whether you are at one or the other cheese factory, you will always find the same quality of products and service, do not hesitate to ask for advice to guide you according to your tastes: sheep, goat or cow cheeses, strong or milder, plain or flavoured, many of which are of local origin, the products sold here will delight your taste buds. A gourmet address to be tested without moderation. It is possible to buy platters to make excellent raclettes or snack platters at very reasonable prices. And if you want to have the Cheese Bar experience, go to Les Halles de Jojo! (see restaurant section)

CHEZ JULIEN
100, chemin de Maquens
✆ 04 68 26 34 32
www.chez-julien-carcassonne.fr
Open Monday from 2: 30 pm to 7 pm; Tuesday to Saturday from 9: 30 am to 7 pm.
Since Julien D'Allasta and his sister Corinne created their temple of gourmet delicacies, the small business has been constantly evolving to the delight of their customers. The shop is located just in front of Décathlon (A61: Carcassonne-West exit) and has a large car park. Those who love good products have made this address a sort of annex to their kitchen where they can find exceptional products. Everything on offer has been meticulously selected to suit all requests and budgets. At Chez Julien, there is of course a very nice range of wines from the region with a nice focus on those of the department but also some beautiful bottles of Bordeaux, Burgundy, Rhone Valley... Also appreciable, the wide choice of wines packaged in magnums, the sweet nectar will be all the better and the effect on the table guaranteed. You will be able to complete your cellar with champagnes from famous houses such as Taittinger, Roderer... as well as small quality producers at more accessible prices. Whiskies, rums, armagnacs and homemade beers also occupy a beautiful place. To accompany the tasting, you will have the choice between a very nice range of fresh or ripened cheeses from Xavier (Master ripener since 1976 in Toulouse and "meilleur ouvrier de France" in 2011), succulent foies gras from Béarn from the Maison Argaud, and Iberian hams including the Bellota reserves, the premium Jabugo de la Jabuguña, black Gascony pork from Haut Vallespir well raised in the open air by Thibault Gonzales, excellent smoked trout from Banka in the Basque Country, spices, jams, chocolates from the house of Nougalet, spit cakes, vinegars, etc. A smart address where you can be sure not to be fooled about the merchandise!
Smart: Julien offers cheese and charcuterie platters made to order, ideal and so delicious for your aperitifs and other occasions.

Wines & Spirits

ARTHUR ET ADRIEN NEW
27, rue Albert Tomey
✆ 06 12 83 68 86
See page 56.

LES BRASSEURS DE LA CITÉ
240, rue Edouard-Branly
✆ 04 30 34 14 21
brasseursdelacite.com
xavier@brasseursdelacite.com
Open Monday to Friday from 8am to 12pm and from 1pm to 7pm. By appointment only. Shooter rental for parties, parties, weddings 30€ for the weekend. Guided tours by appointment only, in French and English, free of charge, by reservation, 12 people maximum. Boxes of 12 from 30€ to 35€. Beers are also sold in 20L and 30L barrels. Carca-Cola & Limonade la Pitchoune: 25€ for 12 33 cl bottles.

Château Auzias (the old cellar and the new cellar).

Carcassonne has been reviving the tradition of beer brewing since July 2015, thanks to Xavier and Désirée Benoist, whose brewery produces homemade beers made with wheat and barley grown in France. They have given their beers the pretty name of Ciutat, which means City in Occitan, and adapt them according to the seasons, with a spring beer, an autumn beer and a Christmas beer. But all year round, you can also enjoy the Classiques: Ciutat Blanche, a refreshing wheat beer, blonde, Pils, a traditional Czechoslovak beer made from 100% barley malt, or Ambrée, with its sweet bitterness and strong flavours. By appointment, you can discover, on site, the entire process of making their beer: the grain germination, the dosage of the hops that gives flavour and bitterness, the brewing, the filtration and the fermentation, all the steps to obtain this ancestral drink that Xavier elaborates with passion. A whole gustatory heritage to discover and share! After brewing, filtration separates the grain peels from the beer, and these residues are then given by Les Brasseurs de la Cité to the farmers of the Montagne Noire to feed their livestock. For children, Xavier has been offering two fizzy drinks since 2017, Carca-Cola (without caffeine) and Pitchoune lemonade, refreshing and slightly lemony.

■ CABANEL – VINS ET LIQUEURS ARTISANALES
72, allée d'léna ✆ 04 68 25 02 58

Open Monday to Saturday from 8am to 12pm and from 2pm to 7pm.

Founded in 1868, Maison Cabanel has been located on the alley of léna since 1905. The place is original, a traditional deccoration, a welcome and sound advice, here, you can find true small pearls: regional wines, champagnes, a multitude of aperitifs, a beautiful range of whisky, rums, vodkas, Gins, homemade liqueurs. The owner Jean-Marc Gazel is the only one who makes the famous Micheline, recipe which would date back to the 4th century, and the Or-Kina, plant-based aperitifs. He also produces 100 %-Carcassonne pastis. Do not leave without having tasted the "Crème de Menthe (Mint Cream)" and the" Crème de Citron (Lemon Cream)", these liqueurs made without additives or colouring agents are very successful, if you try them, you will not drink another thing anymore, word of Fox. The latest of the house, "Le Rigolo" a vermouth made with the cooperation of Gaetan, the head bartender of the five-star Hôtel de la Cité, perfect for your cocktails like the "Spritz". A shop that sweetly smells authenticity, we love it!

CHÂTEAU AUZIAS – CAVEAU
Chemin de Paretlongue
Pennautier (11610)
✆ 04 68 47 28 28
www.auzias.fr – visite@auzias.fr

Open Monday to Saturday from 9am to 5: 30pm. For groups, by appointment only. Outside the above-mentioned times and days, please inform them by phone. The domain also receives camper vans free of charge all year round. Maximum capacity of 5 at a time. Delivery possible. Online shop with the possibility of buying wines directly from the Internet. Follow the link: www.shop.auzias.fr

There is a Wine Tour in the château's vines. This very complete visit consists of a presentation on the history of the Château, a tour within the vineyard (by golf cart – depending on the weather and the number of people). On the way back, you will visit the cellar following the different stages of the production of their wines until bottling. A free tasting of Château Auzias wines will complete this beautiful discovery. In addition to the visit, the place is ideal for shopping and acquiring good and beautiful bottles of local wines from the City of Carcassonne and AOP Cabardès. Possibility to fill your car trunk with bottles and BIB at the preferential price of the property. You will also find exclusively in France, (with the Duty Free Shop of the airports and at Lavinia in Paris), some divine bottles of Chinese wines produced by the family's vineyard in Penglai, Yantai Province in the China Far East: Le Château Reifeng-Auzias. Finally, note that the domain is very connected: facebook, Google +, You Tube... find the latest news on the website: DOM AUZIAS!

▸ **Note:** the weekend of November 11 Exhibition and sale of art, design and decoration at Château Auzias

© Yan EVEN

Aragon.

■ LE VERRE D'UN (RESTAURANT-CAVISTE)
2, rue de Verdun
✆ 04 68 71 43 99
www.leverredun.com
contact@leverredun.com

Open from Tuesday to Saturday. Cellar shop: Tuesday to Saturday from 9: 30am to 12: 30pm and from 3pm to 7pm, Wine bar: Tuesday to Saturday from 10am to 10pm. The bistro-restaurant: from Tuesday to Saturday for lunch from 12pm to 2pm, in the evening from 7pm to 10pm. Delivery possible (5 km around Carcassonne). Privatization of the premises: events, seminars, weddings, a party with friends... Terrace.

Le Verre d'Un attracts your eyes and awakens your taste buds even before you enter the entrance door. Here, you will discover the typical features of the wines and the terroirs, with no less than 400 references, there is plenty to do, at all prices, Cécilia will advise you with the utmost accuracy. Feel free to visit the online shop and use the click and collect, because in addition to the smile, you are put in charge of the car! The vineyard of the south of France is one of the remarkable selections of this cellar, but the most beautiful place is given to the wines of the department: Minervois, Corbières, Malepère, Clape, Cabardès, Limoux, Fitou... Also note, a very beautiful selection of spirits and Champagnes, those who love will enjoy it. Le Verre d'Un is also a restaurant and a wine bar, where you can also come with friends to taste after work and relax. Good plan. Please note the 3 tasting formulas possible: "Découverte" (every day until 6pm, tasting by the glass of 3 wines and tapas board at 20 euros), "Thème", or "Cousu main". An address perfect to know everything about the best wines in the region if you like.

In the surroundings

Aragon ★

■ LA BERGERIE
Chemin de Pech-Mary
✆ 04 68 26 10 65
www.labergeriearagon.com
info@labergeriearagon.com

Qualité Sud de France. Qualité Tourisme. Open from Tuesday to Friday in the evening; Saturday for both lunch and dinner. Closed Sunday and Monday. Few places reservation strongly recommended. Reservation recommended. Menus from 28€ to 34€ (single menu called Market Menu, in 2 or 3 courses. Food and wine pairing extra (3 glasses) 15€/pers. Cassoulet to order (48h in advance) 20€/pers). Children's menu: 10€ (a 3-course menu will be proposed according to the child's tastes). Wine by the glass. 8 rooms from 80€ according to the season and the room – including 1 fitted out for people with reduced mobility -. Breakfast 10€. Swimming pool. Tourist tax 1€ per day and per person. American Express. Labels: Qualit. Groups welcome. Baby chairs. Garden. Terrace. Private car park.

When you arrive on the heights of Aragon, you will immediately understand that you have made the right choice as the village is beautiful, impression confirmed upon arrival at La Bergerie. The restaurant adopts a contemporary style. As for the the bedrooms that are true nests, each bearing a beautiful flower name, you can only fall in love with this modern country house. As for cuisine, the house has a well-justified culinary reputation.

The cuisine changes according to the inspiration of the chef, Fabien Galibert, and seasonal products. La Bergerie offers a unique menu, the market menu, which changes every week, and each dish can be chosen à la carte. For those staying at the address, the menu changes daily. The terroir is ubiquitous in the plates and notes of modernity are looking great. Œuf parfait, crumbled duck, consommé, pork breast cooked at low temperature during 72 h, potato emulsion and mushrooms of the moment, Guinea fowl fillet in vanilla celery version, strawberry-chocolate delicacy... that's an overview of what you can find on the menu. For relaxation, the house has a swimming pool with a view of the garrigue and two of the bedrooms, a private terrace.

Pennautier

Pennautier is a charming small village of about 2,500 inhabitants where we can find one of the oldest wine-growing castles in France located in the heart of the AOP Cabardès and only a few kilometers from Carcassonne. Historically speaking, Pennautier enjoys many assets, with a restored old tile factory, megalithic burials of the Bois de Moure, consisting of a covered alley and a Tumulus, as well as the magnificent castle, built under Louis XIII, called the "little Versailles", and listed as a historical monument with its park since 1972. All this cultural heritage contributes to the influence of this small village, in the department of Aude and the Languedoc-Roussillon region. Local associations lead a very rich sporting, cultural and social life, with a special time during the "Cabardièses de Pennautier" in August, a fabulous piano festival, other events punctuate the course of the year, through the varied cultural programming of the Na Loba theater, which hosts dance shows, concerts and plays. Also noteworthy is the Anne-Marie Almerge multimedia library, which offers a wide range of collections for all audiences (novels, literature, comics, documentaries, local collections, etc.) as well as a multimedia area.

CHÂTEAU AUZIAS – PARETLONGUE

Domaine de Paretlongue

✆ 04 68 47 28 28

www.auzias.fr

bastien@auzias.fr

Open all year round. From 9am to 5: 30pm. Online shop with customer service available 24 hours a day, 7 days a week and free delivery from €199 purchase on: www.auzias.fr. Free tasting and wine sale on site. Wine Tours. Guided tour (groups by appointment by telephone booking). The estate also receives motorhomes free of charge all year round. Maximum capacity of 5 at a time.

Among the Auzias family, wine is a serious business! And for good reason, as this old Languedoc family of Carcassonne winemakers has worshipped this divine drink since 1872, when their craftsmanship began! To follow the development of the different vintages, Château Auzias offers wine tours: visit of vineyards, winery and cellars, an attraction preceding the tasting of its most beautiful wines in the cellar. In addition, Château Auzias, like bees, has spread in eastern China by establishing a vineyard there , the Reifeng Auzias castle (located in Penglaï in Chinese Shandong), whose wines obtained the most beautiful medals of the biggest international competitions, including the famous Gold medal and International Wine Trophy, awarded by the Decanter magazine in the Royal Opéra House of Covent Garden on December 4th, 2013, rewarding the best cabernet franc in the world. 2019 innovation, under the leadership of Poli Perrenoud, a new space has been created on the estate: a place that combines art and wine in which you can discover works by contemporary artists and taste the estate's wines there. Going to the photocall is essential to immortalize this moment at the handlebar of a vintage side car, we love it! The website to shop online is practical. Stay informed about the latest news on the estate by connecting to their Facebook pages (friends and corporate), Instagram, Pinterest, Flickr, Youtube, Google +, Twitter, etc. pages. So, will you follow?

Domaine Auzias.

Château Auzias (the façade of the castle).

MARIONS LES CHOCOLATS
16, rue Pierre-Loti
✆ 06 15 47 62 12
marionsleschocolats@gmail.com
In the centre of Pennautier, right next to the church.

Open from Wednesday to Friday from 10am to 12pm and from 2pm to 6pm; Saturday from 3pm to 6pm. On the Carcassonne market on Saturdays, except in summer. Closed 2 weeks in January. Open on Sundays (only for Chocolate Workshops). Delivery possible (order online; delivery time: 8 days). Chocolate workshop 1 Sunday per month from 1: 30 pm to 4: 30 pm: 35 € for 3 hours. Reservation required. American Express.

In her beautiful shop near the church of Pennautier, Marion welcomes chocolate lovers. She is an artisan chocolate maker and offers candies, marshmallows, fruit pastes, macaroons, orangettes, chocolate decorations, ready-made shortbread jars, spreads, chocolate bars, chocolate to drink and even chocolate to break. And she constantly innovates according to her desires and your desires, according to the events of the calendar and her creativity will seduce you. High quality chocolate, remarkable craftsmanship, for those who love good chocolate. There is a chocolate and wine workshop on request, and workshops on seasonal themes all year round and chocolate maker caterer for your private events. Enjoy it without moderation! For special events, you can win nice chocolate gifts so do not hesitate to follow her on the social networks, it will also be the occasion to see her new creations.

Trèbes

Trèbes is an ancient fortified village located less than 10 km east of Carcassonne. Several bridges span the three rivers running through it. Canal du Midi is part of the landscape. A marina was set and the towpath offers a pleasant stroll in every season. Towards the end of the village, do not fail to see the triple lock, built into the rock wall: its difference in height led to the construction of two mills. You could also see the bridge canal of Vauban and the bridge of Rode. Several types of cruises are offered on Canal du Midi from Trèbes. The weekly market is held every Sunday morning. And every Saturday morning, the sea comes to you with the sale of mussels and oysters. During summer, fireworks are fired along Canal du Midi and in the arenas, night markets and concerts are organized as well as the great Occitan festival Tresbes e Festa d'OC.

EL CAMPO
7, avenue des Capucins
✆ 04 68 78 61 61

Open all year round. Mondays, Tuesdays, Thursdays and Fridays for lunch and dinner; Wednesdays for lunch; Saturdays for dinner. Closed Wednesday evening, Saturday lunch & Sunday. Reservation recommended. Menus from 11,90 € to 30 € (the dinner menu). Children's menu: 7.50 €. Lunch formula: 11,90 € (express formula with a buffet of starters or formula of the day at 13,90 €, business menu at 17,50 €). Pizzas from 8.50 € to 14.50 €, starters from 5 € (green salad) to 15 €, fresh pasta 12.50 €, meat from 15.50 € to 20 €, fish from 14 € to 15.50 €, tapas menu from 4 € to 8 €. Groups welcome (only on reservation). Baby chairs. Garden. Terrace. Take away sale. Wifi.

A must-visit address that has been renamed "el campo chez Poy" by the new owner, a fine connoisseur of the place, for having worked for more than thirteen years alongside the previous owners of this establishment. It is now Patrice and Myriam who welcome you, with a natural kindness, in this beautiful period building at the end of a courtyard. The place is very pleasant and the concept is amazing, as we practice the culinary melting pot, a mix of Iberian and Italian cultures. A nice promise for a meal full of Mediterranean charm, hearty and perfectly tasty. Here, conviviality and sharing are the order of the day, you can enjoy tapas or succulent pizzas that are a delight to eat. You can choose between two authentically decorated rooms, depending on your preference Naples or Barcelona, the upper room with low ceilings, frescoes and Iberian decorative elements reflect the Spanish tradition.

As for the Italian, you will be able to admire the majestic chimney which is set at the back of the room, while the chef is working near the pizza oven. The staff is extremely considerate and will serve you quickly when your lunch break is tight. When the weather is fine, you will have the possibility to settle down on the courtyard side or under the arbour of the terrace, in a quiet area.

- **A private car park awaits you as well as Wifi**
- **Possibility of pizzas to take away.**

LE MOULIN DE TRÈBES
2, rue du Moulin
✆ 04 68 78 97 57
www.lemoulindetrebes.com
contact@lemoulindetrebes.com

Open Tuesday to Saturday for lunch and dinner; Sunday for lunch. Closed: Sunday for dinner and Monday for lunch and dinner (except public holidays). Reservation recommended. A la carte menu: 48 € approximately. Children's menu: 16 €. Lunch formula: 21 € (starter, main course and dessert – 19€ starter + main course or main course + dessert). Wine by the glass. Lunch menu is a unique menu that changes regularly, depending on the products on the market. Starters from 16 to 24€, main courses from 20 to 24€, desserts from 7 to 12€. The room and the terrace are wheelchair accessible, not the toilets. Groups welcome. Terrace.

Pascal and Sophie Ledroit, who have been living at Le Moulin de Trèbes for several years, have revived this place. The place is magnificent, a shaded terrace on the banks of the Canal du Midi, a restaurant that combines the cosy charm of the old with the modern comfort of this old mill. This address is undoubtedly one of the best restaurants in Carcassonne, it must be said that Pascal and Sophie are very demanding both on the dishes they offer and on the quality of service. Here, no tomatoes in winter and scallops in summer but local and seasonal products, the chef favours short circuits and small producers. His cuisine is imaginative, tasty and modern, sometimes with a hint of his native Belgium. Whether you like meat or fish, you will offer your taste buds a festival of flavours. The number of seats are limited to guarantee a meal in the best conditions, it is advisable to book. An address to be visited without moderation all year round!

LOCAVÉLO
3, rue du Plô-d'Orbiel
✆ 04 68 78 68 81
www.locavelo.fr
locavelo@gmail.fr

High season: open every day from 10am to 8pm. Open daily in July and August, on request the rest of the year. Spoken English. Delivery possible. €12/ cycle per half-day, €18/ cycle per day, and €75/ cycle per week. Equipment rental: helmet, tow bar, baby seat... Credit card and cheques not accepted.

Located in Trèbes, in a picturesque setting, in the heart of the old village, between the church and the Canal du Midi, for more than 12 years, Locavélo's credo has been to satisfy the walking desires of all their customers. Whatever your desire, the type of outing you are planning, they will advise you in the best way to find the right type of cycle. Their geographical location offers an ideal starting point for walks and bike rides, at your own pace, to discover the Canal du Midi (towpath) and/or the Audois paths. You will find all the accessories you need to practice the cycle (helmets, puncture repair kit, pump, children's trailer, baby seats...).

DOMAINE DES PÈRES
16, avenue Pierre-Curie
✆ 06 75 99 01 68
http://www.domaine-des-peres.com

Open from Monday to Saturday and on public holidays from 10:30am to 12:30pm and from 3:30pm to 7:30pm. For the shop. Open Sunday from May 1st to September 30th. Shop closed in January. Tourisme & Handicap Label.

Dominique and Jean Bardou opened their shop in 2012 on the banks of Canal du Midi. It is 25 km from there, at the edge of the pond of Jouarres, that are planted 4 200 olive trees bequeathed in the year 2000 to his daughter by the father of Dominique from where the homage to the respective ancestors in the name of the estate. 16 ha of trees that were planted in 1957, after the historical frost of 1956 and which represent the varieties of Lucques, moncita, picholine, cornicabra, aglandau and olivière. They are cultivated in equal parts for the production of oil and table olives (lucques and picholine), at a rate of 25 tons for each during the most prosperous years. The oils come in a blend (ripe fruity) and mono-varieties (lucques, picholine, olive and moncita). Jean Bardou takes as much pleasure in tasting the culinary preparations that are elaborated in the 70 m² laboratory adjacent to the shop (green and flavoured olive pastes) as in looking for ever more original shapes in the containers of his oils. You can enjoy an initiation (by appointment only) and then end with a tasting of the wines of the estate. The Bardou also propose cosmetics that are made from the oil of the estate, do not hesitate to discover them!

Barges along Canal du Midi, Trèbes.

Villalier

Sleeping

LES CABANES DANS LES BOIS
Domaine de Fourtou
✆ 09 70 75 99 00
www.lescabanesdanslesbois.fr
contact@lescabanesdanslesbois.fr

Open all year round. From 9am to 9pm – outside these hours contact the person on duty: 09 74 71 72 75. 29 cabins from 2 to 7 people. Breakfast: €11. Dinner basket "Menu du soir": €20. From €100 to €120. Cabin with terrace for 2 people from €97 to €217/ night – Cabin up to 4 people from €117 to €247 - Cabin up to 5 people from €127 to €247 - Donkey cabin for 7 people from €157 to €277. Tourisme & Handicap Label. Labels: Sud de France and Le Pays Cathare. Three cabins are labelled Tourisme et Handicap. Games for children. Animals accepted (€12 per day). Free WiFi. Food service (a packed lunch service delivered in the huts with menus from €20 to €38 for adults and €13 for children. WiFi is freely available at the reception and on the terraces and secure access in all meeting rooms). Satellite TV. Animations. LED flat-screen TV. Shuttle by electric car to the huts. Possibility of reception for events.

Paradise on earth exists and we have found it! At the gates of Carcassonne, in the heart of a 115-hectare estate, on a plateau with views of Cité de Carcassonne, Canal du Midi and the Pyrenees from far away. Vineyards, farmhouses, cellar, "castle", tower of the 12th century and forest that is gently sloping down towards L'Orbiel... There, in a vast wood that has preserved its original beauty, you will find, hidden beneath the trees, beautiful wooden huts built on stilts. They fit the relief, they blend into their preserved environment. Our child's soul is called, even caught, by these pretty houses that invite us to snuggle there. You enter there, with the same emotion as the one provided by the discovery of a secret hiding place. Inside, great surprise, they are spacious, cozy, arranged and furnished with great taste, nothing is missing, it is a perfect combination between luxury and ecological spirit, even the bathroom with its Italian shower is sumptuous. All have a terrace where the sun plays with the foliage, they are an invitation to put the time on hold. Here, nature tourism takes all its meaning, its most beautiful reputation is given to it, its *resort*spirit is moreover present through the offered services. Quality packed lunches delivered in your hut, many "nature" activities for children and adults, large heated swimming pool of 20 m with massage jets and counter-current swim, a reception lobby worthy of the name. A 3-star address under the trees... A magnificent atypical and eco-friendly achievement that reinvents the hotel accommodation of the 21st century. In spring 2018, the cellar of huts came into being to accommodate groups up to 200 people. The online gift card shop a new thing. An unmissable and romantic experience that you will remember for a long time.

Road to Capitelles.

Villemoustaussou

■ BOULEVARD CAFÉ – CHEZ BOUCA
8, Boulevard Jean-Jaures
✆ 04 68 25 35 49
philippe.boucabeille@gmail.com

Open all year round. Monday for lunch from 8am to 2pm; Tuesday to Sunday for lunch from 8am to 2pm and in the evening from 5pm to 10pm. Late service on Friday evening and Saturday evening. Lunch formula: 14 € (starter + main course + dessert. Starter + main course or main course + dessert: 12. Dish of the day/ 9,50 €). Wine by the glass. Tapas from Friday evening. Pizzas on wood fire in the evening only on site or take away from 7,50 € to 13 € (+pizzas of the month). Groups welcome.

Here, you are not at the Boulevard Café but "Chez Bouca", Philippe Boucabeille and his son Quentin wanted to make this brewery a real place to live, meet and share in the heart of the village on the shaded promenade of plane trees. The bar-restaurant has been completely remade with two pleasant rooms, a large bar and a beautiful terrace. Here, you will be served a homemade cuisine that oscillates between pizzas cooked in a wooden fire (in the evening) and the chef's dishes and tapas. The pizzas are unanimously appreciated, particularly the pizza of the month such as the spring pizza with a cream base, asparagus tips, truffled white ham, black olives, arugula, parmesan, mozzarella. In the kitchen, the chef prepares small gourmet dishes that follow the seasons and his mood. From Friday evening onwards, the choice is broadened by a tapas menu with sausage board from the neighbouring Nègre butcher shop, plancha knives, Catalan snails, grilled chorizo, patatas bravas, camembert in the oven... all of this accompanied by local wines at very fair prices. Don't miss Saturday "Apéro" from 11am with musical atmosphere and tapas. A really nice address that comes alive at the end of the week and during sports broadcasts.

CAUNES-MINERVOIS ★★

■ OFFICE DU TOURISME GRAND CARCASSONNE – ANTENNE MINERVOIS
3, ruelle du Monestier
✆ 04 68 76 34 74
www.grand-carcassonne-tourisme.fr
contact@grand-carcassonne-tourisme.fr

Vignobles et Découvertes. Bike area. April (from Easter) & October 9: 30am-1pm and 2pm-6pm every day, May (Closed May 1- closing at 6pm), June, September 9: 30am-1pm and 2pm-6: 30pm from Monday to Saturday, July & August 9: 30am-1pm and 2pm-6: 30pm every day,. From November to April (until Easter) 9: 30am-1pm and 2pm-5pm Monday to Friday Closed from 20/12 to the end of January. Souvenir shop. In summer: guided tours of the village, visits for children (treasure hunts). Vineyard walks. Reservations and tickets for concerts. Internet access (1.5€ for 20 minutes) and free secure Wifi, map of Caunes-Minervois with the historical circuit and the totem pole circuit. Reservations for the Marble Safaris (commented walks in the red marble quarries). Credit card not accepted. Tourisme & Handicap Label.

Information about accommodation, food, discovery or leisure, you will be very well informed by the team of this pleasant and efficient sub-branch of the Office du Tourism Grand Carcassonne. It will introduce you to a wide range of addresses that are located in Caunes-Minervois or in the surrounding villages. It will guide you on hiking trails, in plain or in mountain, hiking or mountain biking, bathing or fishing lakes... Don't fail to inquire about the "Balades vigneronnes", from June to September, the guided tours of the marble heritage and about the jazz in the cellar (once a month all year round except July and August). The tourist office also has a shop space offering various local products, as well as books.

Dramatized visit and treasure hunt... Follow the Knight of Caunes-Minervois and help him in his quest along the narrow streets of the village! Mysteries and discoveries, a fun and pleasant moment to share with family!

Sightseeing

ABBAYE DE CAUNES-MINERVOIS ★★

Place de l'Église
✆ 04 68 78 09 44
www.caunes-minervois.org
abbaye@caunes-minervois.org

Closed December 24, 25, 31. Open every day: 10am-7pm in July-August; 10am-6pm in June, September; 10am-12pm and 2pm-6pm in April, May, October; 10am-12pm and 2pm-5pm in February, March, November, December. Free up to 5 years old. Adult: 6 €. Child (from 6 to 16 years old): 2,50 €. Group (10 people): 5 €. The bedside, the cloister and the 5 exhibition rooms are accessible to wheelchair users. Guided tour (duration about 1 hour). Virtual reality helmet option: 5 € / person). Shop. Dogs on a leash accepted. Le Pays Cathare label.

The Saint-Pierre et Paul Benedictine Abbey of Caunes-Minervois was built by the abbot Anian in the late 8th century. In a Romanesque style, it has been classified as a historic monument since 1948. It is characterised by its two bell-towers of the 12th century. The meridional bell hosted the treasure and archives of the abbey and as for the bell at the north, it has three floors, and each of the them features a semi-circular gemel window whose white marble tents dates from the Visigoth period. The abbey was acquired successively by the viscount of Carcassonne, the Counts of Barcelona and the Viscounts of Beziers. During the crusade against the Albigensians, the abbort of Caunes received representatives of the pope several times, as they came to preach the Catholic orthodoxy, and Isarn Pierre, one of the last Cathar bishops, was burnt alive in 1227. The 13th and 14th centuries were a very prosperous period for the abbey (despite the power struggles between the secular and religious authorities) where from its remarkable nave and porch. In the early 17th cntury, after a decline period of nearly 3 centuries, the abbot Jean d'Alibert began a series of reforms, restoring buildings, rebuilt the abbey's home and ordered a new Altar. In 1663, the Saint-Maur congregation took possession and rebuilt the monastic buildings and also doubled the nave with a brick arch. In the 17th and 18th centuries, the decor of the interiors was renovated in Baroque style, with lots of polychrome marble. In 1791, the abbey was sold and the church became the community's property. We strongly urge you to admire its beauty from the beautiful esplanade that is right in front.

Please note: The new museum dedicated to Caunes' marble, the visit of the abbey with virtual reality displays, once again this year, the Caunes-Minervois abbey hosts various cultural mediations. From February until the end of May: an exhibition dedicated to the marble of the village. From June to December: for the second year, an exhibition dedicated to cartoon, in partnership with Centre Belge de la Bande Dessinée of Brussels. During off-season, Jazz in the cellar also livens up the abbey with various concerts during one month. In addition, the abbey offers a permanent exhibition of contemporary icons.

The abbey of Caunes-Minervois.

Knife & Fork

LA CANTINE DU CURÉ

16, avenue de l'Abbaye
✆ 07 67 54 94 67
www.lacantineducure.com
benja.taillandier@free.fr

Closed from January to April. Open: April/Nov/Dec: Friday 5pm-2pm & Sat/Sun 11am-2pm. May/Sept/Oct: Thursday/ Friday 5pm-2pm & Sat/Sun 11am-2pm. June: Wed/ Thursday/Friday/Friday 5pm-9am & Sat/Sun 11am-9am; July & August 7 days a week 11am-9am. Open in the evening. Reservation mandatory. A la carte menu: 6 € approx. Dish of the day: 10 €. Wine by the glass. Rib of beef: 32 €. Groups welcome. Garden. Terrace.

Come to us to feel at home! This could be the motto of this tapas bar-restaurant, where Benjamin and his team welcome you on the terrace or in the dining room, here conviviality and a sense of sharing take on their full meaning. Benjamin will advise and guide you as a good winegrower, on the choice of your drink, and if you are lucky, he will make you taste his own organic cuvées (Domaine Benjamin Taillandier in Caunes) at the bend of a game of petanque, on the boules court of the garden. Here, we prefer the short circuits and local producers, the tapas menu changes every week, the canned foods are served at any time and in summer, you can hesitate among more than 150 wine references, or taste a regional artisanal beer from Alaryk. 80% of their wines are made with organic, biodynamic or natural wines, all the authenticity of the terroir and the vine in your glass, a selection is made every week. During the month of April and then from October to December, the terrace is transformed into a cocoon, like a small wooden chalet, near the stove, a cosy atmosphere guaranteed so that with friends we can change the world.

LA MARBRERIE

Avenue de l'Argent-Double
✆ 04 68 79 28 74
otel-la-marbrerie.business.site
contact@la-marbrerie.fr

Logis. Maître Restaurateur. Qualité Tourisme. Qualité Sud de France. Open all year round. Every day from 12pm to 1:45pm and from 7pm to 9pm. Reservation recommended. Menus from €16.90 to €38. Menu: about €33. Children's menu: €8 (up to 12 years old). Formula: €19.90 (terroir formula with bottomless cassoulet!). Wine by the glass. Terroir menu: €23.90; Vegetarian menu €16.90. Assiette de pays €13. Starters from €12 to €16, Dishes from €11 to €20, Desserts from €4 to €10. Reception of groups (from 10 to 50 people). Garden. Terrace. Take-away sale. Shop.

Welcome to this superb village restaurant where everything sweetly smells the Belle Epoque era, the local cuisine of grandma's, with its old-fashioned wooden decor and furniture, because this restaurant was originally a former marble factory. Christine and Robert have managed to give it a new lease of life. You immediately feel at home in this particular place where memories, marble sculptures, wines, books, postcards, artists, locals... Both rooms are bright, the bar is friendly and the terrace under the plane trees is very pleasant, especially soon during the first days of summer. As for the cuisine, it's the very expression of local good food: tasty, copious, just like the Minervois cassoulet with 3 meats that makes the chef proud! Not to mention the succulent delicatessen and meat products of Denis Icher, the butcher of the village, it's great! Red marble is present everywhere here, it is part of the history of the village, so don't miss the visit of the marble quarries, it's fabulous! In order to prolong your stay, the Marbrerie has five bedrooms with private bathrooms.

Shopping

DOMAINE BENJAMIN TAILLANDIER

50, avenue de l'Argent-Double
✆ 06 79 85 99 03
www.vigneron-minervois.fr
benja.taillandier@free.fr

Wine tasting and sale at the estate all year round, 7 days a week by appointment.

Holder of a Viticulture-Oenology diploma and a BA in law and management, Benjamin Taillandier chose organic farming to produce wines of character. His vineyards spread over 16 hectares and are harvested by hand. Cinsault, Syrah, Carignan, Grenache or Muscat grow on schist, clay-limestone and sandy soils and are naturally mature to give wines such as Viti Vini Bibi, a red wine that generously accompanies dishes, Six Roses, a rosé to drink very fresh, or Bulle, a sweet wine based with Terret and Muscat, perfect for aperitif or dessert. The wines can be tasted all year round in the area by appointment, or at La Cantine du Curé, Benjamin Taillandier's restaurant (see restaurant section).

Markets

MARKET
Esplanade de l'Europe

Tuesday, Thursday and Saturday from 8am to 1pm esplanade de l'europe in front of the school. A Christmas market is also organized every year.

In addition to the weekly markets, find a farmers' market in the evening, organized by the Association of Country Producers in partnership with the Chamber of Agriculture of the Aude. You will be able to buy all the local products directly from the producers.

- **Sunday July 19, 2020** from 6pm to 10pm

In the surroundings

Cabrespine ★★

The small village of Cabrespine is located on the borders of Minervois and Cabardès, nestled in the Clamoux valley, between plain and mountain. It belonged to the Abbey of Lagrasse in the era of Charlemagne, until the Revolution. The castle, built in the 11th century, was later a royal garrison, but today, only a few ruins under study remain. However, the parish church, built in the 18th century, is well preserved. Beautiful work in gothic style, inside, a lapidary museum and a painting of Gamelin. The creation of a medieval style garden made this year, in the green space that borders it, adds to the charm of the place. Visitors can discover heirloom vegetables, as well as medicinal plants used in the Middle Ages. The year 2018 saw the creation of Espace Claude Granier, owner and fitter of the giant abyss, a place that gathers a library and a resource fund on the world of caves, mainly composed of the donations of this passionate speleologist. Cabrespine enjoys an exceptional momentum, brought by the municipality that restores, builds and enhances the village, its heritage and its history. Thus, water is ubiquitous in Cabrespine: old wash house, trough and fountain recall the essential role of water that creates the giant chasm of the village (see the "musts" section), known across borders. The narrow and picturesque streets are clean and flowered. These highlights add to the charm of this village typical of Montagne Noire. Environmentally friendly, the municipality has installed two electrical terminals in the car park of the chasm. It should be remembered that Cabrespine has obtained the label "Healthy land, communes without pesticides" which rewards and attests to the efforts made to protect the cultures and the lush vegetation of the village.

GOUFFRE GÉANT DE CABRESPINE ★★★
D 112
✆ 04 68 26 14 20
www.gouffre-de-cabrespine.com
gouffrecabrespine11@gmail.com

Open every day from the beginning of February to the beginning of December. February, March, November and December: from 14h to 17h30; from April to June and from September to October: 10h-12h / 14h-17h30 (last departure), in June extra visit at 13h; July and August: from 10h to 18h (last departure) with regular departures every 45 min. Admission: 11,60 € (children (from 5 to 12 years old): 6,90 €. Young people (from 13 to 17 years old): 9,90 €. Guided tour in French (about 50 minutes). Audio-guides in Spanish, Catalan, English and German (supplement: 1.50 € outside the audio-guided period). Free for children under 5 years old. Children: 6.90 €. Park Adventures (by reservation): Accro Grotte de Cabrespine (from 12 years old): 37€/person; La Rivière Souterraine (from 10 years old): 48€/person. Holiday vouchers. Tourism & Handicap Label. Equipment provided: wetsuit, helmet, harness, gloves. catering (bar and snack bar). Free parking for light vehicles and buses. Charging station for electric vehicles. Souvenirs and regional products shop.

This is the largest developed chasm in Europe, renowned worldwide for its mineralogical richness for more than

Adventure Park, Giant Abyss of Cabrespine.

The Belvedere seen from the entrance, Giant Abyss of Cabrespine.

30 years. Today the abyss is making people talk about it for its breathtaking attractions! The Le Gouffre team makes every effort to impress you and provide you with unique emotions. Apart from the visit to Le Gouffre (an absolute must), you can now enjoy the birds of prey show (from mid-July to mid-August), a feat carried out especially for the abyss and unique in the world, and from August 15, attend the amazing show of "L'envol des chauves-souris", to be seen at nightfall. The most adventurous will set off into the heart of the abyss, well harnessed and in complete safety, to experience an underground acrobatic course with zip line, monkey bridge... a novelty to be discovered since the Easter holidays of 2019. Finally, experience a unique moment as you enter the depths of the abyss in "safari" mode and follow in the footsteps of the first explorers of the abyss, unless you are more interested in exploring the underground river in exploration canoes. Allow about 3 hours for the first route, 4 hours for the second. As for safety, no worries, you are well supervised by real qualified professionals who know the abyss in its every nook and cranny! An adventure to live with family or friends.

Homps

■ EN BONNE COMPAGNIE

6, quai des Négociants
✆ 04 68 91 23 16
www.en-bonne-compagnie.com
♿

Quality Tourism. Sud de France quality. Closed from October to April. Open from Tuesday to Friday for lunch and dinner; Saturday evening; Sunday for lunch. Reservation recommended. Menus from 26,50 € to 45 €. A la carte menu: about 36 €. Children's menu: 9.90 €. Lunch formula: 14 €. Wine by the glass. Cheques not accepted. Groups welcome. Terrace.

On the banks of the Canal du Midi, this beautiful address prepares dishes full of character that combine local and regional products with the ever judicious creativity of the chef. Whether you prefer fish, meat or vegetarian, you will find what you are looking for. The reign of the seasons influences the menus and the à la carte menu of the establishment, but here are a few examples of its gourmet proposals: poached chicken in a Vietnamese style salad, gravlax of salmon marinated in beetroot, hazelnuts of pork tenderloin covered with a sage and onion hash, Thermidor half lobster, chocolate marquise, red fruits and custard. The only constant is the chef's speciality: a banana soufflé with caramel vodka. Obviously, nothing is exhaustive in this suggestion because the menu, in addition to following the seasons, varies according to the chef's mood.

■ LAC DE JOUARRES

Jouarres
✆ 04 68 91 18 98

Open all year round. Supervised swimming in July and August. Pets not allowed.

As soon as the sunny days arrive, Lake Jouarres is a pleasant place to spend a moment with family or friends. The water body of more than 100 hectares offers a magnificent place of relaxation opening onto splendid horizons of pinewood and hills where fans of windsurfing, canoe-kayaking or carp fishing are having a field day. Its supervised green beaches are an invitation to relaxation, sunbathe and swimming... A life-saving splash when the weather is very warm in summer. Its bends have been arranged for walk, an opportunity to enjoy them even in winter. This lake is only two-minute drive from the town of Homps and its harbor - Port-Minervois – which is a high place for those who love sailing on Canal du Midi and the starting point for a walk along the water on traditional gabares. For a few years, every summer, water games are set on the lake to entertain children and adults! Open every day from 10am to 8pm, inquire about the rates.

LA PÉNICHE

19, quai des Tonneliers
✆ 04 68 91 24 34
www.restaurantlapeniche.fr
contact@restaurantlapeniche.fr

Closed from November to March. Open from Friday to Tuesday for both lunch and dinner; on Thursday evening. Open from 9am to 10pm. Closed on Wednesday all day and Thursday lunchtime. Booking recommended. Menus from €23 to €29. Children's menu: €8. Lunch formula: €17. Wine by the glass. Groups welcome (up to 40 people). Baby chairs. Garden. Terrace. Takeaway sale.

The Canal du Midi flows peaceful days in the green in front of this restaurant. La Péniche is unfortunately not a boat but it overlooks the beautiful marina of the village. You have there, on the "front deck", a small terrace decorated with large oleanders where it is good to have a drink. "On board", in the room, you will be seduced by a pleasant country style space, but also by the spectacle of a pizza prepared in front of you and seized in five minutes in a wood-fired oven. It must be said that they are delicious, with their fine dough and generous topping. On the "rear deck", a large garden in the form of a terrace, all very green and shady, i.e. a large part of the terrace can be closed on request. Anne and Alain obviously have a sense of hospitality and make it a point of honour for their team to adhere to the same values, which results in a very attentive waiters and a fast and professional service. In addition to the pizzas, you will enjoy traditional and local cuisine with the must-eat steak tartare prepared in front of you, homemade foie gras, fresh lobster (depending on the arrival) or homemade cassoulet cooked over a wood fire. For dessert, choose the very, very café *gourmand*, Petit Futé's word!

LE CHAI – PORT MINERVOIS

35, Quai des Tonneliers
✆ 04 68 91 29 48
www.lechai-portminervois.com
lechai@cru-minervois.com

Low season: open Monday to Friday from 9am to 12pm and from 2pm to 6pm. High season: Monday to Friday from 9am to 12pm and from 2pm to 7pm; Saturday from 10am to 12pm and from 2pm to 7pm. Delivery possible. Online shop. A tourist information point and the harbour master's office are also present at this same address.

Impossible to leave the Minervois without taking a souvenir of this rich terroir. The Romans designated this land as the most suitable for vine cultivation. Can we prove them wrong? At Le Chai de Port Minervois, also seat of the Minervois vintage union, you will find small pearls at cellar prices. It is among more than 190 references that you will have to make your choice. Pushing the door of the cellar means going to meet the work of the winemakers. The very professional staff will guide you in your choices, while respecting your sensibilities and making you discover the authentic flavors of this land. There is now a range of organic wines, with more than 20 references. Le Chai also offers an organic Discovery box, containing 6 different bottles to give you an idea.

Laure-Minervois

DOMAINE CIRY CATTANEO

9, avenue de la Montagne-Noire
✆ 06 70 36 36 37
www.domainecirycattaneo.com
cirycattaneo@gmail.com

Visit and tasting at the estate by appointment only / Wine bar during the summer weekends from 6pm to midnight with summer cuisine from 7pm to 10pm / Wine tasting at the Pennautier Chocolate Factory Marions les Chocolats from Wednesday to Friday from 10am to noon and from 3pm to 6pm on Saturdays. Delivery possible (wines exclusively from organic farming). From €12 to €20 per bottle. Online shop. Shipping is free from 18 bottles purchased.

An unconditional love of the land, the desire to exhume the soul of the land and a working philosophy based on intra-parcel winemaking, these are the guidelines of the Domaine Ciry Cattaneo, created in 2015 by David Ciry, a professional oenologist and Marion Cattaneo, a chocolate maker. The respect for the culture and life cycle of the vine will lead David to organic farming, artisanal and manual work, on varieties such as Malbec, Syrah, Grenache, Carignan and Tempranillo present in this 2,7 hectare estate in the Minervois region, labeled Ecocert. You will enjoy the Sang Neuf, Malabestia, Les Petites Choses or Les Hirondelles vintages, all produced in limited quantities. These wines, with an intense and concentrated red, offer a generous flavor and reveals a vivid notes of the scrubland such as the thyme or rosemary note, their Languedoc terroir, compound tastes, deep flavors with well controlled expression, and an immense complexity. Beautiful wine food pairings with grilled meats, flavored with Mediterranean herbs, in perspective. New in 2019: a tasting cellar has been created to taste the estate's wines in the best conditions.

Wine and chocolate tastings for groups at the Marions Les Chocolats chocolate factory in Pennautier are available upon request.

Villegly

LE COMPTOIR

NEW

Avenue du Minervois
✆ 04 68 26 46 64
www.lecomptoir-villegly.com
maison.jules.st.martin@gmail.com

Open all year round. Tuesday from 11: 30am to 2: 30pm; Wednesday to Saturday from 11: 30am to 2: 30pm and from 7: 30pm to 10: 30pm. Closed Sunday, Monday and Tuesday evenings. Reservation recommended. Lunch grill: 9,50 €. Wine by the glass. Tapas from 4 to 7 €, Homemade cassoulet 15 €, Grilled meat from 15 to 19 €, Rib of beef 5 €/100g. Groups welcome. Terrace.

Julien is used to surprise us with his ideas and creations, in 2019, he amazed us by announcing the opening of the new "Comptoir" XXL version in the former and superb building of Château Villerambert Moureau, located at the entrance to the village (on the left when you arrive from Carcassonne). But let those who are faithful to the "little" Comptoir be reassured, Julien has understood what his guests love above all: friendliness and good food. You can then find all these ingredients but with, as a plus, a superb cellar where you will find his wines and those of his winegrowers friends, a wine bar to enjoy them, a restaurant with terrace, a baker and even a caterer! An atmosphere of old stones and wood to enjoy the razor clams with parsley, the griddled hearts of duck, the cold meats served on a board... Once the aperitif and the wine tastings are done, in moderation, the embers reddens for tasty and copious grilled meats accompanied by homemade chips and green salad. Beef, duck, pork carbonnade, there is something for all taste buds (6 meats to choose from and 1 fish depending on the day's catch), those who love cassoulet will enjoy that of the house. The address that has already been one of our favorites is now a "super" favorite!

Villeneuve-Minervois

MAISON DE LA TRUFFE D'OCCITANIE

32, Avenue du Jeu-du-Mail
✆ 04 68 72 35 47
www.maisondelatruffedulanguedoc.com
maisontruffe@villeneuve-minervois.com

Sud de France quality. Open all year round. November, December, January, February, March: Monday to Saturday 10am – 12pm and 2pm – 6pm. July and August: every day 10am – 12pm and 2pm – 7pm. April, May, June, September, October: Monday to Saturday 10am – 12pm and 2pm – 7pm. April to June and September to October: Monday to Saturday 10am – 12pm and 2pm – 7pm. Free up to 6 years old. Adult: 6,50 €. Child: 3,50 €. Group (10 people): 4 € (or Carte pass – Group visits by appointment all year round from 10 people). Holiday voucher. Audioguides for blind people (French, English, Spanish, Italian, German and Dutch). Label Le Pays Cathare, Tourism Quality label. Guided tour (interactive visit and projection). Shop. Car and bus parking.

Since 2011, the Maison de la Truffe de l'Occitanie welcomes you in Villeneuve-Minervois, in the heart of the Black Diamond Triangle. In the land of caves and abysses, it is a beautiful space of more than 300 m^2 entirely dedicated to truffles. No less than five themed rooms, equipped with modern facilities, allow visitors to revisit this gastronomic treasure of the subsoil at length.

Good to know: a partnership between the Maison de la Truffe du Languedoc and various restaurants in Villeneuve-Minervois will allow you to enjoy an aperitif or a coffee on presentation of your entrance ticket. Conversely, your bill from one of these establishments, presented to the Maison de la Truffe, will entitle you to a reduction on the entrance fee.

Partner restaurants: L'Auberge de la Clamoux, La Table du Pareur, La Taoulo and Chez Kéké.

MUSÉE DE PALÉONTOLOGIE, MINÉRALOGIE ET PRÉHISTOIRE

12, rue Saint-Mammès
✆ 04 68 26 12 14
www.fossile-minervois.info

Open all year round. By appointment only. Around 1 hour. Free of charge. Weekend or weekly rentals, prices on the museum website. Children welcome. Guided tour. Gift shop. For children: educational visits, moulding workshops...

For 20 years, Xavier, trained as a naturalist, taught at the Museum of Natural History in Paris. He enjoys transmitting his passion and his know-how and we are easily captivated. This small private museum, in addition to impressive archives, minerals, a seabed reproduction, fossils in which the 2000 most frequent of France are represented ... houses exceptional as a Mosasaur lower jaw, a turtle skull, a mammoth jaw ... Xavier offers children a molding workshop. These latter will enjoy a visit as they are allowed to fiddle! As for collectors, they can exchange specimens or have people identify their collection. Passionate guests can also stay on site. An accommodation facility of 3 rooms is rented by the museum, which allows you to enjoy the tours on the theme *Paleontological and mineralogical* discoveries in Minervois offered by Xavier for a day or half a day.

Maison de la truffe d'Occitanie.

LA REDORTE

LA TABLE DE RIQUET

11, Port la Fabrique
✆ 04 68 90 67 64
www.latablederiquet.com
latablederiquet@gmail.com

Open all year round. Low season: Tuesdays, Wednesdays and Sundays for lunch; Thursday to Saturday for lunch and dinner. High season: Tuesday to Saturday for lunch and dinner; Sunday for lunch. Menus from 22 € to 32 € (starter + main course or main course + dessert or complete formula to be chosen from the menu). Children's menu: 10 €.12 € (starter + main course or main course + dessert or 15 €: starter + main course + dessert). Wine by the glass. Groups welcome (upon reservation. Coach parking). Baby chairs. Terrace.

If Pierre Paul Riquet, the creator of the Canal du Midi, was still with us La Table de Riquet would have been his favorite table! Michèle and her daughter Océane have taken over the running of this establishment located on the banks of the Canal du Midi. Michèle is part of the one we have been following since the creation of Le Petit Futé of Aude in 1997 and she has now moved to La Redorte where she has set up her cook's suitcases, assisted by her daughter. On the menu, a seasonal cuisine for both meat and fish is announced, a lunchtime formula to vary the pleasures and small surprises in high season. The menu offers choice: grilled vegetable salad, creamy burrata and dried figs, entrecote a la plancha and homemade sauce, common dolphinfish with dog sauce or John Dory fish with curry-coconut sauce, dishes that invite you to travel but that traditional cassoulet fans can be reassured, Michèle's is excellent. On weekends, suggestions will be offered with for example fresh grilled lobster, 1 kg prime rib and perhaps a Sunday morning brunch formula in summer . As for dessert, Océane will take care of it, pavlova, cheese-cake, tiramisu... They will finish your meal perfectly. A very pleasant address where it is good to stroll on the terrace as soon as the sunny days arrive.

LASTOURS ★★

Sightseeing

LES QUATRE CHÂTEAUX DE LASTOURS ★★★

✆ 04 68 77 56 02
See page 14.

Two of the four Châteaux de Lastours.

In the surroundings

Limousis ★

GROTTE DE LIMOUSIS ★★

51, chemin de la Grotte
✆ 04 68 76 96 63
www.grotte-de-limousis.fr
limousis@wanadoo.fr

Sud de France quality. Closed from mid-November to mid-February. Open all year round by reservation for groups. Every day: 09/02 to 11/11. February and November, visit at 2: 30pm, 3: 30pm, 4: 30pm. March, April, May, June, September and October visit at 10: 30 am, 11: 30 am, 2: 30 pm, 3: 30 pm, 4: 30 pm and 5: 30 pm. July and August regular non-stop departure from 10 am, 6 pm last departure. Free up to 4 years old. Adult: 10,90 €. Child (from 5 to 12 years old): 6,90 € (9,20 € from 12 to 18 years old). Reduced rate: 9.20 €. Label Le Pays Cathare. Guided tour. Other times are possible for groups of more than fifteen people on reservation.

Grotte de Limousis is the largest fitted cave in Pays Cathare. The one-hour guided tour takes you on a journey through the tracks of cave bears (whose scratches are still visible on the walls) and on those of prehistoric man. This one-kilometre route, accessible to all, takes you through seven rooms with very different atmospheres and two wonderful lakes. The Lustre d'Aragonite, the largest set of aragonite crystals, ends this visit with sound and light effects.

Mas-Cabardès

This picturesque village has a rich heritage: the Saint-Etienne church of the 16th century, which is equipped an octagonal tower, the great Tisserands cross dating from the 16th century that testifies to a lost textile industry, houses that are corbelled, half-timbered and with slate roofs... The vast fields of olive trees have also disappeared while, 200 years ago, they were 2,800 in the town, more than 400 in 1870 and no more at present. The oil mill hasn't worked anymore for a long time ago... But the medieval houses on the square and the odd small stone statue at the top of the tower are worth a visit. The ruins of the medieval castle that overhangs the village are in free access.

■ CASCADE DE CUBSERVIÈS ★

Hiking trails.

After having crossed three very picturesque villages of the Black Mountain, you can admire, nestled in the hollow of the mountain, the waterfall of Cubserviès. Some claim that it is the highest in Europe (90 m high), which is probably not true, but does not detract from its exceptional character. You will have a unique panoramic view of the Orbiel valley, the Carcassonne plain and Lastours and the Pyrenees from the summit, where the dolmen of the Roc de Los Caïchos, a witness of the prehistoric era, proudly dominates. A wild, steep place, with an interesting flora. Continue your journey and you will discover a small 12th century chapel dedicated to Saint Sernin de Cubserviès, nestled in the forest. The start of this hike is in the village of Roquefère, dominated by the magnificent 17th century castle built on a rocky peak. A beautiful walk, 4 hours 30 minutes and 13.8 km, in the heart of a preserved nature. Be very careful because the waterfall is not necessarily well indicated.

▶ Departure is from the hikers' car park (mandatory) 300 m from the village of Roquefère, at the level of a rocky narrowing.

Salsigne

The mineral deposits around Salsigne have been exploited since Antiquity, and archaeology allowed to attest that Salsigne was one of the most important mining centers of the Roman province of Narbonne. Iron, copper, silver and lead were extracted from the site whose steel activity dates back to the 1st century BC.

Now known to have been the largest gold mine in Europe, the mine of Salsigne, open in 1892, closed in 2004. From the gold discovery to the beginning of the 20th century, about 120 tons of gold were extracted.

The gold of Salsigne inspired Anne and Serge Golon, the authors of the saga *Angélique, Marquise des Anges*, whose heroes, Joffrey, count of Peyrac, and owner of the gold mines of Salsigne, was accused of witchcraft for the wealth that he gained from his mines.

MONTOLIEU ★★

■ OFFICE DU TOURISME GRAND CARCASSONNE – ANTENNE CABARDES

Place Jean-Guéhenno
✆ 04 68 24 80 80
www.grand-carcassonne-tourisme.fr
contact@grand-carcassonne-tourisme.fr

From Easter, May, and October 9: 30am-1pm / 2pm-6pm from Monday to Saturday Open on the Sunday of the Book Fair – Closed on May 1st June and September 9: 30am-1pm and 2pm-6: 30pm from Monday to Saturday July and August 9: 30am-1pm and 2pm-6: 30pm every day. From November to March 9: 30am-1pm and 2pm-5pm from Monday to Friday, CLOSED from 22/12 to 02/01, Dramatised visits. wi-fi. Tourism & Handicap Label. Label Vignobles & Découvertes.

To best discover the region, ask for free topoguides, which will make you discover Cabardès and Montagne Noire, thanks to the numerous detailed routes and for all levels. The reception staff will also guide you for any information on accommodation, catering, leisure, heritage and numerous activities organized in and around the village. See also their very complete website.

▶ **The fairy of Montolieu...** Follow Montolieu's fairy and help it find the magic formula that will allow it to go back to the pages of the tale from which it has escaped... Following a way that leads you to the shops of the village's booksellers in search of clues, you will discover the enchantment of a tale, for both children and adults. Duration: One hour and half. Ideal for family!

Sightseeing

■ MUSÉE DES ARTS ET METIERS DU LIVRE

37, rue de la Mairie ✆ 04 68 24 80 04
www.montolieu-livre.fr
montolieuvdl@orange.fr

Sud de France quality. Vineyards and Discoveries. Open all year round. Closed on December 25th and January 1st. Open from 1st April to 11th November: Monday to Friday 10am to 12pm – 2pm to 6pm, Saturday, Sunday and public holidays 3pm to 6pm / From 12th November to 31st March: Monday to Friday 2pm to 5pm / Saturday, Sunday and public holidays 3pm to 5pm. Free up to 6 years old (open to the public). Permanent exhibition guided tour 10 € / for school children 5 €. Children (from 6 to 16 years old): 3,50 €. Self-guided tour: 5 €; Guided tour (on reservation) from a group of 8 people: 8 €. Conference temporary exhibitions: 10 €. Permanent exhibitions accessible to wheelchair users, temporary exhibitions on the first floor: not accessible. Children's welcome area. Guided tour. Shop. Animations. Reception in French, English and Spanish.

In the bend of a medieval alley, in the centre of the village of Montolieu, enter the world of Gutenberg. Here for decades, everything is book, everything revolves around ink, paper, pen and typewriter. Welcome to the Museum of Book Arts and Crafts, to familiarize yourself with a world you thought you knew so well. You will discover many details about the alphabet, language, the development of printing through machines, and the book trades that we know so little about. The history of the book will be told from its origins in 3600 BC, in Mesopotamia, to our modern alphabet. Thanks to the guided tours, you will learn a lot of anecdotes about our written communication over the centuries, a fun way to trace the history of printing, from calligraphy to binding, and to observe all kinds of machines on display; some presses are operated for a better understanding during the visit. A permanent exhibition presents the bibliography of François Bernouard, poet, typographer, printer, while upstairs, three rooms are dedicated to an art gallery, with a temporary exhibition, conferences and exhibition openings regularly organized, in addition to creative workshops allow you to learn about graphic arts and book trades.

LA COOPÉRATIVE-MUSÉE CÉRÈS FRANCO

5, Route d'Alzonne
✆ 04 68 76 12 54
www.collectionceresfranco.com
info@collectionceresfranco.com

Open from the end of April to the beginning of November. Open from Tuesday to Sunday and on public holidays from 2pm to 7pm. Exceptional opening on Mondays public holidays. Adult: 7 € (for free visit). Under 16 years old: 4 €. Guided tour 10 € Every Sunday at 4: 30 pm La Coopérative-Collection Cérès Franco offers guided tours of the exhibition without reservation. Meetings of the Cooperative 10 € – Educational workshops 10 €. Children's welcome area (educational workshops). Guided tour.

Since 2015, the Cérès Franco Collection has been housed in an exceptional setting: the former wine cooperative cellar of Montolieu. Resolutely international, the Cérès Franco Collection brings together around 2,000 works from the 20th and 21st centuries, some of which are presented each year on a different theme. Brazilian and European naivety, South American popular art, art brut, self-taught, singular, artists from the CoBra movement or the New Figuration, the provenance of the works reflects an eclectic and independent taste for an art situated on the fringes of the major artistic currents. This collection reflects, with a rare coherence, the gaze of an audacious and demanding collector who has turned to intense works. Each year, therefore, a temporary exhibition, to be held from April 11th to November 1st, is organised with a guest curator who looks at this collection while engaging in a dialogue with other institutions or collections. 2020 is a very special year since it is Céres Franco's own daughter, Dominique Polad-Hardouin, who takes on this role and offers us an initiatory journey through 450 works and more than 150 artists. This exhibition entitled "the Thieves of Fire", will be in the spotlight and will lead us to an artistic profusion accumulated by C.Franco, you will wander through a singular and unique universe, where art no longer has any borders. The place is inspiring, the enhancement of the works is amazing, the reception is very friendly and explanations on the current exhibition are given systematically. To be discovered without hesitation!

Knife & Fork

CASQUETTE ET CHAPEAU

2, place de la Liberté
✆ 04 68 24 76 72
www.casquetteetchapeau.fr
casquetteetchapeau@gmail.com

Low season: open on Wednesdays and Sundays from 10: 30 am to 2: 30 pm; Thursday to Saturday from 10: 30 am to 2: 30 pm and from 6: 30 pm to 10: 30 pm. High season: Tuesday to Sunday from 10: 30 am to 2: 30 pm and from 6: 30 pm to 10: 30 pm. Booking recommended.Fixed-price Menus from €13,50 to € 28 . A la carte menu: about €37 .At lunchtime formula: €16,90 (starter + main course + dessert on the slate). Wine by the glass. Tickets at €12 . Dishes at €18 . Desserts at €7 . Reception of groups. Terrace. Animations. Mezzanine. Wifi.

The restaurant Casquette et Chapeau, is located in the heart of the village, facing the church. We love the current today's bistro-style decoration of the places, it's cozy and contemporary, but we also love the large shaded terrace planted with plane trees, some of which are centuries old. We enjoy traditional recipes revisited and elaborated with quality products. That Sunday at lunchtime on the terrace, there were monkfish with fresh mango, the vegetarian dish made with eggplant and dessert the extra lemon verrine on the menu. As the chef only works with fresh and seasonal products, the menu –short– changes regularly. For the "big eaters", the dishes are not copious. The welcome is pleasant, it's really the perfect place for a gourmet break in a typical Cabardès village. Special mention for the decoration of "little corners", guaranteed reading!

Sleeping

LA MANUFACTURE ROYALE

16, impasse de la Manufacture
✆ 04 68 24 89 67
www.lamanufactureroyale.fr
lamanufactureroyale@gmail.com

4 apartments: from 1,375 € to 2,145 €/week depending on the season and the apartment, 1 studio from 130 €/ night and 2 guest rooms from 90 €/night. Extra bed 20 €/ night. Playground for children. Seminars. Receptions and weddings. Wifi. Food service (restaurant l'Apostrophe in the Manufacture and 3 evenings a week, the guest house offers local dishes and desserts. Barbecue available. In the morning, 2 formulas for breakfast: English style or continental breakfast). For sale. Washing machine. Animations. Equipped home cinema room. Library. Swimming pool of 16 m by 3 m. Free parking. Airport shuttle at extra charge.

Marieke and Bart De Jonge welcome you in this beautiful building, a former woollen-sheet factory, built in the 18th century. The restored place has kept all the charm of the authenticity and the majesty of its architecture. For your

© hanthropos - stock.adobe.com

Montolieu.

stay, you will have the choice between two guesthouses whose surface area is around 30 m², a studio of two rooms with bathroom with bathtub, and four fitted flats that can accommodate 3 to 4 people. If you are decoration and design enthusiast, you will enjoy the elegance of this place where each object has been thoroughly chosen, each paint highlights the unique character of the rooms to give a set in perfect harmony. In addition, La Manufacture regularly features in reports in decoration magazines. The same attention to detail in the park entirely designed by Bart in the shade of tall trees, or at the edge of the swimming pool, rest and *relaxation* are essential. What can be said about the house's table d'hôtes once a week... it's that good taste is also on the plates? Yes, it is! A playground dedicated to children will delight the little ones. La manufacture is a unique place that does not leave anyone indifferent.

Guesthouses

FORGE DE MONTOLIEU
676, Chemin de la Forge
✆ 04 68 76 60 53
www.forgedemontolieu.com
info@forgedemontolieu.com

Gîtes de France (3 épis). Open all year round. 4 bedrooms. Double room from 75 € to 120 €. Breakfast included (included in bed and breakfast (and for unusual accommodation, only the first morning), 10 € TTC and on reservation for those staying in a gîte or unusual accommodation (from the second morning). Served from 8am to 10am). Extra bed: 22 € (per night). Parking included. 2 gites (2 and 3 bedrooms) 120€ to 150€, and 3 unusual accommodations Glamping from 80€ to 110€ (the Dome, the Tiny house or the Cocoon tree) Only from May to the end of September. Games for children. Not admitted. Free Wifi. Restaurant (table d'hôtes on reservation). Sale (bookshop shop on the ground floor). Excursions.

The Forge de Montolieu is a beautiful old industrial site where Napoleon's forge, mills and spinning mills succeeded one another. At the end of the path along a deep river, a natural setting stretches out its arms to you. A superb stone building rises majestically to offer you all the serenity of the place with spacious and comfortable rooms, numerous terraces and a park where time seems suspended. This mansion, fitted out at the end of the 19th century in the last spinning mill of the region, has been recently redone with a sober, elegant and colorful decoration. It offers for the guests part, pretty bathrooms adjoining each room. The masters of the house, Charles Cowen, photographer and musician, and Laure, bookseller in Montolieu village du livre, have been welcoming their guests for several years in a warm, family and relaxed atmosphere. Charles Cowen takes great care in the preparation of the meals he offers, refined and flowery, composed mainly of organic, local and seasonal products. Book lovers will also be able to stroll around the village of Montolieu and stock up on books at La Lettre Volée (Laure bookshop) one of the 14 bookshops in the village.

In the surroundings

Brousses-et-Villaret

LE MOULIN À PAPIER ★
Lieu-dit Cambou
✆ 04 68 26 67 43
www.moulinapapier.com
brousses@moulinapapier.com

Closed on January 1 and December 25. Monday to Friday: by reservation 04 68 26 67 43. Saturdays, Sundays, public holidays and school holidays: Guided tours at 11am, 2: 30pm, 3: 30pm and 4: 30pm. Free up to 4 years old. Adults: 8.50 €. Child (from 5 to 12 years old): 5 €. Group (15 people): 7 €. Sheet paper making workshop: 2,50 € (Make 2 sheets of paper that you take away after going to press), Traces workshop, monotype printing: 12 € (5 pers. min/1 h). Discovery day (3 h) 16 € / child & & 21 € / adult. Children's welcome area. Guided tour. Shop. Animations.

20 minutes from Carcassonne, come and discover "La Magie du papier" (the magic of paper) in the last paper mill of Languedoc. In a preserved natural setting, on the banks of Dure, amidst granite boulders, a trail leads you into "another world" with its hydraulic motors, its ancient machines and the artisanal production of papers. During each guided tour, the magic works as paper sheets arise from old jeans, cotton t-shirts or elephant dung. After the visit, in the workshop, children and adults can shape with their bare hand watermarked paper sheets that they can take home after the session (€2.50). The mill is a meeting place: residence of artists, concerts, exhibitions, conferences...

LE LAUTHIER BAR A VIN RESTAURANT

NEW

Lauthier le Haut
✆ 06 86 66 69 36 – elody_dl@hotmail.com

Closed in January. Low season: open Thursday to Saturday evenings; weekends for lunch. High season: Wednesday to Sunday for lunch and dinner. Reservation recommended. A la carte menu: about 15 €. Groups welcome. Garden. Terrace.

It is a superb stone building, nestled in the foothills of the Montagne Noire, which welcomes you in a green setting, under the watchful eye of donkeys, sheep, chickens and roosters. Here, calm and pleasure reign, welcome to Elody and Yannick's home, the hosts of the place. You will be able to take your place in a superb reception room, with colonnade, a cosy decor and contemporary furniture. The setting is cosy, the purple curtain is very theatrical, in harmony with stone and wood, while the walls are adorned with pictorial works by local artists. In the kitchen, it is Elody who officiates, and will delight you with his variations of tapas cooked around a seasonal product. Thus, you will be able to taste the Assiette de la mer hot or cold, the variation around the shrimp, the boards of cold meats and cheeses to the rhythm of the seasons. Every two weeks, you can set the dance floor ablaze or let your creative side speak for itself during theme evenings with a jazz, tango, karaoke or cabaret programme. A festive and friendly enclave in the Carcassonne region, to be discovered as soon as possible!

- **2 charming gîtes**: The building also houses two superbly restored gîtes offering old-fashioned charm and contemporary decoration
- **Pastry online**: Possibility to order Elody's pastries online via her website www.le7emepeche.fr (possibility of delivery within a radius of 10 km).

LE LAUTHIER GITES

NEW

Lauthier le Haut
✆ 06 86 66 69 36
elody_dl@hotmail.com

2 bedrooms. Night from 50 to 65€. Possibility of weekly rental on request. Animals accepted (small animals accepted). Wifi. Food service. Washing machine, dishwasher. Satellite Tv. Animations. Horse riding centre nearby.

Like jewels in their case, discover two magnificent duplex gites, very recent, with contemporary decoration. Each has a living room with lounge, and a small American kitchen very well equipped, the bedroom upstairs with beautiful dimensions includes a modern bathroom with walk-in shower. Every detail has been carefully thought out, by Yannick the owner, who himself has carried out the work, these apartments are extremely functional and comfortable. The environment is no less important as this magnificent stone building stands in the middle of nature, on the banks of a brook and among some farm animals. A true place of rejuvenation, comfort and services to boot! Possibility to eat on the spot or to settle comfortably around a cup of tea and a homemade pastry made by Elody. A charming residence well kept by attentive and caring hosts.

- Shared washing machine and tumble dryer for the 2 gîtes.

© Phovoir

Pont du Diable, around Montolieu.

■ LE 7ÈME PÉCHÉ NEW
Lauthier le Haut
✆ 06 86 66 69 36
elody_dl@hotmail.com

Open from Monday to Saturday. Order on the website or elody@le7emepeche.com. Delivery possible (free delivery within a 10km radius). From 3€ the classic pastry part to 5€ the special cake part, cupcake workshop: 5€ per child + 1€ per cupcake.

Guy de Maupassant used to say: "Of all passions, the only really respectable one seems to me to be gluttony", with the 7th Sin, you will be satisfied, kingdom of greedy temptation par excellence, you will have only one problem, that of choice! The pastries on offer are each more tempting than the next, and water your mouth immediately. The originality and beauty of execution are particularly remarkable, and make the fame of this online dessert creator. You wish to mark the spirits for an event, to stand out, to make a request official, contact Elody who will be happy to meet your expectations and beyond! Her creations draw their essence from her childhood memories, when she took refuge in her grandmother's aprons, patiently waiting for the results of her culinary preparations, her senses in turmoil and her eyes in wonder. Today, she reiterates these feelings of sweet happiness to her customers with meticulousness and originality.

▸ Pastry only on order or to be tasted at Le Lauthier restaurant (wine and homemade tapas bar).

Cuxac-Cabardès

■ LA TABLE D'ORELISE
28, rue de la Poste
✆ 04 11 20 01 06
www.latabledorelise-cuxac-cabardes.fr
latabledorelise@gmail.com

Open all year round. Closed on Mondays. October to March: open for lunch from Tuesday to Thursday and lunch and dinner from Friday to Sunday. High season: open for lunch and dinner and the bar all day long. Menus from 26 € to 34 € (+ brasserie menu). Children's menu: 6.90 € (to 8.90 €). Lunch formula: 14.50 € (to 17.50 €). Wine by the glass. Reception of groups (on reservation). Baby chairs. Terrace.

Since Elise and Aurélien took over the hotel-restaurant of Cuxac, visitors and local residents have regained their smiles and their appetite and there is reason! Aurélien assisted by Lise, his wife, offers an entirely homemade cuisine with tasty dishes made with seasonal products on the plates. There are great classics of French cuisine such as the œuf en meurette burgundy egg with sauce bourguignonne, the Provençal lamb rack (spring carte) and more summer dishes in summer such as the salmon tartare or the hake with sauce vierge. But what we love above all when coming here is the dishes in sauce and the incredibly tender meat like beef meat, scampi ravioli and foie gras sauce... It's gourmet, it's copious and the plates are well presented, it's just the way we love it to be! You can dine in the dining room or on the terrace. The plus of the address: a bar where you will be served cocktails made by Élise at correct prices, try the sangria, Bojito (Mojito with beer) or the "White Mandarine", creation of Élise. In order to extend your stay, four rooms are at your disposal, also redesigned. A perfect place to discover the charms of Montagne Noire and Carcassonne 20 minutes away.

Fontiers-Cabardès

AUBERGE DE PANTOUQUET
Route de Lacombe
✆ 04 68 26 64 87
www.pour-les-vacances.com/site-4776
dominique.rajol@orange.fr

July and August: open every day for lunch and dinner. The rest of the year open on Friday for dinner, Saturday for lunch and dinner and Sunday for lunch. Reservation essential. Menus from €38 to €48. A la carte menu: about €28. Children's menu: €13. Wine by the glass. Dish of the day: from €18,00 to €28,00 - Wine list: from €10,00 to €37,00. Groups welcome (capacity 150 people). Baby chairs. Garden. Terrace. Gite for 14 people (250 m², 5 bedrooms). From €1 300 to €2 700 per week depending on the season. Week-end from €550 to €650 - Boules court, Children's playground, Park, Private car park, Private dining room – Wifi Internet access, Banquet, Seminar – Pets allowed.

Petit Futé's aim is to discover surprising, sometimes unusual addresses off the beaten track, with a love of quality products, and well Auberge de Pantouquet is all of these things at once: a place where the magic happens instantly as soon as you enter Sylvie and Domi's home. Situated in the heart of the Black Mountain about 20 minutes from Carcassonne, after passing Fontiers-Cabardes, you will follow the small road and you will see the old mill of Pantouquet which shelters within its walls, a luxury gite and the inn with its two beautiful rooms and its covered terrace in the middle of preserved nature. The inn is tastefully decorated, a mountain chalet atmosphere for the first room while the second room is "vintage" oriented. While you are settling in, Domi prepares the wood fire that will welcome your 1kg T-Bone, your duck breast, or your pork spider steak... in short, tempting meats on a nice ember, which will be accompanied by french fries with duck fat. For the starter, let yourself be tempted by an egg casserole with foie gras or snails in Carcassonne way, unless you succumb to the crayfish flambéed in pastis... a delight! Then, Sylvie passes behind you to tie an XXL bib around your neck, so that you can treat yourself without fear of staining your pretty blouse! In low season, we suggest an omelette with porcini mushrooms followed by a pork shank confit with honey... and if you go on to the end, the rum Baba or the tiramisu with chestnuts will complete this gourmet meal in the most beautiful way, it goes without saying that everything here is homemade. An address you never get tired of and that deserves a detour.

Saint-Martin-le-Vieil

■ LA TABLE FERMIÈRE

2, hameau de Villelongue
✆ 04 68 79 34 58
table.fermiere@gmail.com

Maître Restaurateur. Open all year round. Low season: Thursday to Saturday for lunch and dinner; Sunday for lunch. High season: Wednesday to Sunday for lunch and dinner. From November 1 to March 31: booking imperative for evening service before 6: 30pm. Children's menu: €20 (2 courses from the menu with drinks). Wine by the glass. 1 dish: €17. 2 courses: €20. 3 courses: €30. 4 courses: €40. Cheese plate: €10. Dessert: €10. Specific allergic and vegetarian dishes: + €5.

La Table fermière des Bodin is the guarantee of spending a very convivial moment around a generous, tasty cuisine made only from fresh and local products just a few steps away from the Abbey of Villelongue. Fabienne and Philippe make no secret of their joy when it comes to helping you discover their little paradise. It is imperative to reserve your meal as the policy of the house is to work only on a just-in-time basis, here no frozen food, only fresh food and a limited number of guests. The dishes follow the seasons, and you can take undisguised pleasure in tasting them, ballotine of raw salmon marinated with pink grapefruit, avocado mascarpone mousseline, salicornia salad with candied fennel and salmon skin chips, beef shank stew, candied potatoes in the heart of a Comté cheese wheel and to finish, a crispy roasted apricots, chocolate valrona ganache, candied black olive and lemon ice-cream.

Please note, some must-eat dishes are on order only: the gastronomic cassoulet with foie gras, the bouillabaisse, the tripe plate... Special mention should be made of the care taken in preparing the plates, the reception and the pleasant room with its high ceilings, beams and stone walls and the terrace, which is much appreciated in fine weather.

Saissac ★

■ CHÂTEAU DE SAISSAC ★★

4, place de la Mairie
✆ 04 68 24 46 01
www.saissac.fr
chateausaissac@orange.fr

Closed in January. Open: April to June and September: 10am – 6pm. October: 10am – 5pm. February, March, November and December: 10am – 5pm ONLY weekend and school holidays all areas – Feb March – July & August: 9am – 8pm. Free up to 5 years old. Adult: €5. Child (from 6 to 15 years old): €3. Group (10 people): €4 (by reservation and on free visit. Guided tour for groups of less than 17 people: €7. More than 17 people: €4 per person + €50 flat rate for the group). Reduced rate with the passport of the sites of the Cathar country, adult: €4 and child: €2. Children's welcome area. Guided tour. Shop. Animations. Coach parking.

The Cathar castle of Saissac, listed as a historical monument, overlooks from the top of its rocky promontory the Vernassonne ravine, a privileged strategic position on the Black Mountain. Château de Saissac is the oldest and undoubtedly one of the largest castles in the Cathar country. Excavations have established a dating to the year 900, however it was built and completed in different phases over time. In addition to what the castle tells itself, in the central main building, two restored rooms house the museography on the monetary treasure of Saissac, with a fine collection of coins. It also discusses everything related to money: the ore mining, coinage (craftsmen and tools), exchange, the importance of money in trade, conflicts...

■ DOMAINE DE CAMPRAS

Campras

Open all year round. 4 rooms (and a trailer, the trapper's cabin and a loft). Double room 59 €. Breakfast included (for the Loft, the hut and the caravan, possibility of a "home made breakfast" basket at 6,50 €/pers). Extra bed: 22 € (18 € for children under 18 years old. Free for children under 2 years old. Advance booking recommended). Hiring of the caravan (4 pers.), the trapper's cabin (5 pers.) or the Loft: from 70 to 105 € (week-end). Weekly rental. Games for children. Free Wifi. Catering (table d'hôte on request). Garden furniture. Jacuzzi bath.

It is in a small paradise outside of Saissac that the Calas family has laid, stone by stone, the foundations of their estate. To stay here, all you have to do is call or visit the website, and you are spoilt for choice: which formula to choose? One of the four pretty rooms (independent) on the ground floor of the owners' house with a private terrace and a comfortable common room? The astonishing wooden caravan, fully equipped, artisanally designed

© Timbobaggins – Shutterstock.com

Château de Saissac.

and placed in front of the immensity of the decor? The chalet, brand new, built with local wood and natural materials, which will offer you great intimacy and the impression of dominating the world or the new loft with its panoramic view of the Pyrenees and the City of Carcassonne ? Children will be delighted to meet hens, ducks, Igloo and Idéfix the two foals, to discover the pond and to run freely on the lawns of the property. Meanwhile, adults will appreciate the calm and conviviality of the place. Breakfast is 100% homemade, with fresh fruit juice, homemade jams, homemade pastries and freshly baked bread... For a week or for a night, 20 minutes from Carcassonne and an hour from Toulouse, Domaine de Campras is a real favourite.

■ TRÉSORS D'OC
1, place de la mairie
✆ 06 19 33 58 47
patcamilleri504@gmail.com

Open Monday to Saturday from 9:30am to 7:30pm. Terrace. Tasting: €3 maximum per wine. Spread (one starter, two hot salted sandwiches and one dessert) €10. Shop. Crafts. Coffee. Local products. Taste it.

In the heart of the village of Saissac, enter this cave of Ali baba aux mille...Trésors d'Oc. Atypical place, an important social place for the village and intergenerational, where you will immediately be integrated to drink a coffee, or taste one of the wines of producers that Patricia, the boss, particularly likes. An unusual and warm setting, both small in size but large in its choice of wines, handicrafts and other products, you will find the best coffee for the morning, as well as the best wine to start a good aperitif, decorated with "tartinerie" (a starter, two hot salted sandwiches and a dessert) served throughout the day. Patricia will talk to you with passion about all her producers who delight our taste buds, and the richness of her cellar, it is the essential meeting place for locals and travellers, to meet beautiful people during concerts or various cultural events organized here. A place of exchange, simple and atypical, where your mind and your throat are refreshed! So, don't hesitate to take a coffee break on the shaded terrace, on the road to the Cathar castles.

Villeséquelande

■ MUSÉE DE LA CHEVALERIE
1, rue Marcellin-Horus
✆ 04 68 71 48 89
www.musee-chevalerie.fr
contact@musee-chevalerie.fr

Open from February to December. For school holidays information by phone. Open Tuesday to Saturday from 10am to 12pm and from 2pm to 7pm; Sunday from 3pm to 7pm. Closed Sunday morning and Monday. Free for children up to 7 years old. Adult: €6. Child: €4. Groups of 4 to 15 people maximum. Guided tour: €2/ person as an extra charge. Children welcome area. Guided tour. Shop. Animations. Groups on reservation. Pets allowed.

Hear ye, Hear ye, Fine Ladies and Noble Lords! Come and meet Gilles Alessandri, owner and creator of the museum. This true passionate of the Middle Ages welcomes you to this residence in period costumes for the happiness of the children and adults. Relive this Medieval episode which has greatly marked Carcassonne and its surroundings, contemplate these centuries of history through a guided tour and roam among the stunning collections of the host. You will immerse yourself in the daily period-objects, fall for the richly embroidered cushions and curtains, costumes from Jacquouille La Fripouille's period, knights' weapons or the currency in use at that time. Gilles will share his very contagious passion with you and will please the family with his anecdotal stories. A charming immersive link where we learn while having fun; a recreational and pedagogical moment at the same time of which we do not get tired.

▶ **Note that** Gilles organises various activities which groups can book to participate in.

BAGES

This traditional fishing village, located on a rocky spur and surrounded by vineyards and scrublands, overlooks magnificently the pond since the eleventh century. This is the perfect opportunity for you to get away from the tumult of seaside resorts. You can take a walk along its narrow streets and go across the door of the sundial marking the entrance of the medieval village. This dial was offered by Louis XIII to thank the villagers as they treated the wounded soldiers returning from the Spanish Civil War. There, you will find pretty intertwined houses with small openings, which used to form a rempart. You can also admire along the bends of its streets the breath-taking panorama, the colourful flat-bottomed boats, the fishing nets with small stitches (trabacs) drying on the old refurbished port at the entrance of the village. But above all, you should taste the local speciality: *la bourride d'anguilles* (eels). This remarkable site has been attracting a number of artists since the late 80s: sculptors, painters, photographers, sculptors... today as numerous as fishermen. This has led to the creation of many arts galleries. Some buildings of the eleventh century are still visible in the hamlet of Prat-de-Cest. You can stroll on the marked paths or on the roads of Pesquis in the Northwest of the village; when the season is coming, people pick the best asparagus of the area... Follow this pretty road and navigate through the ponds towards Peyriac-de-Mer where egrets, flamingos, mallards and coots come to nest... Enjoy the warmness of the atmosphere, mixing ponds, scrublands, cicadas and accents of the South... As you leave, the only thing you will have in mind is coming back.

Knife & Fork

LE PORTANEL
La Placette
✆ 04 68 42 81 66
www.leportanel.net
leportanel@orange.fr

Open all year round. Tuesday and Thursday to Saturday for lunch and dinner; Wednesday and Sunday for lunch. Reservation recommended. Menus from €32 to €42. Children's menu: €12. Lunch formula: €21 (Clin d'oeil menu served for lunch and dinner on weekdays). Wine by the glass. Local menu "Tasting of Eels" €42 with regional wine for each dish. Le Portanel is also a catering service (wedding, association, 3rd age), ask for more information. Reception of groups (inquire about menus). Baby chairs. Takeaway sale.

Located in one of the small streets of the village centre, Le Portanel is a reference for local people. Like us, you will succumb to this breathtaking view of the Bages pond visible from the restaurant's modernly decorated dining room in natural tones in harmony with the surrounding nature. Jean-Christophe knows how to receive, he knows the codes, the art of the table has no secrets for him and in the kitchen, there is a cutting, slicing, chopping, simmering, in short, here, cooking reigns. Jean-Christophe Rousseau, master restaurateur, creates a daring cuisine, paying homage to the fish in the ponds: wolffish, sea bream... Discover in particular

© Yan EVEN

Route de la saline.

the dish "Autour de la Lisse" the fish of the pond (in Granny Smith apple tartare, smoked and in rillettes with chives)". But the star of the place is the eel. Narbonne eel, eel terrine with sage and green lentil, pan-fried eel from the pond with parsley, eel stew in Fitou and especially its traditional bourride. Here, we only cook with fresh products, and it is only natural that the menu follows the daily arrival of fish and the course of the seasons. The Clin d'oeil menu is the perfect opportunity to discover a sunny and refined cuisine. Do you want a sweet treat? Let yourself be tempted by the Figuette Narbonnaise, a traditional fig and almond dessert that will sublimate your meal.

■ **LES JARDINS DE BAGES**
2, place de Juin 1907
✆ 04 68 70 13 76
lesjardinsdebages@gmail.com
Closed in January. Low season: open for lunch only from Wednesday to Sunday. High season: open every day for lunch and dinner. A la carte menu: about €20. Lunch: starter + main course or main course + dessert €16 - Starter / main course / dessert €19. Wine by the glass. Regional beers, artisanal. Local wine. Groups welcome. Terrace. Shop. Animations.
On the small square at the top of the village, Jardins de Bages is quite atypical as it is at the same time an excellent restaurant, a bar, and a small village grocery store. The dishes offered here are composed of fresh products that have been subtly prepared. For those who love fish, the sea bream with citrus fruits is a must. Carnivores will undoubtedly prefer grilled lamb with herbs or the tagine of chicken or Kefta. For veggies, there is vegetarian tagine, everyone will like the desserts and especially the apple crumble or clafoutis with seasonal fruit, all accompanied by well selected local wines at cellar price (+ €8 corkage fee).
In summer, the terrace is very pleasant, you can enjoy it in the shade or in the sun all day long after a short walk on the pond, but also to appreciate the various concerts that are organised every Thursday from 8.30 pm. A "small village" atmosphere where everyone is invited to share a friendly moment.

In the surroundings

Peyriac-de-Mer

■ **LE COMPTOIR DES ÉTANGS**
7 B, place de la Mairie
✆ 07 77 06 02 61
Closed in January. Low season: open from Friday to Tuesday and on public holidays from 9: 30am (last service at 10: 30pm). High season: Thursday to Tuesday and public holidays from 9: 30am (last service at 10: 30pm). Low season from November to the end of February Closed on Wednesdays. Booking recommended. Pizzas from €9.50 to €13.50. Pizza "Pitchoun": €6. Credit card not accepted.

Did the walk on the ponds make you hungry? Non-stop service at Comptoir des Étangs where you will enjoy the homemade pizzas which are perhaps the best in the department... Here, everything is homemade and their products are rigorously selected; to this can be added a certain know-how in the art of pizza, as well as the good mood of Lynda and Stéphane and a really charming setting. In short, it is one of our " favourite " place! The dough pieces are made with Italian flour, the products that compose them are fresh and cooked on the spot – here, no preservatives or additives with the suspicious code name are used! Here it's pizza à la carte, use your imagination and compose your pizza (except July/August) Finally, the sweet note at the end of your meal is just divine, Lynda's cakes are exceptional! Comptoir des Étangs is also a tea room, so let yourself be surprised by choosing one of the traditional and local lemonades: plain, strawberry-basil, apple-basil... A really nice place, set on the charming square of Peyriac. Visit this place without moderation!

■ **Ô VIEUX TONNEAUX**
3, place de la Mairie
✆ 04 68 48 39 54
Low season: open from Wednesday to Sunday for lunch; Friday and Saturday for dinner. High season: Tuesday to Sunday. Reservation recommended. Menus from €15 to €25 (Chef's menu). Children's menu: €8. Lunch formula: €15 (starter/main course or main course/dessert €13). Wine by the glass. Country platter: €20. Label Café de Pays. Baby chairs. Animations.
It is in the heart of the village, in the small square near the fountain, that David, Christelle and their team welcome you in a simple and friendly atmosphere where villagers, local fishermen, Narbonnais and tourists get together. As soon as you cross the threshold, you will let yourself be carried away by this almost "Pagnolesque" atmosphere where the accents sing, where the sweetness of life is instantly perceptible, where sweet scents already tickle your nostrils. On the terrace or in the room that reminds you of the village's old bistro, you will enjoy a simple cuisine of regional products. Its tapas slate is very appreciated: charcuterie, cheeses, artisanal jams, fried fish... For light meals, the vegetarian plate is very nice. A big hunger? Let yourself be tempted by a beautiful Charolais rib steak or by the creamy kidneys in Madeira sauce and if you come on a Sunday, opt for the Peyriacoise eel bourride, a delight. For the dessert, you will find among other things, the caramelized French toast, excellent! Don't hesitate to stop for a break, if only to taste a glass of wine, a small traditional grape juice produced in the village or for one of the Friday or Sunday concerts depending on the season.

GRUISSAN ★★

■ **OFFICE DE TOURISME**
80, boulevard du Pech-Maynaud
✆ 04 68 49 09 00
www.gruissan-mediterranee.com
From July 1st to August 31st every day from 9am to 8pm. From April 1st to June 30th and September every day from 9am to 12pm and 2pm to 6pm. From February 9 to March 31 and from September 30 to November 4 Monday to Friday from 9am to 12pm and 2pm to 6pm and Saturday and Sunday from 10am to 12pm and 2pm to 4pm. From November 5, 2019 to February 7, 2020 from Monday to Friday from 9am to 12pm and 2pm to 6pm.
You will be welcomed by a competent team who will be happy to inform you, advise you and guide you for activities to do during your stay, whether short or long, or for your installation in the Gruissan city. You will have at your disposal new technology equipment: touch screens, photo screens, virtual reality headphones computers to inform you about cultural, sports, recreational, summer activities, heritage tours, etc. Takeaway brochures are also available on site, as well as wi-fi.

■ **LE DURANDAL** ★
Place des Menhirs
✆ 06 07 31 94 27
www.bateau-promenade-durandal.fr
supercatdurandal@aol.com
Quai d'Honneur pier, place des Menhirs, behind the Tourist Office (pedestrian access).
Open from March to November. In March, May, September and October, departure at 3pm every weekend and public holidays – duration 1 hour. On weekdays on reservation only from 15 people. In April, during the Easter holidays and in June, daily outings (except on Mondays) at 3pm. Adult: €7.50 (to €18.50). Child: €4,50 (to €10,00). Group: €6 (to €17). Group price for children from €4 to €9. Credit card not accepted.
Departing from Gruissan, the Durandal invites you to visit the Aude coastline by sea. Various excursions are available, such as a visit to Port-la-Nouvelle (combined with a small train to visit Saint Lucia, the wild island), or the one that allows you to follow the beach to the cliff of Leucate-La Franqui, its famous Witch Rock and of course the Paradise Cove which is without doubt the most pleasant part of the coast! The catamaran has an underwater space to observe the depths. The duration of the excursions varies according to the programs and departures take place from 9am to 2: 45pm or from 9am to 8pm depending on the destination you choose. Finally, if you want to watch the summer fireworks while on the water, you have to book early, the show is amazing!

Sightseeing

■ **LE SALIN DE L'ILE SAINT-MARTIN** ★★
Route de l'Ayrolle
Le Salin de Gruissan
✆ 04 82 53 10 61
contact@lesalindegruissan.fr
Shop open from mid-February to the end of December. Low season: open from Wednesday to Sunday from 10: 30am

Tour Barberousse.

to 12:30pm and from 2pm to 5:30pm. High season: every day and public holidays from 10:30am to 7:30pm. Night until 10pm in July/August. Free up to 8 years old. Adult: €8,90. Child (from 8 to 13 years old): €6.90. Guided tour (duration 1h20) from the beginning of March to the beginning of November at 11am, 3pm as well as 4:30pm (from mid-April to the end of October) and 6pm (from the beginning of June to the end of September). Restaurant (la Cambuse du Saunier and La Terrasse du Salin).

After crossing the bridge of port Barberousse, head towards l'Ayrolle and after 2 km you will see the salt mine of Saint-Martin island. In an environment protected by a dam that is 1,5 km long, the salt marshes spread over approximately 350 ha. You will discover the profession of salt manufacturer and the importance of the salt industry on the coastline of Aude. Created in 1911, it was used until 2005 by the company of Salins du Midi, now, a SEM revives the site by focusing on the artisanal side of the production. The guided tour of approximately 1h20 takes you on a walking trail in the heart of the salt marshes, and will reveal all the different stages of production: water movement, concentration, crystallization. Special mention for our guide Emmeline, it was a feast to listen to her! Small tricks: In June you will surely have the chance to bump into avocets and from mid-August to the end of September (depending on the weather) you can watch the salt collection. The ecomuseum, where access is free, invites you to go back in time, through a film, photos and tools exhibitions; you will relive salt harvest from 1900 to the present day. The spacious shop will allow you to purchase salt in all its forms: salt flower, flavoured salt, coarse salt... as well as a wide range of local products. On the spot, you can have something to eat or taste local oysters, there is also a bar that offers many concerts on summer evenings. Why not extend your visit to the La Cambuse du Saunier restaurant which offers an incredible view of the salt marshes? The Salt Festival in early July, an event to live if you have the opportunity of being in the region.

■ VIEUX VILLAGE, CHÂTEAU & TOUR BARBEROUSSE ★★

Place Louis-Rachou

https://gruissan-mediterranee.com

Open all year round. Low season: every day from 8am to 6pm. High season: every day from 8am to 10pm. Sunday from 8:15am. Access to the castle can be closed if the wind is higher than 90 km/h. Free of charge.

The old village has kept the authenticity of a medieval village with its Mediterranean circular streets at the foot of the Barbarossa tower. You should let yourself be guided along the narrow and tortuous streets, and take time to admire these ancestral homes of wine growers, fishermen and salt workers who lived there for generations. Built on a steep rock, the castle was constructed in the late 10th century to monitor the coast and protect the city from barbarian invasions that came from the sea. One century and a half later the archbishop of Narbonne reinforced this fortress by adding a tower which is still called Tour Barberousse. Lovers of old stones will enjoy admiring the rusticated stones, true characteristic of the medieval castles of the region, which decorate Tour Barberousse. The remains of this castle are a unique viewpoint of the village, the pond and the scrubland and they still look great!

Knife & Fork

■ LA CAMBUSE DU SAUNIER

Le Salin de Gruissan, route de l'Ayrolle

✆ 04 84 25 13 24

www.lesalindegruissan.fr

contact@lesalindegruissan.fr

Closed from mid-December to mid-February -. In low season: open from Wednesday to Sunday lunchtime. In high season: daily for both lunch and dinner. Oyster tasting or purchase from 10:30am to 5:30pm (high season until 9:30pm). Menu: about 35€. Wine by the glass. Opening hours on the website. Terrace on the terrace.

La Cambuse du Saunier is large tables, bundled dishes and a stunning view of the saltworks. Between Etang de l'Ayrolle, the Saint-Martin island and the Vieille-Nouvelle inlet, you will be dazzled by the beauty of the place! Once you are at the table, the waiters bring a welcome muscat wine glass and a small bowl of raw vegetables, perfect to take time to choose. Here, sea produce and Gruissan salt are favoured. Bulots, mussels, clams, knives, oysters from the Saint-Martin island... You can find every seafood (according to arrival) hot or cold, cooked according to various recipes. We recommend the traditional hot oysters with rouille and cheese, delicious. Here, salt alchemy is also in your dishes: sea bass, sea bream, chicken, duck breast, prime rib... in salt crust and even the desserts are with salt flower like the sheep-milk ice cream, etc. On the wine side, the restaurant favors the wines of the Clapes and its surroundings as well as the wine of Pierre Richard, the nearest neighbor. After a visit to the salt museum and its local products boutique, do not hesitate to impregnate the atmosphere of the masters sauniers and enjoy the divine view or go for a drink at the Terrace des Salins.

LA CRANQUETTE

13, rue de La République
✆ 04 68 75 12 07
www.lacranquette.fr
julien.privat@sfr.fr

Low season: open from Thursday to Saturday for lunch and dinner; Sunday at lunchtime. High season: Tuesday to Sunday and on public holidays for lunch and dinner. Also open on Wednesdays from April to October. Reservation recommended. Single menu at €37. Children's menu: €10 (and €15 according to age). Lunch formula: €25. Wine by the glass. Cheques not accepted. Groups welcome (up to 25 people). Terrace.

We invite you to have a seat in this superbly restored former presbytery where tradition and modernity meet. Julien and Mélanie invite you to pleasantly follow a cuisine of flavor and spices full of elegance, where land and sea combinations are perfectly mastered: no frozen shellfish or fish, only fresh and wild fish. Don't settle for the menu, don't hesitate to pick various specialties from the menu, our favourites are: Mediterranean bluefin tuna caught by line in tartare style, Big Eel fished in Gruissan (Homemade smoked eel portion and parsley cream. Gruissan Bourride Sauce) or the Blond Aquitaine rib steak of the Pyrenees, matured and smoked with juniper berries, detailed roasted lengthwise, adorned and grilled with its sweet onions from Cévennes and fried mushrooms. Even if the portions are generous, it would be a shame to resist the desserts: Blabla au rhum, the baba that makes people talk and whipped cream* with bourbon vanilla "Président" or Dôme fondant with iced white chocolate, caramel with pine nuts and hot muffin with pine nuts. The wine list is very Occitan, with a choice which is mostly based on organic and natural wines from La Clape, we love it! Whether it is on the shady terrace, on the ground floor near the open kitchen or on the first floor in one of the two beautiful bright rooms, we guarantee a pleasant gastronomic moment. Another place in the street (n°10): Cranquette mussels (snack), on the spot or to take away, you will enjoy an original and well-cooked "made in Cranquette" cuisine: Bologna mussels, fish & chips, cuttlefish cassoulet... You can book your table online from the website.

AUX DEUX OLIVIERS

Boulevard de la corderie
Facing the Cave Coopérative
✆ 04 68 75 85 53
www.auxdeuxoliviers.com
auxdeuxoliviers-gruissan@orange.fr

Open all year round. In low season: from Wednesday to Saturday lunchtime from 12pm to 1: 15pm and in the evening from 7pm to 9: 30pm; Sunday lunchtime from 12pm to 1: 15pm. In high season: Tuesday evening; Wednesday to Sunday lunch and dinner. Reservation recommended. Menus from 30€ to 42€. Children's menu: 10€. Lunch formula: 22€. Wine by the glass. Groups welcome. Terrace. Air conditioning.

Plage des Chalets.

Here, we work with quality products and change the menu according to the seasons to respect the freshness of all the ingredients and delight the taste buds. For you; the Emietté of crab with red curry, turnip salad with orange and carrot/ gray shrimp consommé, oven-baked golden can breast, cream of porcini mushrooms and boletus and mashed potatoes in olive oil and the terrific Biscuit moelleux with orange blossom, creamy bergamot and rose jelly, Yuzu lemon ice cream. Vegetarian dish possible in all menus. A very nice address between the port and the old village.

■ LA FLEUR DE SEL

5, rue Jules Ferry
✆ 04 68 75 80 79
madge.sasu@outlook.fr

In high season: open from Saturday to Monday and Wednesday for both lunch and dinner; Tuesday, Thursday and Friday in the evening. In low season: closed on Wednesday evening, Thursday and Friday lunchtime. Children's menu: 9€. Lunch formula: 17€ (starter + main course + dessert). Wine by the glass. À la carte menu + dish of the moment.

When we hear about a restaurant in rather flattering terms like "generous", "gourmet", "tasty"... well let's go! Laurent Boineau will tell you himself, he is not a trained cook but just passionate and self-taught. With his restaurant, he wants to treat his customers as he would do with his friends, he tests, he experiments, he tastes and when the recipe seems perfect to him, he puts it on the slate. La Fleur de Sel is located in the heart of the village, within a walking distance from the market square. You can choose to sit in the dining room or on the terrace. It is therefore a cuisine of inspiration that follows the seasons that will be proposed to you, a love affair for the fresh octopus tentacle, perfectly cooked and melting in the mouth, accompanied by a leek and carrot fondue, a delight. Among the dishes of the moment, the marinated ribs and their homemade barbecue sauce were very tempting. Other dishes are proposed à la carte such as homemade burgers, tuna and its homemade aioli, squid in parsley... You will have a good time in this small unpretentious but generous restaurant.

■ FORMENTERA

Avenue des noctambules
Parking de La Villa
✆ 04 68 49 26 29
www.formentera-gruissan.com
info@formentera-gruissan.com

Open from May to mid-September. May: Fridays, Saturdays and the day before public holidays from 12pm to 2pm (closed on Sunday evening). From June to 15/09: Every day from 12pm to 2pm (closed on Sunday evening). Reservation recommended. Tapas formula from 5€ to 10€. 5 tapas platter: the 6th tapas offered. 8 tapas platter: 1 bottle of Gris-Blanc rosé offered. Wine by the glass. Big plateau of cold meats and cheeses: 14€. Terrace. Heated swimming pool and changing rooms. Deckchair for a fee.

Formentera is a small island in the Balearic Islands located a short distance from Ibiza. It is a paradisiacal and unique place very popular with the bohemian jet-set. It is this atmosphere that the owners of the place offer you here. After a season rich in highlights, Formentera reopens its doors in April, 3 months earlier than last year. For those who are new to Formentera, there is a large heated swimming pool with whirlpools, sun loungers for relaxing and a XXL-size bar where you can enjoy unique cocktails such as "Pink ice Pop – Freixenet©". In the restaurant, the formula is evolving towards a menu of home-made tapas ranging from the most classic to the most cooked, to be savoured at the bar, on the bar tables or by the pool. For this season, you'll find the famous Sunday brunch and new dishes coming on Tuesdays, Wednesdays and Thursdays! Always a clubbing atmosphere with DJs on Friday and Saturday evenings, perfect for a before if you want to spend your evening at La Villa (the adjoining disco), Sundays are more lounges with pool parties in the afternoon. During the 2019 season, Formentera offered Aquafitness courses, find out more about the 2020 season. In short, an innovative concept and a good alternative to the beach, especially on windy days.

■ LA FRITERIE

Plage des Chalets
84, Allée des Aigrettes
✆ 04 68 49 80 41

Open from March 28 to September 30, 2020 - every day! Low season: open every day and on public holidays from 11am to 3pm and from 6pm to 10pm. High season: Monday to Saturday and on public holidays from 9am to 11pm. High season: July / August. Low season: during events such as Défi Wind etc 11am – 10pm non stop; À la carte menu: approx. €12. Children's menu: €8,80. Salad from €7,50 to €13 - Pizzas from €8,50 - Paninis €5,50. Terrace. Take away sale.

La Friterie of Sacha and Virgnia is a snack bar with many "homemade" products where customers from 7 to 75 years old can enjoy a friendly atmosphere! You will meet regulars who have a pied-à-terre at the Chalets, tourists who come to spend the day at the beach, whether at lunchtime or in the middle of the afternoon... in summer, you can nibble sweet or savoury treats at any time! After an afternoon swim, how about a nutella-banana panini or a nice vegetarian salad on the terrace or to take away? Tacos, french fries, pizzas and Pôle Sud ice-cream (traditional Aude ice cream parlour) are waiting for you! In the middle of summer, there can be a bit of a wait despite the great team because everything is freshly prepared... the fresh products must be a little earned. Non-stop service in July-August.

■ MOSQUITO COAST

Plage de Mateille
✆ 06 73 62 77 32

Closed from October to April. High season: open every day and on public holidays from 9am to 12am. Booking recommended. A la carte menu: about €20. Children's menu: €10. Thursday evening burgers €15 - Tapas and salads from €3 to €15 - Plancha from €18 to €21 - Vegetarian combo €15... Checks not accepted.

On the immense beach of Mateille, you will find the Mosquito Coast, a nice restaurant where you can enjoy food sheltered from the wind and the sun on the terrace or with your feet in the sand. Pleasant decoration, simple menu and good food, extra smoothies. We liked the hammocks that invite you to take a nap after a meal! Thursday evening is burger party.

LE PAPARAZZO

Pole Nautique des Chalets
✆ 06 74 65 67 30
paparazzo.gruissan@gmail.com

Closed from November to April. In low season: open at weekends. In high season: every day. À la carte menu: about 25€. Children's menu: 9€. Formula: 21€. Terrace.

In 2020, the Paparazzo is celebrating its 10th anniversary! The Paparazzo is located on the beach of the chalets, on the sea front, and welcomes you in a beach restaurant atmosphere... aperitif, lunch, dinner, and evenings with a DJ, the people from Gruissannais and the holidaymakers have quickly adopted it. Thierry Dozoul is at the helm of this bar-restaurant where you almost have your feet in the water: in the kitchen a menu of fresh products, rather turned towards the sea: grilled sardines with escabeche or whelks with garlic, the mussels and chips, the mussels and chips, scallop skewers and vegetables in the wok, or the grilled wolf, the asparagus risotto, homemade fries... This place is as much for families who want to eat in front of the sea as it is for a clientele of sensible party-goers. Indeed, it is possible to settle down at the bar to have a drink (local wines, cocktails, bottled or draught beers), or several while eating some tapas. Since the last renovation, the Paparazzo offers more space, cosy furniture and a playground for children. Here there is something for all tastes and budgets. The wait can be long in July / August, think about booking! Numerous DJ nights throughout the season announced on the Facebook page. Cross fit, Yoga and muscle building classes in the summer.

LA PETITE BRASSERIE

1, boulevard Victor-Hugo
✆ 04 68 65 24 50

Open all year round. In low season: Sunday, Monday and Wednesday lunchtime; Friday and Saturday evening. In high season: open every day for both lunch and dinner except Thursday lunchtime. Children's menu: 9€. Wine by the glass. Dishes of the day from 14€ according to arrival. Salads from 13€ to 15€. Fish & ships: 16€. Hamburger: 16€. Desserts from 6.50€ to 8€. Terrace. Take away sale.

We predicted a great success for Stéphanie and Eric's Petite Brasserie and we were right! These two passionate people do things with heart, whether it's Eric in the kitchen or Stéphanie in the dining room, everything has to be perfect! We love the decoration of the place, trendy and chic, while the beautiful dishes highlight the chef's creations. In his open (but glassed-in) kitchen Eric prepares beautiful plates that are always gourmet, we find must-haves like the excellent Caesar salad, the Gruissan potato-based salad made with octopus, tellines, mussels, clams and cockles (depending on the season) but also the fish and ships with gribiche sauce, the hamburger with bread from the baker and the omelettes. Other specialities of the house: the linguine of the sea (special recipe of the house) or the veal escalope with mushroom sauce, white ham, raclette cheese and homemade fries, it's greedy and quite copious. If you have a small place left for dessert, we recommend the Tiramisu or the often less classic dessert of the day. We like the setting, we like the food and we like the welcome Stéphanie gives us. In short, this Petite Brasserie is a success!

LE PLAN B

5, rue de la République
✆ 04 68 49 14 26
idem11@gmx.fr

Open all year round. In low season: from Thursday to Tuesday and on public holidays for both lunch and dinner. In high season: every day for both lunch and dinner. Single menu at 27€ (starter + main course + dessert of your choice from the menu). Children's menu: 11€. Suggestion of the day: 15€ (to 19€). Wine by the glass. Cheques not accepted. Terrace.

We like this small restaurant located in old Gruissan, a few streets from Barbarosse Tower. Medhi is a passionate chef who surprises us every time we visit. The dishes are superb, and the products they contain are of impeccable freshness. Whether you are on the terrace or in the dining room, you will be well settled to enjoy your meal. The menu is constantly evolving with traditional and more exotic recipes, as evidenced by the razor fish with butter parsley flavoured with whisky, which could be considered as the house's signature dish. Among the new dishes, we recommend the pan fried cuttlefish, shrimp and spaghetti with cuttlefish with ink sauce or the pork cheek with Banyuls wine, a delight. It should be noted that Medhi plays the "short circuit" menu by offering fishing by Gruissanese fishermen and wines from La Clape. Don't miss the homemade desserts that will perfectly complete your meal. The Plan B is an address where the welcome is not to be underestimated, where we regularly return with great pleasure.

RESTAURANT LES VIEILLES NOUVELLES

19, Grand-Rue
✆ 04 34 27 51 76
lesgruissanaises@gmail.com

Open all year round. Closed the first 3 weeks of January. In low season: from Thursday to Monday for both lunch and dinner. In high season: every day for both lunch and dinner. Single menu at 35€. Children's menu: 12€. Lunch formula: 18€. Wine by the glass. Tapas from 6€ to 12€. Dishes from 19 to 26€ and the famous Parillade de la mer 32€. Baby chairs. Terrace. Animations.

The restaurant takes its name from the Plage de la Vieille Nouvelle linking Gruissan to Port-la-Nouvelle. New leader Pol Ruel and a new menu but still as good as ever! The restaurant has a small room on the ground floor, a terrace on the street side (pedestrian in summer) and a second room upstairs with a bar where the kitchen is located, all decorated in "*vintage*" style and adorned with works by local artists. On the slate, the choice is between tapas and dishes, we notice the mention "all our dishes are fresh and homemade". Must-eat dishes: The seafood parillade ((gratinated oysters, shrimps, razor clams, john dory fillet and sea bream) or the veal sweetbreads on a bed of fresh tagliatelle with pan-fried foie gras and morel sauce, the dishes are served with good seasonal vegetables. To accompany your meal, local wines are available. Finally, homemade desserts – such as crème brulée with chocolate and fresh raspberry or 3-chocolate feuillantine – end with a very pleasant sweet note. An address that develops and offers a cuisine that is increasingly gourmet and generous. Please note that the restaurant is now open all year round.

■ LE POISSON D'AVRIL

At the corner of the Rue du Chat-qui-Pêche
3, avenue d'Occitanie
Les Chalets
✆ 04 68 91 60 01

Open all year round. In low season: Tuesday to Thursday in the evening; Friday and Saturday lunch and dinner; Sunday lunch. In high season: every day for lunch and dinner. In low season: it is recommended to call. Menus from 22€ to 35€. Wine by the glass. Fish soup 10€.

Le Poisson d'Avril is located at the entrance to the village of the chalets on stilts, in a very pleasant setting to go all over during a digestive stroll. But first of all, go to this address with warm and relaxed welcome. Here, there is no fuss, everyone is welcomed and the refined and warm decoration makes everyone feel at ease. However, the seafood is finely selected to offer you delicate and tasty dishes and excellent seafood platters. The fish soup is the must-eat dish of the house, but the griddled cuttlefishes, or the dish of bulots and shrimps are not left behind. Difficult to make a choice! For several years, Diane and Thierry have skillfully managed this address that is inclined to become a must in Gruissan. Restaurant open all year round, it is recommended and remember to book!

■ LE STROMBOLI

1, quai des Palmiers
✆ 04 68 49 46 36
restaurant-le-stromboli@orange.fr
♿

Closed from November to early January. Open every day for lunch and dinner. July and August: continuous service. Card: about 22 €. Children's menu: 10,50 €. Wine by the glass. Terrace. Take away sale.

When you walk past the Stromboli, you think of pizzas and for good reason, they are said to be the best in Gruissan... But the Stromboli is also a generous and gourmet cuisine, where the Mediterranean is given pride of place through small homemade dishes. So you can always find the cream or tomato sauce pizzas, beautiful meal salads, cuttlefish in parsley, mussels, the "dish concept" meal including the 100% vegetarian or the excellent ribs of pork with grape, honey and rosemary sauce from La Clape, a delight! Gourmets will enjoy the "gourmet" burgers and their homemade breads. A restaurant where quality comes first with a large terrace facing the port and late service in high season.

■ LA TABLE D'OLI

Quai du Ponant
✆ 07 67 81 52 60

Open from March to September. Low season: open from Tuesday to Saturday for lunch and dinner; Sunday for lunch. High season: every day and public holidays for lunch and dinner. Reservation recommended. Single menu at €25 (starter / main course / dessert – Starter / main course or main course / dessert €16). Children's menu: €10.50. Dish of the day: €12. Wine by the glass. Or by the jug from the Gruissan cellar as well as bottled wine from local organic producers. Groups welcome (on request (max 30) for all occasions: birthdays, bachelor/ bachelorette parties, etc.). Covered terrace protected from the wind.

The cuisine at La table d'Oli is almost 100% organic (with the exception of a few products, say 70%). Audrey welcomes you on the terrace or in the small glass room and offers you a different formula every day, with a choice of four starters, four main courses and four desserts from the à la carte menu made by the chef with real mastery and a love of work well done. Fresh and local products, such as fish from the gruissannaise fishery and fruit and vegetables from the Estarac gardens in Bages or Sallèles d'Aude. During our visit, the salmon was offered as a tartare as a starter and the line-caught sea bream with white butter and Gruissan saffron, delicious and hearty. Special mention for the careful presentation of the plates decorated with fresh and edible flowers. To accompany the menu, which changes according to the seasons, we recommend the organic white wine from Ricardelle de Lautrec in Coursan or Château Laquirou in Fleury d'Aude. Prices defy all competition on the port of Gruissan with regard to the dishes on the plates, so don't resist the temptation to sit down and test the freshness of the dishes at La Table d'Oli!

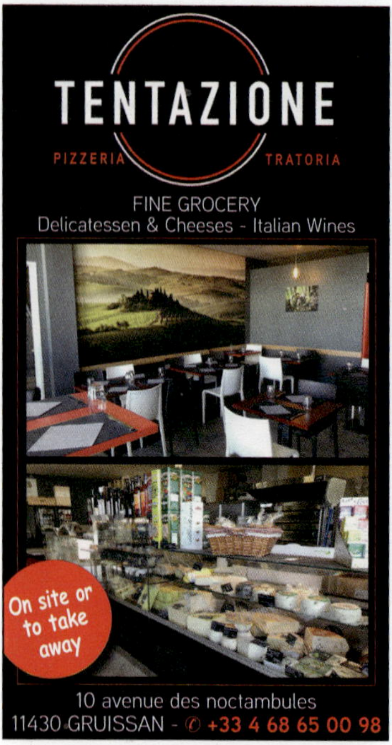

■ TENTAZIONE

NEW

10, Avenue des Noctambules
résidence Ephyra
✆ 04 68 65 00 98
nicolaskraken@gmail.com

Open Tuesday to Saturday for lunch and dinner; Sunday for dinner. Closed on Sunday at lunchtime and Monday. Reservation recommended. Antipasti from €10 to €14 - Salads from €10,50 to €15 - Pizzas from €8 to €24 - Baked pasta from €12 to €15,50 - Desserts from €5 to €11 - Homemade ice-cream from €3 to €12,50. Groups welcome. Terrace. Takeaway sale. Shop.

Oscar Wilde used to say that the only way to free yourself from temptation is to give in to it... Welcome to Tentazione, the aptly named, more than a restaurant, it is the den of good food, in dolce vita style, an authentic restaurant associated with a unique trattoria. Products meticulously chosen by Nicolas, of transalpine origin, who honours his native land, sublimate the flavours in revisited great classics. This address away from the heart of Gruissan is more than a beautiful discovery, it is the assurance of products with controlled origin, a guarantee of freshness and authenticity. This is the intimate address that everyone dreams of getting to know, to keep jealously guarded to treat family and friends, with Italian dishes that will amaze gourmets and gourmands. The master of the place, Nicolas, with his experience in top-of-the-range restaurant, as a private chef, will guide you and offer you beautiful gustatory discoveries, little-known products, tasty recipes, homemade, in short a trip to the land of tradition. The dough of the pizzas are masterfully worked daily, here we give time to time so that the result exalts your taste buds, such as the must-eat "Gian Carlo", enjoy fabulous pizzas or real pastas without forgetting the must-eat *nidi di rondine romagnoli*. There is no doubt that this establishment, once you've passed the door, will remain in a good place in your address book, a guaranteed address for food lovers, petit futé was not mistaken!

- Don't hesitate to order your pizza or takeaway dish
- Delicatessen of Italian products: large choice of cheeses, cold meats, wines, liqueurs, pastries...

■ LA TOUR NOMADE

4, Grand rue
✆ 09 86 36 08 37
latournomade11@gmail.com

Open Wednesday to Saturday for lunch and dinner; Sunday for lunch. Children's menu: €9. Lunch formula: €14 (starter + main course + dessert. Dish of the day: €12). Wine by the glass. Couscous from €13 to €24. Tajines from €19 to €22. Terrace. Takeaway sale. Take away sale on order: -10%.

Do you have the call of the East? Well, push the door of La Tour Nomade and your desires will become reality. You will have the choice between the small terrace overlooking the street (which becomes pedestrian in the summer) or the room with its cosy and oriental decoration. Zhora, the boss and cook will welcome you with a smile and the greatest kindness. She cooks here as she would for her friends or family, her cooking skills, she owes them to her mother, Mestoura, who shared her little culinary secrets with her.

The lunch formula offers a very good value for money, during our visit, we were offered an oriental salad as a starter, a well worked couscous and vegetables as well as oriental pastries for a very reasonable price. Among the specialities, couscous of course, with lamb, fish, keftas, the must-eat Royal and even a vegetarian. Special mention for the cooking of the semolina made according to the rules, steamed several times, making it light and tasty and fragrant with spices. Delicious also, the tajines on order (it should be simmered...) and the grills of La Tour Nomade. Everything here is homemade except for the pastries which come from the best oriental pastry shop in Narbonne. To accompany your meal, local wines are offered but if you want to go to the end of your journey in the Orient, choose a "côteaux du Mascara" (Algeria). A very pleasant and generous address that invites you to travel...

Sleeping

■ SUNRISE BEACH HOTEL

Gruissan-Plage – Les Chalets – Front de Mer
1, allée des Courlis ✆ 04 68 49 13 87
www.hotelsunrise-gruissan.com
sunrisehotelgruissan@gmail.com

Closed from mid-November to February inclusive. 20 rooms (including one PRM room). Double room from 85€ to 110€; triple room from 115€ to 125€. Breakfast: 9€. Extra bed: 22€. Parking. Visitor's tax: 1.25€/person. Animals accepted (6€). Free Wifi. Restaurant (home made tapas menu).

The sparkling Alexandra manages this hotel ideally located on the seafront on the mythical Gruissan chalet beach. The Sunrise Beach Hotel looks great with its large wooden terrace, cosy little lounges and barrels as a high bar. It is the perfect place to take a break and enjoy the view while sipping a small cocktail or a glass of local wine accompanied by a board of homemade tapas to the backdrop of lounge music. Not to be missed in high season: the Sunday after-beach with DJ from 6pm to midnight! The wooden interior is just as pleasant with a large bar and a small lounge with a library. The rooms are simple and equipped with TV, special mention for those on the sea side with balcony and deckchairs facing the Grande Bleue while the others offer a view of the famous chalets. The Sunrise has everything to please and the rates are very correct, we love it!

Guesthouses

■ CHATEAU LE BOUÏS

Route Bleue
✆ 04 68 75 25 25
www.chateaulebouis.com
contact@chateaulebouis.com
Take the exit ZA de Mateille, then immediately to the left, go under the bridge. Immediately after the bridge, turn left and continue straight. The route is then marked out until the estate.

Open all year round. 5 bedrooms. Double room from 74€ to 174€; suite from 134€ to 194€. Breakfast included (in the form of a continental buffet). Parking. Mediterranean restaurant with panoramic view. Visitor's route. Historic vaulted and buried cellars. Wine tourism activities can be booked on the website. Seminars. Receptions and weddings. Free Wifi.

Looking for calm, charm and authenticity with a sea view? What better way to fully enjoy La Clape than to stay at Château le Bouïs nestled in the vines, an estate that once belonged to 5 women winemakers that Frédérique Olivié – originally from the north of France – bought. This little paradise has been perpetuating its tradition for three centuries: charming rooms and suites are fitted out in the old 18th century mansion, the Maison des Demoiselles, and in the former residence of the sharecropper, the Petite Maison du Bouïs. They occupy a special place in the heart of a 2-hectare wooded park. You will appreciate its pretty swimming pool and its Mediterranean garden. His 49-hectare estate produces an elegant and feminine cuvée, the Cuvée Confidences, a Haute Couture rosé labeled Chantal Thomass, a pretty AOP La Clape cuvée, and Prestige cuvées such as Roméo & Juliette. So, take the time to discover these cuvées in one of the largest vaulted and buried cellars in the Clape massif, and sit comfortably on the restaurant's terrace with a panoramic view of the sea and the vines (open in summer only). Also discover the tour route La Légende du Bouïs and all the oenological activities on offer such as the wine blending and creation workshop! Possibility of themed stays around wines and gastronomy.

Campsites

CAMPING LVL- LES AYGUADES

Avenue de la Jonque
✆ 04 68 49 81 59
www.camping-soleil-mer.com
infos@loisirs-vacances-languedoc.com

LVL Les Ayguades is a privileged location by the sea with direct access to the beach! Located between Gruissan and Narbonne-Plage near the natural park of La Clape, our 4-star outdoor hotel offers 120 pitches for tents, caravans or motorhomes, 90 mobile homes and 50 chalets. Our services on site – Food service – Heated aquatic area – Grocery store – Snack bar – Bar – Launderette – Children's playground – Fitness room – Boules pitch – Library – Barbecue area – Multisport field – Entertainment (school holidays) Air-conditioning in all accommodations. And the little "extras" of LVL! Free Wifi throughout the campsite Facilities adapted for people with reduced mobility Animals accepted on the site Opening of the campsite: from 20 March to 8 November 2020. Telephone reception all year round: 9am-12am and 2pm-17pm.

A waterfront campsite with direct access to the sea! Located between Gruissan and Narbonne-Plage, between the sea and the Clape massif. The campsite offers recent mobile homes and bungalows for up to 8 people, perfectly arranged and equipped. This campsite plays the ecotourism card: solar panels for the production of hot water for the toilets and restaurant, biodegradable cleaning products...

This campsite has many highlights: aqua-leisure space with a 25-metre pool, spa, paddling pool for children, restaurant and quality entertainment in July/August, take a look at the programmes on their website. Always in a sustainable development approach, we think of people with reduced mobility, fitted swimming pool, seahorses chairs to ride on the beach and in the water... Smart! One week rentals can start on Sunday or Wednesday or Saturday in July/August. Arrive and leave whenever you want in low season (2 nights minimum). Free wifi connection at the reception, the swimming pool and the restaurant. New in 2020: bicycle, paddle and kayak rental.

Leisure

ACROMIX

Boulevard du Pêch-Maynaud
✆ 06 28 67 49 08
www.acromix.com
contact@acromix.com

Open from the beginning of April to the beginning of November. Open from April to June during the school holidays in all areas and on weekends from 2pm to 6.30pm. From 1st to 09th July from 14h to 19h. From 09 July to 25 August: weekdays from 10am to 7pm / weekends from 2pm to 7pm. Sept / October: weekends from 14h to 18h30. Accrobranche: from 3 to 5 years old: 10 €; from 6 to 11 years old: 15 €; 12 years old and over: 20 €. Laser game: 9 € for a 30 min session. Canyoning: from 40 € to 58 €. Technical equipment provided. Climbing course: 30 € (1h30 to 3 hours of activity). Spirolienne 9 € (-18 years old) 13 € adults.

If the desire to climb trees, go canyoning, go climbing or equip yourself with a laser weapon tickles you, well, Acromix will be able to meet your wishes. The most "popular" activity to do with family is the tree climbing track located on the Gruissan hill in the heart of a protected pine forest. On the spot, you will enjoy a wonderful panorama of Port Gruissan, the sea and the Pyrenees. Departure on foot to join the site from the parking lot opposite the Tourist Office, a small chalet serving as a ticket office is waiting for you there. After this warm-up, you'll be given equipment, you'll be briefed on the safety rules (maximum) and forward for several hours of sensations for children and adults (from 3 years old).

The park focuses on the tracks with zip-line, come and try the Spriolienne, zip-line with turn of 300 meters, there are only three in France! An opportunity to undertake a adrenaline cure. In order to recover from your emotions, you can take a refreshing drink in the refreshement room on the spot and think about your next adventure... canyoning in the gorges of the Aude or the canyons of the Pyrénées-Orientales or climbing in a superb natural site?

JETXTREME

Plage des chalets
Avenue de la Jetée
✆ 07 71 56 54 72
www.jetxtreme11.com
jetxtreme@orange.fr

Open from April to the end of September (depending on the weather). Jet ski: Baptism: 20€ for the 10 min. Initiation: from 55€ to 115€. Hiking: from 120€ to 150€. Towed vehicles: from 10€ to 20€. Hover board 80€. Fly Board: 70€. Reduced rate in the morning before 12pm.

JetXtreme is the specialist in jet skiing and towed equipment such as buoys, sofas, aqua twister and other bumbags from the department of the Aude and Pyrénées Orientales. Since 2004 Jetxtreme has become the reference, the reason for its success: passionate and experienced instructors and state-of-the-art unlicensed machines that will allow novices to enjoy themselves to the fullest and those who are more experienced. The jet ski offer ranges from first ride to ride, we like the ride with the short tasting session of tapas at La Voile Blanche (beach restaurant). If your little child wants to be like dad (or mom), there is a jet ski offer for him, but be careful he will soon like it too much! For even more fun, the flyboard and the hoverboard will give you great sensations, well driven by your instructor, you will quickly get out of the water and think you are a super hero. Still for thrill-seekers: the demonic Raptor boat, fasten your harness and enjoy the 440 HP of the beast (not recommended if you have had a copious meal just before!). Practical: it is possible to order gift cards on their website. And if you want to equip yourself, Jetxtreme is also a Kawazaki dealer, the store is located in Narbonne in the cutting zone.

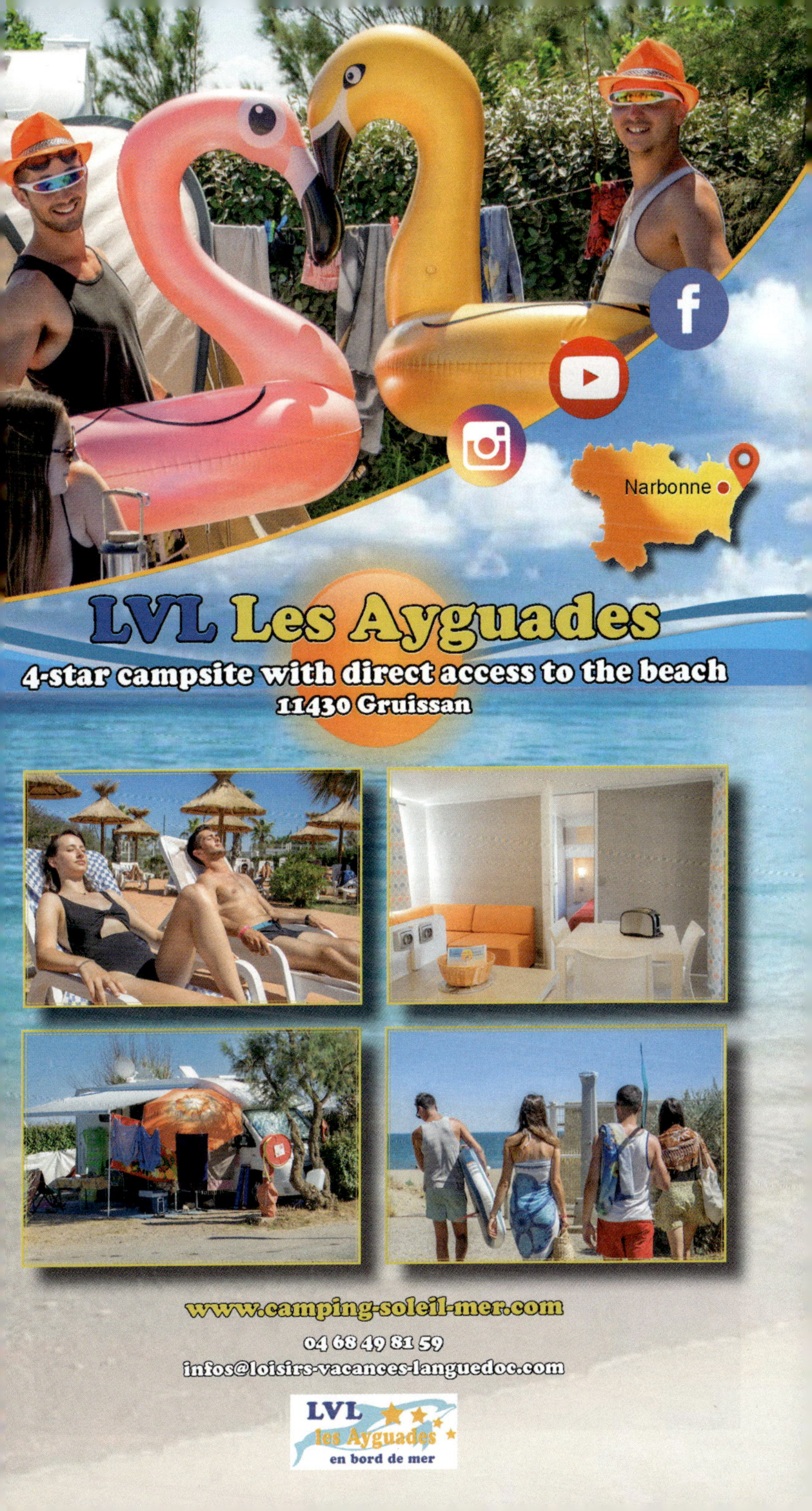
Narbonne
LVL Les Ayguades
4-star campsite with direct access to the beach
11430 Gruissan
www.camping-soleil-mer.com
04 68 49 81 59
infos@loisirs-vacances-languedoc.com
LVL
les Ayguades
en bord de mer

ESPACE BALNÉOLUDIQUE – POOL AND GAMES
Avenue des Bains
✆ 04 68 75 60 50

Open all year round. In low season: open from Wednesday to Monday. In high season: every day. Schedules very variable and subject to change, ask for information. Closed from March 7 to March 21 inclusive. Prices per session: Aquatonic lessons etc from 8€, baby swimmers 8€, access to the weight training area 10€, entry to the pool 25 meters int. 4€ to 5€ adult 3.5€ child under 14 years old, indoor pool + outdoor slides adult 12.50€ – child 5€.

The balneo complex will delight fitness and relaxation enthusiasts as well as those looking for an alternative between the balneo and the beach. On a surface area of 10,000 m^2, several universes are available to you: balneo (see relaxation / fitness), a playful and sporty area. Do you want to work out? You can have access to the cardiotraining and fitness area equipped with the latest high-tech equipment. The 25 m long sports swimming pool offers a view of the sea and the pond and offers many activities: aquatonic, aquapalm, aquabike, aquatic training circuit, baby swimmers, swimming lessons for children and adults… In summer from the end of June to the beginning of September, toboggan, pentagliss, inflatable games, picnic air on a grassy beach sheltered from the wind are pleasant idleness parentheses.

PÔLE NAUTIQUE GRUISSAN (AKILA – BASE MER)
50, avenue de la Jetée
✆ 04 68 49 33 33
www.polenautique-gruissan.com
contact@polenautique-gruissan.com

Closed from November 10 to March 30. Open every day and on public holidays from 9:30am to 6pm. Rentals: Paddle: 14€/1h, Canoe/Kayak: 15€/1h, Catamaran/Funboat (autonomous level required): 45€/1h, Windsurf: 28€/1h. Kite "learning" course 3 days (group: 3X3h / individual: 3X1h): 360€. Bar, surf shop, restaurant.

Facing the sea, just at the end of Plage des Chalets, here is one of the best free ride spots in France. Known and appreciated, thanks to Defi Kite (15 to 17 May 2020) but also by its large gathering of windsurfers: Le Défi Wind, a race with more than 1,800 participants, professionals or amateurs. The famous Tramontana blows more than 200 days a year in Gruissan, well, you who love sensations take note, in 2020, the competition will be held from 21 to 24 May! At Pole Nautique, you can practice kite surfing, windsurfing, catamaran, paddling and kayaking. Whether you are expert or beginner, you can safely move between sea and pond, supervised by unequalled instructors, State-qualified with new high-quality equipment that is tested, approved and adapted (Fanatic North and Cabrinha). Jérôme Serny, manager of the center, is an official tester of the equipment for specialized press. Pôle Nautique is for all, from the age of 6, as group or private lessons. Various activities of handikite are organized, don't hesitate to ask for information!

Relaxation & Fitness

ESPACE BALNÉOLUDIQUE
Avenue des Bains
✆ 04 68 75 60 50

In low season: open from Wednesday to Monday. In high season and school holidays: every day. Schedules very variable and subject to change, please ask for information. Closed from March 17 to 31, 2020 inclusive. Balneo day pass (except summer): 24€; 12€ for 2h30; 12€ from 6pm. Formula: massage (30 min) + balneo (2h30) at 51€. Water park: adult 11.50€, child (under 6 years old) 5€, free for children under 3 years old. All rates detailed on the website.

The Espace balnéoludique delights fans of fitness, relaxation and those looking for an alternative between balneotherapy and the beach. On a surface of 10,000 m^2, several worlds are offered to you: balneotherapy with lavender bath, Vino bath (a nod to the Gruissan winegrowers),

Gruissan.

musical bath, flowing river, hammam, saunas, whirlpool bath... There's something for everyone! Quickly test the new 100 m^2 outdoor Nordic pool with its 31 degree water dedicated to relaxation with bubble deckchairs, weightless zone, water massages... Do you want to exert yourself? You can access the cardiotraining and fitness area equipped with state-of-the-art high-tech equipment before relaxing in one of the massage rooms. The 25 m long sports pool offers a view of the sea and the pond and offers many activities: aquatonic, aquapalm, aquabike, baby swimmer. In summer, slides, pentagliss, inflatable games, beach volleyball, deckchairs on a sod beach are pleasant idleness breaks. Every Tuesday in July and August, a DJ accompanies your relaxation from 4pm!

Going Out

■ FORMENTERA

Avenue des noctambules
Parking de La Villa
✆ 04 68 49 26 29
www.formentera-gruissan.com
info@formentera-gruissan.com

Open from April 27 to September 15. From the end of April to the end of June only on weekends in the evening, then July – August 7/7 from 12 noon to 2am. Restaurant. Animations. Concerts.

Open end of April every weekend in bar, tapas and music mode. Open every evening in July and August, you can attend live concerts, Flower Power evenings, Hype evenings and many other surprises by the poolside! Here you can enjoy the mix of generations in a trendy atmosphere. Follow Formentera's Facebook page, where you will find all the programming.

■ MAMAMOUCHI

Nautical base
Etang de Mateille
✆ 04 68 32 10 95
lemamamouchi@gmail.com

Open every day and on public holidays from 10am to 1: 30pm. Open from April 12 to September 30 minimum. Menu at 19€ for lunch. In the evening à la carte: tapas/entrées between 6 and 21€ and between 11 and 32€ for the dishes. Terrace. Restaurant. Animations. Concerts. Brunch.

If you want your time in Gruissan to be summed up by "Drinking. Eating. Dancing." There's no doubt, it's at the Mamamouchi that you must stop. The place is magical, the terrace made of wood in natural tones is punctuated by cacti and other pouffes. That's right! Le *Mama* offers an extraordinary view between pond and sea. The kitchen is open and all the view is clear. From morning to evening, you enjoy a unique light, every hour a different painting. In the evening the atmosphere rises crescendo, zen at the beginning, then the temperature rises...rises...rises... rises... especially on concert evenings or when a DJ turns the decks, big atmosphere guaranteed! Don't hesitate to taste the Mama Bear, the beer brewed in Narbonne and the image of the place! In the kitchen, you will only be served fresh products, cold cuts and cheeses, but above all oysters, knives, shellfish, and the very fashionable *veggie bowl* to enjoy yourself without excess. The home-made desserts are just like the rest, so don't deprive yourself, in addition, the prices are very reasonable. On Sundays, brunch until 3pm!

■ LE RAFIOT

Quai Barberousse
✆ 04 68 49 11 83

Closed from mid-September to early April. In low season: open every day from 2pm to 1am. In high season: every day from 10am to 1am. In high season: July and August – Open even on rainy days! Free wifi. Terrace. Restaurant. Animations. Concerts. DJ.

Le Rafiot is "the place to be" on the port, it is a bar with the appearance of an old sailing ship where the wood has aged over the years. Le Rafiot has set the pace in the resort for more than 20 years. During the day, the place is quiet, ideal for a drink, an ice-cream or eat some tapas. At the end of the afternoon, as the freshness begins to be felt, the temperature rises at Le Rafiot... Many homemade cocktails, concerts on Wednesdays in July / August, musical and tasting aperitifs on Sunday evenings, consult the facebook page to know about the many theme evenings of the season. A warm atmosphere also in the evenings of sports events, you will have understood it, here, everything is good for a party! On the terrace, on the mezzanine that overlooks the bar, and sometimes on the bar, we dance, we have fun and that's what we also like about Le Rafiot.

■ LA TERRASSE DU SALIN

Le Salin de Gruissan
Route de l'Ayrolle
✆ 04 68 90 54 55
www.lesalindegruissan.fr
contact@lesalindegruissan.fr

In low season: open from Friday to Sunday from 12: 30pm to 7pm. In high season: every day from 10: 30am to 11: 30pm. Terrace. Animations. Concerts.

The Terrasse du Salin offers a breathtaking view of the 400 acres of salt flats which, depending on the period, change colour from pink to white... An show for the eyes not to be missed under any circumstances, so why not take the opportunity to have a good time and enjoy a cocktail? On the terrace, the wicker chairs welcome you and settle you comfortably in front of the saunier's work. Ice cream is good, soft drinks are good. Many activities are planned on summer evenings, such as concerts, etc.

Shopping

■ LA CAVE DE PIERRE – CHÂTEAU BEL ÉVÊQUE

Route des Salins
L'île Saint-Martin
✆ 04 68 75 00 48
www.vinspierrerichard.com
contact@vinspierrerichard.fr

Price range from 12€ to 31€. From December 1 to February 28: Monday to Saturday from 10am to 1pm and from 2pm to 5pm. From March 1 to May 31 and from Oct 1 to November 30: Monday to Saturday from 10am to 1pm and from 3pm to 6pm. From June 1 to Sept 30: daily from 10am to 1pm and from 3pm to 7pm.

According to Pierre Richard, "a fine wine is first of all a good grape" and it was at the Bel Evêque estate that the actor found his happiness in 1986. Loving this authentic, wild and arid site, he made it his living place and his wine estate. Corbières, Syrah, Grenache and Carignan, all these grape varieties mature with the caress of sea breeze. Result: the red wine is both powerful and sweet. Among the rich wine range of AOP Corbières imagined and designed by Pierre Richard, we should mention Château Bel Evêque Rouge aged in oak barrels, ample, generous, with aromas of ripe fruit, and his rosé, smooth and round with notes of raspberry. Our favorite is his "personal vintage" in monovine 100% Syrah. These wines go well with festive meals but also with relaxation aperitifs. For the pleasure of discovering the address and the wine!

■ CHÂTEAU LE BOUÏS, LA LÉGENDE ET LA DÉGUSTATION NEW
Route Bleue
✆ 04 68 75 25 25
www.chateaulebouis.fr
contact@chateaulebouis.com

In low season: open Monday to Friday from 9am to 12pm and from 2pm to 7pm; weekends from 9am to 12pm and from 5pm to 7pm. In high season: every day from 10am to 1pm and from 3pm to 7: 30pm. In low season: from October to May. La Légende du Bouïs 5€ adult / 3.5€ children – many workshops around wine like "the workshop of assembly and creation of wine" 30€/pers.

In this 200 m^2 cellar with magnificent historic vaulted cellars, you can of course taste the estate's grands crus and also amphora-aged wines. The estate's 49 hectares benefit from maritime influences, which favor gentle maturation. Carignan, black Grenache, Cabernet, Sauvignon and Syrah for the reds and rosés, white Grenache, Roussanne and Viognier for the whites which are hand-picked. The reds give off aromas with notes of red fruits, thyme, garrigue and liquorice. The whites are low in acidity, long and fat and have aromas of pear, grapefruit and vanilla. With know-how, the estate's oenologist vinifies and assembles the cuvees with typical scents. We recommend that you taste the Arthur cuvée, made from a selected plot of Syrah, rigorously worked and matured in barrels for twelve months. Its nose of red fruits and vanilla, its very concentrated and elegant palate, its length and persistence give hope for a long life. We also fall in love with its top-of-the-range Juliette cuvée. Discover the Legend of the Bouïs, a multimedia and sensory journey followed by a tasting. Allow 1 hour for a visit. For the little ones, a nature treasure hunt awaits them. It is also possible to eat at the estate in the summer, or to spend a night in one of the superb guest rooms of the château. Ask for more information.

■ MON ÉPICERIE
16, Avenue Joseph Camp
✆ 06 45 71 29 58
monepicerieb l@gmail.com
♿

Gluten-free friendly. Open Tuesday to Saturday from 9: 30am to 7: 30pm.

If you have the desire or the need to do good to your body and mind, we recommend this organic and local grocery store located in the old town of Gruissan. Walk through the door, you are welcomed with a friendly "hello", the shop is nicely arranged and makes you want to discover the variety of references offered. If you need any advice, don't hesitate, Nadine and her daughter Amandine will be happy to help you! At "Mon Epicerie", you can do your shopping for the whole house with organic products and local producers. In the fresh food section, you will find meat from Aveyron and vegetable alternatives, a nice choice of cheeses, organic artisan bread made on the spot (excellent) with sourdough and pastries as well as a very beautiful seasonal fruit and vegetable section.
You can also find everything you need on a daily basis with some bulk products: cereals, olive oil, vinegar, body soap, cleaning products, etc. At Mon Épicerie, it's environmentally friendly. Special mention for the cellar part with a selection of wines from the Aude and the neighboring departments as well as the wines of the owners who are also winegrowers and precursors of organic farming in the region with their Domaine des 4 Rodes de Thézan-lès-Béziers.

INTERMARCHÉ
Avenue des Bains
✆ 04 68 32 83 20
♿

Open Monday to Thursday from 9am to 12: 30pm and 2: 30pm to 7: 30pm; Friday and Saturday from 9am to 7: 30pm. Summer: open every day from 8: 30am to 8pm and Sunday from 9am to 7pm.
In Gruissan, the *Mousquetaires* have flair and a clever mind. Take the opportunity to discover the range of local products highlighted by the "Local Products" label, you will be pleasantly surprised. Various products from the region are on offer such as bull meat from the manade of Tournebelle, oils and olives from the Oulibo in Bize-Minervois, salt from Gruissan, oysters from Bouzigues, melons from Coursan but also everything you need to have a good time with friends: charcuterie from the Tarn, local artisanal beers, local wines.... and this year, a major novelty which is unanimously acclaimed: smoked salmon on the spot as well as tuna, trout, Saint-Jacques... not forgetting the homemade smoked duck breast! Yes, the Musketeers love the wines of La Clape and they are showcasing them, Domaine de Marmorières, Sarrat de Goundy or Ricardelle de Lautrec. Finally, you will be conquered by the butcher's stall which offers meats matured or matured in Himalayan salt for 30 days minimum, the rib of beef is exceptional... the amateurs will appreciate it! L'Intermarché de Gruissan is indeed a supermarket like no other which finds its place in our pages!

TENTAZIONE NEW
10, Avenue des Noctambules
résidence Ephyra
✆ 04 68 65 00 98
nicolaskraken@gmail.com
Open Tuesday to Saturday from 9am to 2pm and 6pm to 10pm; Sunday from 6pm to 10pm. Closed Sunday lunchtime and Monday.
A trattoria that smells good Italy, here authenticity is the key word, and the only problem you will encounter is the difficulty to make your choice, so much the products are of quality and make you salivate. No fear Nicolas Pellegrini, the host of this place resolutely dedicated to Epicure, will advise you with professionalism, you will wander between pasta, olive oil, homemade sauces, fresh cheeses, typical desserts, liqueurs or the unmissable selection of charcuterie that occupies a special place, and will delight the most discerning among you. You will be surprised by the wide range of products on offer, all carefully selected, all from Italy, the Provolone Salumini, Parma black pork ham, Salame Finocchiona, Culatello di Zibello, the smoothness of the real Burrata di Bufala, or the tasty Panforte Margherita dessert with orange peels, candied citron, almonds, honey and spices a real culinary discovery, which will delight the most delicate palates. What can we say about Italian wines, except that these nectars of the gods, famous since antiquity, will make you travel, you will taste the inevitable Chianti of course, but also the very fashionable Spritz, based on a real Apérol, a guaranteed family recipe, and if you like traveling, try Lambrusco, or Chiaro di Stelle. This Trattoria delicatessen will be a real favourite for all those who have made hedonism and traditional good eating a philosophy of life!

LA MER À BOIRE
Zone artisanale des chalets
21, rue de l'Hippocampe
✆ 06 63 09 88 12
www.brasserielameraboire.com
Open from Wednesday to Friday from 5pm to 7pm; Saturday from 10am to 12pm. Free visit and tasting.
Want to immerse yourself in local products? Discover the traditional brasserie: La Mer à Boire and its four beers: white, blond, the red and a light one with a hint of coffee flavor. Respectively, "*L'écume de mer*", with its little citrus taste, the so refreshing "*Oh soleil*"! "*La Barbe rousse*", which roughly means red beard is aptly named, and finally "*La Macar*". Discover seasonal beers such as "*la mer fruitée*", a white beer with peach or apricot, an amber beer with spices for winter, "*la mer givrée*", and a very hopped Ipa, called "*la tram*". Want to share or please yourself? You have the possibility to buy boxes to transport them easily when you return from your holidays, or to enjoy with your feet in the sand, why not? Visit of the factory followed by a tasting of the different beers. For more information, browse its website.

FITOU ★

Knife & Fork

LOU COURTAL DES VIDALS
13, rue des Courtals
✆ 04 68 45 62 58
jean-luc.vidal13@wanadoo.fr
Open all year round. From April 1 to September 30 every day for both lunch and dinner, except Monday and Tuesday lunchtime. Out of season, open on Friday evening, Saturday and Sunday noon and evening. Reservation recommended. Menus from 23.50€ to 35.50€ (food and wine pairing for the tasting menu). Children's menu: 9.50€ (and 10.50€). Wine by the glass. All-you-can-eat buffet 23.50€. Large room for groups.
Visit Lou Courtal des Vidals in Fitou, a former sheepfold converted into an inn, its rustic charm gives it a special touch, with its exhibition of old photographs and its exposed beams and stones. A traditional cuisine with Occitan accents has been found there for more than forty years: the cargolade (snails roasted in their shell), the wild-boar stew, the meats grilled over a wood fire (coustellous, duck breast, rabbit, pièce de boucher according to arrival) without forgetting the griddled fish, the shellfishes and the crustaceans that add to the specialties of the house. We should say that the pond and the sea are very close. The most popular formula is the cascade of buffets, with a salted buffet and a sweet one at will, for children and adults, which will satisfy big eaters at a more than reasonable price. The atmosphere which reigns in this restaurant is unique, you feel almost like at home. You certainly leave here with your stomach filled, but with only one desire, to come back! On fine days, to enjoy the sun's rays and a table in terrace, we recommend that you book.

LE TOIT VERT
Chemin les Pujades
✆ 04 68 70 47 38
www.letoitvert.fr
larouelibre31@yahoo.fr
Closed from December to mid-February. In high season: open every day in the evening. From March to June and from October to November: Evenings from Wednesday to Saturday and Sunday lunchtime. Reservation recommended. Menu: about 35€. Children's menu: 10€. Wine by the glass. Terrace. Animations.
Le Toit Vert is a truly atypical place, a universe where well-being, respect for the customer and love of cooking are paramount. Let yourself be transported by Fabrice Fenoll, a passionate chef. Settle down on the terrace with a breathtaking view of the château or in the room deliciously furnished and decorated with vintage objects. The menu changes regularly, almost every week, depending on seasonal products and arrivals. Here are a few examples of the spring menu that Fabrice offers: local asparagus, soft-boiled farm eggs, shavings of Parmesan and Cécina de Léon or breaded foie gras with almonds, miso broth and poached Leucate oysters as a starter and main course: spaghetti with clams, mussels and poutargue, lamb's lettuce juice or the black mullet fillet from Port Barcarès, sautéed seasonal vegetables with anchovies and olives. As for dessert, how about a beetroot and caramelized orange fondant, ginger syrup and whipped cream with combawa. What imagination and hard work goes into the plates, and it goes without saying that everything you will taste here is of course home-made and that the cooked products come from organic producers in the region. There is also a very nice wine list with no less than 70 biodynamic references. An address apart and an "out of the ordinary" chef who will not leave you indifferent.

Sleeping

LE FUN
Croix du Bayle
✆ 04 68 45 71 97
www.camping-lefun.com
contact@lefun-camping.com
Motorway A9 exit 40 then D6009 towards Perpignan.
Qualité Sud de France. Closed from 2 November to 15 April. Reservation recommended. Reception until 7pm. Guarded 24 hours a day. 130 pitches (including 40 mobile homes). Exposure: half-shaded. Pitch + vehicle + 2 persons (with 10 A) from €16 to €33.50. Mobil-homes without sanitary from €189 to €539 per week; mobile homes for 4 to 8 persons from €239 to €903. July and August €0.35/ day /person + 18 years old. Lodge and Cocosweet tents

from €189. Cheques not accepted. Children's club. Games for children. Animals accepted. WiFi. Food service (snack in high season). Excursions.

This campsite a little far out of summer tourist hustle and bustle offers an exceptional natural setting, in the shadow of pine trees and olive trees, between sea and garrigue! Camping Le Fun welcomes you only a few kilometers from the fine sand beaches of Leucate and La Franqui. Ideal location for convivial holidays: swimming, tanning, walking, water sports and even access *via* the campsite to a windsurfing spot. Kayaks and stand up paddle can be rented on site. In summer, the team offers lively evenings (Wednesday with meals and music), and the campsite is equipped with petanque ground, tennis court, a heated swimming pool and a City-Stade. All that is needed to spend good holidays away from the hustle and bustle but without activities! The little plus: Discover the Lodge tents for a nature, cozy and pleasant atmosphere or the coco sweet housing. Heated closed sanitary block for cooler days. Numerous mobile homes with optional air conditioning, sheet/towel hire possible.

In the surroundings

Salses-le-Château ★★

A gateway to Roussillon, between the pond and the first foothills of the Corbières, the small town of Salses of 2,500 souls is best known for its rectangular fortress. More than five centuries and unique, it was built in plain with brick walls and mortar of a thickness of 6 to 12 meters in order to best adapt to cannonball artillery. With an impressive defense system, it was built by the Spanish in 1497, with the essential role of controlling the narrow passage between Corbières and ponds. It will lose its strategic interest around 1659 with the signing of the Pyrenees Treaty. Restored by Vauban it would serve as a prison and then powder magazine. Visible from the motorway, this is one of the main departmental heritage sites, which hosts more than 100,000 visitors each year.

■ MÉMORIAL DU CAMP DE RIVESALTES ★★★★
Avenue Christian-Bourquin
✆ 04 68 08 34 90
www.memorialcamprivesaltes.eu
info@memorialcamprivesaltes.fr
♿

Open all year round. Closed on January 1, May 1, November 1 and December 25. From November 1st to March 31st from 10.00 a.m. to 6.00 p.m. from Tuesday to Sunday. From April 1st to October 31st from 10.00 a.m. to 6.00 p.m. Monday to Sunday. Free up to 18 years old (and school children, beneficiaries of social minima, journalists, teachers, witnesses, donors, patrons). Adult: 8 €. Reduced rate (job seekers, students, groups from 10 people, heritage pass): 5 €. Free access to the camp (visit outside). Children welcome. Guided tour (French, English, Spanish and Catalan). Catering (snacks and local products). Shop. Activities. Bookstore. Cultural events.

This Memorial is a reference space for the history of internment and forced displacement in France, through the history of the camp and the consequences of the conflicts that forced over 50,000 people considered undesirable into this place. Camp de Rivesaltes was successively a main internment camp of the southern zone from 1941 for Spanish Republicans, foreign Jews and Gypsies, then a depot center for war prisoners of the Axis from 1945 to 1947 and from 1962, a transit camp of harkis and their families.

The camp was destined for destruction when in 1998 Christian Bourquin (1954-2014), then president of the General Council of the Pyrénées-Orientales relayed the safeguarding action of the site, initiated by the civil society, and decided to transform a parcel, island F (42 ha), into a place of memory, hoping that "the memory work will be of use to our youngsters, to all, to humanity". Between the ruins of the barracks of Camp de Rivesaltes, the architect Rudy Ricciotti associated with Passelac & Roque agency, built a lengthy ochre concrete monolith partly buried in the ground. Inaugurated in 2015, the Memorial received in 2016 the Special Prize of the jury of Équerre d'Argent.

The permanent exhibition room was designed so that visitors understand how historical events have caused massive forced displacement of populations and the creation of more than two hundred internment camps in France and in the countries of North Africa, including that of Rivesaltes. A central table has, in addition to the chronology of the camp, documents and objects which trace the internment of colonial troops, Spanish republicans, Jews, gypsies, German, Austrian, Italian, Polish collaborators and prisoners of war, then harkis, Guinean skirmishers, Indochinese Malagasy...

Visitors can also access a set of testimonials from former internees and a large number of archive movies. The memorial encourages reflection on forced displacement of people today.

A cultural, artistic and scientific schedule (temporary exhibitions, conferences, meetings, reading, screenings...) is offered throughout the year.

direct access to the beach	visually impaired disability	take away
bar	mental handicap	room service
laundry	motor disability	fitness room
air conditioning	garden or park	playroom / tv
nightclub	games	modern sanitary
cash machine	washing machine / laundry	water sports
drinking water	bicycle rental	tennis
horse riding	grocery store	

LEUCATE ★

L'HIPPOCAMPE

Left bank ✆ 06 70 94 74 95

In low season: open every day and holidays from 9am to 7pm. In high season: every day from 8am. 6 average oysters: 7€. 6 medium oysters + 6 mussels + 6 clams: 12.50€. Petula spectacular: 3€ per oyster. Wine from 6.50€ to 10€.

L'Hippocampe is the latest addition to the oyster farmhouses of Leucate, it is located on the left bank. It's lead by Lucas Jaulent and Cindy Frances who treat us to oysters that they grow with love. The completely renovated Mas looks great with its wooden facade, the interior room and a pretty terrace that looks out into the channel. Here you will be served oysters, accompanied if you wish by clam mussels and a glass of white (or rosé) Leucate. Real amateurs will enjoy the Petula Spectacular, an oyster (n°0) of extraordinary dimensions that has spent no less than 4 years at sea. Trays can be prepared to take away. A very pleasant address run by a team that is just as pleasant where you can enjoy the sunny terrace sheltered from the north wind.

Sightseeing

CAP LEUCATE ★

Accessible all year round. Be careful on windy days and respect the fauna and flora.

Cap Leucate is a line of cliffs line that peaks at 50 m high facing the sea, between the villages of Leucate and La Franqui. From this protected area of the coastline, beautiful panoramic views of the coastline and the hinterland are available to you. The paradise of those who love paragliding! At the top of the cliffs are an old lighthouse and a semaphore on a huge plateau, overlooking fine sand beaches. This former island has one of the only three cliffs on the Languedoc coast. A location ideal for walks or hikes: trails that leads towards the interior of the land, landscapes of garrigues and vineyards. La Plagette is a dune adjoining the cliff ideally protected from tramontane, making it a place very popular among local people. To access it, head for Leucate-Village. Turn right at the exit of Leucate-Plage and take the road to the semaphore. Parking on a small dirt car park. The descent, a little steep towards the creek, is only on foot. On the promontory, the Le Grand Cap restaurant with chic and uncluttered decoration with the fully glazed dining room offers a breathtaking view of the sea. Chef Erwan Houssin got his first Michelin star in 2018.

© Yan EVEN

Oyster spawning – Oyster port of Leucate.

LES PLAGES AUTOUR DE LEUCATE ★

No animals allowed on the beach. Paid parking in July and August.

In the heart of the Gulf of Lion, its limpid water, its Blue Flag label, long fine sandy beach with its pleasant promenade. Go for a walk on the pier leading to the semaphore, this place is very often photographed in summer and winter. In Leucate, you will also find 7 other beaches: la Plagette, Leucate Plage, Le Mouret and its famous private beaches, the naturist zone, Aqualand beach, La Franqui, Les Coussoules.

- Leucate Plage: The seaside resort takes advantage of the natural shelter provided by the cliff of Cap Leucate. A long fine sandy beach, with good quality water welcomes faithful families, who come here in search of the calm and mild climate, which can also be enjoyed out of season. For a few years now, the straw huts have been used to enjoy good products and cocktails with your feet in the water to the delight of locals and tourists.

Knife & Fork

UN AMOUR DE PLAGE – LE POULPE

747, chemin des Mourets – Leucate Plage

✆ 06 11 20 47 66 – octopus11370@gmail.com

Open from the end of May to mid-September. Open every day for both lunch and dinner. From ten o'clock to one o'clock. Reservation recommended. Menu: about 17€. Wine by the glass. Terrace. Animations. Private beach. Cocktails. Regional wines. Fishing of the day.

Want to enjoy quality home-cooked tapas with your feet in the sand and your eyes on the sea? Go to "Un Amour de Plage". This straw hut is the most chic and elegant on the Aude coast. The finely selected music mixed with a colourful decoration with natural, trendy and design materials promises you a guaranteed change of scenery. The bar offers a wide range of cocktails, beers and a very interesting selection of wines. For the meal, you can choose the dish or the catch of the day according to the arrival, but also summer dishes that will delight your taste buds, Renard likes to take several dishes to share so you can taste everything! If you want to extend your stay in an equally pleasant setting, Cathy and Alex will give you the best welcome in their Hotel**** 19-21 " Un Amour d'Hôtel " in Leucate-village, a surprising and magnificent boutique hotel that will delight lovers of design and decoration.

Cap Leucate lighthouse.

■ L'ATELIER ACTE 2

6, route des Corbières
11510 Treilles (10 min from Leucate)
© 04 68 33 08 59
www.atelier-acte2.com
latelieracte2@orange.fr

Open all year round. In low season: Wednesday and Sunday for lunch; Thursday to Saturday for both lunch and dinner. In high season: Tuesday to Sunday lunchtime and evening. Menus from 29€ to 51€. Lunch formula: 19€ (starter/main course or main course dessert – 24€ starter/main course/dessert for lunch except weekends and public holidays).

Very close to Leucate (10 min) is the small village of Treilles, and at its heart is a charming restaurant well run by an equally charming couple, Sarah in the dining room and Thomas Laffargue is the chef. L'Atelier Acte 2 has something to surprise and delight your taste buds. Fitted out in an old cellar and embellished with two terraces, the restaurant is decorated in a modern style. The terrace at the back is the perfect place to spend a gourmet moment when the weather is fine. In his open kitchen, Thomas cuts, slices, grabs, poach, prepare, in short he cooks! Here, you will only be offered fresh and seasonal products with a menu that changes approximately every two months. Thomas's cooking is imaginative, everything you will find on your plate is subtly cooked, precisely seasoned and the cooking perfectly mastered, as for the presentation of the plates, it is close to perfection. The menu changes with the seasons, here we favour local producers but one must-eat dish, the famous lamb shoulder cooked for 11 hours in aïoli crust like a couscous with candied lemon juice, your mouth is watering, isn't it? In addition, there is a fine selection of wines from the Aude and neighbouring Pyrénées-Orientales and a pleasant welcome. A big favourite and an address that is rising and rising!

■ BIQUET PLAGE

Chemin du mouret – Leucate Beach
© 04 68 33 00 64
www.biquetplage.com

Stand up paddle, pedal boat and canoe rental. Open from the end of May to the end of September. Open every day from 10am to 2am. Children's menu: 10 €. Lunch formula: 26 € (starter + main course + dessert. Poke bowl or salad: 16 €). Wine by the glass. Transat with sunshade: the day 15 €. Grilled fish and meat menu. Seafood. Terrace. Animations.

Biquet Plage is the trendy beach of the department, we love the place because whatever the time of day, the atmosphere is there. Relatively quiet at midday, we enjoy a freshly caught grilled fish à la plancha accompanied by a fresh rosé wine and then we continue with an afternoon on the beach with, for the more adventurous: paddleball rental and for the others: deckchairs. The atmosphere rises crescendo at the end of the afternoon and we move quickly from Charles Trenet to Earth wind and fire, which is not to displease the customers of the place... After having tasted a small O'Toulouse (Gin tonic with violet), you will appreciate the really qualitative cooking that we will propose to you: oysters from the neighbouring oyster farmers, grilled lobsters, knives a la plancha, creamy telines, small cooked dishes, beautiful pieces of grilled meat, poke bowl and copious salads (at lunchtime)... This colourful place also attracts thanks to its offbeat decoration completely crazy, even strange, Biquet loves to hunt and he will always find the improbable object that he will deliciously stage in this ephemeral space. The night usually ends in the best way there is: on the dancefloor ambienced by DJ Claire with turntables from midnight on. An atypical address that attracts all generations.

■ CHEZ GINETTE – LE BEACH PUB

37, avenue de la Côte Rêvée
Leucate Beach
© 06 08 65 17 76
www.ginetteleucate.fr
hello@ginetteleucate.fr

Open from June to September. Open in June Friday & Saturday from 5pm to 2am in July-August from Tuesday to Sunday. Menu: about 20€. Terrace. Animations.

Across the street, facing the famous private beach Chez Ginette is Le Beach Pub de Ginette. Atmosphere Fish & Chips, Burgers, beers, finger food... in short a true pub with a sea view! Darts, billiards, decoration impossible to transcribe if it is not ultra neat atypical, modern and warm at the same time. Go ahead, it's a feast for the eyes! At the beach pub the atmosphere rises a notch during the sporting events broadcasted on 3 giant screens then the music takes over to dance until 2am.

DIGITAL VERSION
FOR FREE!
Get your digital guide book using this tag
Also avalaible at
www.ebookfute.com
with the promo code
ZGJ99P
petit futé
2020 2021
BEST OF
AUDE
OFFER IS VALID UNTIL DISCONTINUATION OF THIS REFERENCE IN FRANCE AND AROUND THE WORLD AND PROVIDED THAT THE NUMBER OF DOWNLOADS IS LESS THAN OR EQUAL TO THE NUMBER OF COPIES. ALSO AVAILABLE FOR SMARTPHONES, TABLETS, E-READERS AND PC OR MAC COMPUTERS.
© PERFECTLAB - SHUTTERSTOCK.COM

LE GRAND CAP
Chemin du Phare
© 04 68 48 13 73
www.restaurant-grand-cap.fr
contact@restaurant-grand-cap.fr

Closed Tuesday, Wednesday all day and Sunday evening. Reservation imperative. Children's menu: 20€. Lunch formula: 39€ (from Monday to Friday). Wine by the glass. Lunch and dinner menus from 55 to 90€.

This restaurant – 1 Michelin star – in an incredible setting, at the top of the Leucate cliff, is run by Erwann Houssin, a chef, and his wife Pamela, a pastry chef. The decoration is sober, refined but delicate, the bay window offers a sea view and the service is very efficient and discreet. And finally, as for the cooking, you can enjoy a real visual show and a delightful taste. For example, according to the menu, you can choose Mediterranean bluefin tuna, in "Retour d'Asie" tartare yuzu/granny apple, creamy avocado/pink grapefruit/young shoots, sea spider crab with fennel and caviar oscière from Neuvic, Galician beef with mature tenderloin sautéed on a griddle, dauphinés with taggiasche olive, green beans from countries linked to candied garlic and anchovy juice from Collioure. As for sweets, we strongly recommend the raspberries country/liquorice/almonds Guanaja chocolate sphere, Sichuan pepper ice-cream. The products are of high quality, seasonal and the dishes are perfectly prepared. The lunch menu offers an excellent price-quality ratio, an opportunity to go and have your first experience at a starred address. A true favorite. And if you want to make a gift, there are gift boxes composed of the different menus. Visit the website for more information.

Sleeping

HÔTEL 19-21
Avenue Francis-Vals
© 04 68 27 68 44
www.hotel19-21.com
info@hotel19-21.com

Closed from January to March. 20 rooms. Double room from 135€ to 290€; suite from 290€ to 325€. Breakfast: 18€. Closed parking: 10€ (per day). Well-being" massage in room: 95€ on reservation. Electric "fat bike" rental: 35€ per person and 50€ for 2. Sauna: free access for Deluxe Rooms and Suites. 15€ per day for the Classic and Superior Rooms. Elevator. Free Wifi. Private beach Le Poulpe with bar and restaurant open from the end of May to mid-September. Sauna.

19-21 is a superb charming hotel fitted out in an old cellar and a mansion where luxury and design are present on all floors. It took Caty, Alexandre and Dominique five years to set up this project and to cater for the smallest details: architecture, choice of materials, the best craftsmen, associations of materials, designers and other artists who contributed to this beautiful realization. When you get in, you will discover a large living room with cozy lounges, a kitchen which opens on a patio where you can have breakfast or enjoy a glass of wine. The three types of rooms are contemporary and cozy and they all enjoy the same comfort, some with private gardens, others with balcony and panoramic views over the village. There are all the necessary equipment and the decoration is a delight. The hotel has a heated swimming pool, a sauna and a cellar where you can taste some local wines accompanied by charcuterie and cheese. In low season, there are no restaurant on the spot but some beautiful tables nearby and from the end of May, the hotel opens its private beach, Le Poulpe, at Leucate-Plage: same atmosphere of good taste, like at the hotel, for the decoration and the dishes. 19-21 is a nice hotel, perfect for a unique stay.

Campsites

CAMPING MER SABLE ET SOLEIL
Chemin du Mourret – Leucate Beach
© 04 68 40 00 90
www.mer-sable-soleil.fr
contact@mer-sable-soleil.com

Labeled Qualité Sud de France and Qualité Tourisme. Open from 16 March to 11 November 2019 inclusive. Reception until 8pm (additional person: €28/week).

© Yan EVEN

Oyster port of Leucate.

Guarded 24 hours a day (electricity, gas and water included in the price). Land of 1.2 ha. 48 pitches. Exposure: half-shaded. Soil: gravel. Landform: flat. Equipment rinsing area. Rental of stand-up paddle. Mobile homes for 1 to 4 people from €354 to €924 per week. Mobile home for people with reduced mobility. Holiday voucher. Kids club. Games for children. Animals accepted (€4). Free wi-fi. Catering (opening of the restaurant le Galion at the end of June). TV in each mobile home. New in 2019: air conditioning in Ophea 34 and 31, new children's playground. Mini golf "zen". Animations. Excursions.

Camping Mer-Sable-Soleil is ideally located between the sea and the pond, 50 meters from a fine sandy beach; it is nicknamed "the funboarders' village". Indeed, here, funboard and kite enthusiasts are the kings and can choose according to their levels and the day's desire between the pond or the sea. As for accommodation, Patrice Besson makes it a point of honor to renew part of his fleet of O'Hara mobile homes and chalets every year, in order to always offer quality rentals. Please note that all mobile homes are equipped with TV. The campsite is eco-responsible: everything is in place to reduce energy and water consumption, such as the use of recyclable products, right up to the choice of new cottages, which are also built in an environmentally friendly manner.

Another highlight of this campsite is the atmosphere! Free sangria evenings with raffles are offered every Sunday evening, for example, to get to know each other; a "zen" mini-golf and the rental of stand-up paddles and mountain bikes are also available. Playground like a small adventure park for the youngest as well as horses and mechanical ponies, an exclusive feature in Aude. It should be noted that the 2020 season will be marked by a major innovation: the reopening of the restaurant Le Galion located on the waterfront opposite the campsite. The campsite team will welcome you in a unique setting to enjoy a simple, good and 100% homemade cuisine, meat and fish tapas à la planchha, cocktails... A really nice campsite where the welcome and quality of service is impeccable.

Shopping

HUÎTRES ALLARY

Right bank
Grau de Leucate
Shellfish growing area
✆ 04 68 40 92 41
www.huitre-allary.com

In low season: open every day from 8am to 7pm. In high season: every day from 8am to 9pm. Formula "assiette de l'étang" at 11€ (6 oysters). Open all year round.

This is a unique production site on the banks of the Grau. Created in the 1970s, it still retains all its typicality with its barracks in rows. Coming from an oyster and mussel farmer, the house Allary Fils is a family story: the grandfather passed on the love of the trade to his grandchildren. Since then, this farm has been modernized: it consists of 6 parks with 4 redesigned tables, ultra-modern equipment and uses new production techniques. Objective: to achieve optimum quality! Just one piece of advice, go and taste the famous "Cap Leucate", a hollow oyster with a fine flesh, nutty flavour and impressive virtues or the "Caramoun", made in Allary: the technique consists in taking it out of the water daily in order to artificially reproduce the tidal cycle, to obtain exceptional gustatory qualities: fine, long in the mouth and much more crunchy! Successful mission, the "Caramoun" has been awarded a gold medal at the Salon de l'Agriculture 2018. Come and taste it with a small glass of local white wine! You can create your tasting platters online at www.huitre-allary.com and collect them from the shop! And as a little gift idea, it is also possible to order and buy gift cards online.

In the surroundings

La Franqui

LE BLEU
19, avenue de la Mediterranee
✆ 07 81 00 81 45
www.lebleucafe.fr
zinouguiri@gmail.com
Open every day. Non-stop service. Children's menu: 10€. Formula: 26€ (starter + main course or main course + dessert. Formula starter + main course + dessert: 29.50€). Wine by the glass. Groups welcome. Terrace. Animations. Concerts and DJ evenings: the first 2 weekends of the month in the pre-season and every evening from 14/07 to 31/08.
Le Bleu is much more than a restaurant, it is a place where regulars, walkers, kite surfers and other wind surfers find themselves with the greatest of pleasures. Zinou and Charlène welcome their customers as they welcome their friends, with respect and professionalism. They are demanding each in their parts: Zinou in the restaurant and in the space dedicated to kite and windsurf rental and Charlène in her shop where she offers the latest trends in beach fashion. In the kitchen, the team is in tune, the dishes are home-cooked from fresh and seasonal products, the portions are generous and the dressage is impeccable. Choose your formula or à la carte and compose your own menu from the dishes on offer. Ceviche of wild prawns with citrus fruits, red tuna or beef tartare, Thai salad with prawns, coriander, ginger... on the plate, there is a choice between meat and fish, for us it will be a baked sea bream accompanied by a gram of Russian caviar, to accompany your meal, Zinou will offer you a very nice wine list from the region and elsewhere ... let yourself be guided. Le Bleu also offers evening concerts where talented musicians take great pleasure in performing here and in front of the sea. A very nice address with a view of the big blue sea that will never disappoint you, Le Petit Futé's word!

LE BUZZ
Chemin des Pitchinos
✆ 04 68 48 08 01
restolebuzz@gmail.com
Open all year round. In high season: every day from 6pm to 2am (last service at 11pm). In low season: ask for information on the FB page or by phone. Reservation recommended. À la carte menu: about 16€. Cheques not accepted.
After a day of relaxation on the beach, you can enjoy a sporting activity, La Franqui is a famous spot of kitesufing and windsurfing, or after a simple stroll on the cliff or at the edges of the ponds, Sébastien Canon welcomes you at Le Buzz where you will find what is needed to recharge your batteries in front of the pond and the scrubland, or in dining room. Tapas board, salad of hot goat cheese, magret en sucettes, steak, big burger or tajine by Buzz, there is something for all tastes. The menu is limited but the products are fresh and the French fries are homemade, a treat! For a drink during your meal, do not hesitate to order a cocktail or a bottle of local wine, you will not be disappointed. For high-wind evenings, it is possible to take shelter in the covered terrace at the back of the restaurant. If it is not always easy to park your car, especially during Mondial du Vent, do not hesitate to join the restaurant on foot to enjoy the atmosphere and the sunset on the pond. Le Buzz is also the meeting place for night owls, jam session every Thursday evening in winter. The best musicians from the area meet to enjoy themselves with guitar, bass, battery... It's time for improvization and conviviality. Various rhums are offered, Don Papa, Dictador, but also more than fifteen beers in bottles, cocktails and local wines.

FISH AND BLUES
22, avenue du Languedoc
✆ 06 36 91 53 77
melinagalindo@hotmail.fr
Open from April to the end of September. Closed on Mondays in high season. Inquire before and after season. Reservation recommended. Children's menu: 10€. Wine by the glass. Suggestion of the day. Tapas from 9€ to 16€. Fish from 20€ to 22€. Meat from 18€ to 28€. Desserts: 8€. Terrace. Animations. Concerts (more info on their FaceBook page).
It took us 4 years to get a closer look at what was going on at the Fish and Blues, and we can say that we lost 4 years! Indeed, this seasonal restaurant literally seduced us! First of all the setting, with an atypical decoration in dark tones, custom-made steel tables and the quirky and highly prized works of art by Ludo, the owner of the place. At Fish and Blues, we also talk about motorcycles and more than words, we live Harley with everything that goes with it, beautiful bikes parked in front of the restaurant, blues and rock concerts, in short this restaurant smells good humor, rock'n'roll and good food! At the stove, Jean-Marc, Ludo's father, treats us to small dishes well worked out and spiced up with spices that breathe the trip, and for good reason, this epicurean cook lives the rest of the year in the Caribbean where he has his restaurant. On the menu, a perfect tapas menu to start with an aperitif and then some well-cooked fish such as tartare with two fishes and wakame, parrot fish a la plancha... As for the meat: bull steak, Iberian black pig ribs, BB king burger... Let yourself be tempted by a nice bottle of wine kept in a cellar worthy of the name. Ah yes, don't leave without going to the toilet, it's worth a look! We love the smiling and professional welcome from the team, the generous portions on the plates and the care taken in preparing the dishes, so don't wait 4 years to go and enjoy the Fish and Blues!

AU GRÉ DU VENT
31, avenue du Languedoc
✆ 04 68 45 64 71
www.augreduvent-lafranqui.fr
Closed in January. In high season: open every day for both lunch and dinner. In low season: open from Thursday evening to Monday evening. June and September: open from Wednesday evening to Monday evening. Reservation recommended. Menus from 35€ to 45€. Lunch formula: 26€ (excluding weekends and public holidays). Wine by the glass. Terrace.

Kite surf.
© Yan EVEN

Au Gré du Vent is very nice semi-gastronomic restaurant! Perrine accompanied by Rodolphe in the kitchen will receive you around a 100% homemade cuisine made with fresh products from their 22 local producers. It is in a room entirely redesigned with a trendy decoration (or on the terrace) that you will take place. On the à la carte menu, the dishes on the menu are mouthwatering. As a starter: organic snails from Perpignan (Le Petit Escargot Catalan) in gingerbread shell and wild garlic flower jelly, marinated scallops and blueberry juice... We continue with a tournedos of bluefin tuna from the boat "Fleur de Sel" of Port Leucate in the Rossini-style, half ice-cream of Rancio from Mas des Caprices and small seasonal vegetables with truffles. To conclude, how about a white chocolate ganache with curry, candied figs roasted with nutmeg, muesli crumble... And if you accompany your meal with a natural wine, (on order because it is decanted for 24 hours) or another biodynamic wine made in Occitania, you will be a satisfied customer! Please note that the menu changes every 3 weeks. An address that is highly acclaimed, think about booking your table!

Port-Leucate ★

Port-Leucate was created in the mid-sixties in order to develop the Languedoc-Roussillon coast. Built on an impressive extent of sand between the sea and the pond, its port is one of the largest in Europe, with 1,200 anchoring places and more than 950 boats. It is therefore a popular destination for yachtsman. The resort is also famous for its winds for the delight of kitesurf, sky-fly, sand yachting or windsurfing lovers. Others will prefer fishing, diving and jet skiing. The place contains another fine treasure: oysters, that you will be able to taste directly in oyster farmers. To finish, Port-Leucate offers a unique international festival dedicated to Cinema voices: *Voix d'Etoiles* (late October).

■ VOILIER LIMNOREIA

Shopping Center
1, Quai Eric-Tabarly
✆ 06 20 60 43 72
www.limnoreia.com
limnoreia@sfr.fr

Sea outings from June 1 to September 30. 1h45 outings: July-August departures at 11am and 3: 30pm – June and September: departure at 3: 30pm (depending on weather and reservations). Outing of 2h30: Sunset cruise: June 6: 30pm (depending on weather). July: 6: 30pm. August: between 6pm and 6: 30pm (depending on sunset time). September: between 5pm and 6pm (depending on sunset time and weather and number of participants). Credit card not accepted.

You can get on board a superb and authentic 1929 schooner to discover the Aude coast and fancy yourself as a true sea dog. So during the day or at sunset, unlike summer activities, you will take a sea trip like never before for two hours. Depending on the period, it is possible to see dolphins but also ocean sunfish. Eric will be happy to tell you about his passion for the sea that has driven him for many years, and you can share it by sailing with him. You will learn everything about the Aude coastline and the history of this boat, one of the oldest in France. So if you are looking for something new and exciting, get on board! Groups can get aboard, it is the ideal place to spend a bachelorette party or just for a romantic or family getaway, or with friends!

■ L'ÎLE AUX LOISIRS

Avenue des Roseaux
✆ 06 20 37 65 19
www.lileauxloisirs.com
lileauxloisirs11@orange.fr

Closed from October to March 31. In low season: open every day and on public holidays from 9am to 6pm. In high season: every day and public holidays from 9am to 7pm. In July and August enjoy Happy Hour canoeing, 1h30 of discovery for only 4.90€. Free up to 6 years old. Canoe / Paddle: 9.90€, equipment provided. Pedal boat: 19.90€ + 1.90€ per person. Boats without permit: 39.90€ + 1.90€ per person. Pass'Loisirs 4 activities, more than 3 hours of animation for only 19.90€ per person. Credit card not accepted.

This island is a true paradise for those who love fauna and flora in natural state... big thrills. Rabbits, herring gulls, predators, birds that set up their nest on the ground... To visit this still unspoiled paradise, canoes, paddles and licence-free boats are available. Discover the marine lake in a playful and informative way. On the spot, explore the biodiversity and environment of Lac Marin with a canoe or pedal boat treasure hunt, with riddles and valuable clues. Children love it and older children quickly get into the game. For a Zen moment, SUP Yoga classes, every Sunday from 11am to 12pm in July and August are offered. On land, you can take a break and relax on the beach or in the shade of the reed cabin in the fishermen's village and quench your thirst or recharge your batteries by snacking with a view of the lake at the Snack, La Cabane du Pêcheur on the waterfront! An exotic paradise corner to discover absolutely.

■ L'ÉCUME

Résidence Les Terrasses du Port
Rue de la Prades
✆ 04 68 40 26 25
www.restaurant-lecume.com
contact@restaurant-lecume.com

♿

Open all year round. In low season: Monday, Tuesday and from Thursday to Saturday for both lunch and dinner; Wednesday and Sunday for lunch. In high season: every day for both lunch and dinner. Reservation imperative. Menus from 22€ to 32€. Children's menu: 10€. Lunch formula: 15€ (dish of the day, cheese or dessert, 1/4 of wine [from Monday to Friday]). Groups welcome. Baby chairs. Terrace. Take away sale.

This is a deliciously traditional address. As soon as you arrive, you will be welcomed with a wide smile and you will be invited to settle in the room or on the terrace. The decoration of the room is rustic, you will spend a moment looking at the paintings, the trinkets, the fresco at the back of the restaurant and small objects that reflect what the owners like about the place. Catherine and Jean-François are so passionate that they have passed on their love of the profession to their children. In the kitchen, Jean-François, assisted by his son, will prepare a traditional and homemade cuisine. As for the room service, Catherine and her daughter are taking good care of their clients. Let's talk about cooking: as a starter, the fisherman's salad is a wise choice and to continue on fish, how about a wolf fillet, scallops salpicon, poached in its white butter. There is also some meat, like the duck breast with honey and spices. L'Ecume is undoubtedly one of the best addresses in the port.

POISSONNERIE CALLI

Rue de la Prade
Shopping centre of the port
✆ 04 68 40 94 93
www.poissonnerie-calli.fr
poissonneriecalli@sfr.fr

Open all year round. In low season: Sunday and Monday from 9am to 12: 30pm; Tuesday to Saturday from 9am to 12: 30pm and from 4pm to 7pm. In high season: every day from 8: 30am to 1pm and from 4pm to 8pm.

Fabienne and Tony Calli's fishmonger's shop is a little marvel! Take a sit on the table and take your time to choose your fish freshly caught by Tony by tasting some small marinated octopus, anchovies, shrimps, whelks... and why not accompany all this with a small glass of white wine selected by Fabienne. Now that you're in the mood, approach the stall and make your choice between Tony's catch of the day, some Atlantic fish or a superb seafood platter. We won't cook you any fish on the spot, we just settle down to have a drink while tasting some tapas from the sea and some oysters from the oyster port of Leucate, just to get you started before you delight yourself to your shopping at home.

LEUCATE AVENTURES

Avenue de la Pinède
✆ 06 10 04 58 50
www.leucate-aventures.com
leucate.aventures@wanadoo.fr

Open from Easter to September 1st. July and August: open every day from 9am to 7pm (cash desk closed at 5pm). For the rest of the year, inquire. Last departure for the tree climbing: 4pm. Adult: €25. Child (from 2 to 6 years old): €12 (€20 for 7-11 years old). Family rate from 4 people only with CLASSIC and ACCRO PASS. Course from 2 years old. Sensational pass from €20, Classic pass and Premium pass. Checks not accepted. Family Plus Label. Equipment provided, duration of the tree-climbing course: 3 hours.

Here is the perfect place to move between sky and earth, on over 280 workshops of increasing difficulty adapted to all audiences and all ages, spread over 16 routes. A playground, the Ouistiti space, allows kids (from 2 years old) to have fun safely. For adults, the difficulty of the paths increases crescendo and ends with the "super noir" route... thrill-seekers and experienced will be able to show their talent! All equipment will be supplied to you on site and you will not run any risk thanks to the "100% security" new system of carabiners; simply wear sportswear and closed footwear. What we enjoy above all in this adventure park is the desire of the management to always want to surprise guests by offering new attractions every year. How about jumping from the 22-meter tower with two 300-meter long ziplines! Let yourself be tempted by the rock for climbing: a unique and tailor-made 8 m creation offering 11 routes allowing beginners and experts to move safely thanks to the automatic rewinders of the latest generation. The Quick Jump is sensational: a 10-meter jump into the void secured by a rope tightly attached to your harness (free fall on 3 meters). Leucate Aventures is a truly pleasant place in the shadow of large pine trees to share strong sensations and emotions with family or friends. Picnic possible on site with drinks and sandwiches at the snack bar (continuous service In summer til 6 pm). Also, note that Leucate Aventures organizes canyoning and rafting routes on natural sites for those who love white water sports.

Giant Zip-line, climbing rock, quick flight (20 m fall), quick jump starting from €5 with Pass.

Port-Leucate marina.

POP'S STARS
NEW

3, rue Dali
✆ 04 30 37 60 15
popsstar.11@gmail.com

In low season: open on Friday and Saturday for both lunch and dinner; Sunday lunchtime. In high season: Monday evening; Tuesday to Saturday lunchtime and evening; Sunday lunchtime. Open during school holidays. Lunch formula: 14€ (starter/main course or main course/dessert + 1/4 wine + coffee. Dish of the day: 12€). Wine by the glass. Tapas from 4€. Board of charcuterie: 12€. Cheese board: 9€. Sea board: 16€.

Pop's stars is for all those who still have a touch of nostalgia for the Yeah-Yeah years and for those who like a slightly offbeat atmosphere. Welcome to Sylvio and Laurence's place, they have made this place a little sour candy that smells like Rock'n Roll and the good food of the south... It is in a unique setting, almost a museum that you will take your place, old Citroën TUB cut out with a grinder and painted in orange, furniture from the 50's that revives in us the memories of the colourful interiors of our grandparents, in short, we take our eyes full of them! Here you won't be served from the big kitchen but a menu of homemade tapas like tortilla, grilled supions, knives a la plancha, patatas bravas, frogs' legs, a beautiful parillade-style seafood board, salads meals, beautiful meat unless the suggestion of the day tempts you more... the portions are generous and the quality-price ratio is excellent. Another particularity of the Pop's Stars: the Sunday lunch dances very appreciated by rock, tango, salsa dancers and the dinner concerts blues, rock, jazz... (All the program on their Facebook page) you will be proposed a unique menu. A perfect address to have a good time with friends or family whatever your age.

© Yan EVEN

Oyster Port of Leucate, Leucate Oysters.

LEUCATE JETSKI
Résidence La Grande Bleue
Parking de la Jetée
✆ 06 84 65 41 62
www.leucate-jetski.com
leucatejetski@gmail.com

From May to September. Jetskiing: 15 min: 40€ – 35 min: 70€ – Hiking 1h05: 120€ / 2h05: 190€. Jetski+ 1 buoy session: from 80€ to 140€. Hiking + Cocktail at Biquet: from 120€. Flyboard: 110€ (25 min). Paddle: 10€ (1h). Towed buoys: 15€ (15 min). Cheques not accepted.

Are you the quiet type or the balloon-bottomed type? It doesn't matter, at Leucate Jetski we adapt to your level and your desires. Here we do almost custom-made! From the 15 minutes discovery initiation formula to the 2h05 hike, be sure, you'll get your money's worth. What we like above all at Leucate Jetski, is the diversity of the offer, there are certainly sensational machines, but there is also the discovery aspect which seduces us. The 2h hike will make you discover the most beautiful places of the Leucate coast: the cliffs at the foot of the semaphore, La Franqui and its famous beach which welcomes every year the mondial du vent, you can even take a break for a swim in the emerald waters of the big blue.
Another offer proposes gourmet hikes (on reservation) with a cocktail break at Biquet Plage (the most incredible private beach in the department) and Leucate oyster tasting on the way back. Finally, for those who want to imitate Franky Zapata (the Flying Man) opt for the Flyboard and go with your best smile, because we are filming you! In short, all these exhilarating activities are accessible from the age of 16 and without a licence with the possibility of a first flight from the age of 6. Smart tip: we strongly advise you to reserve your slot by phone.

LOCA-DÉTENTE
Southern Basin
Quai du Paurel
(located on the port, in the pool opposite the Tourist Office)
✆ 04 68 40 89 73
www.loca-detente.fr
contact@loca-detente.fr

Electric bike rental from €15 (from 1am to 4am) for "classic" bikes: €8 for half a day, €5 for children's bikes. Possibility to rent by the day or by the week. Boat rates without licence: €50 per hour, €80 per 2 hours, €100 per 3 hours, half day €120. Boats with licence from €159 for half a day depending on motorization.

Loca Détente is located on the marina, the place is perfect if you want to discover the Aude coast and the Eastern Pyrenees, a playground which is one of the largest European marinas in the Mediterranean. A refuge and a stopover in the heart of a wild nature that is rich in diversity, and preserved in exceptional landscapes to explore, especially by boat. Loca Détente offers motorboat rental according to what you want with or without license, as well as towed accessories for sport lovers. Be warned, Loca Détente can refuse or shift rentals in case of bad weather, for the safety of all. Electric-bike rental to visit the surrounding areas without forcing! New in 2020: electric fat bike rental.

■ CASINO CIRCUS

Avenue du Roussillon
✆ 04 68 58 17 77
www.casinodeportleucate.fr
vdilct@casino-portleucate.com

75 slot machines. Open all year round. Circus Sport Bar card from €8.90 to €17.50. Brewery formula from €17 to €25. Cocktail from €7 to €9,50. Every day and public holidays from 11am to 2am. Until 4am July/August. Restaurant.

Do you want to play a few euros and win the jackpot? Come and try your luck at the Port-Leucate casino. Slot machines (from €1 cent to €2), electronic roulette, blackjack and other games await you. Circus Casino offers more than 75 latest generation slot machines (90 in summer): mechanical roller machines, video or video poker machine. The atmosphere is pleasant and the staff competent. Every day coffee and tea are offered between 11am and 3pm. Non-players can enjoy the terraces, the bar where cocktails, aperitifs and sweet treats and a snack menu are served during the day. Different formulas are available at the brasserie, for which you can get a game ticket worth €5 or €10. For example, you will eat a sea bream ceviche, a nice meal salad, a monkfish and prawns skewer unless you are more tempted by beef tartare or Circus burger... Various activities take place: dinner-shows, dance evenings, barbecue parties.... Follow the program on their Facebook page.

■ LEUCATE AVENTURES

Avenue de la Pinède
✆ 06 10 04 58 50
See page 107.

■ LEUCATE ÉVASION MARINE

Port de Plaisance
Quai Eric-Tabarly
✆ 06 42 86 37 85
leucate.evasion.marine@gmail.com

June to early September by reservation only on 0642863785. Embarkation before 6: 30pm – 1h15 of navigation. Admission: 19€. Child: 8€. Credit card and cheques not accepted. Restaurant.

Want to enjoy the fresh sea air? Why not come aboard the *Océane II* for an aperitif on the water? On the deck of the boat, enjoy the view, the beach, the cliff of Leucate with the Witch's Rock and her beach.... And then, let's party! Let yourself be carried away by the good mood. On board, taste the delicious "La Cap Leucate" oysters with a hazelnut taste for the amateurs, for the other plates of cooked pork meats of the Country. White wine included. Book your places for aperitifs on the water on the website or directly on the port of Leucate and set sail from 18h30 for 1h15 of navigation.

■ POISSONNERIE CALLI

Rue de la Prade
Shopping centre of the port
✆ 04 68 40 94 93
www.poissonnerie-calli.fr
poissonneriecalli@sfr.fr

In low season: open Sunday and Monday from 9am to 12: 30pm; Tuesday to Saturday from 9am to 12: 30pm and from 4pm to 7pm. In high season: every day from 8: 30am to 1pm and from 4pm to 8pm. Seafood platters from 18€ (the Solitaire/1 pers.) to 149€ (the Royal/6 pers.).

When Tony boards his boat, it is not for sightseeing but to go and haul up his nets for the greatest pleasure of lovers of ultra-fresh fish! From 4am to 6pm Tony doesn't stop for a second, going back and forth with the fish shop he runs with Fabienne, his wife. It is Fabienne who will welcome you in her pretty fishmonger's shop located in the port's market and will guide you in your choice: sole, tuna, sea bream, red mullet, mackerel, brill, cuttlefish, lobster, blue lobster... the fish are of first quality and guaranteed "from the sea to the plate" (except for Atlantic fish offering the same quality). Some very appetizing homemade preparations are proposed as skewers: swordfish tuna with paprika, shrimps with barbecue sauce or cuttlefish with lemon pepper. Seafood platters are offered as well as dishes made to order like bouillabaisse, stuffed squid, paella... Standing oysters and seafood tapas, accompanied by a small glass of white wine to enjoy the atmosphere and the good mood of the owner.

NARBONNE ★★★

Narbonne has a very rich archeological heritage thanks to the diversity of influences it has enjoyed. Today, in particular, medieval masterpieces such as Palais des Archevêques, Abbaye de Fontfroide and many jewels such as Les Halles, the canal, Pont des Marchands... Since its foundation in 118 BC, it has been an essential crossroads and meeting point between Italy and Spain, Atlantic and the Mediterranean, as well as Massif Central and Pyrénées. Narbo Martius is the first colony outside Italy to play an important role for centuries. Narbonne, a place of exchange and trade, saw, from this moment, oils of Bétique, ceramics of Italy, oil lamps, bronze, construction materials arriving on its docks... and exports products from its region, including wine, olive oil, rosemary honey sold in Carthage for its weight of gold, as well as salt, one of the raw materials of Antiquity.

OFFICE MUNICIPAL DE TOURISME

31, rue Jean-Jaurès ✆ 04 68 65 15 60
www.narbonne-tourisme.com
info@narbonne-tourisme.com

Quality Tourism. Opening hours: – from September 15th to March 31st from 10am to 12: 30pm and from 1: 30pm to 6pm from Monday to Saturday, closed on Sundays except during animations and important events. – from 1st April to 14th September from 9am to 7pm every day. Closed on 25 December, 1 January and 1 May. Brand QUALITÉ TOURISME. Tourism & Handicap Label.

It is in the heart of the historic centre, on the banks of the Robine, in the old Entre-deux-Villes Mill (1503), that the Municipal Tourist Office welcomes you. Equipped with a large space where the combination of wood, steel and waxed concrete are of the most beautiful effect, this tool at the service of tourists is equipped with a Wifi space (1h connection/day), a picture wall presenting the earth of Narbonne and giving continuously practical information, an interactive terminal installed at the entrance of the building for information 24 hours a day and even a souvenir shop for many gift ideas or bring back a souvenir from Narbonne. A team of professionals awaits you to immerse you in the heart of the history of the region. In Narbonne, dare an XXL souvenir: selfie lover, go to the passerelle des Barques, follow the instructions: one click on your smartphone and leave with an exceptional souvenir of Narbonne! Free of charge.

CHASSEURS DE TRÉSORS

10, Rue Etienne Billières
✆ 06 52 84 97 32
www.chasseurs-de-tresors.com
contact@chasseurs-de-tresors.com

Open all year round. €15 per box (for a small group or family 3-4 people) €18 if purchased online.

Do you want to discover the city centre of Narbonne in a fun and pleasant way? Go on an adventure and become a treasure hunter! With the help of clues in the box, discover the alleys and monuments of the historic centre in search of the secret of the cat sorcerer: the Matagot. A visit of more than an hour in the streets of Narbonne with a route of about 1.5 km! Children can follow and have fun, and adults will be able to discover the cultural heritage in a different way. Possibility to organize tailor-made treasure hunts for large groups (birthday, seminar...). The boxes are available for purchase online or at several points of sale such as the Narbonne Tourist Office or L'Échoppe médiévale – visit the website for more information. Other hunts are also available in the Aude: Carcassonne, Gruissan and a little further afield, Montpellier, Collioure, Albi and Martigues. Leïla, Mickaël, Vincent and the Louche family are working hard to make you discover the emblematic places of the region. Enhancing heritage and making culture accessible to all, that's a great initiative! Novelty 2020: a new hunt is going to be set up in spring in Narbonne, if you had done the previous one, run to the tourist office to buy the new one!

Canal de la Robine.

LES CHOCOLATIERS CATHARES
ZA du Castellas
Rue Pech-Redon
Montredon des Corbières
✆ 04 68 27 04 04

Open all year round. Guided tour "L'épopée du Cacao" every day at 11am, 2: 30pm and 4pm from July to August, in December and at Easter. Out of season, from Monday to Saturday at 11am and 3pm, by appointment. Free up to 6 years old. Adult: €6. Child (from 6 to 15 years old): €3. Group (10 people): €15. Family rate (2 adults, 2 children and more, from 6 to 15 years old, on presentation of proof): €13. School groups (consult them). Guided tour. Shop. Animations.

Museography of more than $500m^2$ adapted to the whole family on chocolate. Emmy will tell you the history of cocoa over the centuries, she will explain how the old machines presented work, this trip will end with a tasting of course! You will also have the chance to see the workshop in operation through large bay windows (depending on production). Les Chocolatiers Cathares are also very attached to their territory, during the guided tour, you will have the chance to attend a 4D projection on the history of the Aude tramway from Lézignan and through the Corbières: a real journey back in time. No doubt about it, it will make you want to come back to take part in a chocolate making workshop. Nice shop.

LE PETIT TRAIN DE NARBONNE
✆ 06 79 55 93 43

♿

April to June and the month of September departure at 11am, 2pm and 3: 30pm (4: 30pm on weekends). High season: open every day and public holidays from 11am to 6pm. Departure with a minimum of 10 people. Free up to 3 years old. Adult: €7. Child (from 3 to 11 years old): €4. Group (20 people): €5. For a mini-train ticket, a reduced rate ticket for the boat trip on Le Solal. Credit card not accepted. Guided tour.

An invitation to travel in the old districts of Narbonne. The visit commented by a sound system, gives a beautiful overview of the city and its monuments. From Maison des Trois Nourrices in Bourg, at the house of Charles Trenet near the railway, a very pleasant way to discover the ancient Roman city along the Canal de la Robine and to let yourself be guided in the medieval city to the present-day city. Unfortunately, the little train cannot stop to take pictures because it passes through the main traffic arteries, but the tour can guide you and then go for walks. The average length of the journey is 35 minutes and the departure is very close to the city hall, in the shade of the plane trees, on the esplanade of Les Barques. The little train of Narbonne is equipped for disabled guests.

LES VISITES ÉPIQUES
✆ 06 16 65 65 65
www.lesvisitesepiques.fr
visites.epiques@gmail.com

July and August only. Prices and schedules vary according to the visits: Narbonne on Tuesdays at 10: 30am and Saturdays at 5pm – The Abbey of Fontfroide on Wednesdays,

© Yan EVEN

Place de l'Hôtel de Ville in Narbonne.

Thursdays and Saturdays at 10: 30am -. Le Somail on Wednesdays at 5pm – Gruissan on Thursdays at 5pm – Quéribus on Fridays at 11am – Peyrepertuse on Fridays at 2: 30pm – Find their calendar on the website... Free up to 6 years old. Child (6-12 years) from €7, from €16/ adult. Rates vary according to the places and monuments. Credit card not accepted. Children's welcome area. Guided tour. Animations.

Do you want to discover the History of the region in a playful and funny way with guides in period costumes? Alexandre and Jason, qualified guides and actors, will take you on a tour of the emblematic sites of the Aude during exceptional dramatised visits. The two companions are not lacking in humour and are not stingy with anecdotes about the great figures of history but also about the sinister tragedies of Cathar country. During 1h30, let yourself be guided by these merry men to learn while having fun. If you like caustic humour, drama and wild adventures, these dramatized tours are for you. Great lovers of the Middle Ages, the two guides do not lack modernity so, do not hesitate to call them or consult their website to book your tickets.

VISITES GUIDÉES NARBONNE
✆ 04 68 90 30 66
c.cabrier@mairie-narbonne.fr

Open all year round. Planning and schedule of visits according to the seasons. Free for children up to 10 years old. Adult: €6.50. Group (20 people): €6 (on reservation). Guided tour.

Follow the guide! In order to discover Narbonne, a city of art and history, guided tours from 1 to 3 hours are available all year round. Departure from the tourist office or the courtyard of the Archbishops' Palace depending on the seasons and visits. Christophe and his colleagues will tell you about Narbonne la Romaine or Narbonne la Médiévale, for example. Many other themes, it is up to you to choose.

Getting Around

LANGUEDOC VTT ÉVASION

Pont de la Liberté
✆ 06 74 89 75 98
www.languedocvttevasion.com
hugoblanquier@gmail.com

Family and group rates on request. Accessories available for rental (on reservation): baby carrier, luggage carrier, saddlebags. Rental from €10. Cycling: €25 per person. Holder of a state patent. Electric bicycles mountain bike or mountain bike: €30 for half a day or €45 for a day.
Hugo, passionate about mountain biking, hybrid biking and the region, offers you outings along the canal, along the banks of the ponds in Bages, Peyriac, Gruissan, in the heart of the garrigue, but also in the heart of the Clape massif, through the vineyards, in the land of Narbonne but also in the city's track games. Its outings are aimed at a varied public: families, young people, groups, professionals. Hugo also offers a formula for a weekend in Gruissan: accommodation, food service, balneotherapy and mountain biking.
Everyone has his own outing, his own bike, his own level... Practical, the rental stand throughout the summer in Narbonne at the Liberty bridge (corner of the Victor Hugo quay). This is a great alternative to classic hiking and the opportunity to discover the most beautiful panoramas of the region with a real enthusiast! To be tested! Visit his website and Facebook page (@languedocvttevasion) to get all the latest information on current walks and hikes.

Sightseeing

GRAND SUD FM

✆ 04 68 65 03 61
www.grandsudfm.com
contact@grandsudfm.com

Local, regional and national general news radio – music and games -.
Grand Sud FM was created in Narbonne in June 1981, the independent radio station was first of all established in in its first Aude fief, before growing in the 2000s. With 4 different frequencies, Grand Sud FM now covers the most southern part of Languedoc-Roussillon, between Beziers and Perpignan. The 96.1 frequency currently covers the Roussillon plain, and Grand Sud FM, with an adult musical program of the 1970s, 1980s, 1990s and 2000s, has strengthened its editorial policy so as to also satisfy the Catalan listeners including the live broadcast of the USAP and Dragons Catalans matches... Grand Sud FM also gives a privileged place to the local heritage with programs that are fully dedicated to it such as "*Vous prendrez bien un peu de patrimoine*? " (Would you care for some heritage) at 10.10am or "*La Chronique Tourisme*" at 10: 15am on Wednesdays and Saturdays. You know what remains for you to do if you want to stay informed about what is happening on Grand Sud! You can also access live to the programs on the website by simply clicking on "*écoutez*" (listen) or download the Podcasts.

Monuments

ABBAYE DE FONTFROIDE ★★★★

Chemin de Fontfroide, D613
✆ 04 68 45 11 08
See page 8.

CATHÉDRALE SAINT-JUST-ET-SAINT-PASTEUR ★★★

Rue Armand-Gautier
✆ 04 68 65 15 60
www.narbonne-tourisme.com
info@narbonne-tourisme.com

Palace and Cathedral Ticket (Treasure) 6€ adult / 4€ student and children over 10 years old. Guided tour (guided tours organised during the school holidays in zone C, program available at the Tourist Office or on the websites www.narbonne.fr and www.narbonne-tourisme.com).
This cathedral (13th and 14th centuries) is the most prestigious monument in Narbonne. Its Gothic construction was decided in 1268 by Pope Clement IV, former Archbishop of Narbonne. It was dedicated to the young Spanish martyrs Just et Pasteur. It is located in the heart of the current city, an essential place of life in Narbonne where you can admire the 12th century Palais-Vieux building, of Romanesque origin, the keep of the Madeleine built in the 13th century and linked by an arch spanning the passage from the Ancre to the Saint-Martial tower of the early 14th century. The new palace of Gothic origin now houses the Archaeological Museum. The facade was built between 1846 and 1852 by Viollet-le-Duc in a troubadour style. At the corner, the Gilles Aycelin keep dominates the whole from the top of its 40 meters, the view is sublime. At the top of the south tower is the "Bourdon", a large bell weighing 5 tons. It was the only piece to have escaped melting during the revolutionary days of 1793. At around 4 pm., the bumblebee of Saint-Just displays its deep notes from the rooftops in memory of the plague epidemic that devastated the city in 1652. Despite various attempts, this cathedral, which could never be completed, had to extend to the area around the station. Imagine the scale of the project! Do not hesitate to admire the columns and capitals of the recently restored cloister, discover the mysterious acoustics of the Treasure Room.

DONJON GILLES AYCELIN

Place de l'Hôtel de Ville
Palais des Archevêques
✆ +33 4 68 90 30 65
www.narbonne-tourisme.com

Open from Wednesday to Monday from 10am to 12pm and from 2pm to 5pm. Group (10 people): 4€. Pass Palais-Cathedral: €6 reduced rate €4 / Pass Monumentale Narbonne: €10 reduced rate €6 (The pass can be bought at the 1st site visited).
How about a little height? The 162 steps of the magnificent spiral staircase are yours. At a height of 42 meters, you can enjoy an exceptional view of the city of Narbonne. The keep, a powerful square tower, was built between 1295 and 1306 by Archbishop Gilles Aycelin. Its walls contain four rooms: hemispherical room, room known as the Treasury room, the king's bedroom and the defence room.

Cathédrale Saint-Just-et-Saint-Pasteur, Narbonne.

© Cledio

L'HORREUM ROMAIN

7, rue Rouget-de-Lisle
✆ 04 68 90 30 54
webmuseo.com/ws/musees-narbonne
musees@mairie-narbonne.fr

Open all year round. In low season: from Wednesday to Monday from 10am to 12pm and from 2pm to 5pm. In high season: every day from 10am to 6pm. Closed on 01/01, 01/05, 01/11, 11/11, 25/12. Free until 10 years old. Adult: 4€. Narbonne Monumental Pass: 10€ reduced rate 6€ (The pass can be bought at the 1st site visited).

This building was opened to the public in 1976. Visitors can see the remains of the west and north wings, with their respective lengths of about 50 metres for the first, and 38 metres for the second. Each wing includes small openings used as communications and a main corridor with adjoining rooms. The floors are a mixture of gravel, clay and limestone, except for the end of the west wing where we noticed briquettes arranged in fish-bones features. Horreum de Narbonne is considered to be a market or a Gallo-Roman underground warehouse of goods almost entirely preserved, located in the heart of the ancient city, a hundred meters to the south of the forum and Capitoline-temple complex. Its construction dates back to the 1st century BC. Corresponding to a time when Narbonne was long considered as "an observatory and ramparts of the Roman people" (Cicero). The presence of low-reliefs of funerary original are real treasures evoking some old disappeared monuments: amphitheatre, theatre, thermal baths, temples... the setting of the sound and light visit recalls the atmosphere of the Roman markets, evokes the battles of gladiators, the atmosphere of the forum. This is simply magical!

LA MAISON NATALE DE CHARLES TRENET

13, avenue Charles-Trenet
✆ 04 68 65 15 60

Open all year round. In low season: from Wednesday to Monday from 10am to 12pm and from 2pm to 5pm. In high season: every day from 10am to 1pm and from 1: 30pm to 6pm. Closed on Tuesday in low season. For security reasons, the house can only accommodate 18 people per visit. Free up to 9 years old (and jobseekers). Adult: 6€. Child (from 10 to 18 years old): 4€. Group (10 people): 4€. Narbonne Monumental Pass: 10€ reduced rate 6€ (The pass can be bought at the 1st site visited).

"Boom, when your heart goes boom", these words make sense when you enter the native house of Charles Trenet. The atmosphere is intimate, nostalgic and you will pass from one room to the other emotionally. It is like seeing Charles Trenet in the corridors, so much the soul of the singer is everywhere. Many photographs, posters, and winks at the artist are designed for the public. Since August 2011, a new staging with videos, illustrations of Cabu, images in 3D and karaoké have allowed visitors to immerse themselves in the past of the poet. On the ground floor, in the lounge of guests, where a black medium grand piano has pride of place, Trenet tells on screen his town of Narbonne. At the bottom of the staircase, he presents his estate in songs, at a few higher steps, he talks about his childhood, in the dining room, he appears in images with his friends, his mother tells many anecdotes. On the second floor, he invites you to sing *Douce France*, *Le Jardin extraordinaire*, *Y'a d'la joie*... with him. This new museography immerses you in the universe of Le Fou Chantant and we "like the house without the way of the poet!". From downtown, follow the paving stones bearing the effigy of Charles Trenet to go to his native house!

PALAIS-MUSÉE DES ARCHEVÊQUES

Place de l'Hôtel-de-Ville
✆ 04 68 65 15 60

See page 8.

VOIE DOMITIENNE

Place de l'Hôtel-de-Ville

Guided tour.

Covered market of Narbonne.

Via Domitia, the first major Roman road built for military purposes, connected Italy to Spain. It quickly became a major commercial road generating exchange. This road is considered to be the oldest road; drawn in Gaul from 118 BC by the Roman general Cneius Domitius Ahenobarbus, whose name it would bear. Since 1997, part of this Roman route has been built to make it visible. It is now one of Narbonne's essential places. Young Narbonne people meet there, it is possible to have a drink on the terraces all around. In the center of the Place de l'Hôtel-de-Ville, come and discover the time that passes. Before your eyes, a portion of the hard limestone path, which you can observe the wear of the intensive use (deep ruins lined with sidewalks). This location has always been a hotspot: center of the medieval town and the contemporary city. In the middle of Palais des Archevêques and the vast building of the 20th century with the "Dames de France" sign, it is the place of all festivities: concerts, official ceremonies, events, small cafés and restaurants.

Museums

■ COLLECTION D'ART (PALAIS NEUF) ★

7, rue Rouget-de-Lisle
✆ 04 68 65 15 60
Entrance on the Hotel-de-Ville square.

Open all year round. October 1 to May 31: open every day except Tuesday from 10am to 12pm and from 2pm to 5pm June 1 to September 30: open every day from 10am to 6pm. Free up to 10 years old. Narbonne Monumental Pass: 10€ reduced rate 6€. Annual closure on January 1, May 1, November 1 and 11, December 25.

Created in the 19th century by Commission Archéologique et Littéraire de Narbonne, Palais Neuf houses the old apartments that were fitted out for the archbishops from 1632 and artistic collections gathered since 1835. Special mention to the Guard or the Hearing room or with its Louis XIII fireplace decorated with mascarons, the King's chamber and its painted coffered ceiling, the dining room with wood paneling and stucco. Concerning the sculpture and painting works displayed here, we should mention the portraits of the French schools of the 16th and 18th centuries: Van der Meulen, Nattier, David. But also the bust of Louis XIV by Coysevox, parts of the Flemish School: Brueghel, Pickenoy or Italian: Tintoretto, Guerchin, Spanish with Ribera, and the magnificent collection of ceramic tiles of the 17th and 18th centuries. Temporary exhibitions are also arranged, for our greatest pleasure, but what makes the reputation of Palais Neuf is the large collection of oriental works.

■ COLLECTIONS ARCHÉOLOGIQUES (PALAIS VIEUX) ★★

✆ 04 68 90 30 54
Entrance on the Hotel-de-Ville square.

Open all year round. Free individual visits or guided group visits. In low season: Wednesday to Monday from 10am to 12pm and from 2pm to 5pm. In high season: every day from 10am to 6pm. Free until 10 years old. Pass Palais-Cathedral: 6€ reduced rate €4 / Pass Monumentale Narbonne: €10 reduced rate 6€ (the pass can be bought at the 1st site visited).

The archeological collections occupy the oldest part of Palais des Archevêques which dates back to 1833: the Palais Vieux. These collections owe their existence to Paul Tournal, a local scholar who created the Archeological Commission. The most significant elements relate to the Roman era and tell the life and history of Narbo-Martius through the different halls: Fresco paintings from the ancient quarter of Clos de la Lombarde, among the richest in the Roman world, a lapidary collection that evokes the importance of Narbonne, ancient capital of the Roman province, fragments of a triumph arc, altar of peace of Auguste, a portrait of Antoine, former governor, statue of drunk Silene, sarcophagus of Amours vendangeurs, paleochristian sarcophagus, lintel of the primitive cathedral. Also discover tools, mosaics, jewelry, ceramics and an impressive Roman anchor in oak and lead. After the part devoted to excavation techniques and restoration comes an evocation of Roman domestic architecture and an incredible and unique presentation in France of painted and mosaic decors that adorned the walls, the ceilings and the floors of the main rooms of the house with porticoes. Beautifully restored, they are one of the jewels of archeological collections. The transfer of these artifacts to the new museum of Romanité NarboVia is planned in late 2020, whose building of this superb museum can already be seen along the Canal de la Robine.

■ SALLE DU TRÉSOR DE LA CATHÉDRALE ★★

Cathédrale Saint-Just
✆ 04 68 65 15 60

Open all year round. Closed on Sunday morning. From June 1 to 30: visit on request to the caretaker from 10pm to 11: 45pm and from 2pm to 5: 45pm. From July 1 to September 30: from 10am to 11: 45am and 2pm to 5: 45pm. Every day except Sunday morning. Closed on January 1, May 1, November 1, November 11 and December 25. Free up to 10 years old. Pass Palais-Cathedral: €6 reduced rate €4 / Pass Monumentale Narbonne: €10 reduced rate €6 (the pass can be bought at the 1st site visited).

On the upper floor of the Annonciade chapel, in a vaulted brick room with a curious acoustic phenomenon: if you whisper in an angle turned towards the wall, you can be heard perfectly from the diametrically opposite side; absolutely to be tested! La salle au Trésor, as its name suggests, contains a large number of precious objects: elements of medieval sculpture, goldsmith's pieces dating from the 16th to the 19th century, an ivory Gospel plaque carved in the 9th century, a Hispano-Moorish pyxis from the 11th century, the illuminated pontifical of Archbishop Pierre de la Jugie bear witness to the great wealth of the Archbishops of Narbonne. Also worth seeing are two magnificent 16th century Flemish tapestries, including the Creation tapestry. Don't hesitate to pass by the cloister and then go for a stroll in the gardens of the archbishopric and its famous giant bench.

Walks & Strolls

■ CANAL DE LA ROBINE ★★

See page 11.

■ LE JARDIN ET LA SALLE DU PILIER

Through an open door in the west wall of the cloister, you can enter the garden planted at the site of the old ramparts; it has a nice overview of the cathedral and the palace. We particularly note the two round towers built on the foundations of the original enclosures of the city, between which the wing of the synod which is the main building of the New Palace is found. Returning from the cloister into the passage of the anchor, we enter immediately right into a room of which the architectural design of its vaulting, based entirely on a huge central pillar is remarkable. This demarcates four spans intersecting ribs according to a curiously irregular plan. Note the presence of the magnificent tombstone of the Vice countess Algayette (1273) topped by the recumbent statue found at the bottom of the room.

Knife & Fork

■ À LA TABLE DU MARCHÉ

8, rue Emile-Zola ✆ 04 68 43 19 27

Closed during the Christmas holidays. Open from Thursday to Monday for both lunch and dinner. Booking recommended. Menus from €24 to €29 (starter/dish or main course dessert €24 - starter/dish/dessert €29). Children's menu: €10 (dish / dessert / drink). Lunch formula: €14 (starter/main course or main course/dessert €14 - main course €11 - starter / main course / dessert at lunch €17). Wine by the glass. Cheese platter €7. Terrace.

The restaurant is on the side of the halls. The place is pleasant, bright, modern, exhibitions of photos or paintings decorate the walls. The clientele is quite eclectic and rather bobo chic out of season. It is in the mixture of flavours that the chef's know-how is revealed: the menu changes according to the seasons. During our visit, on the programme: cauliflower soup and raisin purée, ravioli stuffed with chestnut cream, smoked bacon consommé and mini chanterelles, crispy pork tenderloin filet mignon with spices, sweet goat's cheese mousse or chocolate fondant with Muscat de rivesaltes bourbon vanilla ice-cream... your mouth is watering, right? In the summer, the dishes are light such as swordfish ceviche and octopus and pimientos de padron. Difficult to choose as everything is delicious! So, when the atmosphere, the setting, the welcome and a quality cuisine with fresh seasonal products are present, we recommend it without hesitation! Terrace as soon as the weather permits, remember to book, places are in high demand. Menus on the Facebook page.

■ L'ART DE VIVRE – CHÂTEAU L'HOSPITALET

Route de Narbonne Plage ✆ 04 68 45 28 50
www.chateau-hospitalet.com

Open all year round. In low season: Tuesday to Friday midday from 12pm to 2pm and evening from 7: 30pm to 9: 30pm; Saturday evening. In high season: every day for both lunch and dinner. Reservation imperative. Menus from 49€ to 89€. À la carte menu: about 40€. Children's menu: 19€. Lunch formula: 29€. Wine by the glass. Vendredis du Jazz: dinner concert in 4 wine and food pairings 9€. Groups welcome. Animations.

If gastronomy is an art of living, l'Hospitalet is the place to be! In the heart of Gérard Bertrand's vineyard, on the road between Narbonne and Narbonne plage, don't hesitate to turn right for a pleasant moment in a unique setting. From aperitif to dessert, you won't be disappointed by the quality of the dishes and pairings that chef Laurent Chabert offers you. Let yourself be guided by your desires, in any case, everything is delicious, often organic and local! At l'Hospitalet, combinations are not only on the plate, every Friday is a musical evening: 4 combinations with food, wine and jazz... Numerous evenings and themed menus throughout the year, such as the "Truffle" menu, the "Easter" menu, etc., which can be found on the website. Booking is compulsory by phone or on the website.

■ BISTROT LA NAUTIQUE

12, rue des Nauticards ✆ 04 68 91 53 73
http://lanautiquenarbonne.com
pavillon-nautique@orange.fr

♿

Closed from January 7 to February 14. Please call for information. In low season: open from Wednesday to Sunday for lunch and dinner. In high season: every day and on public holidays for both lunch and dinner. Reservation recommended. À la carte menu: about 28€. Lunch formula: 16.50€ (starter + main course + dessert at lunchtime except on Sundays). Wine by the glass. In the evening, à la carte only. Groups welcome. Baby chairs. Terrace. Take away sale.

Bistrot La Nautique is an exceptional address, already its location on the small port of La Nautique with a magnificent view of Bages and its pond and then by the atmosphere of the place. The terrace is arranged in the open-air café spirit and the room subtly decorated and furnished with vintage furniture and objects from another time. At the helm of the bistro is Carole Peyrichou who treats us to her seasonal cuisine and good little dishes as we like them: local peach ceviche, grilled Iberian chorizo, you can choose among the three starters on offer. As a main course, we could recommend the cuttlefish stew on a cranquette base unless you are more tempted by the Mediterranean tuna steak, grilled and its sunny vegetables. For the dessert, the homemade chocolate mousse that is served by the spoon is a matter of course.

We like to follow the sommelier's wise advice when choosing wines from a selection of wines from the region. An address that treats us every time we visit.

■ LA BONNE EXCUSE

22, rue ancienne porte de Beziers
✆ 04 68 91 26 73

Open all year round. Closed from December 13 to January 6. Monday and Wednesday to Saturday for lunch and dinner. Closed on Tuesday and Sunday evenings. Single menu at €35. Lunch formula: €15 (starter/main course or main course/dessert – €20: starter+main course+dessert – daily special €13,50). Wine by the glass. Dish of the day: €13,50.
100% fresh and 100% homemade! Here is a new table that will get people talking about it quickly. The restaurant (formerly Le Billot), recently taken over by Johann Saisi, is located in the heart of the city's historic center, close to Place du Forum, and it was therefore after a few months of work that the establishment opened its doors. No terrace but an air-conditioned room and a warm and trendy decoration. As for cuisine, the chef swears by fresh products and short circuits, which gives us a slate that is constantly changing according to the moment and his mood. During our visit at the beginning of summer, we chose as a starter the melon soup "puits d'amour" with basil, espuma with feta cheese and Serrano chips, monkfish with chorizo as a main course, and a pavlova with fresh red fruits as a dessert. Meat lovers had the choice between a duck breast in its buttered herbs and its seasonal garnish or a tender beef fillet "tenderness" cream with ceps... We liked everything, the friendly welcome, the decoration with its chalk fresco by a neighbour and of course the cuisine, from the starter to the dessert!

■ CHAMBOURLETTES NEW

29, cours de la République
✆ 04 68 12 24 86

♿

Open all year round. From Tuesday to Saturday for lunch from 12pm to 2: 15pm and in the evening from 7: 15pm to 9: 15pm. Single menu at 23€ (vegetarian menu 17€). Children's menu: 9€. Dish of the day: 10€ (starter / main course 16€ – main course / dessert 14€ – Starter / main course / dessert 19€). Wine by the glass. Terrace.
Nathalie and Stéphane – Belgians with their sweet accents and passionate about cooking – settled on the boats with the will to work with fresh, local and seasonal products. The restaurant is ideally located on Cours de la République, a pedestrian axis in the heart of Narbonne along Canal de la Robine. Whether you are in the carefully decorated room (a second one is in the basement with a skylight) or on the terrace, you will enjoy the "canaille" cuisine of Chambourlettes, on the menu of well-cooked dishes such as Skrei back on bed of fennel confit espuma with chorizo and many specialties: shrimp croquettes, mackerel fillet with Granny apple and curry sauce, veal with fresh morels... and equally delicious desserts. For your culture, Chambourlette is the one invited to come in, to know more about it, you will have to eat there. You will find the explanations on the carte! Going to Nathalie and Stéphane's restaurant is like going to friends who welcome us warmly and generously, an address that will quickly become a must for the Barques.

CHEZ BEBELLE

1, boulevard Docteur-Ferroul
Les Halles
✆ 06 85 40 09 01
www.chez-bebelle.fr

Open all year round. From Tuesday to Sunday and on public holidays at noon. The bar opens at 8: 30 am and closes at 2 pm. Without reservation. A la carte menu: about €18. Wine by the glass. Bank card not accepted. Bar.
Gilles Belzons, the former captain of the RCNM team, owns one of the most famous restaurant bars in the area. Market atmosphere, rugby atmosphere, good-natured atmosphere, purely "narbonnaiseeee" atmosphere! When we place an order, we are always surprised and enjoy to see Gilles grab his megaphone to order his meat from the stall next door, a butcher's and delicatessen shop also stamped "Chez Bebelle", run by his sister, and yes, here, they like to work as a family. The meat, properly wrapped, flies over your head! The ex-third line then catches the packets as they should be, then passes them to the "plancha" station. It's folkloric, friendly, family, convivial, noisy, atypical... Its formula is simple but all the products come from the halls: meat accompanied by homemade french fries, a small green salad and a slice of bread "con tomate"... Cheese platter, homemade dessert... Arrive early otherwise, you will be good to enjoy one (or two) small glass of white wine while waiting for the available seat, which is not frankly unpleasant. Smart tip: if Chez Bébelle is full, try your luck by going out of the halls in its restaurant, La maison Bébelle.

■ **AU COQ HARDI**
75, rue Droite
✆ 04 68 65 27 38
♿

Open all year round. Closed 3 weeks in November. From Thursday to Tuesday for both lunch and dinner. Reservation recommended. Menus from 25€ to 33€. À la carte menu: about 25€. Children's menu: 10€. Lunch formula: 17€. Wine by the glass. Dish of the day from 12.90€. Cheques not accepted. Groups welcome. Terrace.

This emblematic restaurant Coq Hardi up rue Droite offers Italian dishes since Giovanni has been at the helm. It is therefore in this old building, a remnant of a medieval agricultural building in the town center that you will take your place, with its old stone and exposed beams. You can't resist the wonderful accents of Giovanni and the desire to taste his specialties: Pasta with gambas, basil, tagliatelle with seafood, veal escalope *alla Pulcinella*, gorgonzola and mushrooms, Italian-style entrecote (sliced) rocket and parmesan... Other more traditional dishes are proposed such as Cassoulet, Coq au vin, duck confit... and of course, the must-eat burger and the dish of the day which allows you to vary the pleasures. To complete the picture, charcuterie and Corsican cheeses (guaranteed) are also on the menu with wines from here and from the Isle of Beauty. Small terrace in the pedestrian street in good weather. A very pleasant address with the service sometimes a little slow.

■ **L'ÉCAILLER GOURMET**
15, rue d'Isly
✆ 04 68 90 13 55
lecaillerlacoquille@hotmail.fr
♿

Open from Wednesday to Saturday for both lunch and dinner; Sunday lunchtime. Menu €35. À la carte menu: about 40€. Lunch formula: 22€ (starter/main course or main course dessert – 24€ starter/main course/dessert for lunch outside the weekend). Wine by the glass. Terrace.

Away from the city centre, very close to the beautiful Place Saint-François filled with sunshine by games of petanque, L'Ecailler Gourmet was first installed as a caterer-oyster seller, then as a neighbourhood restaurant. Nicely decorated with a rainbow of colours, this place is very crowded on weekdays by the inhabitants of Narbonne, lawyers (the restaurant is located between the law school and the courthouse) and employees of the surrounding companies... People love its warm welcome, but also the fact that raw foods (before preparation) that will end up in your plate are presented ... a first in Narbonne country! Mussels, oysters gratin, shrimps, large prawns, cuttlefishes with parsley, fish according to the arrival are served either with rice or seasonal vegetables ... It's also possible to order takeaway seafood platters, ideal for celebrations, birthdays, or to only enjoy yourself. A simple and extremely tasty cuisine that we invite you to discover without hesitation.

■ **LA FRINGALE**
7, Place du Forum
✆ 04 68 90 69 31
www.lafringalenarbonne.com
bonjour@lafringalenarbonne.com
♿

Open all year round. Closed all February. Tuesday to Saturday lunch and dinner; Sunday lunch from 10am to 2pm. Brunch on Saturday from 10am to 3pm and on Sunday. Open in the afternoons (tea and coffee room) and for aperitifs. Menu: about 10€. Children's menu: 8.90€. Lunch formula: 13€ (starter + main course + dessert). Wine by the glass. Street food: 5€ to 7€. Veggie dishes: 12€ to 14€. Meat: 15€ to 21€. Fish and chips: 13.50€. Burgers: 12.90€ to 18.50€. Terrace.

Located at the top of the right-hand street, Place du Forum is a haven of good living that is very popular with young people from Narbonne and an active population in the city center. James Bowman, the "boss" understood that he had to target these two types of customers in one place by offering them quality cuisine, fair prices and quick service for the lunch break. The decoration of the place is modern, the atmosphere is warm, you will be offered a well done homemade cuisine and very gourmet burgers like Pulled pork with pork marinated in a barbecue sauce, or Rugbyman with its two special beef steaks large eaters, as well as Veggie burger and its fresh and crisp vegetables. Don't know what to choose? Opt for the fish and chips made according to the rules of the art, simply delicious! Saturday and Sunday are brunch days! Come and compose your meal with pancakes, toasted bread, bacon and eggs accompanied by the famous beans in tomato sauce, there is also homemade Granola, Benedictine eggs, "avocado and salmon toast" etc. A very popular address for Narbonne residents and tourists who love the place for its friendliness and its delicious French and international dishes. Large terrace overlooking the charming square as soon as the sun comes up. An address to fall in love with!

■ L'ENTREPÔT BRAISÉ NEW
16, Place Thérèse Léon Blum
✆ 06 13 53 17 91
www.lentrepotbraise.fr
Open all year round. Tuesday to Saturday for both lunch and dinner; Sunday evening. Children's menu: 6.90€. Lunch formula: 9.90€ (12.90€ and 20€). Wine by the glass. Salads meal from 9.90€ to 12.90€. Entrecôte: (350 gr): 15.90€. Skewer of onglet: 13.90€. Rib of beef (1kg): 22.90€. Whole sea bass: 12.90€. Burgers from 11.90€ to 14.90€. Desserts: 4.90€. Garden. Terrace.
We who thought we had done the trick when it came to the restaurant of charcoal-cooked meat, this one particularly appealed to us... Placed a little out of the historic center, the Braised Warehouse found a place around the Revolution roundabout. A discreet facade hides a pretty room tastefully decorated in a modern and trendy style, a large covered terrace with a stone wall, heated in winter and air-conditioned in summer, and a "garden" which will be very popular in fine weather. During our visit we chose the kebab of beef tabs accompanied by a gratin of seasonal vegetables, the meat (French origin) was perfectly cooked, tender to perfection and served very generously, the same goes for the side dishes. Other very tempting dishes: the burgers made with baker's bread and the rib of beef weighing around 1kg at a price defying all competition. Other dishes on the menu offer an alternative to "non-carnivores": salads, sea bream tartare, whole wolf in Nantes butter sauce... Particular attention for the homemade, even the sauces that will accompany your dish. To complete this gourmet moment, let yourself be tempted by a dessert, for us it will be a banoffee. A generous address where the welcome and the quality of service are second to none and from which you will come out full at a lower cost.

■ LES GRANDS BUFFETS
Rond-point de la Liberté
✆ 04 68 42 20 01
www.lesgrandsbuffets.com
Open all year round. Every day and on public holidays for both lunch and dinner. Reservation by internet from one day to one year in advance. Reservation imperative. Single menu at 39.90€. Children's menu: 19.90€ (from 6 to 10 years old. Free menu for children under 6 years old). Wines served at the table in bottles at producer rate and by the glass. Wine list of 70 references from Languedoc-Roussillon. Cheques not accepted. Tourisme & Handicap Label. Groups welcome (up to 50 people). Baby chairs. Garden. Terrace. Animations.

FROM PLACE TO PLACE

This is an address known and recognized within miles around! Treat yourself to a luxurious all-you-can-eat French feast: lobsters, spectacular rotisserie, tripe, stews, Catalan snails, frog legs, oysters, crustaceans, salmon, organic salads, 6 varieties of all-you-can-eat foie gras, suckling lamb and suckling pig from the Pyrenees cooked on a spit, beef cuts, organic free-range chickens... The majority of the products come from local producers and are transformed on the spot. The desserts are no exception to the spectacular and "homemade" rule by the 6 bakers of the house: paris-brest, saint-honoré, rum babas, cream slices, éclairs, macaroons, canelés, mousses, fresh organic fruits, frozen desserts and a huge chocolate fountain. Les Grands Buffets can now be proud of offering the world's largest cheese buffet with no less than 111 cheeses from France and presented in a spectacular way on 30-meter shelves, a fine entry in the Guiness Book in February 2020! A new timeless space has emerged: the ceremonial tent that takes you back to the Sun King's century. In a Baroque setting, the atmosphere is in the summer garden for your lunch and a candlelit atmosphere for the evening. Note a superb green wall by Amaury Gallon (plant designer at the Musée du Quai Branly). When booking online, you will have to choose between the 3 rooms: Clape, Corbières or Tente d'Apparat. We like the selection of the best winegrowers in the region and the wine at producer prices! Smart tip: all the wines of the list of Grands Buffets are for takeaway sale, and if you buy a box of 6 bottles of the same vintage, the bottle served at the table is given to you!

LE LOFT

86, boulevard Frédéric-Mistral

✆ 04 68 43 99 92

Open all year round. In low season: Monday and Tuesday evenings; Wednesday to Saturday lunch and dinner. In high season: every day and holidays for both lunch and dinner. Closed on public holidays. Reservation recommended. Children's menu: 9.90€. Lunch formula: 17.90€ (starter/main course or main course/dessert – 19.90€: starter+main course+dessert). Wine by the glass. Cheques not accepted. Groups welcome (up to 25 people). Terrace.

Le Loft is located just in front of the SNCF station and close to the city centre. Convenient for a break between two trains, or if you're in town, because you'll find snacks here from 10am to late afternoon, including sandwiches and omelettes at reasonable prices. Where Le Loft is starting to become really interesting is for lunch or dinner: the setting is pleasant, modern, waxed concrete on the ground, a large central bar, contemporary works of art on the wall and designed lighting. In the kitchen, Brigitte is constantly innovating, apart from the Lacaune charcuterie and various salads, we especially appreciate the originality of certain dishes and in particular the vegetables used from the local production of Madame Mijo, from the gardens of Bages. In autumn, you can enjoy a butternut velvety and pan-fried scallops, a trio of tomatoes in carpaccio in summer, squid stuffed with Settoise and its garlic, seshouane tone, grilled meat à la plancha... all accompanied (depending on the season) by freshly picked vegetables such as Jerusalem artichokes, Swiss chard, yellow zucchini, white eggplants... A tip, when you book your table by phone, remember to ask for the daily specials, because here, they in small quantities, which guarantees the freshness of the dishes on offer.

CHEZ LULU

82, rue Droite

✆ 04 68 91 41 81

Open all year round. In low season: Tuesday and Wednesday for lunch; Thursday to Saturday for both lunch and dinner. In high season: every day from 8: 30am to 10pm. Reservation recommended. Menu: about 20€. Dish of the day: 12€. Wine by the glass. Organic coffee / Organic tea (20 sorts). Terrace.

On the very top of the right street, right before Place du Forum Square, Alexandre has opened his little restaurant: a bistro atmosphere, good food and good mood meet expectations. At Chez Lulu, you can come at any time to have a cup of coffee at 8: 30am, enjoy a homemade dish from noon or fall for something sweet with a cup of organic tea during the day. Alex, a well-known restaurateur of Petit Futé (which we have been following since 1998) has therefore chosen Narbonne's good life to settle down and put down his pots. On the menu of simple dishes made from fresh and local produce, the bistro is "100% homemade, 100% fresh and 0% frozen" and Renard confirms! During our visit, the following were suggested (among other things) on the blackboard menu, Narbonne-style beef poire, saithe tartare with lemongrass, oysters cooked au gratin with Bellota and as a daily special, a farm chicken (French) roasted with lemongrass and chardonnay served with tagliatelle of organic vegetables of the moment. It's good, it's copious and it's not expensive, and the blackboard menu changes every week! We also like the atmosphere of the place with popular music of the 1930s and the neat decoration. At Chez Lulu, you can take your time, chat with your neighbours at the table, enjoy the moment, in short, you feel good there. We are willing to bet that this small confidential address will soon become a place very popular among Narbonne residents and tourists, so consider booking..

■ LE MACAR – BAR A VINS ET RESTAURANT
21, cours de la République ✆ 04 68 75 81 23

Open all year round. Low season: Thursday to Tuesday from 9am to 12am. High season: every day from 9am to 1am. Open non-stop – High season: December and July/August. Salad: €10. Burgers: €13. Tapas from €3 to €17.

Le Macar has become in a short time a must visit place in Narbonne, from the good little coffee in the morning to the evening aperitif, without forgetting the lunch break, the little sweetness in the afternoon and the lively evenings. At Le Macar, you will be served for lunch a dish of the day which varies according to the mood of the chef and the market, nice salads, homemade dishes accompanied by vegetables and homemade french fries. For the latecomers, know that for the tapas, the service is continuous, and this until 11pm every day, then discover the slate: patatas bravas or with aioli, camembert in the oven, accras of cod, tortillas, tapenade, pan con tomato with or without Serrano ham, boquerones, board of cold cuts or cheese and even both in a mixed board. Let us advise you the wine, a rigorous selection is proposed in the appellations Corbières, Clapes, Minervois... You don't know what to choose? We advise you, rather woody? fruity? light or tannic? There is always something for you. And if you don't like wine, you should know that the establishment has widened its range of draught beers and bottles. An address that never disappoints, as a couple, with friends, in afterwork... all occasions are good.

■ LE MALLICOLO
43, rue de l'Ancien Courrier
✆ 04 68 49 78 99

Open all year round. Monday to Saturday from 12pm to 3pm. Reservation recommended. Children's menu: 10€ (baroudeur menu). Lunch formula: 13€ (explorer menu). Wine by the glass. Salads 10€, Brushetta 11€, Dish "autour du monde" 16€. Terrace. Vegan friendly.

In the very heart of the historic center of Narbonne, in a shopping and pedestrian street, discover Le Mallicolo. The owners, Nathalie and Éric are frequent travelers, their journey across the South Pacific took them to a small island in the Vanuatu archipelago, the island of Mallicolo. On the menu, a variation of bruschettas (sandwiches), martiniquaise with chicken and curry cream, pineapple, peppers, mozzarella is exquisite. Those who love Bougna (a typical dish of New Caledonia) will be delighted with the Mallicolo plate. Spices, coconut, mango, lime... are the basic ingredients with which Éric prepares his salads of the day, other salads are suggested on a chalkboard menu depending on the season such as the one with marinated shark or the one scallop tartare in summer. Le Mallicolo will delight vegetarians with many suggestions and also vegans with the famous Chapati plate (Indian pancake with vegetable korma) without any animal matter "except the intervention of the cook" according to Eric! Yes, because here, smiles and happiness reign. Seats are not that numerous so consider booking your table on the terrace or inside.

■ LE MOUSSAILLON
19, boulevard Docteur-Ferroul
✆ 04 68 42 43 11
www.lemoussaillon-narbonne.com

Open all year round. Tuesday to Saturday from 9: 30am to 3pm and from 4: 30pm to 9pm; Sunday from 9: 30am to 3pm. Reservation recommended. Lunch formula: 15€ (small tray: oysters, whelks, prawns, mussels). Wine by the glass. Take-away trays from 20 to 109€. Terrace. Take away sale. Shop.

For nearly 20 years, Le Moussaillon has been offering excellent quality seafood in the centre of Narbonne, facing the Halles. In the shell bar or on the terrace, you will treat yourself with oysters, organic shrimps or whelks with a little aïoli. If you prefer some tapas; shellfish and squid in parsley, langoustines à la plancha or some mussels and cheese-topped oysters ... On Wednesday there is pasta with lobster! Better to book before coming as it is most of the time full. Gourmet, slightly spiced and sprinkled with tomato, they are probably the best in the region. There are also some desserts. For special occasions, do not hesitate to order a seafood tray to take away, there are different portions, at different prices and are served with: shallot vinegar, garlic and rye bread. Enjoy a good bottle of white wine with them. Moreover, Le Moussaillon offers a small delicatessen shop: there are fish bisque, aïoli, wine... Don't hesitate to enjoy yourself!

LE PETIT COMPTOIR

4, boulevard du Maréchal-Joffre
✆ 04 68 42 30 35
www.petitcomptoir.com
camille@petitcomptoir.com

Inquire about summer closures. Closed the first week of January. Open from Tuesday to Saturday and on public holidays for both lunch and dinner. Reservation recommended. Single menu at 32€. Lunch formula: 18€ (or 22€ starter-main course-dessert). Wine by the glass. American Express. Groups welcome. Terrace.

Le Petit Comptoir has been part of the Narbonne landscape since 1976, it is one of these select addresses, where people come for dinner and lunch. Here, the culture of cooking still has a meaning: we appreciate the hospitality, the refined setting, the professionalism of the maître d', the know-how of the waiters, the sweetness of the place, the delicacy of the dishes, up to the titles that leave you dreaming... This traditional, local cuisine, constantly innovative by Chef Franck Jeanjean, in order to make you discover new flavours, we have tasted for you (hard job!) the Bisquebouille of mussels and small vegetables, swordfish fillet, pumpkin risotto... and as a dessert of course, the famous pancake puffed with lemon, caramel with mandarin, a real treat! The menu changes every month, just like the à la carte menu, the chef only works with seasonal products. As for the wine list, it reflects our terroir, magnificent! Other pleasures, another atmosphere on the "zinc side", tasting of good wines and tapas cooked from €6 to €35, a must for an evening with friends! Concert every last Friday of the month and DJ every other Friday. These evenings, all of the Narbonne inhabitants 30-50 years old meet, it is not rare to see so many people in it as on the sidewalk!

LA TABLE DE FONTFROIDE

Abbaye de Fontfroide, chemin de Fontfroide RD 613
✆ 04 68 41 02 26
www.fontfroide.com
latable@fontfroide.com

Qualité Sud de France. Maître Restaurateur. Closed from mid-December to mid-February. Open every day from 12pm to 2pm. Dinner: from July 1 to August 31 inclusive, open in the evening on Tuesdays, Wednesdays, Thursdays, Fridays and Saturdays. Every other evening on request (minimum 20 people). Reservation recommended. Children's menu: 12.50€. Lunch formula: 22€ to 26€. Menus from 35€ to 39€. Wine by the glass. Cheques not accepted. In the summer, musical night-time tour in the abbey. Groups welcome. Baby chairs. Garden. Terrace. Take away (snack bar).

La Table de Fontfroide is located in the former sheepfold of the abbey. The decoration respects the authenticity and the simplicity of the simple and elegant place. decorated furniture. Enter the door and you will find that monastic traditions continue... Hospitality, know-how and kindness are the key words of the welcome and the service of this address. As for the cuisine, you will enjoy the gourmet cuisine of Yohan Renard, a renowned chef. All the dishes are refined and made with fresh products, showcasing the Mediterranean. Some dishes of the menu follow a medieval inspiration while others are resolutely modern and of great finesse. Examples include the unmissable ravioles of scallops creamy sauce with morels. The chef offers gluten-free meals every day. The wines you taste are renowned wines of the abbey, there is also a craft beer brewed in the colors of Fontfroide. Fine days will be an opportunity to enjoy the terrace that opens either onto the massif or onto its wonderful garden. For those who are in a hurry, there are quick formulas and snack (sandwiches, salads) served at the bar.

LA TABLE SAINT-CRESCENT

Rond point de la Liberté
68, avenue Général-Leclerc
✆ 04 68 41 37 37
www.la-table-saint-crescent.com
contact@la-table-saint-crescent.com

♿

Qualité Sud de France. Maître Restaurateur. Closed on Sunday evenings, Monday and Tuesday, except in July,

Narbonne, Les Barques rive droite.

August, September – closed on Sunday and Monday and in December. Open Wednesday to Saturday from 12pm to 1: 30pm and from 8pm to 9: 30pm; Sunday from 12pm to 1: 30pm. Menus from 65€ to 95€. Children's menu: 20€ (one drink included). (Business lunch- 35€ served only for lunch, excluding weekends and public holidays). Wine by the glass. American Express. Groups welcome. Baby chairs. Garden. Terrace. Organisation of events for individuals (weddings, baptisms, birthdays etc...) and companies (cocktail parties, inauguration, group meals etc...).

Lionel Giraud, a chef who's on the rise and who has his head in the stars with his two Michelin stars. 2020 also marks the start of a new adventure with a completely redesigned restaurant including the gourmet restaurant and 2 new areas with a resolutely sober and modern decoration: "wine cellar" and "dining cellar". These "cellars" will allow you to come and taste and nibble on tapas and other dishes prepared by the chef. Saint-Crescent's table is located in the sumptuous setting of a former 7th century oratory. Lionel Giraud's gastronomic cuisine has increased in intensity: refined, inventive, demanding, it's a flawless score! A subtle marriage of aromas, flavors and textures. A small extract from the menu during our last visit: oyster from "Pascal MIGLIORE", freshly grilled Estarac pencil leeks with transparent Noir de Bigorre bacon, creamy tetragone cream and grilled rye as a starter. Next, you will always have the choice between meat and fish with, for example, the Aveyron farm hen raised by the Quintard family, candied in black diamond butter, tortellinis with Petit Paris and albufeira sauce or the line-caught hake from La Nouvelle port cooked in a seaweed broth, pink radishes from "Henri BASTELICA" in dry fermentation, candied *daïkons* like an anemone and reduction of bones Juice. And for sweets, let yourself be tempted by the shortbread and hazelnut praline soufflé tartlet, smooth mandarin flower ice cream... We appreciate Lionel's precise cooking and his overflowing imagination to propose exceptional dishes where the good product is king.

■ LES TAPAS DE LA CLAPE

Les Halles

✆ 06 23 47 06 41

http://tapas-narbonne.zenchef.com/

Open all year round. Monday and Friday from 10am (last service at 3pm); Tuesday to Thursday from 8: 30am (last service at 2pm); Saturday from 8am (last service at 3pm); Sunday from 8am (last service at 2pm). Reservation recommended. Children's menu: €8. Brunch on Saturdays and Sundays from 8am to 11am 4 formulas from €5.50 to €19.90. Formulas "Les ración" from €13,50 to €32. Tapas from €5,50 to €17. Vegetarian tapas: €5,50 to €9,50. Mixed boards: €17,50. Salads from €15 to €16. Wine by the glass from €4. Shop.

The halls are an enchantment by their architecture, the typical Narbonne atmosphere that reigns there but also for the quality of the products that you will be served at Tapas de La Clape. Firat, the owner, Master Chef 2013, but also a chef renowned for his "à la plancha" cuisine, offers one of the most beautiful showcases of Clape wines (30 producers and 80 references) that goes perfectly with the good products of Les Halles. Take a seat on the high tables and start with some tapas from the land: homemade foie gras, duck heart, grilled chorizos... If you are more attracted by sea products: grilled razor clams, oysters au gratin, prawns, tuna tataki... You will also have a choice of skewers, salads (we recommend the gersoise) and dishes from the land or the sea or both. As a main course (el ración), special mention for the Wagyu de Kobé beef, tuna steak with citrus fruits or the quadrilogy of the oldest pork butcher of the halles aka Robert Laforgue. Mixed boards are a good compromise to taste a little bit of everything. Cheese lovers, don't hesitate, you will be served here the delicious cheeses of Le Hâloir (cheese maker of the halls). A gourmet address where the "food and wine" pairings make us happy. Voted the best wine bar in the Languedoc in 2015, this is a very nice place not to be missed in Les Halles! New for 2020: The Week-end Breakfast in Les Halles, Firat and his team offer on Saturdays and Sundays from 8am to 11am tailor-made brunches from Basic to Je me casse le ventre! To be tested as soon as possible.

■ LA TRATTORIA – SUCRÉ ET SALÉ

22, boulevard Gambetta

✆ 06 12 57 90 72

https://www.latrattorianarbonne.com/

trattoria@gmail.com

Open Monday to Wednesday from 9.30am to 3pm; Thursday to Saturday from 9.30am to 3pm and 7pm to 10pm. Menus from €19.90 to €27.50. A la carte menu: about €15. Children's menu: €10. Lunch formula: €13.50 (pasta / dessert or Poke Bowl / dessert). Wine by the glass. Takeaway pizzas and pasta. Terrace. Take away sale. Shop.

It is in a Haussmann-style building that Nicolas and Odile Galati welcome you with the kindness that characterizes them. Walk through the door and you are in the heart of the deep Italy of the 1970s, icons of Ennio Morricone on the wall, high ceiling, stone columns, it smells like olive oil, basil and parmesan! You can sit at the bar, at the table in the big room or on the terrace (soon covered). The maestro puts on a show, he cooks only fresh products in front of you, and the dishes are prepared under your eyes. His great mastery of cooking and flavours makes a simple pasta dish unique... Italian genius! Among the specialities, pasta of course, penne with porcini mushrooms are the best, but the lobster bisque ravioli are worth the detour. The portions are generous, the plates are beautiful and the taste buds go wild! On Friday evening (from 7pm) we like to meet there for an aperitivo italiano with DJ, to taste a spritz or a glass of wine (local like Castelmaure, organic with Pech Redon, or Italian bottles to be tasted imperatively) with antipasti and cold cuts, a delicious moment where we quickly forget the daily routine... Wellness formula for lunch: Poke Bowl + dessert.

■ T – SALON DE THÉ & RESTAURANT
21, rue de l'Ancien courrier
✆ 04 34 44 45 14

Open all year round. In low season: Tuesday to Saturday from 10am to 7pm. In high season: from Monday to Saturday from 10am to 7pm. À la carte menu: about 15€. Dish of the day: 11€ (to 14€). Soup of the day from 13€ – Quiche of the day 13€ – "côté light" 8.50€. Terrace. Take away sale. Shop.

You may know the tea room side of the "T", so go and try their different lunchtime formulas. Wraps, salads, every day a hot dish including the famous Fish and Chips (not greasy!) or the chicken burger, quiches, salted clafoutis, soups in winter, cassolettes. For those with a sweet tooth, try Heidi's famous cheesecake, carrot cake, banana bread or cupcakes! Small terrace overlooking the pedestrian street. Good to know, at the T, we welcome you in French, English and Spanish!

Sleeping

LE C BOUTIQUE HÔTEL
15, rue de Suffren ✆ 09 67 17 56 54
www.hotel-le-c.com
boutiquehotellec@gmail.com

Welcome until 8: 30pm (24 hours a day with digicode and key box). 10 rooms (including 4 junior suites (4 persons)). Breakfast: 12€ (8€ until 12 years old). Extra bed: 20€. Parking: 12€ (closed at night). Standard rooms: 99€ to 135€. Luxury rooms: 109€ to 140€. Junior suites: €139 to €175. Free Wifi. Satellite TV.

"C" is a magnificent boutique hotel located in a quiet and residential area just a few steps from the historic center. C Boutique Hotel is the former Hotel Le Régent, only the exterior walls, roof and Art Deco staircase ramp have been preserved, everything else has been completely redesigned by Chris and Cécile to offer their guests a cosy little cocoon in a chic and modern style. From the standard rooms to the luxury suites, all offer a personalised decoration where the combinations of colours and materials are of the most beautiful effect. The Junior Suites and Luxury Rooms have a small lounge, the "-1" room is independent and has a private "garden-terrace", the others have a rooftop on the top floor with a 360° view of Narbonne and the Clape Massif. The bathrooms are equipped with a large Italian shower and Rituals beauty products. As far as equipment is concerned, there is nothing to complain about, everything is there: minibar, TV, air conditioning, wifi and courtesy tray. Breakfast consists of pastries, homemade jams, cheese and cold meats from the Narbonne market. The welcome of Chris and his team is pleasant and professional. Le C has a small private car park, a tip, remember to book. A small but pleasant hotel that deserves a particular attention.

HÔTEL LA RESIDENCE
6, rue du 1er Mai ✆ 04 68 32 19 41
www.hotel-laresidence-narbonne.fr
hotellaresidence@free.fr

Open all year round. Tourist tax 1.65€ per day and per person. Welcome 24 hours a day. 26 rooms. Double room from 89€ to 158€. Breakfast buffet or in room: 12.50€ (coffee break 7€). Extra bed: 20€. Garage: 9€ (6€ for a motorbike). American Express, Diners Club. Animals accepted (9€). Free Wifi. Sale (local wines).

Hôtel La Résidence is undoubtedly the most charming hotel in Narbonne. Ideally located in the heart of the historic center of the city, just a stone's throw from Canal de la Robine, Palais des Archevêques and the pedestrian streets. A successful blend of styles in this tastefully renovated address, the 19th century architecture of the premises is sublimated by the new decoration, both chic and contemporary. The same spirit applies to rooms where the materials chosen are noble and of high quality, they are air-conditioned and equipped with good bedding. Special mention for the breakfast to take in the new, completely redesigned area where excellent organic products are offered: Iberian ham in a bowl, cheese from Montagne Noire, pear and apple juice, homemade pies... If you want to take the opportunity to discover the city and its treasures, different formulas are available to you, the "prestige" includes 2 nights, breakfasts, a half bottle of champagne and 2 Monuments and museums passes at a special rate. Finally, the hotel offers you a small lounge where you can taste a selection of wines at producer prices. A good address where good taste is resolutely on every floor.

Campsites

■ CAMPING LA NAUTIQUE
254, Avenue des Étangs ✆ 04 68 90 48 19
www.campinglanautique.com
info@campinglanautique.com

Open from March 1st to October 31st. Minimum stay of 2 nights from April to the end of June and from September to October. One week stay from Sunday or Wednesday in July and August. Reservation recommended. Reception until 8 pm. Guarded 24 hours a day. Land of 13.8 ha. 390 pitches. Exposure: half-shaded. Relief: flat. Parking on pitch – Individual sanitary facilities – Outdoor swimming pool heated by solar panels. Pitch + vehicle + 2 persons (with 10 A) from 22,50 € to 49,50 €. 86 mobile homes for 1 to 7 people from 264 € to 1,092 € per week. 9 different types of accommodation from Coco Sweet to Soléo. Tourism & Handicap Label. Children's club. Games for children. Animals accepted (except category 1. 5 €). Area for motorhomes. Free Wifi. Animations. Excursions.

Close to the south exit of the motorway, between Narbonne and Etang Bages-Sigean, Camping La Nautique enjoys a strategic location, a perfect starting point for exploring Pays Cathare or enjoying Mediterranean beaches. With its stunning view of the pond, its comfortable facilities, and its atmosphere, the campsite offers the opportunity to spend good holidays with family. The campsite offers mobile homes with the best comfort, spacious and separate pitches, as well as individual toilet and showers. Always keen to meet the expectations of its demanding guests, a heavenly beach in postcard lagoon style was inaugurated in 2018! While those who love water sports will indulge in their favorite activities on the pond, whereas others will enjoy aquagym courses in the heated swimming pool or the new wellness path of 2.5 kms, while children continue waterslide descents, others refine their tan by the brandnew and spectacular lagoon of La Nautique-Plage… in the quiet. The latter is perfect during days of strong winds when the beach can't be reached. During this "relaxation" moment, Cool Kid will be taking care of your children by offering them many workshops and games. Isn't life beautiful?

Leisure

PARC AQUATIQUE ESPACE DE LIBERTE

Rond-point de la Liberté
Route de Perpignan
✆ 04 68 42 17 89
www.espaceliberte.com
client.espace@legrandnarbonne.com

♿

Open all year round. Except December 25 and January 1. Monday to Friday from 12pm to 8pm; Saturday and public holidays from 10am to 7pm; Sunday from 10: 30am to 6pm. The Olympic Basin opens at 8: 30am Monday, Wednesday, Friday. Holiday periods: indoor pools from Monday to Friday from 10am to 8pm; Saturday from 10am to 7pm; Sunday from 10am to 6pm. Adult admission: €6. Admission child for under 2 years old: €1.50, child from 2 to 11 years old: €3.90. Package 12 tickets: €60. 10h package: €29. Summer rates: €8.20. Admission for children under the age of 2: €2, for children from 2 to 11 years old: €6. Water Jump with extra charge.

The Aquatic Park of the Espace de Liberté is a must-visit for all lovers of aquatic pleasures. Whether you practice swimming or you like to relax in the water with your children, or to experience some gliding sensations, everything is planned! In the indoor aquatic area, a 25-metre swimming pool, 6 lanes, heated to 29° is at your disposal, lines for swimmers, a "Swimming School" for all levels for children and adult. Families will also discover an aqua-family area with slides, whirlpool bath and Slash Pad for safe fun. But also, O'Tonic a special aquafitness pool with innovative and trendy activities such as aquabike, crosstraining, pilates,... With online courses booking. Outdoor, swimmers will enjoy doing swim lengths in the open air in the Olympic pool (50 meters) exposed south and heated all year round (the Philippe Lucas team trained there for 5 years to prepare for the Olympics).

This pool, equipped with competition lines, hosts sports camps all year round during the school holidays. The Espace de Liberté "sport" group trains in this pool from January 1st to December 31st. In summer, the most beautiful slides are provided on the giant slide and the 4-lane water slide. The 300 m² Slash Pad aqua'kid park specially designed for children dominates the Olympic pool. For relaxation: the solarium, and the shaded picnic area. Since the summer of 2019, a new sensational new activity is offered: Water Jump. Composed of 4 exceptional tracks from 9 to 12m high (white, green, red and black), it will allow you to perform incredible jumps and tricks before a dive in the brand new pool. Not to be missed under any circumstances!

Espace de Liberté

The Espace de Liberté is a flagship sports and tourist site in the Aude department and the region, offering an ever-wider range of activities to satisfy the greatest number of people, adults and children alike: leisure park and indoor/outdoor aquatic complex, heated Olympic pool open all year round, Water Jump, giant slides, Aquafitness center, ice skating rink open from October to April and go-karting on ice, 12-lane bowling alley with scenography. It is located at the entrance of the city, on the Narbonne-Sud motorway exit side. It can be seen from afar with its glass pyramid. Come and discover the new bowling lanes, a pool dedicated to aquagym and novelties such as the "Splash-Pad" or the Waterjump which are unanimously appreciated by the youngest (up to 7 years old) as well as the oldest! You will also find an English pub, perfect for after-work or in the evening to enjoy delicious cocktails comfortably seated in the cozy armchairs. Every Thursday groups perform in a very good atmosphere. On the spot the famous "Grands Buffets" with the spectacle of a kitchen open to the room. All these services will bring you pleasure, leisure and delicacies.

▸ www.espaceliberte.com

PATINOIRE ESPACE DE LIBERTÉ

Rond-point de la Liberté
Route de Perpignan
✆ 04 68 42 17 89
www.espacedeliberte.com

School period: open on Wednesdays from 2pm to 5: 30pm, Fridays from 9pm to midnight (karting), Saturdays from 2pm to 5pm then from 5: 30pm to 7: 30pm (karting) and from 9pm to midnight and Sundays from 2pm to 5pm and from 5: 30pm to 7pm (karting). Short holidays: open every morning from 10am to 12pm from Monday to Friday and every afternoon from 2pm to 5: 30pm and evenings from 8: 30pm to 11: 30pm (karting or skating). Entrance fee: 6,50 €. Child: 6 €. Skates included. Restaurant. Cloakroom with lockers.

In this beautiful leisure park that is the Espace de Liberté, the ice-skating rink is still the only one in the Narbonnais. Both sporty and playful, it is addressed to everyone. Don't be surprised to meet Philippe and Olivia Candeloro, the dancers come regularly for the preparation of their ice shows. An atmosphere of sounds, light shows and DJs to accompany children and adults in the joys of sliding on an 800 m^2 ice track... At the Espace de Liberté ice rink, we offer you two ways to slide: on skates or... in a kart! Yes, six electrically-powered go-karts allow acceleration and skidding on ice transformed into a circuit... Sensations guaranteed for children and adults! The ice rink is also well anchored in the sporting life of Narbonne with its two hockey and figure skating clubs. So, dear beginners or experienced, everybody, let's skate! The ice rink welcomes individuals, groups or companies wishing to organize events and seminars.

LES PETITS BATEAUX DU CANAL

32, cours de la République, Promenade des Barques
✆ 07 67 57 36 96

Rent 1h: Boat 5 pers: 29 €. Boat 7 pers: 33 €. Extra hour: 20 € boat 5 pers. 25 € boat 7 pers. Half hour rental: 17 € for 5 pers. and 19 € for 7 pers.

After walking through the historic centre of Narbonne, what would you say to a little boat trip on the Canal de la Robine which, let's not forget, is the junction between the Canal du Midi and the sea and is classified as a UNESCO World Heritage Site? This walk will be an opportunity to discover the city from a different angle and in a fun way, children love it, especially when they take the helm. After a short tour on the side of Pont des marchands and the footbridge "Between two cities", you make a "U-turn" and go towards the sea (which you won't reach: too far). These small boats are eco-friendly because they are electric, comfortable and you will of course be equipped with life jackets. A nice moment to share with friends or family.

Going Out

ESCAPE YOURSELF

17, route de Lunes
✆ 07 78 90 46 23
www.escapeyourselfnarbonne.fr
escapeyourselfnarbonne@gmail.com

Open Monday; Wednesday to Sunday. Monday and from Wednesday to Friday: Sessions at 2pm, 4pm, 6pm, 8pm. Saturday: Sessions at 10am, 12pm, 2pm, 4pm, 6pm, 8pm, 10pm. Sunday: Sessions at 10am, 12pm, 2pm, 4pm, 6pm. Admission: 18 € (to 30 € depending on the number of players and timetables). Groups of 10 or more people are possible outside the normal opening hours.

Escape Yourself has recently opened in Narbonne in the city centre in front of the Leader Price, this place may not leave you indifferent. The Escape game's principle is simple, form a team, forget your mobile phone in the locker room and try to take up the challenge: solve a mysterious enigma in 60 minutes! There are three possible puzzles: the cabinet of curiosities or a friend (whom you've probably forgotten) sends you the following message: "Take the first plane and meet me quickly at my cabinet, I've made a discovery that could challenge the whole of humanity! I can't tell you anything before you come, it's too risky! " The other riddle, and our favourite, is that of your late great-aunt Ernerstine who has just left you her sumptuous manor house, the one where nobody ever goes and which frightens the children... 3rd riddle The "Lost in Space" room or how to survive when you wake up too early from your hyper-sleep phase and your space vacation destination is not yet reached! So, which one do you choose? The sets are very realistic and you get into the game instantly. Perfect for group cohesion but especially for a good game of fun with friends or colleagues. A unique experience to live without delay if you're smart and cunning, a bit like us...

Kids

ESPACE DE LIBERTÉ

Rond-point de la Liberté
Route de Perpignan
✆ 04 68 42 17 89
www.espaceliberte.com
client.espace@legrandnarbonne.com
Motorway, exit Narbonne Sud.

Open all year round. Variable hours, see the various articles in the guide. Aquatic Park – Skating rink – Bowling – Karting on ice (5 € to 17 €).

A flagship sports and tourist site of the department of Aude and the Region, Espace de Liberté offers an ever-wider range of activities to satisfy as many people as possible, adults and children alike: leisure park and indoor/outdoor aquatic complex, heated Olympic pool open year round, Water Jump, giant slides, Aquafitness Center, ice rink open from October to April and ice karting, 12-lane bowling alley with scenography. It is located at the entrance to the city, at the exit of the Narbonne-Sud motorway. You can see it by from a distance with its glass pyramid. Come and discover the new bowling lanes, a pool dedicated to aquagym and new features such as the "Splash-Pad" or the Waterjump which are unanimously enjoyed among little children (up to 7 years old) and adults! You will also find an English pub, perfect for an after-work or in the evening to enjoy delicious cocktails comfortably seated in the cosy armchairs. Every Thursday, groups perform in a very good atmosphere.

On site, the famous all-you-can-eat "Grand Buffets" with the show of a kitchen opening onto the dining room. All these services provided will bring you pleasure, leisure and delicacies.

Tea Rooms

DÉLICE CAKE
4, rue Marcelin-Coural
✆ 04 68 91 67 40

Open all year round. Tuesday to Sunday from 10am to 7pm. Every day Brunch €18 for sweet – €21 for salty. Lunch dishes: €15 approx. pastry: between €5 and €6. Wedding cake, traditional pastry, custom-made pièce montée. Terrace. Shop.

At Délice Cake, everything is deliciously thought out and both female and male customers enjoy it. Both tea room and restaurant (small catering), we are here in a *cosy* little boudoir with girly decoration, a cocoon where it is nice to meet for a gourmet break. At lunchtime, you can choose a formula or the special dish of the day: salmon cheesecake, mushroom crepe, mixed salad, sandwiches and croque-monsieur, but the speciality is sweet treats. American-style cupcakes (with fruit, Kit-Kat™, coconut...), banoffee, crumble, cheesecake, meringue, macaroons, apple crunch, millefeuilles, bubble waffles. We no longer know where to look, everything is as good as it is beautiful, and homemade! No matter the calories... Délice Cake makes wedding cakes, party and birthday cakes made to measure (and to order), best seller of the moment *number cake*, guaranteed effect! Finally, every day, it's brunch from 10: 30am to 3pm. An excellent address to visit at any time of the day, from breakfast to after-work in the powder-coloured room or on the small terrace with its antique furniture. The Facebook page will whet your appetite! True info: some customers complain about the welcome, for our part, we have nothing to complain about, have we been lucky?

T – SALON DE THÉ & RESTAURANT
21, rue de l'Ancien courrier
✆ 04 34 44 45 14

Open all year round. From Tuesday to Saturday from 10am to 7pm. Dish of the day from 12€. Exhibition, sale of Théodore tea, decorative objects, teapots... Free Wifi. Terrace. Shop.

Heidi was dreaming of a tea room in downtown Narbonne! A dream come true for several years now, the American has opened a classy-design-cosy establishment where you can enjoy lunch with colleagues, tea with friends, or a snack with children. The selection of teas is excellent, a real work is done to offer you fruity, tangy or spicy flavours. Every day, the team proposes a dish, a salad, a quiche of the day but also different recipes of wraps, bacon, cheddar, salmon. In winter, Heidi offers a different soup every day: Tartiflette-style potato with bacon and Reblochon cheese perfect for a nice winter day... A treat at a low price! In the summer, we recommend iced teas that can be taken away. For sweet treats, there are cupcakes, cheesecake, pine nut pie, carrot cake and big cakes like in the movies. Pastries are accompanied by a Theodore tea, capsule coffee, freshly squeezed fruit juice or soda made in the USA. The motto of the house: "You can't buy happiness, but you can buy cupcakes, and it's kind of the same thing". The take-away formula can also bring a little happiness home. We recommend!

Bars & Pubs

LE MACAR – BAR A VINS ET RESTAURANT
21, cours de la République
✆ 04 68 75 81 23

Open all year round. Low season: Thursday to Tuesday from 9am to 1am. High season: every day from 9am to 1am (non stop opening). Open every day in December and July-August. Salad from €10. Dish from €12. Tapas from €3 to €23. Terrace.

"To know that a glass of wine is too much, you have to have drunk it! " This is the motto of this wine bar in the heart of the Barques. We like to come with friends for the afterwork, to nibble tapas served non-stop, to have a drink or a hot drink during the day... in short, it is the trendy meeting point for 30-45 year olds. Relaxed and friendly atmosphere. In summer and winter, the terrace, sunny all day long, on the Promenade des Barques is very pleasant. In bad weather or for those who are sensitive to cold, a small room welcomes you inside.

Note the excellent selection of wine by the glass: Château Camplazens, Château Caraguilhes, Domaine de Couderc,. . .

O'BRIANS – IRISH PUB
9, boulevard du Général-de-Gaulle
✆ 04 68 75 96 57

Open all year round. Tuesday to Sunday from 5pm to 2am. Drinks from €3.50 to €8 - Snacks "Savoury delights of the small grocery store" from €2 to €12. wi-fi. Animations.

Near the courthouse, the Irish pub is warm, the wood is dark and patinated, the vintage armchairs offer a *so British* decor. The pretty library is open to everyone and matches the elegance of the waiters. As in any good pub that respects itself: 24 beers of your choice (bottle or draught) with the must-drinks Guinness, whisky, rum, vodka, match nights on its three screens... without forgetting the little wink of the South: boards with sausage, tapenade and pâté. As for the atmosphere, on Wednesdays, don't miss the Karaoke evening, DJs on Fridays, Saturdays and Sundays evenings, bachelor parties, *blind test* evenings or sports events. Here, you've understood it: everyone has their own atmosphere and at each moment, all the information on the pub's Facebook page (O'Brians Pub).

V AND B
Forum Sud
Chemin du Quatourze
Road to Perpignan
✆ 04 68 58 42 59
www.VandB.fr
narbonne@vandb.fr

Open all year round. Monday from 3 to 8 pm; Tuesday and Wednesday from 10am to 12: 30pm and 2: 30pm to 8 pm; Thursday to Saturday from 10am to 12: 30pm and 2: 30pm to 8: 30 pm. Late closing on special evenings. Terrace. Animations. Concerts.

FROM PLACE TO PLACE

Want to leave your home for V&B? You will not be disappointed as there are various activities offered to you all year long. We can talk about the famous Saint Patrick who attracts crowds of people dressed in green every year, Music Day; sports repeats; aperitif-oysters; magic shows, nuit de la Barbe, Halloween... We love the Happy parties of Tuesday like the Happy Wine with glass of wine at €2. V&B is also waiting for you every evening, an *afterwork,* until 8pm and 8.30pm on Thursdays, Fridays and Saturdays! When the bell rings, it's time to recommend a drink before it's too late. Feel free to visit their Facebook page to learn more!

Bowlings

■ BOWLING ESPACE DE LIBERTE

Rond-point de la Liberté
Route de Perpignan
✆ 04 68 42 17 89
www.espaceliberte.com
client.espace@legrandnarbonne.com
Highway, exit Narbonne Sud.

Open all year round. From 2pm until midnight or 1am. School holidays from 2pm to 1am. Party at 6,50 € shoes rental included.

Open every day, it promises you entertaining, friendly afternoons and festive evenings. The 12 fluo tracks are adapted to children thanks to removable rails, launching ramps and light balls, to play in optimal technical conditions. Beautiful lighting design. The bowling alley welcomes individuals, groups or companies wishing to organize events and seminars. Good deal evenings (except school holidays and public holidays): Sunday from 6pm "Bowling no limit", unlimited games at €10 and from Monday to Friday, enjoy the "Happy Bowler" with 3 games at €10. Just next door, the Private Bowling Pub invites you to spend a moment in peace and quiet in a typically Victorian setting, with more than twenty different types of beer, draught or bottled, and numerous non-alcoholic drinks. We advise you for the after-works, some days from 6pm to 8pm, with wines from local producers and quality charcuterie! It's the ideal place for a relaxing family moment right in front of the bowling lanes.

■ PRIVATE BOWLING PUB

Route de Perpignan
Rond-point de la Liberté
✆ 04 68 42 67 25
www.espaceliberte.com

Every day from 6pm to 9pm Afterwork. Open all year round. School period open Monday and Tuesday from 6pm to midnight, Wednesday 2: 30pm to midnight, Thursday and Friday from 6pm to 1am, Saturday from 1pm to 1am and Sunday from 1pm to midnight. School holidays every day from 4pm to 1am except Sunday from 2pm to 1am. Concerts (rock and blues on Thursday evenings from October to May).

The vintage decor, its wooded furniture and its warm atmosphere, make Private Pub very appreciable. But people meet here especially for all these blond, brown or red beers. They are all there! The young waiters advise you on the beers, whiskies and on the impressive beer-based cocktail and other spirits menu. Every Thursday, from 9: 30pm, concerts are organised: jazz, swing, rock... Local or from elsewhere groups share the stage, in a friendly atmosphere (sometimes, the music can be too loud). Another disadvantage, it is sometimes difficult to find a seat on the banquettes and other armchairs, but it is always possible to settle at the bar. The advantage for bowlers is that they can wait until a track becomes available that they are called while enjoying their drink inside or right on the track. Bowling lovers can also watch the alleys directly from the pub. Our favourite is their after-work, this friendly event to discover the 16 wines of our region. The pub has a conservation window that allows you to serve yourself a glass of wine from 3 cl to 12 cl with a prepaid card. This tasting is accompanied by nice, varied appetizers and deli meats, the whole is at will and offered.

Shopping

■ VUE SUR COURS

5 bis, cours Mirabeau
✆ 06 52 68 48 20
www.vuesurcours.com
contact@vuesurcours.com

Open from Wednesday to Saturday from 11: 30am to 6pm; Sunday from 10 am to 1 pm. Or by appointment... for the most popular ones!

Under the initiative of Claude, the creator of the address, the gallery-shop Vue sur Cours took place in Narbonne 4 years ago, setting with her a new concept in the region. Within walking distance from the covered markets and opposite Canal de la Robine, an apartment has been fully renovated to create the cosy and intimate atmosphere of this art gallery of which the idea is to highlight the best artists in the area. Here, you will find creations in all forms: paintings, photographs, sculptures, ceramics, contemporary jewelry, bags and accessories, textile, concrete or cardboard furniture, hats, but also creations for children. Do you want to offer a pretty, unique and artistic gift, or to pamper yourself? All you need to do is climbing the few steps to reach this place. Please, note that the creators presented change every three months, and that various events are planned; do not hesitate to visit the website. More than a year after its installation, Vue sur Cours has become a must-visit place for art lovers with new exhibitions such as Muriel Persil's ceramic works that combine poetry, floral decorations and delight.

Gourmet Basket

■ LA CAVE DE L'AMPHORE

19, avenue du Maréchal-de-Lattre-de-Tassigny
✆ 04 68 32 46 34
www.langovino.fr
cavedelamphore@orange.fr

Open Monday to Saturday from 9am to 8pm; Sunday from 10am to 1pm. Cheques not accepted.

If you are looking for a cellar and a delicatessen, La Cave de l'Amphore should meet your expectations. Located in the heart of the neighborhood of Cité, close to Rond-Point de la Révolution, Jocelyne Lardé's cellar contains small treasures. Are you rather red wine, white or rosé, do you like them with much roundness, aged in oak barrels or light? Express your wishes and you will be better guided according to your tastes and desires. The selection of the wines is rigorous, no false notes among the wines of the region, Corbières, Fitou, Clape, Minervois-Faugères, Cabardes, Malepère and beautiful bottles in Alsace, Bourgogne, Bordeaux, Cote du Rhône... We also love the wide choice of whisky, rum, Armagnac... and champagne you will say, well there are some and good ones! And to complement all this, a beautiful selection of salted and sweet gourmet products. An address very popular among Narbonne residents, both for an exceptional gift and for a daily purchase, or simply for these tasting workshops whisky, rum and champagne, every Friday evening. We also love the little corner of good bargains, the pump wine of Domaine de Longueroche (Corbières) and the sound advice of the team.

■ LA FERME COTÉ PRODUCTEURS

1, rue Panhard
✆ 04 68 41 75 19

♿

Open Monday to Saturday from 9am to 1pm and from 3pm to 7pm.

Are you a locavore, or do you simply love the good products of the region? Go to La Ferme Côté Producteurs: here, we promote short tours and local products. A real mini-market, you will find everything you need: meat, fish, fruit and vegetables, honey, biscuits, soap, but also finer products: foie gras, dry duck sausage plain or with Espelette pepper, wines... Discover also the pasta of Lasbordes, the melons of Coursan or the pumpkins of Ouveillan (according to the season), the cheeses of Corbières or the peppers of the Garden of Clairette, their pastries, or the soups of Peyriac. All the products on sale in this shop come from the Aude and the Pyrénées Orientales, so it's ecological and economical, but it's also a good taste plan when the products are of superior quality. A good plan for the planet and the taste buds! Numerous tastings are organised: ask for more information. In a zero-waste approach, remember to bring your fabric bag with you.

■ FROMAGERIE LE HALOIR

Les Halles
✆ 04 68 32 10 01
nabonnefab@free.fr

Open Tuesday to Sunday from 7am to 1pm.

Located in the famous Narbonne market, the Haloir makes you discover the best cheeses from the region but also from France and elsewhere! Rather cow's milk? goat's milk? sheep's milk? Soft or hard cheese, pasteurized or not, here there is something for every taste and every palate. Goupil has a soft spot for fresh goat cheese and truffled Brie and what about Comté and Tomme with Berry flowers... a delight! Fabienne and Bernard Nabonne also offer quince paste (without colouring or preservatives!), butter, Italian cheeses, homemade whipped cream, cottage cheese sold by the ladle and superb "aperitif" trays to order. A very popular address for amateurs, where the welcome is always courteous and professional, so don't deprive yourself of it!

Wines & Spirits

■ L'ANTRE DE L'ÉCHOPPE

4, rue Benjamin-Crémieux
✆ 04 68 91 67 92
echoppemedievale@wanadoo.fr

Open Thursday and Friday from 6: 15 pm to 1 am. Price range from 2 € to 5 €.

L'Antre de l'Echoppe – both factory and beer tavern – is just steps from Echoppe Médiévale, right next to Place des Quatre-Fontaines in the pedestrian city center of Narbonne. You will be surprised by the place, once you are through the door, you need to go down a few steps to discover a completely atypical dining room in the basement. For nearly 9 years, Renaud and Céline have been welcoming you with conviviality and love for work well done! Vault, exposed stones, vats, board games and a lot of beers. Twelve draught beers are offered as well as mead wines, organic juice and soft juice. Here, organic and local are favored, but there are also more classical beers. A crush for La Fée Bistande both for its legendary name and for its taste. When the place turns into tavern, it is possible to have a pizza delivered at your home or come with your meal. If you do not come for the aperitif, you can also take a guided tour and discover the history of the place and also the techniques of making beer. Very instructive! Smart information: no telephone network at L'Antre, claustrophobic people should refrain from coming on busy days.

V AND B
Forum Sud
Chemin du Quatourze
Road to Perpignan
✆ 04 68 58 42 59
www.VandB.fr
narbonne@vandb.fr
♿

Open Monday from 3 to 8 pm; Tuesday and Wednesday from 10 to 12: 30 am and 2: 30pm to 8 pm; Thursday to Saturday from 10 to 12: 30 am and 2: 30pm to 8: 30 pm. Tapas plate 5 € (Iberian charcuterie and cheese...).
V& B "(Vi) and (Bi)" which means "Vins et Bières (Wines and Beers)" is a concept offering the sale of alcohol to take away or to consume on site in a pleasant brick setting with a wine "cellar", beer cases, barrels and a very large bar. With no less than 400 beers listed, from the most ordinary to the most unlikely, it is not easy to make a choice, this is where Hortense and her team come in to guide you as best as possible. Recently, V&B has positioned itself as a discoverer of rare pearls: a team travels the roads of France and Europe with the sole aim of bringing back small treasures: microbrewery beers called "craft beer", wines from "small" independent producers, the opportunity to impress your friends who love beers or wines! V& B is also a very popular place after a good day's work, an "afterwork" that is now a must in Narbonne where you will be offered boards of Iberian charcuterie, cheese and tapas to accompany your drink. Note the Friday evenings (2 per month) from 7pm to 10pm, theme evenings, concerts, sports broadcasts, beer, rosé, primeur festivals... and the must-attend event: St. Patrick's Day in March. Finally, every Thursday is tapas night, and on Tuesdays: Happy craft or Happy wine evenings. In short, great moments in perspective.

Markets

LES HALLES DE NARBONNE
1, boulevard Docteur-Ferroul
✆ 04 68 32 63 99
www.narbonne.halles.fr
leshalles.narbonne@wanadoo.fr
Open from 7am to 1pm. Open every day. Even on Christmas Eve and New Year's Day. Monday is a minimum service day.
From 7am, the halls are busy. On the stalls, the best products of the region are installed. This metal building, in the Baltard style, was completed in 1901. Today, the halls are home to nearly 70 food shops: pork butchers, butchers, pastry chefs, bars, tapas, market gardeners, tripe growers, poultry farmers, pizza makers, florists, caterers, wine merchants, cheese makers, restaurants... Every day, it's lively, especially on Thursdays and Sundays. You can fill your basket, but you can also have breakfast, an aperitif, lunch... All the soul of Narbonne!

MARCHÉS DE PLEIN AIR
www.narbonne.fr/marches-foires
A pleasant atmosphere, fragrances, colors... our outdoor markets are numerous. These different merchants settled on both sides of the Robine. On Promenade des Barques and Cours Mirabeau (7am to 6pm on Thursday and 7am to 2pm every Sunday) at Plan Saint-Paul, every Thursday until 1pm, opposite the hospital, you will find our producers of fruit, vegetables, shellfish, butchery and delicatessen. Every Tuesday morning, at the parking lot of La Charité, second-hand clothes market. Every Saturday morning (8am to 1pm), at Place du Forum, you have the organic market, with quality and local products (temporarily moved to Place de l'Hôtel de Ville during the work). Every day in the covered halls in the city center. In addition, each summer, at the beginning of August, a big sell-off is held in the city center which has all the shops in the area and many stallholders in a festive atmosphere. In December, Christmas market is held on the Barques and offers many stands that are open every day: hot drinks, waffles, pancakes, arts and crafts... These are the terroir's friendly events you should not miss.

In the surroundings

Armissan

DOMAINE SARRAT DE GOUNDY – WINE ESTATE AND TABLE
46, avenue de Narbonne
✆ 04 68 45 30 68
www.sarratdegoundy.fr/
contact@sarratdegoundy.fr

At the entrance of the village of Vinassan.

From June 13 to September 15. Open from Wednesday to Saturday evenings. Single menu at 37 €. Wine at cellar prices. Tapas from 6 € to 15 €. Various grills.

Do you know the principle of winegrower restaurants? Olivier vigneron welcomes you in his "so chic" cellar with a contemporary and vintage atmosphere, the decoration is neat 10 minutes away from Narbonne – very nice terrace! Domaine Sarrat de Goundy is a unique place on the Narbonnais, a wine estate offering a beautiful range of wines from white vintage "Jolies Mômes" to the "Petits Canons" in 3 colours, all light and aromatic, easy to drink and so perfect for aperitifs. For those who love red wines, we recommend La Combe au Louves, a wonder and undeniably the "prestige" vintage of the estate. Come and dine there with 2 different formulas: either tapas or the unique menu which will always include a grill (octopus, T-bone steak...). Not to be missed is the Wednesday evening package which will allow you to visit the estate's vineyards in Massif de la Clape, enjoy a tasting, return to the cellar and visit the cellar to finish with a food and wine pairing meal for €50.

Bizanet ★

■ J'EMMES LES MINÉRAUX ★★

RD 613
Domaine de la Source
✆ 04 68 42 14 46
www.jemmes.fr

Low season: open every day from 10am to 12pm and from 2pm to 7pm. July and August: every day from 10am to 7pm. Free exhibition and screening. Mini golf: €5. Treasure beach: €2,50. Shop.

Françoise and Norbert settled in an old wine cellar more than 10 years ago to share their passion for minerals and crystals. Here, you will discover different areas dedicated to the stones of the world with the largest exhibition of amethysts in France and a tour of the old wine vats with plays of light that make the precious crystals sparkle. Then, you can take a seat in the projection room where you will be offered films on the origin and extraction of minerals... You can end the tour with a visit to the shop where you will of course find jewellery, blocks of rough stones cut or not, fountains, statues and more than 250 varieties of stones, offered to lovers of lithotherapy... (also on sale on www.géode.com). Still for the shop, you will discover the "singing bowls", they are crystal bowls that emit sounds... bewitching... Concerts are regularly given, ask for dates on their website (www.jemmes.fr). Finally, to prolong this moment, well kept and landscaped exteriors are at your disposal as well as a miniature golf course (€5) and, for children (under 10 years old), a treasure beach (€2.50) where a real gold nugget, rough diamonds and fine stones are hidden! An address to discover with your family where you can even have a picnic on the spot (snack in July and August)!

Narbonne-Plage

■ OFFICE DE TOURISME – ANNEXE DE NARBONNE-PLAGE

Avenue des Vacances
✆ 04 68 49 84 86
www.narbonne-tourisme.com
ot.narbonneplage@mairie-narbonne.fr

Qualité Tourisme. Open from April 1st to September 30th. From 1st July to 31st August: open every day from 9am to 7pm. From 1st April to 30th June and from 1st to 30th September from 10am to 12:30pm and from 1:30pm to 6pm, Monday to Saturday. Closed on Sundays except during events.

The Tourist Office of Narbonne-Plage welcomes you from April 1st to September 30th. You will find all the information you need to have a pleasant stay in the resort. At your service: an interactive information terminal accessible, 7 days a week, 24 hours a day outside. wi-fi connection (1h/day).

■ AQUAJET

Route de Gruissan
✆ 04 68 49 33 61
www.aquajetnarbonne.com
contact@aquajetnarbonne.com

Open from 16 June to 2 September. From 16/06 to 01/07: open only on weekends and Wednesdays. Adult: 15 € (and 25 € with unlimited access to water-jump). Children (up to 4 years old): 6 €. Free for babies. Free parking. Transat free of charge. Snack bar on site.

Palm trees, tropical plants, a hectare of greenery, all facing the sea, welcome to the unmissable amusement park narbonnais. A change of scenery and good time guaranteed, Aquajet offers multiple water games with water slides: the Anaconda, the Rapido or the Boa, and the two slides created in 2016: the Canaïma and the Salto Angel, which can accommodate up to four people at the same time! Since 2019, there are new features with 6 water jumping ramps at 8, 10 and 12 meters and their 300 m^2 pool! For the little ones, two swimming pools and a paddling pool secured by lifeguards, four inflatable playgrounds, trampolines and waterless playgrounds are proposed. While the children are having fun, parents can enjoy the deckchairs and the brand new solarium sheltered from the wind and facing the sea. Finally, for a meal or a snack, you will find picnic areas and a snack bar on site. In the winter, the park gets a makeover to offer you something new every time it reopens! We like the freedom that this park offers with the possibility to leave the park without any problem all day long and the free deckchairs.

■ ENTRE MER ET GARRIGUE

2, avenue du Languedoc
✆ 09 83 77 04 15
bruno.ruppert712@gmail.com

♿

Open all year round. Closed in January. Low season: Monday to Friday evening; Saturday lunch and dinner. High season: every day for lunch and dinner. Open for lunch on reservation in low season – High season from Easter to October. Single menu at 28 €. Children's menu: 12 €. Dish of the day: 13 €. Wine by the glass. Mussels with homemade french fries 10 €. Holiday vouchers, Restaurant vouchers. Groups welcome (on reservation). Terrace. Air conditioning.

What we like here is the originality of the cuisine, the chef starts from the principle that when you go to eat in a restaurant you have to find something else on your plate that you can eat at home. Bruno masters the art of matching seafood products with those of the land spiced up with spices from here and there, you may find touches of Asia, a country he loves. For example, you will enjoy roast mackerel, rolled pork belly with soy milk espuma or wolffish stuffed with squid ink and coconut-chorizo milk sauce... The fish comes from the local fishing industry. Here we opt for the short circuits, then the locavores-carnivores will revel in a beautiful bull steak with sangria sauce from the nearby Tournebelle manade. Other specialities of the chef: revisit the great classics, such as the Paris-Brest which you will find here under the name of Paris-Narbonne plage. The wines are local and the emphasis is on clape wines. A pretty bistronomic table to discover.

Lifeguard station, Narbonne-Plage.

■ RESTAURANT DE LA CLAPE

4, rue des Fleurs
✆ 04 68 49 80 15
www.restaurant-delaclape-narbonne.fr
hoteldelaclape@gmail.com

♿

Logis. Closed from December 15 to March 15. Low season: open from Monday to Saturday evenings. High season: every day in the evening. Sunday brunch at lunchtime from June to September. Reservation recommended. Menus from €35 to €50. A la carte menu: about €35. Children's menu: €10. Wine by the glass. Menu that changes according to seasons/arrivals. American Express. Reception of groups (on reservation). Baby chairs. Terrace.

This restaurant with its sheltered patio offers a cuisine that smells of the sun, the dishes are prepared in a "dietetic" way, both original and generous like grilled fish or scallops... Everything here is homemade, the tapenade and garlic are made according to the recipes of the country, no frozen food, but a market cuisine, accompanied by a judicious selection of wines from the region. In addition, Corinne and Nicolas have taken a real ecological approach throughout the establishment, we welcome the initiative! If you wish to continue your stay or not take the road after a good dinner, the 6 suites and 24 rooms of the Logis de France hotel are waiting for you... just like the swimming pool. From €51 the room and €148 the suite with terrace.

■ LA TERRASSE DE SÔ

1, boulevard du Front de Mer
✆ 04 68 75 09 29

♿

Open all year round. Low season: Sunday, Monday and Thursday for lunch; Friday and Saturday for lunch and dinner. High season: daily for lunch and dinner. Single menu at 26,90 €. Lunch formula: 15,90 € (starter + main course or main course + dessert. Full formula: 18,90 €). Groups welcome.

The restaurant La Terrasse de Sô is the ideal place if you want a table with a view of the Grande Bleue. The establishment is recent and everything has been thought of to make the customers feel good. La Terrasse de Sô is open all year round (which is rare in Narbonne beach)

and therefore seducing the local clientele in search of good food is a priority. The setting is pleasant and refined, whether you are in the dining room or on the terrace (veranda), you will enjoy modern and comfortable furniture. In the kitchen, only fresh products are prepared and everything is homemade (guaranteed). Here, you will choose your slate formula which evolves according to the market and the season. The seafood products have the beautiful share with for example oysters au gratin, tuna in tartare or tataki decorated for one with fresh fruits and for the other with fresh herbs and ginger-soya sauce. Asian and oriental inspirations punctuate the menu with, for example, prawns in curry sauce or meats prepared in a tagine style. To accompany your meal, a fine selection of La Clape wines is offered. The welcome is perfect and the value for money is undeniable.

The little extra: in summer, you will enjoy the concerts organised by the town as the stage is just opposite as well as the fireworks on July 14th.

HÔTEL DE LA CLAPE

4, rue des Fleurs
✆ 04 68 49 80 15
www.hoteldelaclape.com
resa@hoteldelaclape.com

Sud de France quality. European Ecolabel. Logis. Quality Tourism. Open from mid-March to mid-December. 24 rooms (and 6 suites). Double room from 51 € to 95 €; triple room from 78.50 € to 117 €; suite from 95 € to 165 €. Half-board (from €54). Buffet breakfast: €10. Extra bed: 12 €. Parking. Communicating rooms for 4 or 5. American Express, Cheque Vacances. Tourism & Handicap Label. 2 casseroles. Animals accepted (5 €). Cleaning service. Restaurant.

Petit Futé recommends this hotel-restaurant every year because it makes you feel good. The hotel is well sheltered from the wind, which is not insignificant in the department and the beach 5 minute walk away. The rooms are structured around a patio with a Mediterranean atmosphere, it is at your disposal all day long for a relaxing break by the small swimming pool, to immerse yourself in your novel or for lunch or dinner. No fuss for the classic rooms, they are simple, clean and quiet. The six suites take you somewhere in the East, they are comfortable, air-conditioned and equipped with canopy beds and beautiful bathrooms with walk-in showers. We recommend the restaurant of the address where a traditional homemade cuisine made from fresh produce will be served. After a small cocktail with appetizers, you can enjoy, for example, a tartare of oceans with citrus fruits, frogs' legs garnished with parsley (only on order) and on a plate, grilled fish or beautiful pieces of meat, all accompanied by finely selected wines from the region. Corinne and Nicolas' welcome is very courteous, and they will be able to advise you on the most beautiful spots in the surrounding areas. Hôtel de la Clape is part of an ecological and responsible approach and we welcome them!

Marina, Narbonne-Plage.

■ CAMPING LA FALAISE – TOHAPI
8, Avenue des Vacances
✆ 04 30 05 29 85
www.camping-falaise-narbonne.fr/

Open from 4 April to 27 September 2020. Reservation imperative. Reception until 7pm. Guarded 24 hours a day (in season). 393 pitches. Exposure: shaded. Relief: flat. Pitch + vehicle (with 6 A) from 26 € to 50 €. Pitch + vehicle from 24 € to 48 €. Mobile homes for 4 to 6 people from 207 € to 1 756 € per week. Tourist tax: 0,40 € (per day and per adult person). Games for children. Bathroom for babies. Animals accepted (from 1,60 € to 2,10 €). Area for camper vans. Free Wifi.

The children are kings: aquatic area with swimming pool, water park with slides, pool and games for children. A children's club and a new wooden playground are waiting for little children. Adults are not forgotten with a wellness area with a whirlpool bath, sauna, hammam and massages. Park your vehicle and let yourself be carried away, enjoy your holiday! La Falaise is a 2-star Tohapi campsite 300 meters away from the beach easily accessible on foot! This campsite has several advantages: a very friendly, family, peaceful welcome, proximity, shaded, large surface area, spacious pitches, recent mobile homes, brandnew Ecoluxe tents and is located a stone's throw from all the amenities of Narbonne-Plage like the shops, the tourist office and all the resort's activities.

■ L'ENSOLEILLADE
Boulevard de la Méditerranée
✆ 04 68 49 82 83

Open every day and on public holidays from 8: 30 am to 1: 30 pm and from 4: 30 pm. Open from Easter to mid-September. Open on Sundays.

With its red and yellow facade, hard to miss it, L'Ensoleillade is Narbonne Plage's unmissable delicatessen shop. For more than 15 years, Remy Rodriguez has been putting the small dishes in the big ones to delight loyal customers and tourists passing through. Of course, you will find the great classics of this type of business here, but what we like are the house specialities: boles de picolat (Catalan speciality), paella, bouillabaisse (on order) and gardiane de baureau (bull stew). Barbecue lovers will have a choice with, among others, Toulouse sausage made on the spot, marinated skewers, beef made in France, local lamb and matured rack of beef. Some delicatessen products are offered such as the excellent Granhota vinegars made next to Narbonne or specialities cooked in jars and Occitan charcuteries. A very good address that you will also find in the covered market of Saint-Pierre-la-Mer.

■ AQUAJET
Route de Gruissan
✆ 04 68 49 33 61
www.aquajetnarbonne.com
contact@aquajetnarbonne.com

Open from 16 June to 2 September inclusive. From 16/06 to 01/07: open only weekends and Wednesdays. Open from 10am to 7pm. 6 € for children under 4 years old, free for babies. Entrance: 15 € (and 25 € with unlimited access to the new slides (water jump)). Cheques not accepted. Free parking. Baby area free. Baby space. Shaded area. Snack bar on site.

Palm trees, tropical plants, a hectare of greenery, all facing the sea, welcome in the amusement park in Narbonne. A change of scenery and a good time guaranteed for everyone, whether you come with your family or for young people in search of thrills. Aquajet offers multiple water games including water slides: the Anaconda, the Rapido or the Boa, and the two slides created in 2016: the Canaïma and the Salto Angel for up to four people at the same time! Since 2019, there are new features with 6 water jumping ramps at 8, 10 and 12 meters and their 300 m^2 pool! For the little ones, two swimming pools and a paddling pool secured by lifeguards, inflatable playgrounds, trampolines and games are offered. While the children are having fun, parents can enjoy the deck-chairs and the completely rebuilt swimming pool and the brand new solarium sheltered from the wind and facing the sea. There is also a new "sweet bar" where pancakes and waffles are served. The snack corner and picnic areas are at the disposal of the guests. Plan the day so that you can make the most of the activities.

We like: Once your bracelet is placed on your wrist, you can come and go as you please during the day, you can leave the park freely to go for example to take a dip in the sea.

To know more: There is no age limit to enjoy the slides (except water-jump) as long as the youngest are accompanied by their parents.

Salles-d'Aude

L'ARDOISE – CUISINE LIBRE

50, avenue de Fleury
✆ 07 69 72 69 93
audrey.viel@live.fr

Open all year round. Low season: from Wednesday to Sunday for lunch and dinner. High season: every day in the evening from 7pm to 10pm; Friday to Sunday for lunch. Single menu at 25,50 € (discovery menu starter + main course + dessert or 19,50 starter + main course or main course + dessert). Children's menu: 9,50 € (made with fresh products). Wine by the glass. Suggestions among a dozen dishes from 14€ to 22€. Garden. Terrace.

If you want a true good plan that combines all the ingredients for a successful meal, book a table at L'Ardoise! Whether or not you pass through Salles-d'Aude, Ardoise is worth a visit! A resolutely vintage atmosphere inside and out with furniture from different periods. But what we appreciate most of all is Audrey's good food. The facetious (and professional) Kako will propose you the menu of the day or the discovery formula which is renewed every 3 weeks to follow the local productions, the seasons, but also the Chef's creativity. Traditions, creations, exoticism and fresh products are à la carte. During our last visit (in November), we chose to come on a Wednesday evening because that evening is cheese! Raclette, fondue, tartiflette and other cheeses in the oven accompanied by charcuterie, green salad... a delight (in low season only). But the particularity of L'Ardoise is that you will be offered a "free kitchen" which means "no labels" with a menu that is constantly evolving! Audrey likes to make her clients travel by offering them dishes from other countries. Greece was on the menu a few weeks ago, followed by Portuguese specialities and the next destination announced is Italy (follow the program on their Facebook page). Audrey's cuisine is precise, generous and tasty, and Kako's welcome deserves a nod... In L'Ardoise, you can enjoy yourself, discover new flavours in a relaxed atmosphere. This year le Petit Futé fell under the spell again!

Vinassan

CHATEAU DE MARMORIERES

Route de Fleury
✆ 04 68 45 23 64
www.marmorieres.com
marmorieres@orange.fr

Open Monday to Friday from 10am to 5: 45pm. Possibility of booking events / meeting room and tasting. Delivery possible.

Château de Marmorières, the largest wine estate in La Clape covering 150 hectares, is well known to lovers of Languedoc wines. Since 1826, it has been the family estate of the Woillemont family, whose ancestor was the originator of this same appellation. At the bend in the road, surrounded by vines in the heart of Mediterranean flora, the land blessed by the gods of the Château de Marmorières can be seen. A formidable tasting cellar awaits you amidst olive trees, the scents of the garrigue, sea spray and peacocks, the hosts of the place. In 2005, a former commandery of the Order of Malta (12th century) and its vineyard located on the heights of Saint-Pierre-la-Mer, joined the possessions of the Woillemont family, in the heart of the Clape massif, overlooking the Mediterranean. Victor Hugo used to say that "God only made water, but man made wine". Indeed, at first confidential, then quickly recognised unanimously and internationally, the wines produced and matured today by Ombline and Jehan de Woillemont, the 8th generation of winegrowers, are the fruit of hard work, of a passion for this ancestral land at every moment. Their vineyard, certified "High Environmental Value", allows them to highlight a particular aromatic exaltation, through the twenty or so grape varieties produced, a rare complexity of blending. Unanimous rewards crown their vintages, from the "Marquis de Raymond", of great elegance, with notes of red fruits and spices perfectly mastered, to the white cuvée "Les Pinèdes" mineral and aromatic. Unique wines to discover and appreciate without any moderation.

▶ Every year in April, **Château de Marmorières** takes part in the "Ma vigne en musique" festival and hosts a concert on the estate followed by a wine tasting session.

CHEZ PIERROT

48, rue du Four-à-Chaux
✆ 04 68 45 35 10
www.chez-pierrot.fr
chezpierrot@orange.fr

Open from June 11 to September 6. Open every day in the evening; weekends and holidays for both lunch and dinner. Without reservation. À la carte menu: 18€ approximately. Children's menu: 5€ (the dish). Wine by the glass. Pizzas from 7.50€ to 11.40€ – Salads XL 11.70€ to 13.30€ – Burgers 13.50€ single 17.50€ double. Groups welcome (on reservation). Baby chairs. Garden. Terrace. Take away sale. Animations.

It was grandfather Pierrot Soulé who created Chez Pierrot. Today, this restaurant, which opened 43 years ago, is a veritable institution run by the third and fourth generation. Chez Pierrot is a huge open restaurant with a "guinguette" spirit set in a pine forest that can serve up to 1,200 covers a day in high season, with fast service provided by a hundred seasonal workers! We appreciate the place under the pines, the inflatable games for the children, so parents can take their time while the little ones have fun! But where Pierrot is strong, it is that in addition to having fun, we enjoy it despite the number of meals served! The menu improves every year, in addition to the must-eat pizzas and mussels that have made their success, we also like salads (XL or XS), beef tartare, fish-based dishes, burgers, gargantuan pancakes, pasta, wood-fired grills and desserts that will satisfy even the most demanding gourmets... to liven up your meal, Gérard Bertrand wines are a must. The address is very popular with the people of Narbonne from the opening in June and with holidaymakers passing through, and for good reason: here, it's good, it's festive, it's cheap and it's a paradise for children. An atypical address where you always have a good time.

PORT-LA-NOUVELLE ★

OFFICE DE TOURISME
1, place Paul-Valéry ✆ 04 68 48 00 51

Qualité Tourisme. Low season: open from Monday to Friday from 10am to 1pm and from 2pm to 5pm. High season: every day from 9am to 7pm. And during the holidays of all Saints' Day, open on Saturday from 10 am to 1 pm and from 2 pm to 5 pm. From 1st April to 31st May: Monday to Saturday from 9am to 1pm and 2pm to 6pm, Sunday and public holidays from 9am to 1pm. From 1 to 30 June and from 1 to 30 September: Monday to Sunday from 9am to 6pm. Tourism & Handicap Label.

The tourist office is located in front of the Mediterranean Sea. An ideal setting to advise you on your stay in this friendly seaside resort of La Narbonnaise Surprenante Méditerranée. Don't hesitate to come and meet our stay advisers, they will give you tailor-made advice to organise your fantastic holidays: beaches, the Robine canal, nature walks in the Regional Nature Reserve, discovery of charming villages and vineyards, etc. On site, make the most of the free Wifi and varied documentation.

BATEAU LE CATHARE
parking island Sainte lucie ✆ 07 82 09 13 51
https://bateauxcanalmidi.com
contact@bateauxcanalmidi.com

Cruises from 29/06 to 30/08. Open every day. Departures at 11: 15am and 2: 45pm. Free up to 3 years old. Adult: 14 €. Child (from 4 to 11 years old): 8 €. Credit card not accepted. Wheelchair: on request. Guided tour.

Embark aboard the *Cathare* – a 43-passenger panoramic boat – from the car park on Saint Lucia Island and discover the regional nature reserve of Saint Lucia Island via the La Robine canal. Between sea, pond and canal, during 2 hours, you will pass a lock and discover exceptional landscapes. Smart tip: take your picnic, go down to Saint Lucia and don't come back on the next boat! The return time must be decided when you buy your ticket. Possibility of privatizing the boat with the organization of a dinner aperitif to live unforgettable moments with friends or family.

Sightseeing

L'ILE DE SAINTE-LUCIE
Office de tourisme ✆ 04 68 48 00 51

The access can be closed in case of major fire risk.

The Regional Nature Reserve of Saint Lucia, a site protected by the Conservatoire du littoral, is an area of almost wild nature. It is located in Port-la-Nouvelle, where it offers a variety of natural environments and magnificent landscapes: huge and wild beach of the Vieille Nouvelle, old salt marsh and Saint Lucia island, covered with scrubland and pine trees. It offers a splendid view of the lagoons of Ayrolle, Bages-Sigean and the surrounding mountains. Managed by the Narbonnaise Regional Nature Park in the Mediterranean and the municipality of Port la Nouvelle, the island has been developed to be open to the public. A car park is located less than 500 metres from the lock, the only access to the island. We advise you to climb up to the Saint-Antoine rock, which offers an exceptional view of Narbonne, Gruissan and its ponds, to discover this land on a guided tour, where its rich past will be revealed to you, namely more than 20 centuries of human occupation, as shown by the ruins of the salt workers' canteen, the buildings of the wine estate and the remains of a church. So, the magic of the "thousand scents" island will immerse you in its ancient splendor! Two circuits of 3 and 6 kilometres allow a walk (bring walking shoes) or mountain biking in a unique setting. In order to protect the area from fire danger, access to the island is sometimes prohibited during the summer season and during extreme winds. For your safety and the beauty of the area, please follow the instructions. Dogs are not allowed on the island.

Port-la Nouvelle beach.

Knife & Fork

L'ADRESSE
10, rue Roger-Rapin ✆ 04 68 45 39 35

Open all year round. Low season: Monday and Tuesday for lunch; Thursday to Saturday for lunch and dinner. High season: Monday and Tuesday for lunch; Wednesday to Saturday for lunch and dinner. Menu: about 25 €. Children's menu: 9 € (up to 10 years old). Lunch formula: 14 € (for lunch and excluding weekends [starter+main course+dessert+glass of wine or coffee]). Wine by the glass. Terrace.

What a nice surprise when we walked through the door of this restaurant. The exterior does not look like much, but when you go through the front door you discover a very pleasant interior, decorated in a modern, vintage and refined spirit. At the helm of this restaurant, Ong (the cook) and Vincent (the wine expert) wanted this place to reflect their image, a place where conviviality, good humour and sincerity are the order of the day. While Vincent is at the bar serving the aperitif to the first customer, Ong is busy in his open kitchen. Here, we offer you a semi-local, semi-asiatic cuisine, the dishes are copious, difficult to combine starter and main course and dessert unless you are a great eater. Among the specialties of Ong, a dish is really unanimous: the sea bass (wolffish) in Thai way, allow 10 minutes of preparation since it is freshly cooked. More classic, the gourmet rib steak with its marrow bone, grilled pata negra breast and a fried egg, cuttlefish a la plancha and parsley, or the succulent beef wok. We highly recommend the assortment of spring rolls and samoussas! The lunch formula is perfect to vary the daily pleasures without spending much money. To perfect your meal, a very nice selection of wines from the region and elsewhere is offered to you, with this year again, some little marvels in the cellar. Let Vincent advise you, oenologist and enthusiast, he will surprise you for sure. A favourite address that really deserves the detour.

L'ARCHIBAR
22, rue de la République ✆ 04 68 70 69 27

Open all year round. Every day from 7am to 1am. Lunch formula: 14,90 €. Terrace. Animations.

Located on the square where the market is held, this emblematic bar of the village has become a trendy brasserie where Fabio and Jannice are waiting for you from the morning coffee. What we like here is that everyone, from the horse-racing enthusiast (PMU) to the company director, can find something to their liking. Jannice and Fabio, the two young bosses, are not short of ideas for building customer loyalty and attracting new customers. Settle down in the dining room, on the terrace or in the new space they call "Le Chalet" and enjoy the kitchen of the chef, Maxime. In the lunch formula with his dish of the day and his dessert, the chef will offer you small seasonal dishes, very copious and gourmet. Not to be missed under any circumstances: the chalet's pierrade to share (or not) with its 400 g of grilled meat, vegetables, chips and homemade hot sauces. Other Archibar musts, the cassoulet del Carmen, the chef's lamb mouse, roasted Camembert, squid à la plancha with parsley, turbot steak and beautiful salads. Everything is homemade here, so let yourself be tempted by the tapas menu: slates of charcuterie, "Simmental" entrecote, small pans like Basque squid... So as you don't miss any events, go to their Facebook page. An address where good mood rhymes with good food!

LE P'TIT BISTROT
1172, avenue de la Mer ✆ 04 30 37 47 22

Closed in June. Low season: open from Thursday to Monday for lunch and dinner. High season: daily for lunch and dinner. Reservation recommended. Menu: about 25 € (fondues and raclettes between 16,50 and 20 €). Children's menu: 10 €. Groups welcome. Terrace.

Marjorie Bergon, a native of Port la Nouvelle, has managed to make her restaurant an unmissable address on the port side of town. An adorable welcome, a warm chalet-style decoration, subdued lighting, a mezzanine reserved for children, so that parents can spend a quiet moment and a terrace. The cuisine served here is just as friendly with dishes that follow the seasons and specialties such as marrow bone grilled with coarse salt and garlic, snails in parsley, lamb shank roasted with thyme, a mussel menu ... For burger lovers, this is the place to be, the bread is homemade, the meat is of good quality and cheese is a pure delight! In the summer, you can enjoy the nice salads, they are delicious and generous or for the fish of the day from the nearby fish shop unless the bull's rib of about 400 g tempts you more... In winter, special mention for the Savoyard fondues and the raclettes declined in 6 different ways made with good cheese and served with quality charcuterie a treat! In short, a perfect address for an evening with family or friends.

Sleeping

Campsites

CAMPING CAP DU ROC
1700, route de La Palme
✆ 04 68 48 00 98
www.camping-cap-du-roc.com
capduroc@aol.com

Sud de France quality. Closed from October 1st to March 31st. Reservation essential. 90 pitches. Exposure: shady / half-shaded / sunny. Soil: grassy. Relief: flat. If you wish to buy a mobile home, different models are available. Pitch + vehicle + 2 persons (with 6 A) from 11 € to 32 €. Mobile homes for 2 to 8 people from 200 € to 995 € per week. Mobile-home "acapulcos" with private spa. Holiday vouchers. Booking fees 25 €. TV rental: 30 € per week or 5 € per day. Children's club. Games for children. Animals accepted (2 to 4 € per day). Area for camper vans. Wifi for a fee. Food service (snack bar). Animations.

The Cap du Roc campsite has more than one asset, already its location close to the sea and ideal starting point to discover the treasures of the Cathar country and the Pyrénées-Orientales without forgetting the African reserve of Sigean at about 15 minutes. But what we like most of all about Cap du Roc is the cliff that protects you from the north wind, which is particularly present in the department ... The campsite is very well maintained, the trees provide good shade in summer. Another strong point of the campsite: its playground with ping-pong tables, playground... and its aquatic area with a heated pool allowing the more sporty to do some laps in the morning and its slide very appreciated by the youngest. Clever tip: 4 mobile homes (for 4 people) equipped with private whirlpool baths (hygiene issue because the water is changed very regularly)... In high season, many activities are offered: dance, karaoke, bar... We like the colorful theme of the campsite like Mexico and the games of petanque which often end at the bar of the campsite for the winner's (or loser's) tour. A well-kept campsite where the management will bend over backwards to make your stay unforgettable.

Going Out

L'ARCHIBAR
22, rue de la République
✆ 04 68 70 69 27

Open all year round. Every day from 7am to 1am.

In addition to being a brasserie where you will be served quality homemade cuisine, L'Archibar is the place to be for a drink with friends.

We love the afterwork and especially the lively theme evenings. Fabio and Janice will always welcome you with the greatest smiles and will make you have a great time, Petit Futé's word!

Shopping

AUDE MARÉE – LE CHALUTIER

178, rue de la Mairie
✆ 04 68 70 14 59
aude-maree@orange.fr

Low season: open from Tuesday to Sunday from 8am to 12: 30pm. High season: Monday to Saturday from 8am to 12: 30pm and from 5pm to 7pm. Open all year round.

Not far from the town hall, it's one of the oldest fish stores in La Nouvelle. Now, Aude, José Micheau's granddaughter offers you a wide range of fresh fish from the Mediterranean, seafood platters from Canot, Sapinou and Chalutier, directly supplied from the fish market. Daily arrival. Takeaway seafood platter and tasting space.

In the surroundings

Portel-des-Corbières

CHÂTEAU DE LASTOURS

✆ 04 68 48 64 74
www.chateaudelastours.com
contact@chateaudelastours.com

Closed from December 23rd to January 5th. Low season: open from Monday to Friday from 9am to 12: 30pm and from 1: 30pm to 6pm. High season: every day and holidays from 10am to 1: 30pm and from 2: 30pm to 7pm. Restaurant telephone ✆ 04 68 48 64 77.

Château de Lastours is located in the heart of Massif des Corbières on the former communication route: Via Mercaderia which connected Narbonne to Spain in the 12th century. It was a rallying point for the lookout towers of Americ and Viala of Laurède that marked out the Domitian road dating from the 2nd century BC. This unique estate in Corbières stretches over 850 hectares, 100 of which are dedicated to vine and 10 hectares dedicated to olives. Since 2017, Château de Lastours has engaged in an approach of conversion to organic farming.

Its vineyard, which is based on the natural qualities of the site, located on terrace on steep hills and deep gorges, overlooks the sea. The cellar of 1,400 m^2 was designed in an energy efficient logic (natural light, isolation, half-buried cellar). All these elements sublimate its wines. You can follow the progress of the grape harvest and the wine making on the facebook page of the castle. The estate is also renowned for its 90 km of dirt tracks and its all terrain activities. For many years, the famous Paris-Dakar has made its way through. Today, those who love Quad, 4x4, motorbikes, electric bikes can practice these leisure activities in a pleasant natural setting and led by qualified instructors. And of course, here, wine is combined with wine tourism, its gourmet restaurant "La Bergerie" offers you a seasonal cuisine with its chef Jérémie Lefèvre and their cottages and guest rooms are ready to accomodate you upon reservation.

TERRA VINEA ★★

15, Chemin des Plâtrières
✆ 04 68 45 87 68

See page 16.

LA BERGERIE

Château de Lastours – Domaine de Lastours
✆ 04 68 48 64 77
contact@restaurantlabergerie.fr

♿

Closed in January. Low season: open from Wednesday to Saturday for lunch and dinner; Sunday for lunch. High season: Tuesday to Sunday. Reservation recommended. Menus from 27 € to 68 €. Children's menu: 12 €. Vegetarian menu: 20 €. Groups welcome.

The restaurant is located in the heart of the Estate of Lastours, a mythical place which hosted the Paris-Dakar pilotis a few years ago. It is in the old sheepfold of the castle, dating from the 12th century, that you can discover a traditional, varied and gourmet cuisine. The chef, Jérémy Lefèvre, serves the best of the local products that surround him like Cathar lamb, goat cheese from Thezan, honey from Jean Soulier de Portel... Whether you are a meat lover, fish lover or vegetarian, you will be delighted. We enjoyed the back of salmon cooked in the smoke of Beech, with apple in oil and cottage cheese in dill and then the excellent rack of roast pig honey, mustard and fondant potato or the holy stone roasted in saffron accompanied with lobster boulinade and a light aïoli, it is simply perfect! The strawberry raspberry shortbread and white chocolate ganache ended our meal marvellously but the gourmands will undoubtedly appreciate the chocolate soufflé with a caramel heart and salted butter... If you want to prolong this moment, Héléna who is the wife of Jérémy, the chef, offers superb guest rooms and a guest-house with designer decoration (see the Villas of Lastours Castle).

TERRA VINEA

15, Chemin des Plâtrières
✆ 04 68 45 87 68
www.terra-vinea.com
resaterravinea@gmail.com

♿

Low season: open every day from 10am to 5: 30pm. Closed from Christmas to the beginning of February.

The Terra Vinéa grocery store is a bit like the Ali Baba cavern of local products, but more spacious! Among the hundreds of products presented, you will find an enjoyable treat. There are, of course, the wines of the Rocbère cellar, such as the Grand Opera or the Thesaurus, which have been aged in barrels in the underground galleries under the shop, but also from producers of the whole region and even organic wine, it is ideal to accompany the artisanal preserves of Castelnaudary cassoulet, the sausage but also the different tapenades and olivades of the neighboring Pyrenees. Bird appetites may turn more towards teas, ceramics or soaps. All accessories related to wine are available on-site, one can find glass bottle caps in different forms, decanters and even "crocodile-style" isotherm handbags to transport your bottles!

© TERRA VINEA

Terra Vinea.

© Yan EVEN

Vue panoramique - Portel des Corbières.

© Yan EVEN

Chai of the Château de Lastours.

RELAIS DE TAMAROQUE
112, avenue des Corbières
✆ 06 73 91 20 13
www.relaisdetamaroque.com
contact@relaisdetamaroque.com

Gîtes de France. 5 bedrooms (including 3 suites with 2 bedrooms that can accommodate 4/5 people). Single room 75€; double room 90€; triple room 113€. Breakfast included. Extra bed: 20€. Closed parking included. Room for 4 persons 135€. Animals accepted (on request and with extra-cost). Free Wifi. Large relaxation room with TV, table football, board games, fridge, billiard room.

In Occitan, tamaroque means "the broken rock", so, this former post house takes place between river and mountain. At the entrance of the village, the establishment is ideally located to visit the beautiful country of Corbières. From this beautiful and large building with blue shutters, Brigitte and Jean-Luc made it a welcoming residence full of charm and a special soul. Perhaps it is the large volumes and the unique retro decoration, perhaps it is its dream location above the Berre gorges or simply the warm welcome of your hosts, in any case, you quickly feel good there. The rooms are spacious, personalized and comfortable. Like the whole house, they display a look of yesteryear, the furniture is carefully selected to create unique atmospheres. The Corbières room is the smallest but has a breathtaking view of Berre, the Jardin Secret suite is ideal for small families, just like the Vent Marin, in blue shades. In a very friendly spirit, the large common room with terrace is a meeting and exchange place around the billiards. The other privileged moment is the sharing of the generous breakfast in the dining room or, most importantly, on the terrace with its breathtaking view of the gorges. Brigitte's amazing and delicious jams, French toast and other little extra will be important for a gourmet breakfast. An address for those who love nature, mountain bike riding enthusiasts, moto enduro or hiking. Within walking distance from Terra Vinea, the African reserve and the 4x4 loop of Chateau de Lastours.

Sigean

At the foot of the Corbières massif, between garrigues and ponds, Sigean occupies a privileged geographical location: 5 kilometers from the sea and only 70 kilometers from the Pyrenees and Spain. This small town of Corbières is named after the Gallo-Roman era: the villa "Sejanum", important agricultural area. A beautiful spotlight on the region, following the opening in the seventies of the African Reserve. But Sigean has many other assets: Hiking and discovery trails, a renowned vineyard, a rich heritage with its seventeenth century church whose organ is classified and its old walls... Not to mention its unmissable site: the oppidum of Pech Maho, located on the bank of the Berre near the pond!

LIEU D'ART CONTEMPORAIN (LAC)
Hameau du Lac
1, rue de la Berre
✆ 04 68 48 83 62
https://lac-narbonne.art/

Closed from December to March. Closed from December to March except by appointment for schoolchildren. April – May: Open every day from 2pm to 6pm. Closed Tuesday – July to the end of September: every day from 3pm to 7pm. Closed Tuesday – October and November: Open on weekends from 2pm to 5pm. Free until 15 years old. Adult: 5 €.

In 1991, Piet Moget, a Dutch painter, and his daughter Layla fell under the charm of this old character wine cellar, in Corbières Maritimes. In this vast place, the most unexpected one, on two levels, they have organized contemporary exhibitions. It now houses a permanent collection particularly rich: works related to meetings of Olivier Debré, Dado, Matias Spescha, André Lote... and many other trends that have become flagship so far. The old vats have become small showrooms, ideal for confidential works. Each exhibition is accompanied by a selection of the collection, from Mondrian to today's creation. Visit the website for further information. We strongly recommend this stopover with wine flavors, in this cutting-edge place, where contemporary art takes its full dimension! At the end of 2015, Piet Moget died, leaving behind him and in the good hands of Layla, the LAC, but also many paintings and so many souvenirs for the premises: the art lover and painter liked to represent Port-la-Nouvelle. When the sky was gray, his canvas was always hung on his truck, and he held his brush with an expert hand.

LE POTAGER
28, avenue de Perpignan
✆ 04 68 48 42 76
www.restaurantsigean.com

Closed from October to March 31. Low season: open from Friday to Sunday for lunch and dinner. High season: Tuesday to Sunday for lunch and dinner. Reservation recommended. A la carte menu: about 30 €. Children's menu: 12 €. Lunch formula: 16 € (starter + main course or main course + dessert). Wine by the glass. On weekends: à la carte dishes. Groups welcome.

Behind the large walls of this former winegrower's building hides a small treasure. Past the patio where the large barbecue for the beautiful grills is located, you will cross the beautiful restaurant room with its fireplace and large zinc and, at the very end, a terrace overlooking the house's vegetable garden. Take the time to go around before eating so that you can see the vegetables you will later find on your plate... guaranteed appetizer! We like the neat decoration made by Christine where the art of mixing the modern, the old and the atypical (see the lustre of the patio) is of the most beautiful effect. In the plates, the vegetables from the garden, therefore, and, if they are lacking, it will be those from the neighbouring vegetable gardens, provided they are organic. The bright red tomatoes with fresh sheep's cheese and fine herbs are sublime, the vegetable escalivada from the sun and its basil pesto whet our appetites and, as a main course, try the mussels over a wood fire unless a nice grilled meat or the fish of the day (à la plancha) tempt you more. In low season, dishes that simmer, cassoulet, cranquette soup (small crabs), leg of lamb on string, etc. This restaurant has some nice surprises in store, including the Boutique du Potager: unique and colourful creations. An address really unlike any other to frequent without moderation!

■ **RESERVE AFRICAINE DE SIGEAN**
19, Chemin Hameau-du-Luc
RD 6009
✆ 04 68 48 20 20
www.reserveafricainesigean.fr
contact@reserveafricainesigean.fr

Open all year round. Low season: every day and public holidays from 9am to 4pm. High season: every day and public holidays from 9am to 6: 30pm. Free up to 4 years old. Adult: 32 €. Child (from 4 to 14 years old): 23 €. – Disabled rate: 13.50 €. Tourism & Handicap Label. Restaurant. Picnic area.

For 45 years, Réserve Africaine, a large wildlife park, has welcomed you to discover the world of wildlife! On board your car, then on foot, you will observe how animals feed, court, mate, raise their young, communicate with each other, adapt to their environment... Lions, zebras, wildebeests, giraffes, impalas, buffaloes, springboks, white rhinos, ostriches, cheetahs, African wild dogs, chimpanzees, meerkats, porcupines, wallabies, sitatungas, alligators, greater flamingos, pelicans, storks... Throughout your visit, you will discover more than 140 animal species that live on a vast 300-hectare estate. VIP guided tours are available upon prior reservation. Travel the safari car in a minibus with a Park guide who will introduce you to the animals of the Réserve africaine de Sigean. Smart Tip: buy your tickets on the internet and save €1 / person.

LA MAISON ROUGE 1852
1, avenue de Narbonne
✆ 04 68 48 20 29
www.lamaisonsigean.wordpress.com
lamaison1852@gmail.com

Open all year round. Every day from 6: 30am to 2am. Monday to Wednesday may close earlier. Animations. Concerts.

In Sigean, the inhabitants were surprised to see the Rotunda, a famous café over 30 years old, disappearing in favour of La maison 1852. Marcel, Dimitri changed everything. Red curtains and vintage club chairs have found their place. The stage, surmounted by an old piano, is the essential place in the room, which preserves its paintings and mouldings from the early 20th century. At the time, the place was a brothel. Today, music is in the spotlight with groups from Montpellier, Perpignan or Toulouse on a Friday evening every 15 days, from October to June: program on the facebook page. The atmosphere is warm, friendly, different beers and local wines are offered. Originality of the place, here you will only be served to drink, to eat, you can pick up to take away in the nearby restaurants and come and eat at La Maison 1852! In a few years, Dimitri imposed his style and atmosphere on Sigean. Every Thursday of the summer, the unmissable event is the "market mixx" evening with DJ, tapas, tatoo, oysters and vegetables. Dimitri wants his Maison to be a place for children and families and offers workshops for children on Sunday mornings.

■ **LA FERM'ATTITUDE**
16 ter, rue Marcelin-Albert
✆ 04 30 37 42 59

Open from Tuesday to Saturday from 9am to 12: 30pm and from 3pm to 6pm.

Ferm'Attitude is a producers' store located in Sigean. Here, you will find local produce, mainly from the Aude but also from Pyrénées-Orientales and Tarn. The vegetables are from Névian, Puichéric or Peyriac-de-Mer, and follow the course of the seasons and the climate. You will also find there the Carcassonne lemonades Pétillo of Boissons Ortiz, but also cold cuts, Tarn meat, milk products, honey and jams of Corbières and various kinds of pasta made in Lasbordes and recently, fresh bread and viennoiseries. The farm is run by Aude producers who offer quality products. A must for locavores and epicureans who are curious to taste local and quality products.

FROM PLACE TO PLACE

© Shen MENG – Adobe Stock

African Reserve of Sigean.

SAINT-PIERRE-LA-MER

Knife & Fork

■ L'ASTERIE

10 bis, rue du Rocher
✆ 04 68 49 14 04

Open all year round. Low season: Thursday to Sunday for lunch and dinner. High season: every day and holidays for lunch and dinner. Reservation recommended. Single menu at 22,50 €. Children's menu: 12,50 €. Wine by the glass. Fish on the slate. Chef's suggestion for lunch. Cheques not accepted. Groups welcome (upon reservation). Terrace. Take away sale.

Very small and charming, the restaurant L'Astérie owes its success to the cuisine of Mehdi and the good mood of Cathy, the two owners of the address. Griddled fish, the parillada (the key dish of the house, unmissable for those who love fish), the fisherman's pot or the fresh lobster (upon order in off season)... and yes, here, you eat fish and what a fish! Cathy will also offer you some good traditional delicious meals. Tapas with local deli meats and wine from the area. An address guests enjoy for the quality of the dishes served and the hostess' welcome which is always friendly.

■ LA BOUCHE'RIT

6, Avenue de la Mer
✆ 04 68 91 17 28

Open Monday to Saturday for lunch and dinner. Menu: about 35 €. Lunch formula: 17 € (starter / main course / dessert – 14.90 € starter / main course or main course / dessert). Tapas to share 18.90 €.

Are you familiar with the concept of the butcher's shop? Lovers of good meat, come and discover and taste at the Bouche'Rit in Saint Pierre la Mer. The meats are French -entrecôte, burger, steak tartare – but also baked camembert with homemade charcuterie and fries, farmhouse salad, The "pierrade" barrels with 400 gr of meat per person (beef, pork, lamb and poultry) will reserve you a nice evening with friends. Generous portions. Nice terrace away from the hustle and bustle of the resort. Concert and karaoke in summer. Reservation recommended in summer.

Leisure

■ GLISSE & KITE

Base de loisirs
Etangs de Pissevaches
✆ 04 68 49 22 31
www.glisseetkite.com
accueil@glisseetkite.com
Behind the municipal campsite of Pissevaches, not far from the motorhome area

From April 1st to October 31st (open from Easter to All Saints' Day). Closed from November 1st to March 30th. Open every day and on public holidays from 9am to 7pm. Nautical activities from 15 € / h for paddle and kayak rental. Restaurant.

Opened in 2013 by Géraldine and Christophe, located on the edge of the Pissevaches pond, you will be able to rent paddle, giant paddle, kayak, kitesurf equipment for free use in complete safety. Depending on the chosen activity, you will be at sea (kite and its beach park) or in the pond (ski lift). Glisse & Kite is well known in the kite surfing world that you will be able to practise here in 2h30 lessons or in small groups or even in autonomous and supervised navigation and for the less adventurous, try the tandem baptism. During the school holidays there are Optimist sailing courses for children, windsurfing and catamaran courses for children and adults. A ski lift park is also available for lessons or sessions, always with a friendly instructor. For the youngest from 6 years old, the towed buoy is waiting for them! Laughter guaranteed! Possibility to privatize the ski lift park for a birthday, a challenge with friends... Group welcome on reservation. A small restaurant awaits you on the spot from May to September, you can taste the famous homemade kite burger at the beach bar with panoramic view on the ponds. Family atmosphere where children, teenagers, adults and groups of friends get together.

Shopping

■ BUBBLE CAFÉ

Boulevard des Embruns
✆ 04 68 90 55 36

Open all year round. From 6: 30 am to 7 pm. In high season, closed at 2am.

Bubble Café is one of the few establishments open all year round in Saint-Pierre-la-Mer, summer and winter, it is possible to enjoy the sunny terrace in front of the market. You can have hot drinks, eat homemade pancakes or waffles for a snack, but also smoothies made with ice and fresh fruit. The ice cream is homemade. The prices are correct, the welcome is pleasant. Good news, Bubble Café is expanding and now offers take-away sales to extend the pleasure to your home!

■ CHÂTEAU D'ANGLÈS

Route des Cabanes-de-Fleury
✆ 04 68 33 61 33
www.chateaudangles.com
info@chateaudangles.com

All year round, Monday to Friday, 8am to 4: 30pm, Saturdays by appointment. July and August, Monday to Saturday, 11am to 7pm. Guided tour by appointment only. Price range from 12.90 € to 22.50 €.

In the heart of vineyards of forty hectares, you will discover Château d'Anglès. Three things are mixed there for a success recognised and rewarded with many medals and specialised guides. First of all, the setting: a beautiful country house between vineyards and sea, clape and pond. Then, the soil: a clape with maritime influences. And finally, the know-how: that of the former technical director of Lafite Rothschild, Eric Fabre. Here, we choose grapes harvested by hand, carefully sorted, combining the best of tradition and technology. You will discover the wines of the estate in the beautiful cellar made in 2016. You will contemplate the cellar with barrels from the bay window and will listen to the explanations of Vianney on the wines of the estate and the story of Château d'Anglès. Here, pedagogy is highlighted, you will leave there delighted of having discovered character wines prepared with passion and you will know more about the different grape varieties of Clape like Bourboulenc or Mourvèdre. Wines that are considered as references: "The Great wine" that is red and white, aged in barrels, which develop a great aromatic complexity of spices and candied fruit, winning medals for several consecutive years. The "Classic" vintage in red, rosé and white, is fruity, accessible and fresh. We then recommend a stopover at the castle for a moment of pleasure and to complete your cellar with beautiful bottles or just to take a bottle of rosé to be enjoyed fresh in the shade of a stone pine!

■ L'ENSOLEILLADE

Les Halles
Face au marché de Plein Vent.
✆ 04 68 49 82 83

Open every day and on public holidays from 8am. Closing of the halls around 1: 30pm. Open on Sundays. Open from Easter to mid-September.

Are you on vacation? Don't feel like cooking? You're bound to find what you're looking for at L' Ensoleillade in the halles de Saint-Pierre. The caterer is a must, and this year it is celebrating its 15th anniversary in Saint-Pierre and Narbonne Plage. Mathieu Bernard, a butcher and trained cook, offers traditional dishes and other typically Mediterranean dishes like boles de picolat (a Catalan speciality), paella, bouillabaisse (to order) and gardiane de baureau, all homemade. Who says holidays, says necessarily barbecues, Mathieu will cut you a beautiful piece of beef (French origin) unless the homemade Toulouse sausage, the marinated skewers or the duck breast tempt you more... You will also find cooked dishes in jars, Occitan charcuteries, fresh pasta, cheese... in short, enough to sustain you by varying the pleasures.

In the surroundings

Coursan

■ GRANHOTA – L'ATELIER DU VINAIGRE

16, rue Béranger
✆ 06 32 92 62 20
www.granhota.com
contact@granhota.com

Open from Tuesday to Saturday from 9am to 12pm and from 2pm to 6pm.

Laurent Faure, a graduate of an engineering school of statistical economists in Paris, a lover of good wines and gastronomy, has combined interest and passion under the Granhota banner. A new profession, as much as a life project, which led him – or brought him back – to his native village of Coursan. Settled since 2013 in an old cellar, the young man created his vinegar factory to create balsamic vinegars and wine vinegars flavoured with fruit or spices. Laurent Faure applies ancestral methods to his work, with the ambition of restoring the reputation of this condiment. He selects wines from the Languedoc region, whose tannins, warmth and vigour ripen for many months in oak barrels, without sulphites, preservatives or colourings. The Granhota range of vinegars is available in different flavours, for which the natural is once again preferred. Only rare fruits, peppers and spices, aromatic herbs or saffron from the Corbières, for example, are used to flavour the young craftsman's creations. On his online shop, we find promising bottles: star anise ginger vinegar, muscatel vinegar, special oyster vinegar – with lemon touches – and old-fashioned mustard made with brown mustard seeds harvested from the Narbonne area.

THE REGION OF CORBIÈRES-MINERVOIS

BIZE-MINERVOIS

■ L'ODYSSÉE DE L'OLIVIER
4, hameau de Cabezac
✆ 04 68 41 88 88
www.loulibo.com
resp-tourisme@loulibo.com
♿

Open all year round. Departure visit: July – August: 11am, 3pm, 4pm, 5pm, 6pm. June and September: 11am, 3pm, 4pm, 5pm. Off season: 10: 30am, 2: 30pm, 4pm (January/ February only on reservation). Adult: 6 €. Child (up to 15 years old): 4 €. Group (20 people): 5 € (family package at 16 or 14 €). Guided tour. Shop. Animations.
Since the 1940's the olive cooperative L'Oulibo has been passionately producing olive oil and table olives, particularly the Lucca variety, with a desire for excellence. L'Oulibo invites you to live the adventure of olive and olive oil on its guided tour site: L'Odyssée de l'Olivier – 5 stopovers for a journey into the world of the olive tree. You will follow your guide step by step in an olive grove of 400 trees to discover the secrets of the tree blessed by the gods: the harvest, the varieties, the care, and all the steps to follow the olive to the mill. You will go back in time from ancient Greece to our times and follow the olive adventure on the Giant Screen. The sound and light show allows you to experience the effervescence of the mill as it would be during the harvest period... The last stage is undoubtedly the best since it is an introduction to olive oil and olive tasting! You will be able to take up the challenge and set off with your family in pursuit of the green diamond, the new treasure hunt for 6-12 year olds but also the dramatized visits in July/August on Tuesday mornings and Thursday afternoons with the presence of 2 actors in disguise to live an unforgettable moment and a return to the past. Possibility to buy the visits on the website. Meet at the Oulibo for a visit.

Knife & Fork

■ AUBERGE DE LA SELETTE
Locality La Selette
✆ 04 68 46 28 64
www.laselette.fr
♿

Low season: open Monday and Tuesday for lunch; Thursday to Sunday for lunch and dinner. High season: Thursday to Monday lunchtime and evening; Tuesday lunchtime. High season (April to November). Reservation recommended. Children's menu: 11 €. Lunch formula: €16.50 (lunchtime during the week). Wine by the glass. Lunch Menus €16.50 and €23.50 - Evening Menus €27.50 and €37.50. Groups welcome. Baby chairs. Terrace. Takeaway sale.
Katrien and Kris, straight from Belgium, welcome you in all simplicity. We come here for the setting: in winter, we treat ourselves in the large room with its warmly decorated fireplace, or in the veranda to take advantage of the fine weather of the South. In summer, we meet on one of the two terraces. On the plate, rather classic but very well

presented dishes, made up of excellent quality products, we come here for its matured meats. The Salers prime rib for 2/3 persons from 1.5 kg at €60 is excellent! Dessert lovers like me will be spoiled, gourmet desserts with an original presentation. The little extra for this address: a large car park is at your disposal. Don't hesitate to reserve for special occasions, the menus are always very tempting for Christmas, New Year's Eve or Valentine's Day!

LA GRANGE RESTAURANT

La Bouillette
✆ 04 68 48 18 90
www.la-grange-bize.com
info@la-grange-bize.com
♿

Open all year round. Low season: Thursday to Sunday evening; Sunday at lunchtime. High season: Wednesday to Friday evening; weekend for lunch and dinner. Reservation recommended. Menus from 26 € to 35 €. Children's menu: 10 €. Wine by the glass. Groups welcome (up to 80 people, on reservation). Baby chairs. Garden. Terrace. Animations.

This restaurant with Occitan accents is a refurbished old barn that is located well before the entrance to the village. As soon as you arrive, you will be immersed in the world of local winemakers and historic events of 1907 which marked the region, it should be noted that Marcelin Albert is from the neighboring village, Argeliers. La Grange is a spacious and bright place. A large glass bay opens onto a lovely terrace and on a garden of totems, reeds, palm trees and olive trees. Here, the cuisine is both traditional and original and the products served follow the seasons. Beef parmentier in sauce, split pea soup, trilogy of foie gras, duck breast with pepper, there is nothing but delight here. You can also get tempted by the " all duck " menu. The new cocktail bar of Chiringuito, with Cuban looks, is the perfect place for an aperitif or a drink at the end of the evening. Many concert evenings announced on Facebook.

Shopping

CHÈVRERIE COMBEBELLE

✆ 04 67 38 05 38
combebelle@gmail.com

Open Monday from 10am to 12pm; Tuesday to Sunday from 10am to 12pm and from 4pm to 7pm. Open from March to the end of October. Range from 2,60 € to 5,10 €. Credit card not accepted.

At the exit of Bize-Minervois on a pretty narrow road surrounded by scrubland, you will find this small artisanal exploitation. As soon as you arrive, you will be welcomed by the hens of the sheepfold: yes, happiness is in the garrigue! Children and adults will not want to miss the milking of the goats, every day from 5pm. An exceptional moment, both playful and fascinating. In the barn, photos show the evolution of the sheepfold, while the list of mother goats and their kids born during the year shows some funny names. The visit of the cheese dairy is limited to the first room, where you can observe the different stages of production: the goat's milk collected during milking, filtering, curdling basin, draining and maturing. Then, it's time for tasting and after tasting the different goat's cheeses (crottin tout affinage, faisselle tome, from the freshest to the driest), you will be tempted to buy everything, especially as other local products are also on sale: wines, honey, almonds, fruit juices and the latest addition: goat's cheese yoghurt... The Ecu of the Cathar country and the Caprichon a soft goat's cheese are very appreciated. It's a pleasure to share this visit with your family.

L'OULIBO

Hameau de Cabezac
✆ 04 68 41 88 88
www.loulibo.com
contact@loulibo.com

Living Heritage Company. In low season: open Monday to Friday from 8am to 12pm and 2pm to 6pm; Saturday from 9am to 12: 30pm and 2pm to 7pm; Sunday from 10am to 12: 30pm and 2pm to 7pm. In high season: every day from 8am to 8pm. June and September every day from 8am to 1pm and from 2pm to 7pm. Guided tour L'Odyssée de l'Olivier: Adult: 6€. Child (up to 15 years old): 4€. Group (20 people): 5€ (family package at 16 or 12€ depending on its composition). Free entrance to the shop.

Created in 1940, this olive-growing cooperative, labelled Entreprise du Patrimoine Vivant (Living Heritage Company), is ranked among the 10 most visited companies in France. L'Oulibo invites you to travel in L'Odyssée de L'Olivier. For 80 years, this cooperative has been crushing its olives with granite millstones. L'Oulibo is 1,700 member-cooperators, 80 tons of picholines, 100 tons of oil and 350 tons of Lucques PDO whose luminous green, crunchy flesh, buttered hazelnut side make it the Green Diamond of the region! L'Oulibo gets its traditional oil, tapenades and other local delicacies from this beautiful Aude products. Every year, L'Oulibo obtains many medals at the Agricultural Show for the Lucques but also the picholines, oils... We highly recommend the instructive and fun guided tour "L'Odyssée de L'Olivier" (with its treasure hunt for children), which will take you on a journey through 5 stops in the world of the olive tree. L'Oulibo is also a beautiful showcase of local products in which you will find fresh produce such as cheeses from the nearby goat farm, honey from the Corbières, local wines, beauty products, olive wood kitchenware, home decoration and even a range of clothing! Since 2019, L'Oulibo has an online shop allowing you to enjoy it all year round wherever you are in France.

In the surroundings

Argeliers

LE CHAT QUI PÊCHE

Rue du Port
✆ 04 68 45 37 42

Open from April to early September. Open from Thursday to Monday for lunch and dinner. Reservation recommended. Menu: about 25 €. Children's menu: 10 €. Formula: 19 € (starter + main course or main course + dessert. Starter + main course + dessert: 24 €). Wine by the glass. Cheques not accepted.

On the port of Argeliers, on the edge of the Canal du Midi, Le Chat qui Pêche has to be earned, it has to be found! We welcome you in a bucolic setting on the terrace to enjoy the Canal and the passage of barges on sunny days or in the cosy room for the winter. Here no noise, just water and dinner at sunset, you will come back! Warm atmosphere with local cuisine, fresh and seasonal products: snail cassolette, duck confit, salmon lasagne, homemade fries. I was about to forget the retro atmosphere given by the music from the record player and vinyl records from the 60s to the 80s, which add an extra charm to the place. Particular attention for the attentive service and the smile.

Mirepeisset

■ CAMPING LE VAL DE CESSE

Locality la Garenne
✆ 04 68 46 14 94
campinglevaldecesse@homair.com

Open from April 4 to September 13, 2020. Reservation imperative. From 3pm to 7pm. 114 pitches. Shaded. Mobile homes for 4 to 6 people from 203€ to 980€ per week; mobile homes for 4 people from 182€ to 917€. Discount on the website. Children's club. Animals accepted (1 only dog, except cat 1 and 2, with vaccination book, 5€/day). Wifi for a fee. Children's club in summer. Bicycle hire for children and adults. Animations.

Le Val de Cesse is a campsite full of charm, friendly, quiet but lively, where all members of the family will have the pleasure to meet. A breath of fresh air and well-being for a relaxing and natural holiday. Here, the sea is 25 kilometres away, so why not take advantage of the swimming pool or the river Cesse for a swim? Children love it, adults can fish or laze in the shade of the trees. At Le Val de Cesse campsite, many activities are organised to brighten up your days: dancing meals, pétanque, aquagym, fitness, sports tournaments, belote... A wellness area is at your disposal from June to September.

Saint-Marcel-sur-Aude

■ LA DISTILLERIE – CHEZ BARBÉ

3, chemin des Coopératives
✆ 04 68 45 97 52

Low season: open Tuesday to Saturday for lunch; Thursday to Saturday for lunch and dinner. Menus from 18 € to 65 €. Dishes from 9 to 11 €. Children's menu: 6.50 €. Lunch formula: 14,50 €. Wine by the glass. Groups welcome. Terrace.

We have been waiting for a few months for the reopening of La Distillerie and it is done. Stéphane Barbera, the new owner, is already well-known to the locals since his restaurant in Narbonne was already a reference in the city: Lou Castel. At La Distillerie, he satisfies his desire for space and outdoors. The place is remarkable, the decoration is extremely neat and the architecture has been preserved, we find the superb metal framework and even a still (look up...). Those who know "Barbé" can rest assured because in terms of cuisine, he continues with what made him so successful in Narbonne: meat grilled over a wooden fire, scoundrels such as veal head, tripe or beef tongue, generous portions and all homemade. The other highlight of La Distillerie is its huge shaded terrace with a large bar and a second fireplace. As an alternative to grilling and grilled fish, a menu of homemade and cooked tapas will be available. Musical atmosphere with concert or DJ on certain evenings will allow you to spend enjoyable moments with friends or family.

Sallèles-d'Aude

■ AMPHORALIS ★

Allée des Potiers
Musée des Potiers gallo-romains
✆ 04 68 46 89 48
www.amphoralis.com
amphoralis@legrandnarbonne.com

Closed every Monday, November 11 and May 1. Closed during the Christmas holidays. In low season: open from Tuesday to Friday from 1: 30pm to 5pm; weekends from 10am to 12pm and from 2pm to 6pm. In high season: Tuesday to Sunday and public holidays from 10am to 12pm and from 3pm to 7pm. Numerous activities all year round (see website or Facebook profile). Free up to 6 years old. Adult: 5€. Children (from 6 to 26 years old): 3€ (as well as students, unemployed on proof of employment). Group (10 people): 3€. Subscription card: 11€. Gravel path but without major difficulty. Seat cane on free loan. Large car park. Guided tour (1h30). Shop. Free on the 1st Sunday of each month.

Between the vineyards, olive trees, pines and very close to the junction of Canal de la Robine and Canal du Midi, you will find Musée des Potiers, Amphoralis. In the 1970s, a couple of winegrowers discovered many shards of antique potteries while ploughing a plot. For about twenty years, archaeologists would patiently uncover the remains of an ancient factory of potteries, including vine amphorae, building materials and everyday tableware. In 1992, a museum overlooking the remains opened to the public and archaeological experimentation projects were gradually set up in the museum's park, much to the delight of visitors who can discover reconstructions of ovens, houses and ancient gardens. This artisanal complex is a retrospective of the lifestyle of potter generations for more than three centuries (1st to 3rd century of our era). Many activities and events are offered all year round: guided tours, earth workshops, ceramic workshops, conferences, screenings, tastings, story time. Feel free to visit the website to find out the dates of the events. In summer, they are numerous and for all ages! Don't forget to download the "Amphoralis" application for a free digital tour of quality and suitable for all ages; the application is also available on a tablet on loan at the museum. Also to be discovered on site: augmented reality device on excavations, educational videos, game booklets for children.

Amphoralis, the museum of Gallo-Roman potters.

LA MAISON DE L'ÉCURIE
Route de Mirepeisset
La jonction
✆ 07 87 72 69 68

Open from 1 May to 30 September. Low season: open on weekends. High season: daily for lunch and dinner. Reservation recommended. Starter from 7€ to 12€ – Main courses from 13 € to 18 €. Desserts between 7€ and 8 €. Wine by the glass. Tapas board: 18 € the large one, 12 € the small one. Tapas from 4 € to 15€. Reception of groups (on reservation). Garden. Terrace. Animations.

It is after having skirted the canal de la Robine that your road (by car) stops, you just have to walk 5 min along the canal to reach the junction with the Canal du Midi. It is here that you will find La Maison de l'Ecurie, which was once used as a stable and "bar" for the horses. Today, La Maison de l'Ecurie rests us with its bucolic setting, treats us to homemade food and drinks good local wines. The vocation of the place is still there... You will take a seat right on the canal in the small lounges made of cosy palettes, perfect for tasting the Domaine La Bouysse's cuvée Floréal accompanied by homemade tapas or boards of cold meats and cheese. Under the pergola, you will be offered a reduced menu with, for instance, salads, "gourmet" or "brunch", *vongole linguini* from the smoked beef steak with pine thorns, roasted hazelnuts... to finish, the apple-ginger crumble with rosemary ice cream is a delight. Outside of mealtimes, you will be served waffles or pancakes, ice cream and something to refresh you. This is an address like no other, zen and romantic, where tourists passing through on foot, by bike or by boat can take a gourmet break with a view of Pierre Paul Riquet's work and his canal, classified as a UNESCO World Heritage Site.

Le Somail

OFFICE DE TOURISME DU SOMAIL GRAND NARBONNE TOURISME
168, allée de la Glacière
✆ 04 68 41 55 70
www.visit-lanarbonnaise.com
lesomail@grandnarbonnetourisme.fr

Bike area. Vineyards and Discoveries. Qualité Tourisme. July and August, Monday to Sunday from 9am to 7pm, June and September, Monday to Sunday from 9am to 1pm and 2pm to 6pm, November to March, Monday to Friday from 10am to 1pm and 2pm to 5pm. April, May and October, Monday to Saturday from 9am to 1pm and from 2pm to 6pm, Sunday and holidays from 2pm to 6pm. Closed for Christmas holidays.

The tourist office is located along the canal in a pretty mansion built around 1830. You will regularly be able to discover exhibitions of quality art, and don't miss the space of mediation around the three canals of the Great Mediterranean Narbonne with the touch-screen tablets, the "trades" terminal and, the highlight of the show, the hologram of Madame Cradock. Recreational and informative! At Somail, you can participate all year round in many activities and enjoy various renowned and widely appreciated activities: on Easter weekend, don't miss the "*Artistes au Somail*"; local festival on the last weekend in June; 3rd week of July, the Convivencia festival and the many concerts, jazz, classical guitar, Cuban music... In September, take part in the gourmet trip, find out more so you don't miss out on anything during your stay near the Canal du Midi!

BATEAU LA CAPITANE
Allée de la Glacière
✆ 07 82 09 13 51
https://lacapitane.com
contact@bateauxcanalmidi.com

Cruises from mid-June to mid-September – duration about 1h30. For group cruises from April onwards. Follow the facebook page for special events between April and June. Cruise Ecluse de la Cesse: from 15/06 to 12/07 departure 1: 45pm and 3: 45pm. Château de Ventenac from 13/07 to 13/09 (with tasting of the château's wines). Free up to 3 years old. Adult: 13€. Child (from 4 to 11 years old): 8€. Motorised disabled access: 3 steps. Guided tour. Animations.

Embark aboard La *Capitane* and enjoy the gentle way of life on the Canal du Midi from the pretty port of Le Somail. This entirely wooden gabarre is a replica of the 19th century and can accommodate up to 50 passengers. For movie lovers, La *Capitane* has been filmed in the

Rivière Espérance. The Lock of the Cesse cruise will allow you during 1h30 of commented navigation to discover: the Canal du Midi and the Canal du Jonction, the Cesse Aqueduct, the Patiasses spillway and finally to experience a lock passage! Smart info: the barges have a canvas roof to protect you from the sun or... showers. New in 2020: Sail in the direction of Château de Ventenac with a wine (or grape juice) tasting break and a visit to the winegrowers' attic. Possibility to visit the cellar and the barge Marie Thérèse moored in Ventenac. Follow the facebook page of La *Capitane*, exceptional cruises are proposed in the season such as "Music and tapas" and "Gourmet Stops".

- Tip: Save time and buy your tickets on the website.

LE COMPTOIR NATURE

1, chemin de Halage
✆ 04 68 46 01 61
www.comptoirnature.free.fr
lecomptoirnature@hotmail.fr

Open from 1/04 to 30/10. In April: closed on Sunday evening and Monday lunchtime. From May 1 to October 30: open every day. Children's menu: 11€. Lunch formula: 15€ (except Sunday and public holiday). L'Assiette de Pays du Comptoir Nature 19€. Alaric Menu 18€. Riquet Menu 24€. Cathar Country Menu 34€. Boat hire. Terrace. Silent electric boat rental 22€ per hour.

Along the canal, this guinguette-style place will quickly take you out of time. This year, the restaurant has changed hands but not concept, the local products are always in the spotlight, giant salads, local dishes, a la plancha blood sausage of Pays Cathare, homemade cod brandade, griddled grilled meat including the lamb Red Label of the tarn... Le Somail is not only famous for its wine (terroir of Minervois) but also for its gardens and its orchards: you will be served the wellknown fruit juices of Le Somail, but also organic syrups, traditional aperitif like Carthagène, Baies de Sainte-Lucie... To close the chapter on sweets, do not leave without tasting the homemade ice-creams, whith sheep milk, with milk jam-salt flower, sorbets with Saint-Jean-de-Minervois muscat, with fig, walnut with honey... In front of the show of ducks and geese, the quiet passage of barges, this place is ours... but we share it with great pleasure!

- Possibility of renting small electric boats on site to take a short trip on the canal.

PÉNICHE EPICIÈRE TAMATA

Allée de la Glacière
✆ 06 69 53 67 18

Open every day and holidays from 7am to 9pm. Open from April to October.

Ownership change in 2019 for the grocery barge. This beautiful green and yellow 24-metre-long, black-hulled Dutchwoman dates from 1927 and is an integral part of the Somail landscape. You will find all you need to do your daily shopping with bread, pastries, basic groceries, wines, but also regional specialities: honey, cheeses, cakes, sweets, baskets, postcards, local delicatessen... even small originalities or small gifts.

A great idea for yachtsmen who call at the port of Le Somail in fine weather and for people who love curiosities or simply want to taste the products of the region. Go to Le Somail to discover the floating grocery store! New since 2019 for breakfast in the morning, a few restaurants on the bank are waiting for you.

© Yan EVEN

Le Somail.

L'Ô À LA BOUCHE
Allée Cyprès
✆ 04 68 46 00 09
www.loalabouche-somail.com

Open all year round. Low season: Monday, Tuesday and from Thursday to Saturday for lunch and dinner; Sunday for lunch. High season: every day for lunch and dinner. Closed on Wednesday and Sunday evening. Menus from 25 € to 32 €. Lunch formula: 15 € (starter + main course or main course + dessert). Wine by the glass. Groups welcome. Terrace.

L'Ô à la Bouche is a beautiful address situated on the banks of the Canal du Midi in the charming village of Le Somail. The restaurant has a beautiful terrace which is very pleasant on sunny days and a large dining room fitted out in an old cellar with an atypical decoration where works of contemporary artists are displayed. Amaury will welcome you in this charming place. As for the cuisine, the chef concocts dishes that oscillate between tradition and exoticism. Here, everything is prepared from fresh and seasonal products and you will appreciate the particularly neat presentation of the plates. In the summer, you can enjoy hearty salads, beautiful meats accompanied by seasonal vegetables, fish such as this delicious Thai red tuna and exquisite homemade dishes. Sometimes, we travel with Caribbean, Cuban, Thai or other specialities. We appreciate the evenings "Let's toast! " on Friday evenings where a winemaker is honored, it is then the opportunity to have a good time around tapas (always homemade) and good music (programming on their website). Keep a place for the desserts, they are divine. And if you want to extend your stay at Le Somail, a superb 80 m² gîte for 8 people is at your disposal. The new l'Ô à la Bouche has conquered us.

LE TROUVE TOUT DU LIVRE
28, allée de la Glacière
✆ 04 68 46 21 64
www.le-trouve-tout-du-livre.fr
trouve.tout.livre@wanadoo.fr

Closed from 15 to 30 November. Closed December 25th and January 1st. Open every day and on public holidays from 9am to 12pm and from 2: 30pm to 6: 30pm. Free admission.

Raymond Gourgues had a dream, a passion: opening a bookstore of old books, wish granted in 1980 in this beautiful hamlet of Somail, along Canal du Midi. Now, this is his little daughter, Nelly who is the guardian of this true treasure. Do you like old books? Touching them, smelling them and reading them? Between old and recent, more than 50,000 books found refuge at Le Trouve Tout du Livre: ancient magazines, original editions and beautiful works on Canal du Midi, rare books, fine art books, comic books, books for children... but also works of art by local artists... You're inevitably gonna be unable to resist! This bookstore is a coup de cœur: 1,000 m² on two levels, a large mezzanine, shelves that are 6 meters high, shop windows, an atmosphere, a smell, a culture... Some appropriate arrangements: a nice little corner for children and a space for pocket books with local novels. Undoubtedly, this place is always a wonder of every moment!

DURBAN-CORBIÈRES

In the surroundings

Cucugnan

CHÂTEAU DE QUÉRIBUS
1, rue Achille-Mir
✆ 04 68 45 03 69
See page 12.

THÉATRE ACHILLE MIR
1, Achille-Mir Street
✆ 04 68 45 03 69
communication@cucugnan.fr

Open every day. February: 2-5pm; March 2-6pm; April 10am-12: 30pm / 2pm-7pm; May to end of September 10am-12: 30pm / 2pm-7: 30pm; October 2pm-6: 30pm. Full price: 3.50 € for 1 film, 5 € for 2 films. Children

© Weblody – stock.adobe.com

The village of Cucugnan.

– 6 years old free. Free ticket for 1 film with the ticket of the castle of Quéribus. Tourism & Handicap Label.

In the heart of the village, a former house has been converted into a theatre dedicated to Achille Mir, an Occitan writer of the 19th century, famous for his poems and regional tales, in langue d'Oc, especially *lou Sermoun del curat of Cucugnan*. The Achille Mir theatre offers a multimedia show every half hour – 2 films are available: *Le curé de Cucugnan*, 17 minutes of a truly unusual journey through the crusade, catharism and the history of the homily of the priest of Cucugnan (revisited version of the Languedoc poet Achille Mir, who reminds us of the one published in 1869 by Alphonse Daudet in *Les Lettres de mon Moulin*) and *Les Clés de Quéribus*, a 27-minute documentary on the history of Château de Quéribus, sublime images shot by drones. Every year, during July, three days are dedicated to shows: musicians and storytellers have fun and entertain us. Feel free to enquire about it on the website.

■ MOULIN À VENT OMER – BOULANGERIE LES MAÎTRES DE MON MOULIN

Rue du Moulin
✆ 04 68 33 55 03
www.farinesdemeule.com
Parking at the bottom of the Village. Then walk to the Mill.

Low season: open from Tuesday to Sunday from 9am to 7pm. High season: every day from 9am to 7pm. Annual closing December 24th to mid-February. La Fournée is ready around 11: 30 am in low season – 2 batches in high season 10: 30 am and 11: 30 am. Visit of the mill possible – please contact the Boulangerie.

This pretty little mill, whose last restorations date back to 2003, left no one indifferent in this famous village of Cucugnan. Roland Feuillas is more than a baker, he's a man with a mission on earth. Going up to Cucugnan and tasting its bread is a path that transforms you, and not just for the taste buds. It's a life lesson... Indeed, here, ethics and quality are emphasized in order to offer "healthy" flours and bread. Wheat is grown organically, only old seed varieties are used and everything is stone-ground. A perfect alliance between tradition, health and taste. Noted that the bread keeps for a week. Would you like to discover the entire bread-making process? A guided tour is possible, ask at the bakery. It is also possible to order online: flours, breads, biscuits, cakes... Treat yourself! For the most curious, we also offer you the opportunity to learn how to make your own bread during different 4-day courses at the Ecole du Pain, don't hesitate to ask for more information on the site or by phone. Clever tips: come preferably in the morning at batch time if you want bread, it happens that the bakery is robbed very quickly! Wooden tables in front of the bakery to taste on the spot the breads and biscuits like the Diamond (round biscuit with sugar around it with different flavours). It is preferable to order at the latest the day before you come.

Fontjoncouse ★

L'AUBERGE DU VIEUX PUITS

Avenue Saint-Victor
✆ 04 68 44 07 37
www.aubergeduvieuxpuits.fr
reception@aubergeduvieuxpuits.fr
♿

Closed from January to March 19. Low season: open from Wednesday to Saturday for lunch and dinner; Sunday at lunchtime. High season: Tuesday for dinner; Wednesday to Sunday and on public holidays for lunch and dinner. Reservation recommended. Menus from 185 € to 215 € (excluding drinks). A la carte menu: about 160 €. Children's menu: 27 €. Lunch formula: 125 € (weekdays – excluding public holidays). Wine by the glass. American Express. Groups welcome. Baby chairs. Shop.

It can be said that Gilles Goujon has accumulated awards, Best Worker of France 1996, elected by his peers Chef of the Year in 2010 and, the consecration: the third star. Despite all these trophies, the man knows how to keep it simple, he buys products in Lézignan and his inventive local cuisine follows the rhythm of the seasons. It is difficult to "tell" you his cuisine as it is surprising, refined and technically flawless, we will only mention a few dishes. As a starter, the famous "rotten" Carrus chicken egg with truffles on a mushroom purée and summer truffles, warm briochine and cappuccino to drink, followed by a duo of Mediterranean bluefin tuna in "chichoumey", basil tomato and ratatouille "cristian" sorbet, tuna tripe, Catalan-style juice and bottarga croutons. As for the land products, enjoy the roasted back of black pig, puffed rind, mousseline gratin with blood sausage, potato in the air, potato on the ground, andouille quail, Lucca olive juice. Finally, don't leave without tasting the chocolate leaf shortbread with its surprise of raspberry and sparkling "Tannéa", accompanied by a "choc o'tea" sauce and raspberry sorbet. Or perhaps you will be tempted by Mr. Magnani's fake "Folfer" cherry in puffed sugar, chabrot with spices and sorbet, tiramisu mascarpone with verbena and fleur de sel shortbread! We're so excited about it. Stop the ordeal there, book your table right away on their website!

Thézan-des-Corbières

CHÂTEAU SAINT ESTÈVE

D611 – Château Saint Estève
✆ 04 68 43 32 34
www.chateau-saint-esteve.com
contact@chateau-saint-esteve.com

Open every day and on public holidays. From 9am to 6pm. Open on Sundays. Delivery possible. From 7,5€ to 41€ per bottle.

In Thézan-des-Corbières, at the bend of vineyards and a stony path, let yourself be guided by the sun's rays, in the heart of the rugged Corbières, where the earth reveals the character of men of passion and exalts the blood of the vine, welcome to Château Saint Estève in the Boutenac cru! The Latham family welcomes you in the center of a magnificent stone building, in a cellar steeped in history and a tribute to Henry de Monfreid, adventurer and writer, one of whose vintages bears his name. The welcome and availability of the owners is equal to the wines they make: generous. Don't miss the tasting of the vertical cuvée Ganymède, an exceptional vin de garde with blackberry accents and tannic structure, and discover all the secrets of the Carignan grape variety. You will be able to let yourself be captivated by the finesse of the Altaïr or Astréos vintages with their spicy aromas. The complexity of these wines has undeniably seduced a good number of well-informed amateurs and seasoned professionals who have not been mistaken, and have been widely rewarded: Gold Medal of independent winegrowers for Ganymède, 2019 and 2020 Excellence Prize at the Paris Agricultural Show for the overall quality of the vintages. It is worth noting the LPO certification of Château St Estève, which validates the environmental actions undertaken in favour of birds and amphibians.

▶ Summer jazz evenings, after-work aperitif dinners and oenological discovery walks are organised from spring onwards! Red, rosé and white wines in the Corbières and Boutenac appellations, for all budgets and all palates (sparkling wine without alcohol and pure grape juice made for children).

Tuchan ★

CHATEAU WIALA

Rue de la Gare
✆ 04 68 45 49 49 – www.chateau-wiala.com

Open every day from 4pm to 8pm.

By taking over a 20 hectare estate in this exceptional site in the Upper Corbières, Wiebke Seubert and Alain Woorons have realised their dream: to become winegrowers! The adventure began: they restructured the vineyard, opted for more traditional farming practices and above all for sustainable agriculture. Château Wiala is mainly made up of two islands of plots and benefits from the complementary nature of the terroir: different grape varieties and exposures. In a modernised winemaking cellar, a powerful and racy red AOC Fitou (80%) and a fruity and vanilla-flavoured Muscat de Rivesaltes are produced. The Harmonie cuvée (red) rewarded with a gold medal at the Concours Agricole will make you see all the colours! This summer (July/August) a show is proposed to you in the cellar of the Sensatio estate: a fresco on biodiversity, the beauty of the Corbières, the love of a terroir... So, see you at 6: 30 pm!

LAGRASSE ★★★

This ancient cultural capital of Corbieres is ranked among the Most Beautiful Villages of France. It is a medieval city located in the beautiful valley of Alsou, watered by the Orbieu. Lagrasse has many attractions like the twelfth-century bridge, paved streets lined with Renaissance facades that lead up to a beautiful square with classified houses, the Gothic style Saint-Michael parish church, the covered market and the famous abbey of Sainte-Marie-de-Orbieu. Today, the village is promoting arts and crafts through its many shops... It is delightful to discover such a heritage and a way of life. Do not hesitate to get more information about Mitounes that offer an old legend of several centuries to the village.

VINAIGRERIE CYRIL CODINA

16, Boulevard de la Promenade
✆ 04 68 75 83 66
www.vinaigrescodina.com
vinaigrerie.cc@gmail.com

Vineyards and Discoveries. Closed from 6 to 19 January. From November to March: open every day except Thursdays from 11am to 6pm. April, May, June, September, October:

every day except Thursdays from 10 am to 7 pm. July and August: every day from 9: 30am to 8pm. Free of charge. Shop. Animations. Vinegar, wine and olive oil tasting.

Located on the main street of the village, with its modern storefront, it is impossible not to see this lovely shop from which the fragrances come out onto the sidewalk. Cyril Codina is a passionate and exciting vinegar maker. Come in and enjoy! More than 35 types of vinegar, how about a balsamic vinegar with wild blackberry or combava and vanilla vinegar? Here, it is difficult to leave empty-handed, the choice is so great.

You can find Cyril Codina's vinegars in many restaurants in the region, notably at the Le 1900 Restaurant, located on the other side of the street down below.

Sightseeing

■ ABBAYE SAINTE-MARIE-D'ORBIEU (PUBLIC PART) ★★★

4, Left Bank
✆ 04 68 43 15 99
www.abbayedelagrasse.com
abbayedelagrasse@wanadoo.fr

The abbey is divided into 2 parts. The timetables below therefore concern the public part. Closed from mid-December to mid-January. From mid-January to the end of March and from November 1 to mid-December: 10am to 5pm. From April 1 to mid-June and from mid-September to the end of October: 10am-6pm. From mid-June to mid-September: 10am-7pm. Last visit 1 hour before closing. Free up to 5 years old. Adult: 5€. Child (from 6 to 15 years old): 2.50€. Group (10 people): 3.50€. Passport ticket for the sites: 4€. Guided tour (on reservation from 15 people, 2.50€ + extra-cost 1.50€). Shop. A ten minute walk is necessary to reach the abbey from the obligatory car parks.

The Benedictine abbey founded in the 8th century under the protection of Charlemagne grew rapidly thanks to donations from powerful lords. From the 8th to the 18th century, 64 abbots succeeded one another there, and they actively participated in the political and religious life of the Languedoc and Catalonia regions. During the Revolution, the monks were driven out, and the abbey was split and sold in two lots. The division still exists today. The oldest part, owned by the department of the Aude, includes the oldest buildings: the rich abbey palace and its "small cloister", the dormitory of the monks in inverted vessel hull, the cellar, the bakery, the ceremonial room.... The upper gallery leads to the abbey chapel of the late 13th century, a true jewel of Gothic art. 11 spaces, restored and highlighted, are open to visitors. The second half of the building is once again occupied by a community of religious. It can be visited independently. A pleasant time visit, history, and which can also be spiritual. Enjoy being in the village to discover the medieval atmosphere that reigns there!

■ LOGIS ABBATIAL ET DORTOIR ★

✆ 04 68 43 15 99
www.abbayedelagrasse.com
abbayedelagrasse@wanadoo.fr

Visit included with that of the Abbey of Lagrasse Public Part. Opening hours see Abbaye de Lagrasse Partie Publique. Shop in the courtyard.

In the heart of the former lodging house is located a fanciful small garden surrounded by two galleries with columns surmounted by Romanesque capitals, one of which represents luxury. Above this is the abbey chapel of the late thirteenth century, walls decorated with frescoes and floor covered with varnished terracotta tiles with various motifs – centaurs, deers, men... New buildings were built around the garden: storerooms, cellar, bakery and a superb dormitory. The visit takes about 20 minutes. The abbey is connected to the village by two bridges above Orbieu including a magnificent hump-backed one dating from the 11th century which makes the reputation of Lagrasse.

FROM PLACE TO PLACE

Abbey of Lagrasse.

LE MONASTÈRE
✆ 04 68 58 11 50
www.chanoines-lagrasse.eu

Open all year round. On Sundays and holidays, mass is celebrated at 10: 30am. On weekdays, mass is at 9: 30 am. Every day, Vespers is at 6: 30 pm. Mass and services are sung in Gregorian. Low season: weekends and holidays from 3: 15 pm (last visit at 5: 25 pm). High season: Friday to Wednesday and public holidays from 3: 15 pm (last visit at 5: 25 pm). In low season: during local school holidays, open every day except Thursday. Free up to 16 years old. Adult: 4 €. Child (from 16 to 18 years old): 2,50 €. Group (10 people): 2,50 €. Children's welcome area. Guided tour (for groups).

To access the monument of the monastery and the parts open to visitors, do not hesitate to use the pink sandstone gate. This stone, which is present throughout the monastery, is characteristic of the sobriety and brilliance of the buildings of the convent and the main courtyard. It is possible for you to visit the cloister which offers calm, serenity, its restoration dates only from the 18th century but it is worth a visit. The Gothic church was built in the 13th century on the foundations of a Carolingian basilica and opens onto an 11th century Romanesque transept. Three Romanesque absidioles (small chapels) from the 11th century display their charm on a monastic garden that has been worked by the monks every day since 2004. Finally, the lapidary museum contains the famous historical capital of the Master of Cabestany representing Adam and Eve expelled from Paradise, the lid of a 6th century sarcophagus but also the capitals of the former Gothic cloister. Do not hesitate to stay, in the monastery the atmosphere is relaxing and spiritual. We strongly advise you to attend a Gregorian Chant Mass, a melodious experience!

Knife & Fork

LE BASTION
50, Boulevard de la Promenade
✆ 04 68 12 02 51

Maître Restaurateur. Open from Wednesday to Saturday for lunch and dinner; Sunday at lunchtime. Menus from 32 € to 52 €. Children's menu: 9 €. The blind menu – 52 € – must be chosen by all the guests of the restaurant. Terrace.

On the very pretty promenade of one of the most beautiful villages in France, Lagrasse, a new address was opened in the summer of 2019. In the heart of a historic medieval building with stone walls and modern furniture, you will be warmly welcomed by Valentin Renaud and Fabien De Bruyn (former chef of the Gaia in Narbonne), both cooks and pastry chefs and childhood friends. The setting is perfect: the kitchen open onto the room gives off gourmet fragrances, a room upstairs quieter, a pretty terrace. The chefs work with local producers and winemakers, so you can enjoy a mackerel marinated in Kina- Karo from the vinegar maker Cyril Codina (from Lagrasse), then a snacked beef faux filet, calçot grilled with lava stone and to finish, a vacherin with kiwis and Sichuan pepper. You will find the menu of the day on the facebook page. We'll be back very soon to test the brand new "blind tasting" menu and its mystery dishes served on weekends and dinner during the week with 6 courses!

LA PETITE MAISON
12, boulevard de la Promenade
✆ 04 68 91 34 09
lapetitemaison.david@gmail.com

Closed from December 15 to February 13. Open from Friday to Wednesday from 9am to 6pm. Reservation recommended. Menus from 15 € to 23 €. Lunch formula: 14 €. Wine by the glass. Vegetarian and gluten-free dish. Terrace.

It is simple and effective: a table d'hôte atmosphere with this "very open" kitchen, seasonal and homemade products, simple and tasty dishes, all in a very friendly atmosphere. The lunch formula consists of a meal salad, the one with the homemade pie is unanimously popular, but the Petite Maison also offers three types of lasagne that is always different every day, for instance: lamb and Espelette pepper, chicken-curry, organic goat cheese from the Sérviès en Val goat farm... and a mince parmentier with duck confit deglazed with balsamic vinegar from the nearby vinegar farm. After lunch, the restaurant takes on the appearance of a tea room and offers excellent pies, homemade cakes, homemade ice creams and Granny "Vic"'s must-have fluted creams. Inside or on the terrace you will appreciate this small gourmet break in the shade of the large plane trees of the promenade.

General view of Lagrasse.

RESTAURANT LE 1900
13, boulevard de la Promenade
✆ 04 68 12 17 67
www.restaurant1900lagrasse.com
chris.cros@live.fr

Open from Thursday to Monday for lunch and dinner. Closed on Tuesday evening and Wednesday. Reservation recommended. Tapas from 5 to 12 €. Boards from 8 to 15 € (26€ with foie gras).

Instead of the former 1900 museum in Lagrasse, the Restaurant Le 1900 opened its doors in the spring of 2018. In a decor that is both retro – some will recognize part of the decoration of the old museum – and modern, Christophe, Valérie and Romain welcome you. A choice of tapas version with duck hearts, parsley knives, for instance, boards of cold meats, cheese boards or a brasserie version with grilled meats, fish a la plancha, parillade (for 2), hearty salads without forgetting for our part a very good gourmet tea... the dishes are gourmet and here, everything is homemade. It should be noted that many dishes are made with the vinegars of our neighbour, Cyril Codina. Our tip for sunny days, the tables in the small patio full of charm at the back of the restaurant are very pleasant.

In the surroundings

Montséret

MIELLERIE DES CLAUSES ★
Hameau des Clauses, 8, pech de la Garrigue
✆ 04 68 43 30 17
www.miellerie-des-clauses.com
mielleriedesclauses@wanadoo.fr

Qualité Tourisme. Bienvenue à la Ferme. Qualité Sud de France. Open every day from 9am to 12pm and from 2pm to 6pm. Discovery pony ride 30 minutes. Free up to 11 years old. Adult: 5.80€ (complete visit of 1h15). Bee theatre July and August: visiting hours: 10: 30am, 2: 30pm, 4pm and 5: 30pm. Weekends in July and August: visiting hours 10: 30am, 3pm and 4: 30pm. May, June and September: visiting hours: 2: 30pm and 4pm – 7 days a week. Credit card not accepted. Tourisme & Handicap Label. Company benefiting from the "Valeurs Parc Naturel Régional" label.

Welcome to the world of bees! Miellerie des Clauses, masterfully handled by passionate beekeepers, offers a discovery of bees' life in the small village of Corbières. More than a museum and without taking the risk of being foraged, here, they make you discover live (and with exciting commentary) the interior of the hives with a webcam, it's bees' theater! This visit is carried out by the beekeepers themselves! Through an observatory, the beekeeper comments on the bees' lives in a specially dedicated workshop, and the beekeeper will not hesitate to open a beehive inhabited by bees, which you will watch safely behind a bay. You will also discover the honey from its extraction from the hive to its conditioning. In summer, several activities are offered to you, children can go on pony back for 30 minutes to discover the scrubland and the plants that bees are gathering pollen from, while adults can wear beekeeper garb to approach the beehives (on reservation every Wednesday morning from 9am to 11: 30am), a unique experience in the sector. The less courageous can be content with a honey, gingerbread, mead or little candy tasting... Impossible to leave empty-handed. You are advised to visit the website, as well as to book your tickets on the online ticketing to save time during peak periods (July and August).

Saint-Laurent-de-la-Cabrerisse

LA BONBONNE NEW
36, avenue de Talairan
✆ 04 68 70 61 41

Closed from December to February. Open from Thursday to Monday for lunch and dinner. Booking recommended. A la carte menu: about 25 €. Garden. Terrace.

A brand new, very bucolic address! When the weather is nice, the service is done in the garden overlooking the Nielle. Breathtaking view of the river and the heart of the village. In the kitchen, regulars and locals know well, the menu is original, not easy to choose between a Bangkok salad (salad of green mangoes and raw vegetables, vermicelli, spicy peanut sauce and shrimp brochette), the Bouyiourdi (feta cheese, peppers, onions, tomatoes and crispy filo pastry), the superb plate of the sea, the sea bream ceviche with coconut milk (excellent!). You will also find a divine burger. The concept is to share the dishes, the prices are attractive because the portions correspond to starters, count 2 dishes per person and 1 dessert for good appetites. Flavours are there. We'll come back in the fall to dine indoors in the cosy decor.

Talairan

LA TALARIANE
8, avenue du Termenès ✆ 04 68 45 82 19
latalariane@orange.fr

Open all year round. Closed 1 week in February. Low season: Tuesday to Saturday for lunch and dinner; Sunday evening. High season: every day for lunch and dinner. A la carte menu: about 20 €. Children's menu: 9 €. Formula: 13 € (starter/main course or main course dessert – 15 € starter/main course/dessert for lunch outside the weekend). Wine by the glass. Entrecote limousine 26 € (huge!) T-bone steak (1 kg) limousine 36 €. Terrace. Take away sale. Free Wifi. Animations and concerts.

Located in the centre of the village, La Talariane is not just a restaurant, it is a place where locals and passing walkers meet. Here, the friendly atmosphere and the local cuisine guarantee a good evening. Here, we are locavore and the cooked products are of good quality, whether it is the enormous XXL rib steak, the cargolade (snails), the must-eat cassoulet, the cuttlefish and its homemade aïoli or the tripe à la catalane... Here, everything is homemade, even the french fries! This summer, the chef Jérôme Castille whispered to us that white truffles would be in the spotlight during a special truffle evening... to be continued. La Talariane is also a wine bar where you can taste wines from the region, carefully selected and sold at very reasonable prices. Parties (concerts, DJs, etc.) are regularly scheduled as well as sporting events broadcast on the big screen. An address where authenticity and friendliness are the order of the day. Visit the Facebook page to follow the program!

Villerouge-Termenès

CHÂTEAU DE VILLEROUGE

✆ 04 68 70 09 11

See page 14.

LA RÔTISSERIE MÉDIÉVALE

Le Château ✆ 09 81 64 09 11
www.restaurant-medieval.com
contact@restaurant-medieval.com

December to February only by reservation. Low season: open from Thursday to Tuesday for lunch. High season: every day for lunch. Open in the evening only on reservation (from 1 meal). Reservation imperative. Menus from 35 € to 42 € (drinks with and without alcohol included). Children's menu: 16 € (under 14 years old. drinks included). A la carte menu. Groups welcome. Animals accepted.

Housed in the ceremonial room of the Villerouge castle, the restaurant of the lady Audrey and master Thierry will transport you to the 14th century. A surprising place, the service is performed in period costumes, the furniture, the decoration, the musical ambiance, everything has been studied in details. Moreover, you are invited to (freely) dress up, swords and helmets of knight are lent to children. Then, you can sit around a large table made of solid wood, where you are served rose wine, wine spiced with cinnamon, ginger (a clarification, everything is homemade apart from the "vinasse gouleyante" served at will), once you have taken the appetizer, your meal can begin. Paté du viandier or Tourte du Roi Manfred (with chicken liver)... copious! Coming up next, the roasted cockerel and its sauces, accompanied by seasonal vegetables which are served on trenchers (thick slice of round bread used as a plate cooked on site in the morning), to enjoy with fingers for even more authenticity, children love it! Wooden spoon and knife can be provided. Get prepared to "feast" The desserts close the banquet, pear with hippocras, "crespes" with red-fruit coulis or flan pie. The meals are generous and it is sometimes difficult to end, but don't worry, here, you do not waste anything! Your leftovers are given to pigs or compost, like in the Middle Ages! Time travel guaranteed! Be careful, in summer, it can be too hot in the ceremonial room.

LEZIGNAN-CORBIÈRES

Lézignan-Corbières, a town of 12,000 inhabitants, is situated at the crossroads of the Corbières and the Minervois. The historic centre was built in the form of a "circulade" around medieval fortifications that surround the church of Saint-Félix-de-Gérone. Lézignan is not a city that you adopt at first glance. It has its own character and you have to take the time to discover it: we like its Avenue de la République in the shade of the plane trees where you will find a wide network of shops, restaurants and entertainment, we like its traditional market on Wednesday mornings with its stalls covered with fresh fruit and vegetables from local producers under the open market hall, but our favourite goes to the Maison Gibert, a former 19th century wine-producing estate, which presents quality artistic exhibitions and cultural events all year round. And if you're here for Pentecost, don't miss Prom'aude, a major gourmet festival of local products.

www.lezignan corbieres.fr

Knife & Fork

LO TIRA TAP

Boulevard Chateaudun
✆ 06 70 40 95 38

Open Monday to Friday for lunch; Thursday to Saturday in the evening. Room upstairs fitted out for groups. Evening menu at 30 €. Lunch formula: 16 € (pan con tomato and ham + starter + main course [dessert extra 3 €]). Wine by the glass. Take away sale.

Located in the centre of Lézignan, in a small alley slightly off-centre, Lo Tira Tap is a place to be discovered absolutely! Maria, the owner, is an exceptional woman, dynamic, smiling, welcoming, generous, with a nice little Portuguese accent. Her cuisine is fresh and delicious! On the menu, a wide choice of homemade tapas: let yourself be surprised by the cod fritters, duck casserole, aubergine caviar puff pastry, shrimp or prawn casserole, pissaladière, fish terrine, pan con tomato, scallop... She masters all the Latin specialties! The express lunch formula is excellent for a very good value for money. The editorial staff has tested: a plate of pan con tomato and ham as appetizer, a poached egg, French fries and homemade tomato sauce as a starter. And as a main course, honey-roasted duckling leg with basil pasta. A treat! And to top it all off, her husband, an oenologist, has selected quality wines. As for the sweet treats, her must-eat homemade pancakes and her Tarte Tatin are real delights! On the terrace in the summer, in the hall in the winter, the atmosphere is always warm. Attention, small precision: the menus are unique, if you have particular tastes, remember to ask for the menu of the day before sitting down.

Sleeping

MAISON DES JEUNES ET DE LA CULTURE – CENTRE INTERNATIONAL DE SÉJOUR

25 rue Marat
✆ 04 68 27 03 34
cis@mjc-lezignan-corbieres.com

Arrivals from Monday to Friday from 9am to 7pm (no reception on weekends for new arrivals). Price 18 € per night with WC and shower in the room. 22 € night + pdj – 33.50 € half board. Sheets are provided. Free Wifi in the common areas. Washing + drying linen 5 € (8 kg)

A youth hostel located in the heart of the town of Lézignan-Corbières, in the middle of greenery, close to shops, restaurants, cinema, not far from sports facilities (swimming pool, tennis, gymnasiums, stadiums ...). The train station is accessible in 20 minutes on foot. Rooms with 2 or 4 beds (total 58 places), in which there is a shower room. The windows overlook the public garden. A large dining room will allow you to spend a pleasant moment around a good meal if you take the formulas pension or half-board. Fully equipped rooms can be rented for meetings, training, dance and shows.

Leisure

CHUTEXTREM
Aérodrome de Lézignan-Corbières
Route de Ferrals
D611
✆ 06 81 65 33 86
www.chutextrem.com
tandem@chutextrem.com

Open from March to the end of November. Open from Friday to Sunday and on public holidays. 249 € the tandem skydiving jump – Initiation jump with 2 instructors + video 349 €.

Do you want to live a unique experience rich in adrenaline? Then come skydiving at Chutextrem! The jump is practiced in tandem, with a certified instructor. After several minutes of explanations about the freefall jump, the instructor will equip you and prepare you for the big jump. Don't panic, everything is under control! You climb between 3000 and 4000 meters of altitude by plane (duration: 20 minutes), then you take a deep breath, and you jump! It's off for almost a minute of free fall at 200 km/h, a unique sensation. You then have 4 to 6 minutes of flight under canopy to get back to dry land. Enjoy the breathtaking scenery! Possibility to buy the jumps directly on the internet, they are valid for one year but note that Chutextrem closes in December, January and February. New: Boeing 737-800 simulator. How about taking orders from 49 €? Conforming replica of a Boeing 737-800 NG cockpit, the sessions are supervised by professional pilots.

■ FLYZONE
Aérodrome de Lézignan-Corbières
✆ 04 68 48 20 41
www.flyzone.fr
info@flyzone.fr

Open all year round. On reservation only. Every day from 9: 30 am to 5: 30 pm. Price from €29.90. Available from 5 to 90 years old. Freefall simulator. F1 simulator. Restaurant. Accomodation.

Flying? It's no longer a dream thanks to the FlyZone freefall simulator. Without jumping from a plane and in complete safety, experience this incredible feeling and impression of being weightless in every way similar to that felt by parachutists! Let's go for an unforgettable experience! A stay in weightlessness where the body floats in the air! The experience is accessible to everyone, children from 5 years old, adults without age limit, amateurs and experienced parachutists! Did you know that every time we do two simulator flights, it's like we've had three parachute jumps! ! ! Note that on the aerodrome of Lézignan-Corbières and a few meters from Flyzone, you can live the real experience of free fall with "Chutextrem" for parachute jumps and "Languedoc Aviation" for tourist flights to enjoy the region from above as well as flying courses. Recently, two new activities have been added to the site: a dynamic F1 simulator to experience an exceptional race and a Boeing 737 simulator that allows you to take the controls like a flight captain and travel around the world! ! ! Feel free to follow the Facebook page, Flyzone regularly makes exceptional offers with prices, also in free fall.

■ LANGUEDOC AVIATION
Aérodrome de Lézignan-Corbières
Plaine de Conilhac
✆ 06 43 98 71 09
www.languedoc-aviation.com
info@languedoc-aviation.com

From the age of 5. Sightseeing flight 30 min: 80 €. (1pers) 149 € (2 pers) family (3 pers max): 210 €. Video of your flight: 30 €. Flying course from 15 years old: 299 €. Catering.

Languedoc Aviation invites you to get up high. Enjoy a plane ride over the region's must-see sites! It is on board a DA40 that you will take your seat to discover the jewels of the department from above. Different routes are proposed: flying over the Cathar Castles, the City of Carcassonne, the Pyrenees mountains, the Canigou massif or the coast! Choose what you want and take off for a unique visit between land and sea. Equipped with a helmet with a microphone, your pilot will comment on the ride and help you discover the cultural and historical heritage of Languedoc Roussillon. You enjoyed the flight and would like to take lessons? Languedoc Aviation also offers flying courses! Based on the aerodrome of Lézignan-Corbières, just off the motorway exit, you will find here a whole complex dedicated to aviation: Freefall Simulator, Tandem Skydiving, Skydiving School, Formula 1 Simulator and Boeing 737 Simulator! You will be filled with exceptional sensations and memories.

Shopping

■ MAISON BERTRAND
Rue Alfred Nobel
✆ 04 68 27 57 63
https://www.maison-bertrand.com
boutique@maison-bertrand.com

Open from Tuesday to Saturday from 9am to 12pm and from 3pm to 7pm.

La Maison Bertrand, butcher's shop – charcuterie, is a real institution in Lézignan. Father Marcel and his wife opened the store in the town centre (still in business) in 1966 and then expanded and opened this department store in the shopping area. There you will find homemade products (charcuterie, canned foods, cured meats), poultry, quality meat but also a beautiful delicatessen area with local products and a wine cellar. There is also a nice selection of cheeses. Nelly – the daughter – and her husband have since taken over the reins of this beautiful family business. Will you be tempted like us by a "round trip" of dry sausage? There are many gift ideas in the form of boxes of good products (charcuterie, canned foods, delicatessen...). For your events, we advise you the boards of cold meats and cheeses, nicely presented, just put them on your tables!

- **City centre shop** (with delicatessen department) – 18 avenue Barbès – Tel: 04 68 27 04 75 - Open from 8: 15am to 12pm and from 3: 15pm to 7pm.

In the surroundings

Boutenac

Sleeping

LA CORBIÈRE VACANCES
15, route de Ferrals
✆ 06 19 98 27 78
www.lacorbiere.eu
contact@lacorbiere.eu

Open all year round. For 5 persons (90 m², 2 bedrooms). From 450 € to 950 € per week depending on the season. 2 nights minimum from 70 € per night (except July / August – 7 nights from Saturday to Saturday). Credit card not accepted. Free wifi. Garden furniture, dishwasher. Satellite Tv. Plancha, deckchairs, numerous tourist information, high chair, cot, bath, changing mat, toys available free of charge on request.

How about a nice holiday rental with a swimming pool in a village well known for its excellent wines? In a beautiful 1882 winegrower's house, Gwénaëlle offers you a 90 m² cottage located on the ground floor with 2 bedrooms and each with their own bathroom, a large living room with open plan kitchen opening onto a south facing terrace with plancha. We liked the modern and bright decoration and the large, well-equipped kitchen.

At the back of the house, a pretty garden with its swimming pool (3.50 x 3.50 m) and its cosy corner ideal for a nap awaits you! You won't be far from the major sites to discover in the department: Canal du midi, Châteaux Cathares, Carcassonne, Narbonne... Gwénaëlle knows the region like the back of her hand and will be happy to give you many tips for visits, whether it be cultural places, such as unusual places, the addresses of winegrowers or good tips for food lovers. For your evenings, many board games, books for all ages.

Shopping

CHÂTEAU LA VOULTE-GASPARETS
✆ 04 68 27 07 86
www.lavoultegasparets.com
chateaulavoulte@wanadoo.fr

Open every day from 9am to 12pm and from 2pm to 6pm. Open on Sundays. Bottles: White 8.80€ / Rosé 7.30€ / Red 9.40€ to 19.90€.

Park in the courtyard and ring the bell in front of the big door that serves the cellar. Indeed, to keep the barrels and bottles at the right temperature at the Reverdy's, we caulk ourselves! From the 60 hectares of vineyard, Patrick Reverdy and his son Laurent offer many vintages that are highly appreciated in the region and far beyond. The two best known are the AOC Corbières Boutenac reds: the cuvée Romain Pauc and a cuvée Réservée. You will find the "vins de la Voulte", as they say here, in many Aude restaurants, from starred restaurants like Gilles Goujon's Auberge du Vieux Puits to village restaurants. In addition to these two references, the estate also offers whites and rosés. Ask to see the cellar, a superb achievement.

Conilhac-Corbières

AUBERGE CÔTÉ JARDIN – RESTAURANT
7, avenue 113
✆ 04 68 27 08 19
www.auberge-cotejardin.com
contact@auberge-cotejardin.com

Qualité Tourisme. Maître Restaurateur. Tables & Auberges de France. Qualité Sud de France. Restaurant: From May to September: closed Monday lunch and Tuesday lunch. From October to April: closed from Sunday evening to Tuesday lunch. Hotel: open every day from May to September. Closed on Sunday evening from October to April. Reservation recommended. Menu from 30€. Inspiration menu: 60€. Children's menu: 15.50€. Dish of the day: 17.50€ (except weekends and public holidays "basket of the day": 19.50€ starter + main course or main course + dessert and 24.50€ starter + main course + dessert). Groups welcome (up to 45 people). Baby chairs. Garden. Terrace.

If you're visiting Aude, don't miss David Prevel's establishment! Both a charming hotel and a gastronomic restaurant, good taste and mastery of the trade are on every floor! David is a demanding, even uncompromising chef when it comes to the products that make up his dishes. The plates are superbly prepared and his cuisine follows the seasons. His creativity has been rewarded many times, notably with the regional innovation prize for his cassoulet revisited, based on bean purée, shredded duck and Toulouse sausage. From the starter to the dessert, you will be enchanted by this festival of flavours that will move all your senses. We can mention in particular the homemade foie gras with its vanilla tomato jam, following, the roast spring veal, cut in the square, sprinkled with its cooking juice, with the garnish of the moment and its Maury juice, and for dessert, depending on the season, we propose a pan-fried strawberry slightly spiced with Penja pepper, cubism of faisselle and crispy meringue... In 2015, Julie Andrieu and her famous "Carnets de Julie" honoured her work and her cooking during the show broadcast in October. An address that makes epicureans, lovers of good food and beautiful places, happy.

Fabrezan

LES CALICOTS

17, rue du Commerce
✆ 04 68 49 18 54
www.les-calicots.com
lescalicots@orange.fr

Closed from November to March. Open every day (for lunch and dinner) except Tuesday. Reservation recommended. Menus from 22 € to 35 €. Children's menu: 12 €. Lunch formula: 15 € (during the week with coffee or 25 cl of wine). Wine by the glass. Groups welcome (up to 35 people). Baby chairs. Terrace.

With Les Calicots, those who love confidential addresses will be served! Nestled in the heart of the village of Fabrezan, in a small street between the church and the medieval castle near the 12th-century tower, the restaurant of Géraldine and Olivier is a true delight. A former mercery, once held by Géraldine's grandmother, became a restaurant full of charm and authenticity. When the weather is cold, you are received in the dining room, lit by a skylight, when it is warmer you will find your happiness in the small courtyard shaded by tropical vegetation. You will enjoy Olivier's cuisine: for starter, foie gras with knuckle of ham with fig chips, salad of calicots with hot goat cheese from the farm of Carrus, pesto and honey, for main course, pike-perch with horns of mushrooms and bacon, spring rolls with duck confit, pork cassoulet and beans from Pays Cathare, and for dessert, the famous crème brûlée with lavender. Large choice of local wines only for beautiful discoveries.The reception is warm and generous. Don't forget to go down a level to discover the exhibitions or events organized in the great vaulted cellar, where Fabrezan wines have a special place like La Delicatesse or Le Marcelin that you can take at owner rate. Do you have an event to celebrate with your friends? Do not hesitate to book the room that can accommodate up to 35 people!

DOMAINE PAUL HUC

37, avenue de Lagrasse
✆ 04 68 90 57 04
www.domainepaulhuc.com
domainepaulhuc@gmail.com

Open all year round. From 4 to 6 people. Low season: from 990 € to 1,030 € per week. High season: from 1 400 € to 1,500 € per week. Possibility to rent for a weekend from 510 €. Breakfast: 9 €. Closed parking included. One apartment is fully equipped for wheelchair users. Playground for children. Animals accepted (15 € per stay). Free Wifi. Private terrace. Shop. Tearoom. Service on request (shopping, various rentals...). Garden furniture, tumble dryer, dishwasher. Reception room and equipped kitchen.

Do you want to spend a few days in the heart of Corbières? In Fabrezan, Domaine Paul Huc welcomes you for a stay in the quiet and a guaranteed change of scenery. The former wine estate of Paul and Alice Huc has completely been restored to accommodate 22 people in 5 independent apartments. The decoration is fancy, the owners, Aude and Florence, the great-grand daughter, wanted to preserve some furniture of their ancestors by giving the whole place a touch of modernity. Aude has managed to turn the old beams away to make them stools and bedside tables, the frames of the enormous barrels were transformed into TV furniture while the armchairs and carpets of the 19th century found a new life thanks to the care of the owners. The apartments are all fitted with at least two rooms, with a new and very comfortable bed, the bathrooms and shower rooms are equipped with a hairdryer and a straightner, reversible air conditionings will ensure coolness in summer and heat in winter, unless you prefer to make a little blaze in the fireplace. Finally, in summer, you can eat fruits and vegetables directly picked in the garden, not far from the swimming pool and the outdoor terrace.

Ferrals-lès-Corbières

MAISON DE LA ROCHE

27, avenue de Carcassonne
✆ 04 68 90 60 88
www.maisondelaroche.fr
enquiries@maisondelaroche.com

Open all year round. Three gîtes for 4 or 5 people. Reception on Saturdays from 3pm. From 790 € to 1,700 € per week depending on the season.

Right in the centre of the village of Ferrals, it's hard to imagine that there is a dream house, a real luxury establishment. Behind the gate, a tree-lined courtyard strewn with gravel, Bob the dog of the house and the smile of Honor Marks, the mistress of the house, give the impression that we are here in an exceptional place. The dog barks in English but our hostess speaks French and knows the country much better than some natives. The whiteness of the buildings reflects the sun of the Corbières. We are in an old wine estate entirely restored with taste and finesse, as our British friends know how to do. The three gîtes are spacious, chic, with high ceilings and authentic terracotta tiles. Everything has been thought out for comfort, including picnic baskets and cool bags. For those who are more sensitive to the cold, the swimming pool is heated at the beginning and end of the season. The reception is at the height of the services offered. Honor will also be able to advise you on wine or tourist discoveries in the region and will even lend you bicycles to take full advantage of the scenery.

Sud de France
THE BEST OF OCCITANIA
"ALL IN THE GAME
REGIONAL CONSUMPTION."
ROMAIN NTAMACK
Ambassadeur de la marque Sud de France
La Région
Occitanie
Pyrénées · Méditerranée
sud-de-france.com
FOR YOUR HEALTH, EAT AT LEAST FIVE FRUITS AND VEGETABLES A DAY. WWW.MANGERBOUGER.FR

CASTELNAUDARY ★

LE BOAT
the large pool
quai du canelot
✆ 04 68 94 52 94
www.leboat.fr
castelnaudary@leboat.com

Navigation on the Canal du Midi from April 1 to October 31, 2020. Every day: 08: 30am-12: 30pm and 2pm-6pm – week-long cruises (7 nights) departing from Castelnaudary, Homps, Trèbes or Narbonne. From Castelnaudary: 13h (31 locks) to our base in Trèbes / 20h (45 locks) to our base in Homps / 27h (61 locks) to our base in Narbonne. Cruises on the Canal du Midi, boat rental without licence.

Do you want to discover the cultural heritage of the Aude in a different way? Welcome aboard the Boat Fleet, and let yourself be guided along the beautiful work of Paul Riquet, the Canal du Midi, listed as a UNESCO World Heritage Site. Renting a boat without a licence allows you to sail in complete peace and quiet, cruising serenely through the department of Aude, dotted with works classified as Historic Monuments. You will be immersed in a real open-air museum, throughout your journey! Your river holidays will take place at the rhythm of a series of picturesque and secluded landscapes, small peaceful villages, dynamic towns, privileged historical witnesses, full of charm. All you have to do is let yourself be carried along by the waves.

Knife & Fork

HÔTEL-RESTAURANT DU CENTRE ET DU LAURAGAIS
31, cours de la République
✆ 04 68 23 25 95
www.hotel-centre-lauragais.fr
hcl11@live.fr

Open all year round. Monday to Saturday lunch and dinner; Sunday lunch. Reservation recommended. Menus from €18 to €39. A la carte menu: about €35. Children's menu: €12 (served to children under 10 years old). Lunch formula: €18 (or €19.50 and €22.50. Served only from Monday to Friday for lunch, except on public holidays). Wine by the glass. Menu "Cassoulet": €25. Starters from €9.5 to €19, main courses from €13 to €27.50, desserts from €6.50 to €9.50. Terrace. 10 rooms from €69 to €104 up to 5 people. Evening stopover.

Ideally located in the center of Castelnaudary, this restaurant is one of the most popular in the town. It is thus in a large room with baroque, black and white decoration, or on the terrace that you will take your place. The tables are well set, the fabric tablecloth and the pretty crockery announce the color, the cuisine that you will be served here is of course traditional, but the young chef can also express his sense of modernity, and he does not deprive himself of it.

We recommend without restriction the house's musts: the cassoulet of Castelnaudary with two confits, the Lauragais squab with ceps, the veal kidneys with chanterelles or the fish cooked in a unique way a la plancha. The chef also proposes more original, gourmet dishes of great finesse, such as the Gravlax Salmon, avocado mousse with lime, corn blinis and apple fruit, or to follow the Risotto "Camaroli" with prawn tails and reduced shell juice, a real delight!

All the dishes make you want, so it is imperative to come back as soon as possible. The ten rooms of the hotel have been completely redone to offer more comfort and more space, they will be perfect for a getaway in the Lauragais land.

LA MAISON DU CASSOULET
24 cours de la République
✆ 04 68 23 27 23
www.maisonducassoulet.com

Open all year round. Arrivals from 6 pm to 9:30 pm; departures before 11:30 am. 9 rooms (including 1 family room for 3/4 people). Double room from €48.50 to €52; triple room from €54.50 to €59.50. Half-board (67€ to 77€/pers depending on the season). Breakfast : 6,50 €. Extra bed: 5 €. Free public car park at 50 m. 1 baby bed available on prior request. Visitor's tax: 0.30 € per day and per person. The hotel is not accessible to PRMs. Animals accepted (free of charge). Wifi free of charge. Food service (menus from 14 € to 36 €; children's menu: 8.90 €). Canal +. Terrace.

Located in the centre of Castelnaudary, only 300 metres from Canal du Midi, the hotel of La Maison du Cassoulet has 9 comfortable and well-equipped rooms that will charm you with their modern and simple layout, they have an LCD satellite TV, as well as a private bathroom, equipped with a shower and free toiletries. A Wi-Fi connection is available free of charge in the rooms, you can enjoy a bicycle room and a continental breakfast. This address is ideal for a gastronomic stopover or a relaxing stay to discover the heritage of the Chaurian capital, a medieval city on the Lauragais plains. We advise you to choose their half-board packages which will delight your taste buds as well as your curiosity. This hotel is modest but it is a very good value for money plan.

Sleeping

■ HÔTEL-RESTAURANT DU CENTRE ET DU LAURAGAIS

31, cours de la République
✆ 04 68 23 25 95
www.hotel-centre-lauragais.fr
hcl11@live.fr

Logis. Open all year round. Languages spoken: English, French, Spanish. 10 rooms (including 2 suites). Double room from €69 to €84; triple room from €79 to €99. Half board: €28 (extra charge per person). Breakfast: €9. Public car park nearby. Baby bed: €10/night. VRP stopovers from €90 to €125 depending on the season / pers. Pets allowed. Free Wifi. Food service. Satellite Tv.

In the heart of the Chaurienne capital, in the main street, you will find this large building, at the corner of the Cours de la République, with a pink facade, housing on the ground floor a traditional gourmet restaurant, and upstairs a charming 3-star hotel. The 10 rooms and two suites, with their very refined modern decoration, were renovated in 2016. They offer all the comfort you can look for with air conditioning, TV, and bathroom, in soothing tones, they allow rest and serenity. You can enjoy the bar or the outdoor terrace on sunny days and eat on site. You will be only a stone's throw away from the Canal du Midi and the activity in the center of Castelnaudary, an ideal place to stay as a starting point for discovering the Lauragais lands.

Shopping

■ LA FERME DU PAYS D'OC

38, cours de la République
✆ 04 68 23 56 12 – www.fermedoc.com
fermedoc@fermedoc.com

Open Monday to Saturday from 9am to 12:30pm and from 3pm to 7pm; Sunday from 9am to 12:30pm. Sale on line. Delivery possible (delivery throughout France or collection in store. Recipe ideas on their site and offers discovery every month lots at exceptional prices to allow you to discover or rediscover Aude local products).

Wishing to discover the Aude products, being sure of their origin and quality, welcome to the Ferme du Pays d'Oc! Located in the heart of the city, opposite the tourist office, this excellent showcase of Castelnaudary crafts and food products will show you the best of the Aude region. Here, we prefer short circuits, since this delicatessen is a group of local producers and craftsmen, who promote an ancestral know-how in a concern for traceability and total quality. A wide variety of products awaits you in this temple of good food, you will have difficulty to choose, everything is mouthwatering: the traditional and authentic cassoulet of course, as well as salted meats, foie gras, ready-made meals such as Lauragais lentils with two confits... For the sweets, you will not be left out with a range mixing confectionery, cakes, nougat, honey... carefully prepared by neighbouring farms, or by your grocery store itself.

MAISON ESCOURROU

Artisanal zone of En Tourre
9, rue Jean-Baptiste-Perrin
✆ 04 68 23 16 88
www.escourrou.com
maison@escourrou.com

Open Monday to Friday from 8am to 12pm and 2pm to 7pm; Saturday from 9am to 12pm. The shop in the town centre is open Monday from 8am to 12pm, Wednesday to Saturday from 8am to 12pm and from 2: 30pm to 7pm, Sunday from 8am to 12pm. Delivery is possible (see the bargains catalogue for bargains that allow you to take advantage of the special discount prices). Gourmet boxes and online shop.

Maison Escourrou, a Castelnaudary family cannery since 1963, treat the most gourmet to their "local" specialties with the flavour and originality of our local products. All its specialties are handmade and French, and have been awarded many times at Aude Gourmande. You will not be able to resist the terrines, foie gras, canned food, ham, preserves and ready meals. When the temperature drops, a small cassoulet from Maison Escourrou seems ideal to warm you up; cassoulet but also fevoulade or lentils with confit. Escourrou makes its cassoulets with Gers confit, Castelnaudary beans and makes its own sausage, but the must remains the cassoulet in terrine, made with the same recipe for over half a century, to share authentic tastes and flavours. You will find these recipes everywhere in France through the online shop.

▶ Maison Escourrou is a member of **Confrérie du cassoulet de Castelnaudary**.

In the surroundings

Belflou

LE CATHARE

Lac de la Ganguise
La Barthe
✆ 04 68 60 32 49
www.auberge-lecathare.com
contact@camping-lecathare.com

Open all year round. Every day and holidays. For those not accommodated, only by reservation and for a minimum of 8 people. Reservation imperative. Menus from 22,50 € to 28,50 €. Wine by the glass. Cathar menu (homemade cassoulet with duck confit): 25,50 €. Menus from 14,80 € for hotel guests. Possibilities for weddings, baptisms, communions, etc.

An authentic inn in a former 16th-century priory where you enjoy regional and homemade dishes prepared with local products, cassoulet cooked on wood fire, foie gras, homemade charcuterie; duck breast grilled on charcoal stove, *poule au pot*, cabbage soup, stuffed chest… You can also turn back the hands of time by trying a good boiled chicken or one smoking cabbage soup, prepared according to traditional recipes. Of course, the famous dishes match the wines of Corbières, Malepère, or Blanquette de Limoux... But to taste, you will need to be 8 minimum at table if you are not staying on the spot! It must be said that the large restaurant room is itself ready! A countryside atmosphere reigns with the stones and beams and an imposing fireplace, and very long tables are arranged on special occasions.

LAC DE LA GANGUISE

lac de la ganguise
✆ 06 08 63 79 65
www.ganguise.com
cv.ganguise@wanadoo.fr

Sessions in group lessons (45€ optimist, dinghy, windsurf or catamaran [1h]) or free rental dinghy 1h 35€, canoe 1h 15€, paddle 14€... From March to December, come and discover their different boats: catamaran, dinghy, windsurf, funboard, paddle, pedal boat, canoe, mountain bike; for hire, lessons, regattas or at school.

Do you want to do a racing breaststroke, windsurfing or paddle? Everything is possible at Lake Ganguise, halfway between Carcassonne and Toulouse, in the communes of Baraigne, Cumiés, Gourvielle and Molleville. The 280-hectare dam lake forms the artificial reservoir of the Estrade, surrounded by pine forests, sunflower and wheat fields, with guaranteed open air. This horseshoe-shaped body of water collects mainly the waters of the Ganguise to the southeast, and forms the largest body of water in the department. The two arms that form the lake meet at the dam to the northwest. A small island is visible in the southern arm, where you can find grey herons but also kingfishers, two protected species whose observation is a delight for ornithologists. For sports enthusiasts, sailing, windsurfing, tennis, horse riding, fishing, mountain biking are some of the activities that the local nautical base offers. Not to mention swimming during hot weather (unsupervised) and fishing, even at night in some places (contact the AAPPMA of Castelnaudary with Mr. Paraire by phone).

Labastide-d'Anjou ★

HOSTELLERIE ÉTIENNE

1, chemin Saint-Jammes
✆ 04 68 60 10 08
www.hostellerieetienne.com
♿

Open all year round. Tuesday to Sunday from 12pm to 1: 30pm; Wednesday to Saturday from 7: 30pm to 8: 45pm. Closed on Sunday evening, Monday all day and Tuesday in the evening. It is advisable to call for the other evenings of the week. Reservation recommended. Menus from 17 € to 29 € (the 17 € menu only during the week; cassoulet menu at 25 €). Children's menu: 8 €. Starters from 5 to 13 €, Main courses from 10 to 25 € – Cassoulet to take away 2, 4, 6, 8 and 10 portions 8 € per portion + terrine deposit. Holiday vouchers, Restaurant vouchers. Groups welcome (capacity: 150 place settings in the dining room and 70 on the terrace). Baby chairs. Garden. Terrace. Take away sale. Park with trees. Specially adapted to group meals. Room rental.

© jojojo07 - Adobe Stock

The Canal du Midi in Castelnaudary.

In a former country house surrounded by a wonderful park, Eric Rousselot invites you to discover the true cassoulet, which he simmers for hours until the aroma is perfect. The secret recipe was taught to him by his father, Etienne, a former saucier of the Queen of England and a master in the art of cassoulet, people come from all over the world to taste his excellent cuisine and many television channels come there for programs on the preparation of cassoulet. The menu that offers true values hardly ever changes and that is good, because people come here to taste the specialties of the chef. Whether you choose the Imperial cassoulet (at will), frog legs with parsley, prawns with Rousselot, grilled duck breast or Tournedos Rossini, you will be filled and satisfied. Meals are served in the dining room that is completely soundproofed or in the beautiful park shaded by centuries-old trees. You can order a cassoulet served in the traditional cassole, hot or cold, as take-away. It is highly recommended that you book.

Mas-Saintes-Puelles

POTERIE NOT

Locality La Poterie
✆ 04 68 23 17 01
www.artisan-aude.fr
philippe.not@neuf.fr

Living Heritage Company. Open Monday to Friday from 8am to 12pm and from 2pm to 6pm. Open Saturday and Sunday by reservation only. Closed in August and from 24/12 to 02/01. Credit card not accepted.

One of the last potteries of Lauragais has remained for two centuries. Created in 1830 by the Perrutel family, several family units have succeeded one another at the head of this company. Nowadays, the Not brothers, former workers, perpetuate this ancestral tradition. Through the windows of the workshop with a special atmosphere, you can admire the shaping with clay of the pots "edges", jugs, ornament vases as well as the famous "cassole", used to prepare the local emblematic dish: cassoulet. This is the only place in France where it is turned by hand. "Cassole" is the ideal local object whose creation belongs to the potters of Issel, in Lauragais, it dates back to the 19th century. Poterie Not also produces dishes made to order, for food professionals as well as for private individuals who love local gastronomy, you can then discover saucepans with lids used to cook cockerels or any other more unusual product.

Montferrand

SEUIL DE NAUROUZE – LIGNE DE PARTAGE DES EAUX ★★

Walking area with free access.

Seuil de Naurouze, 12 km west of Castelnaudary by the D 611, sometimes also called Seuil du Lauragais, is an istmo, which separates the Atlantic Ocean from this beautiful Mediterranean sea... A strategic location where water is reluctant to flow to one catchment area or the other. One day, Paul Riquet watched the waters of Fontaine de la Grave, between the oceanic and Mediterranean watersheds, which were divided into two streams, one flowing towards the Garonne and the other towards the Aude. Thus Riquet had the first thought of establishing there, the highest point of the construction of his Canal du Midi, it was then sufficient to bring the stored water to St Ferreol, to supply the two watersheds of the canal. At this point, an 8-hectare octagonal basin had been dug and completed in May 1673, Paul Riquet had even thought of building a prestigious city all around, which would have served as a port. The basin is no longer and in this place with its century-old trees, Paul Riquet's heirs had an obelisk built in his honour in the 19th century. Nice walk in perspective!

Saint-Papoul ★

ABBAYE DE SAINT-PAPOUL ★★
5, place Monseigneur de Langle
✆ 04 68 94 97 75
www.abbaye-saint-papoul.fr/index
abbaye.saintpapoul@orange.fr
At 7 km northeast of Castelnaudary and at 30 minutes from Carcassonne.

Closed from January 1 to 31. Closed during the Christmas holidays as well. In high season: open every day from 10am to 7pm. February, March, November, 1 to 15/12: open every week from 10am-12pm/ 2pm-5pm closed Sunday morning – April/May/June/Sept/Oct: open every day from 10am-12pm/ 2pm-6pm (Oct closed Sunday morning). Other times are listed on their website. Free up to 5 years old. Adults: 5€. Child (from 6 to 15 years old): 2€. Group (10 people): 5€ (partner and group on self-guided tour (more than 10 people: 4€). Child from 16 to 18 years old, student: 3€ – Children and school groups: 1€. Groups welcome all year round on reservation. The cloister, the church and the exteriors are accessible to people in wheelchairs (on the same level). Adapted sanitary facilities are located on the square. Guided tour. Shop. Animations.

An exceptional site, Saint-Papoul is a must-visit monument in the Aude, a treasure of Romanesque art! Classified as a historical monument in 1840, this small Benedictine abbey, whose first written mention dates back to the 9th century, quickly became prosperous. As a result, it is made up of many sculptures by the Master of Cabestany, an itinerant artist from the late 12th century, of whom there are some very beautiful sculptures here. The cloister, inspired by the Gothic style, dates from the 14th century. In July, August and September, the abbey hosts various cultural events, so in August you can attend theatrical meetings in the main courtyard of the former episcopal palace, while the Rires et Patrimoine festival, which offers shows accessible to all, will take place in the abbey and the palace. In September, in addition to the Heritage Days, Saint-Papoul hosts the festival Les Troubabours chantent l'Art Roman. Near Castelnaudary, in the heart of the Lauragais, a Cathar land, Saint-Papoul Abbey is a cultural place, a true jewel of the Aude heritage.

New: Feel free to download 2 free mobile applications, including 20 exceptional sites from the Aude (10 castles, 7 abbeys, 2 medieval cities, 1 museum) for a total cultural and heritage immersion, in a fun way.

FANJEAUX ★

Sightseeing

MONASTÈRE NOTRE-DAME-DE-PROUILHE ★
Lieu-dit Prouilhe ✆ 04 68 11 22 62
www.prouilhe.com
monastere@prouilhe.com

Closed from September 1 to 15. Open every day from 8am to 12:30pm and from 2pm to 7pm. Liturgical offices throughout the day. Shop open weekdays from 9:30am to 11:45am and from 2pm to 5:15pm, Sundays from 11am to 12pm and from 2pm to 5:15pm. Guided tour. Boutique.

Whether you are a believer or not, in accordance with the Dominican doctrine, the monastery welcomes all its curious visitors or people seeking spiritual healing for stays of different duration. Notre-Dame-de-Prouilhe is a Dominican hotspot whose existence dates back to the 12th century when Saint-Dominique preached in Lauragais to eradicate the firmly implanted Catharism. Besides the

© Iuliia Sokolovska – stock.adobe.com

The village of Bram.

visit of the Basilica with neo-Byzantine architecture – its construction started at the end of the 19th century has remained unfinished – you will have the opportunity to share the daily life between work and prayers of fifteen religious people living on the spot. You enter here into religion for a while, you enjoy the silence, you attend the celebration of the services in the sacristy. For accommodation on the spot, you will have a very simple room with washbasin (hot water included) and W.C. on the same floor. Rates are based on the possibilities or generosity of individuals. Note the presence of a shop offering books, religious objects (crosses, medals, prayer beads, etc.), small pretty cribs from the world for Christmas, but also crafts of Prouilhe (icons, ceramics, cakes), and products of the monastery (cosmetics, honey, sweets, jams, fruit jellies).

In the surroundings

Bram

CUISINE D'ICI ET LÀ
2, impasse de la Malepère
Lauragais Business Park
✆ 04 68 78 68 83
www.cuisineicietla.com
restaurant@cuisineicietla.com

Open Monday to Thursday for lunch; Friday for lunch and dinner. Reservation recommended. Menu: about 22 €. Children's menu: 11 €. Lunch formula: 15,50 € (2 formulas: one large starter, main course and dessert, a small one at 14€ Starter + main course or main course + dessert). Wine by the glass. Vegetarians welcome. Groups welcome. Terrace. Take away sale. Orders possible 48 hours in advance by tel. Delivery in Bram until 11:30am +5 €.
Two beautiful rooms with about thirty place settings were waiting for me, a contemporary and warm atmosphere due to the woody notes of the decoration, but there's more. An astonishing concept, the art of revolutionizing the fast food lunch break kitchen with a truly inventive cuisine that gives pride of place to short circuits and seasonal products. Tanguy Lagasse and his team offer you a creative cuisine where local products, in an unexpected but successful way, rub shoulders with spices from elsewhere, Asian flavors and exotic fragrances. The meats come from producers of the Montagne Noire, as do the seasonal mushrooms, and the fruit juices, entirely natural, made in Fanjeaux, in Lauragais. In terms of recipes, the chef will delight you with his sushi specialties that can be enjoyed on Friday evenings, unless you opt for a plate prepared to your liking. His credo? *"Anything's possible as long as I'm having fun!"*. From starter to dessert, Futé has licked his lips!

■ EBUROMAGUS – MAISON DE L'ARCHÉOLOGIE
2, avenue du Razès
✆ 04 68 78 91 19
www.eburomagus.com
eburomagus@villedebram.fr

Qualité Sud de France. Open all year round. Annual closing from November to March. Tuesdays and from Thursday to Saturday from 2 to 6pm; Wednesdays from 10 to 12am and 2 to 6pm. Closed on Sunday & Monday. Adult: 4€. Child (from 6 to 15 years old): 1€. Group (10 people): 2€ (4€ with guide). Students, people with disabilities: 2€. Tourisme & Handicap Label. The whole building is accessible to people with reduced mobility. Children welcome. Guided tour (for groups). Shop. Educational workshops on different themes.
Come and discover the history of Eburomagus, which Bram's ancestor at the archaeology house, right in the centre of the village. Visit the museum and you won't be disappointed! Young and old will really like it as everything is interesting and instructive. You will travel back in history with the most diverse objects. In sum up, Eburomagus which is now Bram, is in Antiquity the most important agglomeration situated on the Aquitaine road between Toulouse and Carcassonne. With more than 800 archaeological pieces that are presented, a quarter of which have been restored, the permanent exhibition retraces, in 6 themes, the history of Bram and the western Aude from Prehistory to the end of the Middle Ages. You will discover the daily way of life as well as commercial exchanges or funeral rites. The section concerning Antiquity is particularly fascinating. Temporary exhibitions. Visit of the research laboratory during the Heritage Days.

■ TELESKI NAUTIQUE BRAM
Rue des Fleurs, Lac de Buzerens
✆ 04 68 79 74 14
www.teleskinautiquebram.net
teleskinautiquebram@gmail.com
Open from April to the end of October. High season: open every day. Water skiing 18 €/1 hour and 28 €/2 hours, paddle rental 10 € / 1 hour. Private lesson on 2 pulleys 15 € for 15 min. Terrace and toilets accessible to people in wheelchairs or with reduced mobility. 7 years old and over. Restaurant. Snack bar open 7 days a week in high season for lunch and dinner from Friday to Sunday.
Things are moving in Bram at the water ski lift on Lake Buzerens. The owners of the place have a lot of ideas and are developing the place into a real leisure base. Every year new investments are made, in 2016 Jason and Fred invested in a new installation: a ski lift forming an 800 m loop that completes the ideal return cable to start with. This will allow more fluidity and amateurs will be able to indulge in wakeboarding, skateboarding, water skiing and other knee-boarding. Those who are more active will be able to practice paddling, petanque or idleness. Playgrounds for the youngest are also available as well as a bicycle path that relays the Canal du Midi. Here, there is something for everyone, even for experienced or beginners wishing to perfect their skills and follow wake classes supervised by state-qualified instructors. If you're a little or very hungry, you can enjoy a good burger, grills or tapas in the shade of the weeping willow. You'll find something to get over your emotions, and why not enough energy to start over! Everything is designed to make you want to come back! Don't miss the "ça Bram pour toi" evenings organized by the Wake Asso Bram, don't forget to check out their Facebook page.

CHALABRE ★

The medieval village is founded in the 11th century on the lands of the Trencavel house in the midst of catharism, but one must wait until the year 1350 for the walls and fortifications of the village to be completed. It seems that the name of the village comes from one of the three streams that cross it, the Chalabreil. The second is the Blau, which it is necessary to follow in order to enjoy the facades of the most beautiful and ancient Chalabre houses. And finally, the Hers. The grain hall, in the heart of the old village, also worth a detour, many markets are organized there all year round. Lovers of history and architecture can visit the castle and enjoy the many animations that take place there!

■ **CHÂTEAU DE CHALABRE** ★
Allée du Château
✆ 04 68 69 37 85
www.chateau-chalabre.com
chateau.chalabre.info@gmail.com

Closed in July. Open to the general public from July 5 to August 31, Zone A spring school holidays and Ascension weekend. In high season: open from Sunday to Friday from 12 noon to 6.30pm. All year round by reservation for groups and schoolchildren. Free up to 4 years old. Adult: 16€ (19.9€ with tree climbing). Child (from 4 to 11 years old): 14€. Group (12 people): 15€ (18.9€ with tree climbing). Reduced rate: group of 12 people minimum, disabled person, student. The videos of the castle will be subtitled in French and English for the hearing impaired public. Children's area (fun and educational workshops). Guided tour. Restaurant (picnic area, large car park). Shop. Animations. Exhibitions.

Become Jacquouille la Fripouille during an afternoon at Château de Chalabre! Located in Cathar lands, it offers visitors a total immersion, through interactive medieval activities and entertainment, which allow them to become an actor in the life of the castle. Visit various exhibitions spread over the 2,500 m^2: spices, historical costumes, medieval garden, war machines, as well as the knighthood show in the late afternoon during the summer. Come to learn and participate in all the activities: calligraphy, heraldry, medieval dances, history of the Castle, fire master, weapons room training, knightly tournament, archery, medieval jet machines... From 1pm to 6.30pm, dressed in costumes, your children will become the new knights of the castle. They will discover equestrian techniques of this kind as they ride ponies.

▶ **New for 2020**: discover without moderation the 1st "accrobranche médiéval" (medieval tree climbing) and the "trappe du courage" (courage trapdoor). A variety of sensational aerial activities, testing your sense of balance, your adventurous instincts, a fun challenge for all budding knights, in complete safety, from 12 years old. Those who are under the age of 12 can immerse in the daily life of a knight and train on pony back, on an initiatory course of chivalry, with spear and period costume. This year, a large zip line is offered to you, free access!

LIMOUX ★

At the gates of Haute Vallée de l'Aude, at the edge of this same river, Limoux probably originated as a large city of the Roman era. The first known mention of the name of the city dates back to the middle of the 9th century, and an urban development was undoubtedly affirmed from the 11th century, near the Saint-Martin church which is now located in the middle of the old centre of the city. Fortifications were mentioned at the beginning of the next century, and around the same era, "an upper town" was formed in the North-West of the first agglomeration. But this upper town was definitively removed following the military episodes of the Crusade against the Albigensians, in the late 1220s. At this period, Limoux was an important hearth of catharism and opposed a strong resistance to the king of France and the Church. The neighbourhood of the right bank of Aude which is now called "Petite Ville" appeared around 1240. This sector firstly hosted activities linked to leather making, one of the most flourishing economic sectors of the city, with the production of woollen sheets and the wood transportation by floating on the Aude. In 1355, during the One Hundred Year Old War, Prince Noir took and devastated the city, and the fortifications should be rebuilt. Between the end of the Middle Ages and the Revolution, Limoux was ranked among small cities of Languedoc populated by 5,000 to 8,000 inhabitants.

Both geographical bolt and land of History, Limoux is the capital of a microregion with strong identity. This subprefecture, which has approximately 10,000 inhabitants today, is the inevitable stage to reach Haute Vallée de l'Aude. The city is famous for its blanquette attested since 1544, and its carnival mentioned for the first time in 1605, and which lasts from January to March. Here, the landscape is more wooded and the climate undergoes both Mediterranean and Atlantic influences.

■ **CARNAVAL DE LIMOUX**
Place de la République
See page 22.

Limoux.

Sightseeing

INSTITUT DES ARTS DU MASQUE

18, rue du Palais
✆ 06 11 68 15 60
iam-limoux.fr
institutartsdumasque@gmail.com

Open on Saturdays (2pm to 6pm) and Sundays (10am to 12pm and 2pm to 6pm) during the carnival period from the end of January to the beginning of April. Open from July 22 to August 9, 2020. European Heritage Days (18/09) to All Saints' Day (11/11) open 3 days a week V S D afternoon – from 2pm to 6pm. Free of charge. Thematic exhibition during the carnival period with free entrance. New temporary exhibitions planned for autumn 2020. Children welcome. Guided tour. Animations.

Guillaume Lagnel, director of the company L'Arche de Noé-Patrimoine et création, has been a loyal servant of theatre and heritage for more than fifty years. Over time, his creations have been accompanied by the manufacture of hundreds of masks, sets and costumes, which to date constitute the initial foundation of the Institut des arts du masque. Located in the former court of the Blanquetière city, this cultural centre invites visitors to discover the carnival in a different way. Indeed, the city of Limoux has a very codified carnival tradition, which dates back to the 15th century, and prides itself on having the longest carnival in the world. This thematic convergence around the mask as a symbol of carnival has led Guillaume Lagnel to imagine and develop a place that combines tradition and creation, modernity and knowledge. This Institut des arts du masque, inaugurated in January 2017, gathering more than 500 masks of limouxin goudils, and many costumes, is unique in France and becomes the living conservatory of an artistic know-how, place of memory, intended for a broad influence throughout the world, confronted with other civilizations and rites of the mask in the world. You can't participate in the Limoux Carnival without venturing to the Institut des arts du masque, to better understand all the subtleties of it.

Exhibition: "Mémoires de carnaval", during the winter 2020 carnival.

MUSÉE DES AUTOMATES

4, rue Anne-Marie-Javouney
✆ 06 70 39 01 74
www.lemuseedesautomates.com
museautomates@yahoo.fr

Open all year round. High season: every day and holidays. Low season: call ahead. Free up to 4 years old. Adult: 6 €. Child (from 4 to 12 years old): 4 €. Groups every day by appointment. Groups from 10 people, adults: 5 €. The whole museum is accessible for PRMs, except the toilets. Children welcome (workshops). Guided tour (from 1h to 1h30). Food service (in summer, a small bar area is open to visitors). Video on the history of automatons since the 18th century: duration about 30 min.

The Musée des Automates is a private museum which opened in July 2006 on the initiative of a family of enthusiasts. Jean-Jacques Achache and Martine Morand gave life to their automatons, each one more beautiful than the other. Today, it is their daughter Judith who has taken up the torch with such passion. The museum is housed in a former industrial building from the 1930s, a flamboyant baroque decor that welcomes you in 1,500 m² of enchantment and transports you to an imaginary world. More than one hundred and fifty characters in movement set to a series of variations of light, music and imagination. Enter a universe where characters inspired by myths and other phantasmagorias meet, they play and come to life in a musical atmosphere. The latest scenography allows you to discover new automatons, all colorful. Enter the laboratory of the imagination and let your mind dream and

Institut des Arts du masque.

wander freely, become for a few moments the child in you. You will also be able to enter the workshops, which we call "The maternity of the automatons"... New this year: the giant puppet workshop where you can build your own puppet. An experience that will not leave you indifferent.

Knife & Fork

CHEZ STEPHAN (WINE BAR)

6, place de la République
✆ 06 25 80 07 76
stephan.maitret@gmail.com

Annual closing in November. Open Wednesday from 10 am to 3 pm and 6 pm to 10 pm; Thursday from 10 am to 4 pm and 6 pm to 11 pm; Friday from 10 am to 4 pm and 6 pm to 2 am; Saturday from 10 am to 3 pm and 6 pm to 2 am; Sunday from 10 am to 3 pm. Open from December to May from Thursday to Sunday, in May/June from Wednesday to Sunday and in high season until November: from Tuesday to Sunday evening. Reservation recommended. Children's menu: €10 (up to 10 years old). Wine by the glass. Tapas from €2 to €19. Salad meal from 11 €. Home made Cassoulet €22. Burgers from €13.90. Groups welcome (on reservation, 15 people maximum). Terrace. Animations. Wine bar, tapas.

In the old centre of Limoux, under the arcades of the Place de la République, the wine bar and restaurant Chez Stephan, is a must with its atypical concept and idyllic location. The traditional lunch menu will delight the most gourmands among you, dishes prepared by the chef using fresh products that make you want to taste everything! You can sit out on the terrace or in the room with its wine bar – bodega atmosphere, around barrels, high bar and among bottles of regional vintages. The dishes are nicely presented, carefully prepared and made with products that are freshly worked, which titillate both the taste buds and our nostrils, with tasty aromas. In the evening, the tapas atmosphere reigns and it is in a convivial atmosphere that we enjoy the cooked tapas to share, a real treat. A plate of foie gras, Jabugo ham, pan-fried foie gras... Two menus are available throughout the year with, in summer, a salmon ceviche, skewers, tuna tartare with citrus fruits, hearty salads, and, in winter, a roasted Camembert PDO, duck breast skewers marinated with honey, a traditional cassoulet. All this is complemented by a friendly, fast and professional service, for a more than reasonable bill. A favourite address, which has become a safe bet over time.

▸ Note that the restaurant offers its "traditional" menu for lunch and home-cooked tapas in the evening.

■ LA TAVERNE À BACCHUS

Château de La Monèze Haute
Route de Malras
✆ 04 34 21 90 44
celine.benedan@sfr.fr

Open from Wednesday to Sunday and on public holidays for lunch and dinner. Reservation recommended. Menus from €36 to €46. Children's menu: €15. Garden. Terrace. Every 20th of each month: "Le 20 c'est vin" (even on closing days).

The tavern in Bacchus has left the village of Pieusse to welcome you in a real wine storehouse of a castle near Limoux. The new version of this restaurant, well known by the locals, has some nice surprises in store for you with a larger space, a private car park, and a shady park for outdoor concert projects, as well as a marquee for your most important events. This is the new outfit for this restaurant with a well-established reputation. Don't worry, the spirit of the house remains the same, the owners Céline and Eric still offer you the best products, exceptional meat pieces, Corsican and Iberian delicatessen, which are alongside those made by Eric himself, foie gras and many other homemade dishes that will make your taste buds tingle. The centerpiece of the restaurant is the fireplace from which emanates the tempting scents of grilled meats, sausages, goat's cheese, and many other preparations such as peasant soups to die for. After you have feasted on delicatessen, Eric cooks in front of you, your dish... a can, suckling pig on a wood fire, or a rabbit that tempts you? Perhaps you would prefer a good cassoulet, stuffed cabbage or a good calf's head... the choice is vast. And what about homemade desserts apart from "yum"? Everything is served to you in superb old-fashioned dishes that seem to have come straight out of your great-grandmother's wedding trousseau. Ah! Here, a smile is not an option, it is an integral part of the qualities of this authentic place with its rural and friendly atmosphere. A return to the roots, to the land and to the good products that are sometimes unjustly forgotten...

Sleeping

LE MAUZAC CHAMBRES D'HÔTES NEW

1 bis, rue du Razès
✆ 06 14 01 62 88
jeanpierrelemauzac@yahoo.com

Open all year round. Reception 24 hours a day (late arrivals possible). 5 rooms (price according to seasonality). Double room from 55 € to 65 €. Breakfast included. Parking space. For 2 persons (12 m², 5 rooms). Only an umbrella bed can be added. Free Wifi. No tv.

After having been a hotel, Le Mauzac reunites with its historic owners, the Tournié family, to become a bed and breakfast at the beginning of March 2019. These changes accompany the history of a renaissance announced in an establishment that was, a few decades ago, a local institution. Built in 1963 on a former vineyard, on the hillside at the entrance to the town, it was natural to give it the name of a grape variety. To date, 5 guest rooms will perpetuate this family property with a new decoration, a warm welcome and relaxation assured in this old hotel structure. Very luminous, the cocooning rooms with their neat and refined decoration, all different, benefit from a shower room or a bathroom, a tray of indulgence at your discretion and all the necessary linen. Specially designed for one or two people, you will be able to offer yourself a break of serenity. A breakfast room on the ground floor as well as a living room with television are at your disposal and open onto a terrace overlooking the city. For an event, for a visit, for a desire, do not hesitate to take the step!

New in 2020: a gîte is born with two bedrooms, a laundry room, a living room, a kitchen, a dining room, each bedroom has its own bathroom and in addition a separate toilet. Rental of 3 nights min.

Shopping

L'ATELIER DES VIGNERONS

2, place de la République
✆ 04 68 20 12 42
www.atelier-des-vignerons.com
contact@atelier-des-vignerons.com

Open Monday to Saturday from 10am to 12:30pm and 2pm to 7:30pm; Sunday from 10am to 1pm. Delivery possible (in Germany, Austria, Belgium, France, Italy, Luxembourg, Netherlands, United Kingdom). Tasting evening: 15 €, reservation recommended (40 people max). Afterwork on Friday evening.

Who said that wine was a man's business, certainly not us and even less the team of the Atelier des Vignerons de Limoux. Much more than a wine shop, you will find here the quintessence of the best in wine and spirits. Laurence Turetti is a true passionate person, she is now accompanied by a "big wheel" in the world of wine, the sommelier Cédric Vernice who, after having worked in great starred restaurants, has joined Laurence to make us discover Wine with a capital "V". The shop is refined, the wood combined with soft lighting is the perfect setting to discover the 400 references of wines all in reasoned, organic and biodynamic farming methods. Gourmet and playful tasting evenings are regularly organised with winegrowers from the region, and food and wine pairings are then offered: wines and cheeses, wines and desserts, Tout en Gin... New features since 2019: the "Battle entre 2 vins" (monthly) or the "Pépites du sommelier" every Sunday morning. Also to be discovered is a beautiful range of whiskies and gins, including the "Petit Grain" distilled in Saint-Jean-de-Minervois. An unmissable address in Limoux from which you can come out with much more than a bottle... Note the afterworks on Friday evening and the possibility of ordering online and have your order shipped to France and to 7 European countries.

OUSTAL ANNE DE JOYEUSE

34, promenade de Tivoli
✆ 04 68 31 11 30
www.annedejoyeuse.fr
oustal.limoux@cave-adj.com

Open Monday from 10am to 12pm and from 3pm to 7pm; Tuesday to Saturday from 9am to 12pm and from 3pm to 7pm. Free tasting, groups accepted, 15 people maximum.

Cave Anne de Joyeuses (labelled Pays Cathare) was created in 1929. The winegrowers, realizing the exceptional quality of their terroir, started in 1972 the first plantations of noble grape varieties like merlot, cabernet sauvignon and chardonnay. It then became the first and the most important southern vineyards to engage its entire resources in a local selection known as "à la parcelle". In 1989, the classification of its wines as white AOC Limoux rewarded the efforts and the work provided, like the quality of the products. Fifteen years later, its red wines were in turn classified as red AOC Limoux. A well-deserved recognition for the wines of L'Oustal Anne de Joyeuses whose wine growers preserve biodiversity and the environment, it's a commitment symbolised by the Protect Planet® charter. Thus, fauna and flora continue to develop through maintaining vegetation cover. The cellar will present you the red AOC Limoux "La Butinière", which has a dark-red purple colour with garnet-red reflections; with raspberry, violet, black cherry flavours, and mellow flavours of red fruit, prune and spices, in the mouth. The wines of Anne de Joyeuse are regularly awarded at the General Agricultural Competition.

In the surroundings

Alet-les-Bains ★★

It seems as five fairies have always been watching over this village! One gave it its water with virtues known since the Roman era, the second one a peaceful natural environment, the third one a welcoming micro climate, the fourth one a well preserved architectural and a historical heritage, and the last one an initiative spirit to share this wealth here as elsewhere.

ABBAYE ET CATHÉDRALE NOTRE-DAME-D'ALET

Avenue Nicolas-Pavillon
✆ 04 68 69 93 56
www.aletlesbains.com
accueilabbaye@aletlesbains.com

At the time of writing this guide, the opening days and hours for the year 2019 are not yet known. Times are for information only. From April to June and from mid-September to October: 2pm-6pm except weekends and holidays: 10am-12: 30pm and 2pm-6pm. From July to mid-September: 10am-12: 30pm and 2: 30pm-7pm. November to March: Tuesdays and Thursdays: 2pm-5pm; Sat: 10am-12pm. Free up to 12 years old. Adults: 4€. Child (from 13 to 18 years old): 2.50€. Group (10 people): 3.50€. Guided tour (for groups and individuals). Shop. Animations. Animals accepted. wi-fi.

The history of Alet is closely linked to that of its Benedictine abbey – probably founded around the year 813 - dedicated to Notre-Dame and an important pilgrimage center in the 17th century. The sculpted decor is of ancient and medieval inspiration. Becoming a cathedral in 1318, the Romanesque abbey church harbours an imposing Gothic choir. In fact, it never ceased been built , demolished and rebuilt... and was demolished for good in 1792. Today, there are still the very beautiful and impressive ruins in ochre sandstone, considered by some to be "the most beautiful ruins of France". They can be visited and are a fabulous natural scenery for musical and theater performances each summer. The reception hall of the abbey has a shop space in which you will find a wide choice of books on the region and the Middle Ages, especially for children, but there are also postcards and local products like the lemonade made in Alet, with the spring water of the village, and the *biscotins d'Alet*, delicious little dry cakes that deserve to be tasted.

Brugairolles

CÔTÉ RESTO – DOMAINE GAYDA

Chemin de Moscou
✆ 07 80 32 73 98

High season: open from Monday evening to Saturday evening for lunch and dinner. Reservation recommended. Children's menu: 8 €. Wine by the glass. Reception of groups (reception of groups. Outdoor space and terrace. Parking). Terrace. Shop.

Since its opening in 2006, the Domaine's restaurant has established itself as one of the best spots to eat, offering a superb setting and quality cuisine. This year, the kitchens were taken over by a new chef, initiating a simple but effective menu featuring succulent grilled meats, accompanied by homemade french fries. Specialities include Tim Burger with farmhouse tome cheese, cassoulet with duck confit, beef tartare and fish from the catch of the day. We also like the bar in Charcut, very cosy, with sofas and vintage armchairs, the panoramic view of the Pyrenees chain. It is the right place to have an aperitif between "potos" and share charcuterie board made of Serrano, Iberian Belota, fricandeau, Catalan terrine and other pork, all well served with wines from the estate... of course! A simple and casual restaurant in a chic and surprising place.

Vignes de Limoux – Antech.

DOMAINE GAYDA (WINE ESTATE)

Chemin de Moscou
✆ 04 68 20 65 87
www.domainegayda.com
guillaume@domainegayda.com

November to April: open Monday to Thursday from 10am to 5pm; Friday from 10am to 4pm. May to October: Monday to Friday from 9am to 5pm, Saturday from 9am to 4pm.

The Domaine, which has been certified for Organic Agriculture since 2011, is located in the heart of the Malepère region. While some estates highlight their age, Domaine Gayda relies on the quality of its wines, which are meticulously made and aged by Vincent Chansault, a graduate of Cognac's School of Viticulture and Oenology. A passion for wine based on sustainable, respectful and instinctive viticulture. It is inspired by the diversity and complementarity of its terroirs, as well as the tastes and aromas of its grape varieties, to produce PGI Pays d'Oc of quality and many times award-winning. The grapes, selected from the soils of Malepère, La Livinière (Minervois) and Roussillon, give life to beautiful ranges called Sélection, Chemin de Moscou, Figure Libre, En Passant or Cépages. Domaine Gayda is also a restaurant created in 2006 and which has always been able to meet the expectations of its guests in search of the best food and wine pairings. This year, the cuisines were taken over by a new chef, initiating a simple but effective menu featuring succulent grilled meats. Come to the estate to enjoy this exceptional site with a panoramic view from the Malepère plains to the Pyrenees, and discover the refurbished and extended shop, which showcases the estate's wines and wine-tourism activities such as wine tastings and a visit to the cellar...

PUIVERT ★

Sightseeing

■ CHÂTEAU DE PUIVERT ★
✆ 04 68 20 81 52
www.chateau-de-puivert.com
infos@chateau-de-puivert.com
Park at the foot of the castle, then 5 min walk with a very slight difference in altitude.

Closed from November 15 to December 20. From December 15 to Easter weekend: every day from 10am to 5pm closed on Saturdays outside school holidays all zones – From Easter weekend to November 15: every day from 9am to 7pm. Free up to 11 years old (within the limit of 2 children for 1 adult). Adult: €7. Child (from 12 to 18 years old): 5€. Group (20 people): 5€. School groups: 5€ per child. Reception of handicapped persons. Children's area. Guided tour (unusual visit "Sur les traces des troubadours" at 3pm from May). Shop. Animations. Myliame proposes an original visit of Puivert castle and the Quercorb museum, combining commentary on history, architecture, medieval music and troubadour songs.

Château de Puivert is one of the castles known as Cathar, Quercorb, Aude hinterland, it is classified as a historical monument since 1907. Private, it is composed of a ruined old castle from the 12th century whose remains are still visible and a new castle from the 14th century, one of the best preserved. In the 11th and 12th centuries, it belonged to the Congost, lords of Puivert, protectors of Catharism and in 1210 became the property of Lambert de Thury (Simon de Monfort's companion), then of Pons de Bruyères. At the beginning of the 14th century, a new castle was built, the sculpted decorations of the musicians' room in the keep testify to the refinement to its layout, intended for the functions of a seigneurial residence. An important assembly of Pays d'Oc troubadours is reported to have met at Château de Puivert in 1170. Access is via a square gate tower with a harrow and stunner, initially equipped with eight flanking towers, five of which remain in a very good state of conservation to this day. Under an apparent external rigour, the keep, originally adjoining the seigneurial dwelling, has four magnificent vaulted rooms, and has kept its full height (35 m), the interior is almost intact. There are four floors, occupied by the castle chapel, or the musicians' room reserved for the reception. The vaults fall on eight historical bases where characters playing different musical instruments are represented, unusual in a military fortress! Through its immense farmyard, the Château de Puivert, reminds us of the tournaments and games dear to the Knights. For all these exceptional assets, it is resolutely a must-visit. It has been used as a backdrop for many films such as "The Ninth Gate" with Johnny Depp. To complete the visit of the castle, the Musée du Quercorb, in the heart of the village of Puivert, offers a permanent exhibition on the history and architecture of the monument as well as reconstructions of the instruments in the musicians' room.

Shopping

■ BDQ TAPROOM
4, route départementale 117
✆ 06 31 30 19 18
www.brasserieduquercorb.com
contact@brasserieduquercorb.com
♿

From April to November: open every day except Monday, from 11am to 10pm. From November to the end of March open on Friday/Saturday/Sunday from 3: 30pm to 9pm. Groups on reservation. Theme evenings. Possibility to rent Beer-Truck. In high season, the brewery organizes free concerts every Sunday afternoon from 5pm. Shop. Bar. Terrace. Bottled beers from 3.60€ (33cl) to 7.50€ (50cl) 22 references & 4 references draught beers.

Located in a renovated former 1920s agricultural garage on the main road, this artisanal brasserie offers a bar where you can taste 4 draught beers and the whole range in bottles. In a rustic but skillfully staged setting, in the middle of stainless steel tanks you will be warmly welcomed to enjoy a natural, unfiltered and unpasteurized artisanal beer. The beers are authentic with surprising tastes that you won't find anywhere else. Naturally closed, the traditional recipes have been revisited to create beers with a unique taste and rich in flavour; 25 beer recipes, with a revisited traditional style, that Paul and Jayne call Occitan names. Everything here is in a "melting-pot" sauce, a clever mix of England and Cathar terroir. You can nibble without fuss: cold meats, cheeses, bread loaf warmed on the stove.... Every Friday and Saturday evening, enjoy pizzas cooked over a wood fire, fish and chips, concerts. To prolong the pleasure, you can rent the Beer-truck for your private events, transport the concept home, with this vintage J7, to have a nice moment with friends!

QUILLAN

■ SERVICE TOURISME PYRÉNÉES AUDOISES
Square André-Tricoire
✆ 04 68 20 07 78
www.pyreneesaudoises.com
tourisme@pyreneesaudoises.com

In low season (January / February / March / October / November / December): Monday to Friday from 10am to 12pm and from 2pm to 5pm / closed to the public on Thursdays – Mid season (April / May / June / September): Monday to Saturday from 9: 30am to 12pm and from 2pm to 6pm. In high season (July / August): Monday to Saturday

The Saint-Bertrand Leisure Centre

Since the summer of 2017, it is possible to enjoy a vast leisure base. In Saint-Bertrand, more than 22 hectares welcome you to relax, exercise or have fun. On both lakes, you can swim, play paddle (available for hire) or take advantage of the beach to laze around. There are no sand castles here, only small pebbles. A cycle track and footpaths allow you to fully enjoy the area. You will also find on the spot a health trail as well as weight-lifting equipment, if you are more relaxing than you spend. Don't hesitate to come and picnic with the barbecues that have been built! A little extra: toilets and showers are available. Nature is enhanced here, the setting is pleasant with different species of trees, shrubs and plants, for family activities in the welcoming little town of Quillan.

from 9:30am to 6pm, Sunday from 9:30am to 12:30pm. Tourisme & Handicap Label.

The tourist office of the Aude Pyrenees is located in Quillan, square André Tricoire, in front of the station car park. Created in 1906, it is one of the very first tourist information offices in France. Located in the city's former shower baths, built in a Moorish Art Deco style, the Maison du Tourisme was awarded the departmental prize for Heritage Ribbons in 2000 for the renovation of this former building.

In the centre of the country of the Aude upper valley, the tourist office of the Aude Pyrenees invites you to discover all its treasures. You will find an abundant offer of leisure activities, as well as a free Wifi connection, a shop with topoguides, postcards, an exhibition room, and useful services for motorhomes. It is a one-stop shop where you have at your disposal resident advisors to guide you, help you in your search for accommodation, catering, leisure, culture... It also has seasonal information offices in Axat from June to mid-September and in Roquefeuil. It is the ideal gateway to your holiday destination or business stay.

Sightseeing

■ DÉFILÉ DE LA PIERRE-LYS ★

Classified natural site.

Magnificent! That's the first feeling that is going to overwhelm you when you are going to take the road between Quillan and Axat, the entrance to the vertiginous corridor of this exceptional site creates a surprise. Very beautiful gorges, about 4 kilometers from Quillan, were patiently forged by the Aude river, which has eroded the limestone rock over millennia, thus creating high vertical cliffs from 400 to 600 m ending with sharp rocky spills. In some places, the width of the passage does not exceed 20 metres, feeling of being closed is possible. This parade, of about 5 kilometres long, has long remained impassable. The first blow of a pickaxe was given in 1781 by the priest Félix Armand, opening a trail to the upper valley of Aude and Roussillon. After the work was interrupted during the French Revolution, they resumed as early as 1814. When you look at the rock, you still see the blows of many pickaxes that attacked the stone. This thoroughfare, followed by the construction of a railway link, was going to allow this region, hitherto landlocked, to participate fully in the adventure of the industrial age. At the bottom of the road, the Aude always flows into a fast torrent, greatly appreciated by fans of strong sensations, practicing white water sports such as rafting, hydrospeeding or kayaking.

Knife & Fork

■ LA CHAUMIÈRE

25, boulevard Charles-de-Gaulle
✆ 04 68 20 02 00
www.pyren.fr
lachaumiere@pyren.fr
♿

Qualité Tourisme. Annual closing from the beginning of January to the beginning of February. In low season: open Monday and Friday evenings; Tuesday to Thursday and Saturday for both lunch and dinner. In high season: Monday and Friday evening; Tuesday to Thursday, Saturday and Sunday for both lunch and dinner. In low season Closed on Monday evenings, Friday evenings and Sunday. Reservation recommended. Menus from 20€ to 35€. À la carte menu: about 35€. Children's menu: 10€. Starter + main course or main course + dessert: 20€. Vietnamese menu: 25€ (starter + main course + dessert). Terroir menu: 35€ (starter + main course + cheese + dessert). Nems to take away: 1€/piece. American Express. Groups welcome. Baby chairs. Terrace. Take away sale.

In a rustic and pleasant setting, push the door of this establishment, which has been a veritable institution in the city of three skittles for more than half a century. At the helm, the Castel family has managed to breathe a breath of modernity, with a refined cuisine that combines the pleasures of the local soil with much more distant flavours and spices, the Asian version of which is sure to titillate our taste buds. You will revel in the fabulous home-made cassoulet with duck confit, Quillan sausage and garlic crouton or travel with Vietnamese specialties such as *Cha gio hanh san*, prawn ravioli or beef marinated in satay and lemongrass, to finish with a much more classic touch, but not to be missed with, for example, the lemon meringue tart. On the wine side, you won't be outdone with the enlightened advice of Olivier, who will know how to make you appreciate the most subtle food and wine pairings. Don't forget to make a reservation, because with its tasty cuisine, the success of this restaurant is well established, and it's the right address to go to with friends, like a secret that you only share on the sly, to make sure you eat well.

In the surroundings

Axat

EAURIZON-SUD RAFTING
2, route départementale 117
✆ 04 68 49 99 82
www.eaurizon.eu
contact@eaurizon.eu

Le Pays Cathare Label. Open from April to the end of October. Reservation recommended. Open every day from 9: 30am to 7pm. Canoeing from 12€/1h to 32€/day, 45€ with supervision. Canyoning from 37€ to 55€ for half a day. Climbing or caving from 31€ for a half day. Credit card not accepted. Reception in French, English and Spanish.

Eaurizon, is a dynamic club of experienced professionals who will share with you their passion for nature and whitewater sports. They have two sports sites, including their main base in Puichéric between Carcassonne and Lézignan-Corbières, open all year round, and that of axat on the banks of the Aude river in the upper Aude valley during the summer season. You can discover or rediscover rafting, hydrospeed or canorafting trips with your family or friends at your leisure and if you prefer the mainland, there is always climbing, caving or canyoning. Don't hesitate any more and embark on the river's tumults, during sessions of about 2 hours to live a unique experience, experience the fauna and flora in a different way, for unforgettable memories, guaranteed sensation!

Bugarach

FERME DE JANOU
Chemin de Cugurrou
✆ 04 68 69 81 69
www.fermedejanou.fr
serviceclientele@fermedejanou.com

© Yan EVEN

Quillan.

Tables & Auberges de France. Open on weekends. Evenings by reservation before 6pm. Reservation recommended. Menus from 18€ to 35€ (Vegetarian menu, Menu at 35€ on Sundays and public holidays at noon). À la carte menu: 30€ approximately. Children's menu: 10€ (for children under 10 years old). Credit card only accepted in the gourmet shop. Groups welcome. Garden. Terrace. Take away sale. Shop. Online sale of gourmet products and wines at producer prices, range of Foie Gras, Pâtés, Rillettes, Confits, Ready-made meals. Free Wifi.

If the Bugarach region is famous for its mystical aspect, people enjoy going there to discover the beautiful landscapes and its history, why not take this opportunity to discover another aspect of the village by visiting the farm of Janou? Here, they raise poultry, grow ancient and forgotten, like root vegetables according to the seasons. A shop allows you to buy cooked dishes and various farm products but what you're going to prefer is getting something to eat in the restaurant located on the farm. You are offered a local cuisine with, of course, all the products of the farm cooked with know-how and love, you can particularly find foie gras, the cassoulet, a poularde sauce with morels or the unmissable beef cheek confit à la vigneronne… For dessert, let yourself be tempted by the profiteroles made like before… You will enjoy this address in winter sitting by the fire and in summer on the shady terrace facing the famous peak.

Couiza

LE CARNOTZET
69, route des Pyrénées
✆ 04 68 74 13 13
www.le-carnotzet.com
le.carnotzet@orange.fr

Open all year round. Monday and Tuesday from 12pm to 2pm; Thursday to Sunday from 12pm to 2pm and from 7pm to 9: 30pm. Closed on Monday evening, Tuesday evening and Wednesday all day long. Open 7 days a week in July and August and during school holidays. The rest of the year closed on Monday evenings, Tuesday evenings and Wednesday all day. Reservation recommended. Children's menu: 9.50€ (up to 10 years old). Lunch formula: 15€ (dish of the day 9.80€). Wine by the glass. Savoyard specialities from 15€ to 25€. Starters from 8 to 16.50€, Fish from 20 to 23€, Meat from 18.50 to 25€, Rib of beef from 600g 39€, Desserts from 6 to 9€. Groups welcome. Terrace. Animations. Free Wifi. Private car park.

Once you have passed the door, you find yourself in a superb mountain chalet with a carefully designed contemporary decoration, where it's good to relax. The room upstairs is warm and cozy, the peace and quiet that emanates from this establishment and the possibility to eat on the terrace as soon as the first rays of sunshine appear are real assets for this atypical place of exception. In the kitchen, Franck cooks 100% home-made seasonal dishes, the cooked products are carefully chosen, because here only the best is served to the customers! Among the dishes on offer are great classics of French cuisine, from Occitania, the Basque country, the Alps and elsewhere. You can enjoy the Savoyard fondues, Raclette or reblochonnade, or the pierrade, but the fox particularly appreciates the house specialties such as the 5A andouillette and its mustard sauce, the Catalan "El Xaï" lamb and its garlic juice, the Gambas flambéed with Pastis Naturel "Figanis", or the fabulous Magret de canard braised with orange. Note the gourmet novelty, fresh homemade pasta, which will make you salivate with happiness with the seasonal ravioli declined in 4 original recipes. A beautiful selection of wines is offered to accompany your meal, let yourself be guided by Véronique, your hostess who will be able to advise you for the most pleasant food and wine pairings. To finish your meal, the homemade desserts are exquisite, especially the homemade chocolate and almond profiteroles. A favorite address that we never get tired of!

Espéraza

Halfway between the sea and the mountain, nestled up in a bend of the Haute Vallee of Aude, 280 metres above the sea level in a corrie with wooded hills, sits a fine little village called Esperaza. The municipality extends on both banks of the Aude river, between the Pyrenees and the Corbieres and it is a prehistoric place. It is a village from which many hiking trails leave. It has two museums and offers pleasant summer entertainment (Feast of Saint Jacques in July and Saint Michael in September). Haute Vallee is full of history, starting with the Charlemagne era, marked by the creation of many abbeys (Saint-Hilaire, Saint-Martin-Lys, Alet). In 813, Esperaza got its own priory. In the Middle Ages, the town lives thanks to the the work of "carrassiers" or "radeliers", who conveyed trains of logs and trunks between Quilllan and the sea. Wood was first of all meant for heating, then from the seventeenth century for shipbuilding. In the mid-nineteenth century, Esperaza became a centre for the manufacture of wool and felt hats, occupying the second world rank of hat making! In 1989, paleontological researches revealed thousands of dinosaur bones in the area; it is a new dawn for Esperaza. The excavations now extend up to Campagne-sur-Aude and contain one of the most important fossil deposit in Europe!

■ LE MUSÉE DES DINOSAURES ★

1, place Maréchal de Lattre de Tassigny
✆ 04 68 74 02 08
www.dinosauria.org
contact@dinosauria.org

Closed from January to February. Open during all school holidays. Workshops for children offered. Low season: open from 10: 30am to 12: 30pm and from 1: 30pm to 5: 30pm. High season: every day from 10am to 7pm. School holidays: from 10: 30am to 5: 30pm. Low season: from January to the end of June and from September to December. High season: July and August. Free up to 4 years old. Adult: €9. Children (from 5 to 12 years old): €6,50 (student and disabled). Family ticket: €27 for 2 adults and 2 children. Excavation workshops for children from 7 to 12 years old from €3 to €6. Visit of the Bellevue excavation site on request: adults €4.50, children from 3 to 12 years old €3.50 to €6. Tourisme & Handicap Label. Children's welcome area (educational visits). Guided tour. Shop. Animations. Labels: Qualité Tourisme, Le Pays Cathare and Qualité Sud de France. Coach parking. Pets allowed.

45 kilometres south of Carcassonne, the Dinosaur Museum offers you an immersion in the world of "Jurassic Park", opened since June 1992 three kilometres from France's largest dinosaur deposit. It offers a permanent exhibition area of 2,500 m^2 devoted to dinosaurs and other fossils of reptiles, mammals, invertebrates and plants discovered in the four corners of the planet. The museum offers a real journey back in time to the origins of life on Earth nearly 3.5 billion years ago. It is aimed at all generations: from the youngest who meet their favourite dinosaurs, to adults immersed in the heart of this long history of life on Earth. The museum's paleontologists share and exhibit here the results of 30 years of research. Workshops are offered, to better discover the profession of palaeontologist and participate in real excavations. It is managed by the DINOSAURIA association, whose main objectives are scientific research, training and dissemination of knowledge in palaeontology.

- For all budding Indiana Joneses, be sure to follow the DinOblog: www.dinosauria.org/blog.
- Exhibition "Belles de Dino" until November 1, 2020: 150 years of dinosaur history through comic strips.

© Yan EVEN

La Tour Magdala, Rennes-le-Château.

© Yan EVEN

Eglise de Rennes-le-Château.

© Yan EVEN

Asmodée, Eglise de Rennes le Château.

Luc-sur-Aude

■ CHOCOLATERIE NOUGALET
8, rue des Gourmets, La Tuilerie
✆ 04 68 74 02 63
www.nougalet.com
nougalet@nougalet.com
Open Monday to Friday from 9am to 12pm and from 2pm to 6pm. Open from Monday to Sunday during the month of December, non-stop from 9am to 6pm. Sale on line.
Founded in Alet in 1951, Nougalet, which takes its name from its village of settlement (nougat in Alet), later moved to Luc-sur-Aude. In 2008, Éric Monterrat, a native Burgundian with exceptional know-how, took over the reins of the company to make it a flagship in the world of artisanal chocolate. As soon as he arrived, he updated the entire product range, rewrote a manufacturing process and formalised the different production stages. Raw materials are chosen according to their quality: cocoa beans from Ivory Coast and Ecuador, hazelnuts from southern Italy, almonds from Andalusia, vanilla from Madagascar. The diversity of the products ranges from praline chocolates to macaronias (macaroons made from marzipan and chocolate coated with royal icing), confectionery and caramels, as well as the multiplicity of packaging: from boxes to baskets and cases, 250 tons of "chocolates" come out of the various workshops every year. A brand has even been created: Paris Chocolat, which showcases sophisticated boxes, and recently, a boutique has opened in Monterey, Mexico. The shop of the craft company is not left behind and is very popular with local customers, loyal from generation to generation. Here, we are in the true haute couture of confectionery, with a rare work of old-fashioned chocolate, to be tasted directly at the chocolate factory and on the online shop!

Rennes-le-Château ★

This charming little village has been attracting researchers and curious visitors worldwide since 1960. The Abbé Saunière's "mystery" has already been written, has aroused meticulous excavation and raised many questions. How did this atypical country priest who officiated at the village in the second half of the nineteenth century and who had been called to order several times by his superiors become so rich? What family secret or treasure did he find so as to restore the Sainte-Marie-Madeleine church, to construct a rectory, gardens and a real domain: Bethany House, Orangery, Gothic style Magdala tower ... Questions remain. The only person, except the abbot himself, who knew the secret, was his faithful servant Marie Denarnaud who remained silent until her death. Her only words were that "the abbot had discovered documents and maps". Is it a Visigoth or Templars treasure, perhaps that of Cathars or that of the nobles who exiled during the Revolution? Many assumptions, including the most unlikely ones, are tracked onto the subject. A captivating plot that continues to evolve over the years. Questions around this mystery are piled in layers of all backgrounds: religion, ancient treasure, coding, esotericism, topography, geography and especially art and painting. Many books have been written about this mystery, the most famous are the "Da Vinci Code" by Dan Brown and "The Untold Story of Rennes-le-Chateau" by Henry Lincoln. This last author made the world crazy for this mystery. Curious people from around the world come here "just to see", others try really to clarify this mystery. Moreover, for a long time, the town had to take measures to prevent illegal excavations that would ransack the village. However, although inconveniences it may meet, this charming village also takes advantages of this mystery. It is indeed a significant asset for its economy. Anyway, it worths a visit for its real beauty and mysteries buried under a thick of lead blanket, hidden within it!

■ DOMAINE DE L'ABBÉ SAUNIÈRE ★
Rue de l'Église
✆ 04 68 31 38 85
www.rennes-le-chateau.fr
tourisme.rlc@orange.fr
Qualité Sud de France. Open from mid-March to mid-November and during the end of year holidays. Low season: open on Sundays from 10am to 12:30pm and from 1:30pm to 5pm. High season: every day from 10am to 7pm. May-June-September: from 10am to 6pm. Free up to 10 years old. Adult: 5 € (free visit). Child (from 11 to 18 years old): 4 €. Group (10 people): 4 €. Reduced rate 4 €. Visit with digital tablet 8 €. The church is in free access and free of charge. Cathar country label. Guided tour (French, Spanish and English). Museum shop: books, regional products, souvenirs.
The visit includes the Magdala Tower, Villa Béthanie and the oratory, the presbytery, the Sainte-Marie-Madeleine church, the Orangery, and various other showrooms. With a single ticket, you will have access to all these places. Maybe, one of them has the answer to the mystery of this strange abbot ... Three car parks are recommended before you enter the village, and another car park on a panoramic viewpoint is reserved for the reception of visitors with disabilities.

Sougraigne

■ RANDONNEE ENTRE SEL ET VERRE
La Voutoulo, Route D74
✆ 04 68 69 84 55
Open all year round. A course intended for PRM, Departure: N 42.891872° / E 2.395795°.
Situated in the north of the commune of Sougraigne, the archaeological site of the glass factory of Les Salines, which was built around 1650, by order of the Marquis de Montesquieu, was in operation until 1765. In the heart of the Hautes Corbières, this place is home to the Sals, a salt spring which has always attracted the attention of the neighbouring populations. Discover this singular site, once frequented by many people: glassmakers, jet miners, charcoal burners, lumberjacks, shepherds, peddlers and of course, smugglers and gabelous from the general farm on their heels. This site allows you to understand the life of the people of this country at the time of the Gabelle, to discover the salt spring, but also a site of glassmaker's workshop and archaeological site.
▶ **Association "Salicorne"**, guided tour possible: 04.68.69.82.94 - www.salicorne-en-aude.fr – contact@salicorne-en-aude.fr.

INDEX

A

B

C

D - E

F

G

H

© Yan EVEN

Canal de la Robine in Narbonne.

La place Carnot, à Narbonne.

The rooftops of Narbonne.

CONTRIBUTE TO THE NEXT BEST OF AUDE

CONTRIBUTE TO THE NEXT BEST OF AUDE

CONTRIBUTE TO THE NEXT BEST OF AUDE

CONTRIBUTE TO THE NEXT BEST OF AUDE

CONTRIBUTE TO THE NEXT BEST OF AUDE

CONTRIBUTE TO THE NEXT BEST OF AUDE

CONTRIBUTE TO THE NEXT BEST OF AUDE